Cataloging with Copy

CATALOGING WITH COPY

A Decision-Maker's Handbook

SECOND EDITION

ARLENE G. TAYLOR
with the assistance of
Rosanna M. O'Neil

1988

Libraries Unlimited, Inc. — Englewood, Colorado

LIBRARIES UNLIMITED, INC.
P.O. Box 3988
Englewood, CO 80155-3988

Library of Congress Cataloging-in-Publication Data

Taylor, Arlene G., 1941-
    Cataloging with copy.

    Bibliography: p. 337.
    Includes index.
    1. Copy cataloging. 2. Cataloging. I. O'Neil,
Rosanna M., 1957-   . II. Title.
Z693.3.C67T38 1988   025.3   88-13840
ISBN 0-87287-575-X

To the memory of
ALLIE BETH MARTIN
who first sparked my interest
in cataloging

and to
KATHRYN LUTHER HENDERSON
who fanned that spark
into a flame

CONTENTS

INTRODUCTION

"May I never again have to hear that kneejerk piety 'but that's the way LC does it.' "[1]

"The use of standardized, externally provided catalog cards or information without change is significantly cheaper and better than either original cataloging and classification or the attempt to review, edit, or adapt externally provided copy or cards."[2]

These two opposing viewpoints were used to open the introduction to the first edition of *Cataloging with Copy*, published in 1976. Though the statements are now more than 14 years old, they still express sentiments felt by many librarians. The dilemma of speeding items through processing to make them available, and at the same time attempting to provide good access through the local catalog, still exists. In a 1987 discussion of some issues in library school education, Kathryn Luther Henderson observed:

When, beginning in the 1970s, libraries joined groups known as bibliographic utilities, they came to accept, often without alteration, bibliographic records from among the millions of records created by LC and many other libraries.... Soon many professional catalogers were replaced by paraprofessionals with instructions to accept what could be found in the database. Often forgotten was the fact that individual records do not a catalog make and, although much is gained through cooperation, we have yet to determine whether much may not also be lost in consistency and the meeting of local needs.[3]

In addition, libraries continue to view their missions as being different. Although consistency is useful for scholars who use more than one library, there are libraries, not particularly serving those scholars, whose patrons have diverse needs.

Like the first edition, this edition attempts to provide a framework to aid individual libraries in coming to grips with the implications of these opposing viewpoints. To those called upon to reconcile divergent opinions on the use of cataloging copy, it suggests benefits and liabilities that will result from any decisions made, so that they may be weighed in the light of the unique situation of the decision-maker's library. Planners may make more sound decisions if they have systematically evaluated as many of the effects as possible, rather than waiting to discover them, for better or worse, during or after implementation.

Noncataloging librarians will find here a delineation of the complications arising from choosing to alter or not to alter outside copy. They are also given a look at why it takes time to integrate copy into a local catalog in such a way that the item can be found when needed. In a majority of cases, little time is spent matching the description with the item. Description is usually not only adequately done by an outside source but also is done for a high percentage of materials acquired by most libraries. Thus, individual libraries do not have to generate their own descriptions. Matching access points on the copy with those already in the catalog, however, is another matter.

Library administrators and systems analysts will find here an explanation of the potential consequences, and in many cases the impossibility, of using outside copy exactly as it appears. Cataloging instructors and their students will find textual material to supplement the traditional cataloging texts that emphasize original cataloging of a unique item. The discussion of the process of maintaining the viability of an existing catalog while integrating copy from an outside source should complement discussions of original cataloging. Practicing catalog librarians are given here a framework for decision-making when faced with the responsibility of integrating externally produced cataloging into a local existing system. Finally, both professional and paraprofessional catalogers will find some procedures and possible alternatives for the integration problems that arise daily.

Maintaining a useful catalog is a time-consuming process because rules for description, rules for access points, subject heading lists, and classification schedules are not static. The cataloging and classification of today often does not mesh easily with the cataloging and classification of yesterday. Even a new library is faced with integrating cataloging copy for retrospective materials, which were cataloged in earlier eras, into the same catalog with new copy. Available cataloging copy does not always get revised when changes are made by the source, and copy already in the local catalog remains until steps are taken to change it, either by an individual decision of someone responsible for catalog data or by corporate decision to make a computer comparison of catalog headings with those found in an authority file.

Although the authors' preferred solutions are obvious in some cases, for the problems identified in the text there is seldom a best solution for all libraries. In finding a solution, problem-solvers and decision-makers must take into account the type of library, its size, budget, clientele, ability of available technical services and/or public services personnel, open or closed stacks, type and arrangement of catalog, presence or absence of branch libraries, presence or absence of a weeding policy, present state of technology, anticipated state of technology for the near and distant future, and many other factors. For example, a medium-sized public library serving a well-educated clientele should do different things with its catalog than a medium-sized public library serving a population that is much less privileged. Among academic libraries, there should be differences in treatment of copy depending on such things as whether the library is more research-oriented or more curriculum-oriented. A research-oriented library needs an in-depth, carefully constructed, well-referenced catalog. The personnel of a curriculum-oriented library often have responsibilities in addition to cataloging; there is simply neither the time nor the need for the catalog to be as in-depth. This book attempts to offer a variety of possible solutions, taking varying factors into account. Some potential solutions to problems are, no doubt, missing from the text, as are some potential copy cataloging problems. I would appreciate hearing about these so that the deficiency may be corrected.

The book is arranged in nine chapters. Chapters 1 and 9 present overviews of the procedures and personnel needed to integrate externally produced cataloging, the necessity for changing an existing catalog, and the usefulness of local copy cataloging units. Noncatalogers may find these chapters most useful, and perusal of the examples in the remaining chapters will help them develop an understanding of the perplexities of copy cataloging. Those with a deeper interest in daily copy cataloging decisions should profit from the entire work. Chapters 2 through 6 present a detailed discussion of integrating the description, main entry, name and title access points, subject headings, and classification/call numbers into an existing system. Chapter 7 particularly addresses use of copy that did not originate from the usual source. Use of such copy has become more prevalent as cataloging networks have become more widespread and as their members have made wider use of each other's copy. Chapter 8 is completely new to this edition. It addresses issues particularly related to using copy from online sources.

Much of the text for this edition has been completely rewritten. The changes that have occurred since 1976 are almost overwhelming. There have been new editions of the rules for description, subject headings lists, and classification schedules. Many more libraries are now cataloging in online environments, and some of those have online catalogs. These changes require new kinds of evaluation and innovative solutions. In addition, the changes have, in some cases, created new problems that must be solved. I was astonished, however, at the number of considerations mentioned in the first edition that remain as points needing decisions: only the context has changed.

Because so much copy cataloging today is completed online using records in the MARC format, many of the examples in this edition are in that format. I am very grateful to OCLC for permission to use records from OCLC and in the OCLC format. This format was chosen because of its readability. There are also many examples in card format. Numerous libraries still have card catalogs, and others continue to work entirely in a card environment. Therefore, I hope that a mixture of examples will speak to all who need to use this book.

Most of the examples used in the text are Library of Congress (LC) cataloging. I hope that the principles discussed will be equally applicable in libraries using copy from some other source. It is inevitable that, as the largest and most visible among us, LC is held up for examination (and complaint), as well as being a model. LC's cataloging is, for the most part, consistently done. Thus, because I give many examples in this book of the errors and other problems that can occur with LC copy, does not mean that I believe LC copy is wholly unreliable. LC copy has errors because it is created by human beings. I have tried to provide, where known, data about the incidence of errors of various kinds. For the most part, percentages of error are low. Most of the examples are not actually illustrations of *errors*, but rather are shown to illustrate how things are and have been done and the resultant action that is required of someone using that copy.

The reader will likely find in the examples some errors or problems other than those pointed out by the authors. Except where noted, I did not edit the examples but used them as I found them in the OCLC system. I chose each example to illustrate a particular point. If some other problem, not related to the topic under discussion, occurred in an example, I seldom noted it.

I wish to acknowledge gratefully the assistance of Rosanna M. O'Neil in the preparation of this edition. Ms. O'Neil completed the basic writing of Chapter 8 and did much of the revision work for Chapter 7. In addition she read and commented on the draft copies of manuscript versions of the other chapters.

The expertise and recent experience that she brought to this work is deeply appreciated. I also appreciate the excellent index completed by Bettie Jane Third, Adjunct Professor, School of Library Service, Columbia University.

I wish also to thank Charles Simpson, Assistant Director for Technical and Access Services, State University of New York at Stony Brook. The research we did on the incidence of errors on LC copy helped to provide many of the examples for this edition. Mr. Simpson also provided helpful comments and much moral support. Another person who gave help that I deeply appreciate is Mark R. Watson, Head of Copy Cataloging, University of Oregon, Eugene. He read the manuscript and made very helpful comments.

My thanks go, too, to the staff of Libraries Unlimited, Inc., for their patience, expertise, and helpfulness. I am particularly grateful to Bohdan S. Wynar for his continuing support.

Finally, I wish to thank my husband, A. Wayne Benson, for his wonderful moral support, and, in addition, for preparing meals when I was engrossed in writing, for not objecting when I shirked my share of the household responsibilities, and, as the deadline approached, for typing many of the manuscript changes into the computer.

—Arlene G. Taylor

* * * * *

Chapter 8 of this book can be considered a useful tool in preparing documents for local practice in the use of machine-readable copy. This chapter does not, of course, cover specific needs of the individual library and is in no way exhaustive. Instead, what I have done is address the use of the MARC record in the most practical and economical way, because the use of technology in copy cataloging was meant to bring it to this point. Collections and needs vary; therefore, it is my hope that Chapter 8, in conjunction with other chapters in this book, will be used as a starting point by those who have never used MARC copy, and as an evaluation tool by those who have already established their local practices.

I would like to extend my gratitude to Ichiko Morita at the Ohio State University Libraries for giving me the opportunity to spend eight hours a day solving copy cataloging questions.

I would like to acknowledge the following colleagues from OCLC who so willingly spent the time and effort to answer questions that arose from this revision: Ellen Caplan, Carol Davis, Rich Greene, and Jay Weitz from Online Data Quality Control, and Gloria Steriti from Profiling. Very special thanks go to Glenn Patton in Cataloging and Database Services at OCLC, who will never cease to amaze all who know him with his breadth of knowledge in all aspects of cataloging, OCLC, and the MARC Formats. Appreciation is also extended to Kay Guiles, Senior Descriptive Cataloging Specialist at the Library of Congress, who has come through time and again, never once asking me to lose his phone number. Because most of my cataloging career was spent using OCLC, I would like to extend special thanks to Robert McDonald at the University of Michigan and Mary Brady at Northwestern University, who shared their experience with the use of copy on RLIN. And, finally, thanks to Nancy G. Thomas, my friend and coauthor (*Notes for Serials Cataloging*), who was a constant source of encouragement, and to Arlene G. Taylor for this opportunity to work with her again.

—Rosanna M. O'Neil

NOTES

[1]Alan Fox, [Letter], *Library Journal* 99 (November 15, 1974): 2918.

[2]Theodore C. Hones, "Evaluation of Processing Services," *Library Trends* 22 (January 1974): 308-9.

[3]Kathryn Luther Henderson, "Some Persistent Issues in the Education of Catalogers and Classifiers," *Cataloging & Classification Quarterly* 7 (Summer 1987): 16.

1

CATALOGS, PROCEDURES, AND PERSONNEL

INTRODUCTION

At one time or another most libraries face decisions about the kind of catalog that will be used as an index to the collection and the sources that will be used for cataloging copy. The cataloging policies to follow and the personnel to carry out these policies must be determined. Libraries must not remain static, however. A vigorous self-analysis must be pursued, especially considering the rapid technological developments that have occurred recently. Besides technological developments, there are always local changes which necessitate reevaluation. Some libraries may anticipate a tremendous increase in growth rate, or may face a change in emphasis (e.g., from a reading room atmosphere to a research-oriented one). Established procedures should not become ends in themselves, never to be reconsidered. And, of course, a new library must consider such questions for the first time.

TYPES OF CATALOGS

A question many libraries face today is whether to replace the type of catalog currently in use with another type. The variety of catalog types available is the greatest it has been in history, and each type has characteristics that make it advantageous in certain situations.

Card Catalog

The card catalog is still the most common type of catalog and has many advantages, especially over book and microform catalogs. Many of its advantages, though, are quickly and easily achieved with an online catalog. However, online catalogs are expensive and require a new kind of expertise to create and maintain, while card catalogs are made with readily available materials and skills, and therefore, for many libraries, may continue in use for some time.

Following is a list of advantages that card catalogs have over book or micro-form catalogs. It should be kept in mind, however, that points one through three are advantages only if the catalog is small enough that the filing can be kept up-to-date.

1. New entries can be added at any time; therefore, the catalog can be updated regularly.

2. Entries are on movable units (i.e., cards) and new entries can be interfiled among the old. This means that subsequent searching is done in only one place, not in several supplements.

3. Cards can be removed at any time, making it possible to withdraw entries immediately upon discarding materials. Cards can be changed or replaced by new cards; therefore, the catalog can keep pace with changes in forms and in terms used as headings.

4. The alphabet is distributed over a larger area (i.e., many drawers), so that more patrons can use it at the same time in that one geographic location.

5. Print is usually larger and easier to read.

6. There is usually more information about the cataloged item at each entry point than appears in a book catalog or COM catalog.

7. More "informal" flexibility is possible (e.g., interfiling of similarly spelled headings).

Book Catalog

Book catalogs, as a form, were abandoned in American libraries around the turn of the century, due to the cumbersome process of typesetting and printing as catalogs grew. However, in the 1960s it became economical and feasible to use computer batch processing to again produce book catalogs. Especially as catalogs increase in size, a book catalog can provide certain advantages over a card catalog:

1. It is portable and can be located and consulted in any part of the library. If not of unusual size, it can be taken to another location to be perused at leisure.

2. Multiple copies can be made. These can be available in numerous parts of the library, branches, university departments, classrooms, book-mobiles, etc.

3. Entries are so grouped that the eye can scan a page quickly, in contrast to the relatively slow process of turning one card after another.

4. It occupies much less space than card catalogs.

5. Clerical filing time and errors can be eliminated if arrangement of entries is done by computer. However, the filing time saved may be replaced by computer inputting time, depending on the system used.

Microform Catalog

This form of catalog is often referred to as a COM (computer output microform) catalog. It can be either on film or fiche, and, of course, requires a microfilm or microfiche reader for its use. It has some of the same advantages as the book catalog. Numbers 3 through 5 under "Book Catalog" also apply to microform catalogs. Number 2 is applicable *if* the library can afford to place a reader in all of the branches, departments, etc. In addition, the microform catalog offers the advantage of being cumulatively updated periodically, so that supplements do not have to be searched in addition to the main catalog. However, cumulations rather than supplements can prove to be expensive.

Online Catalog

A number of large libraries have developed online bibliographic systems that can truly be called online catalogs. Such systems are being sold to or shared with other libraries. In addition commercial systems are flourishing. Many of these are especially geared to smaller libraries. Advantages realized from online catalogs will vary from system to system and can include the following:

1. There are minimal to no delays due to filing time, reproduction time, or binding processes.

2. Instant updating is possible.

3. Authority control over names, series, and subjects can be more efficient, often with semiautomatic assistance from the system.

4. All like entries appear together; there are no supplements to search.

5. The amount of information given can be varied to suit the needs of each user (i.e., a user can specify, for example, "index," "short," or "full" bibliographic record length).

6. Terminals can be available almost anywhere, subject to cost.

7. It is possible to give much more information, such as whether an item is checked out and when it is due; and the system can be used to gain management information so that efficiency of operation can be achieved.

8. Online catalogs can offer enhanced access to bibliographic information through searching capabilities that permit users to perform keyword and Boolean operations on or across single and/or multiple fields.

Makers of all catalogs face many of the same problems of integrating old and new forms of various headings; the assignment of call numbers presents the same decisions to be made, no matter what form the catalog takes. The decisions all libraries face are discussed in Chapters 2 through 7. Makers of online catalogs and those who use the computer as the basis for cards or for book and COM catalogs face additional decisions. These are discussed in Chapter 8.

SOURCES FOR COPY

Most librarians today find that they must rely on cataloging prepared outside the library (usually called *copy cataloging*) in order to get new material on the shelves quickly and to keep their catalogs up-to-date. They do not have the personnel, time, or money to do their own cataloging in-house (usually called *original cataloging*) for everything they acquire. For most of the twentieth century, American libraries have relied on the Library of Congress (LC) as the primary source of copy. The dependence has been so great that most libraries (especially academic libraries) have adopted the practice of following LC policy in their own original cataloging so that the LC copy could be integrated easily into local catalogs.

The extreme reliance on LC for copy is gradually changing with the growth of computer networks such as OCLC (Online Computer Library Center), RLIN (Research Libraries Information Network), Utlas International (formerly University of Toronto Library Automation Systems), and WLN (Western Library Network). In these networks, member libraries input original cataloging when they cannot find LC or other copy already present for an item being cataloged. Gradually, more and more libraries are accepting this *member copy* (also called contributed copy) as the basis for their own catalog records.[1] It is still true, however, that there is a great amount of pressure to follow LC practice when creating member copy. This ensures a certain amount of standardization that will then allow other libraries to use the copy with a minimum amount of alteration.

Library of Congress copy is available from a number of sources. If a library has access to the Library of Congress book catalogs and National Union catalogs, LC cataloging can be located in these and copied by hand or photographed. There are various kinds of equipment that will allow a library to photocopy directly from the book catalog.

Library of Congress copy can be obtained from several other sources as well. Single copies of LC cataloging are available through the LC Cataloging Distribution Service (CDS) Alert Service and from Machine Readable Cataloging (MARC) tapes. Some companies offer LC cataloging on microfiche, which can be printed out on reader-printer paper or reproduced directly onto card stock. Other companies offer a variety of local computer systems that provide access to MARC databases. The newest source of LC cataloging is on compact disc, read-only memory (CD ROM), which provides the entire LC MARC database and allows card production and printing of spine labels.

Library of Congress cataloging data have become more readily available in the publications themselves. Called Cataloging-in-Publication (CIP), the data are usually printed on the verso of the title page. (For an example, see the verso of the title page of this book.) Originally begun by the Library of Congress in 1971, CIP is now being produced in several other countries. There is further discussion of CIP and its possible uses in later chapters.

Cataloging data also can be found in *Weekly Record* (New York, Bowker, 1974- ; weekly). Prior to 1974, the *Weekly Record* appeared as a section of *Publishers Weekly* (New York, Bowker, 1876-). Titles with CIP data are listed in *Weekly Record* much more quickly than other titles, but, of course, lack the physical description. Other titles are listed as soon as they appear in MARC. If *Weekly Record* does not receive LC cataloging information within a reasonable time, then the *Weekly Record* staff prepares its own cataloging; such entries are marked in *Weekly Record* with an asterisk. When examining *Weekly Record*, then, it is important to know that all entries, except those marked with asterisks, represent LC cataloging.

Because of the availability of LC cataloging on MARC tapes, some LC copy can be acquired as already-completed card sets from the jobber or processing agency that supplies the libraries with books and other library materials. There are also companies that sell such card sets (usually based on LC cataloging) independently (i.e., without an accompanying book order).

For many years there has been some cataloging copy available that was not originally created at LC. The *National Union Catalog* has contained since 1956 copy sent in by cooperating libraries for items not owned or cataloged by LC. More recently, the massive set of *National Union Catalog: Pre-1956 Imprints* has published cooperative copy sent to LC before 1956. This copy was often called *co-op copy* and usually received different treatment than strictly LC copy did. The more current equivalent of co-op copy is the member copy, mentioned above, that is available in computer networks. In addition, some of the processing companies that supply cataloging with book orders do original cataloging for items not cataloged by LC.

TRANSITION FROM COPY TO CATALOG

Once outside copy has been located, it must be prepared for the local catalog. The intellectual decisions that must be made in order to do this are discussed in the remaining chapters of this book. After the intellectual decisions have been made, the physical process for getting the copy into the catalog depends upon the type of catalog.

Card Catalog

There are three basic methods by which catalog card sets are made ready to be filed in a catalog:

1. Master unit record altered in-house to suit, then sent outside for card set (which may or may not be returned with headings already printed).

2. Master unit record altered and duplicated in-house, with headings added in-house.

3. Card set purchased from outside; headings may be typed on in-house or the set may be purchased with headings already printed.

1. **Master unit record altered in-house to suit, then sent outside for card set.**

In order to use this method, the library must have a ready source of master unit records. It must also have personnel for preparing the master and may need personnel for typing headings, depending on which system is used. Library of Congress cataloging, cooperative cataloging of some sort, and original cataloging are the usual sources of copy.

In one kind of system using this method, masters are altered if necessary for the local situation, the call numbers are typed on, and the masters are then sent out of the library to a duplicating service. Card sets returned to the library from these services consist of exact duplicates of the master copy. Any headings required must be typed on after return of the card set.

The other kind of system using this method is a computerized operation such as that used by OCLC. In this case, cataloging copy is called up at a computer terminal, where any alterations desired can be keyed in to appear directly on the screen. Then by giving a "produce" command the library orders a set of cards, complete with alterations, from the central computer. These cards are produced according to the needs of the library. Each card of the set need not be a complete unit card, as is necessary for cards provided by duplication methods. Batches of cards arrive in the library with headings already placed at the tops and arranged in order for each catalog, ready to file.

2. **Master unit record altered and duplicated in-house, with headings added in-house.**

Libraries that duplicate card sets by xerography or offset printing methods, may use a master for reproducing card sets, after making any alteration that might be locally required and after typing call numbers on the master. If a multilith method is used, the cataloging must be completely transferred via typewriter to a stencil, which is then used for duplication. After card duplication, a typist is usually needed to type added entries and subject headings at the top of the cards and to make special notations on shelflist cards. Some of this typing has been eliminated in libraries that use highlighting or guide card methods. (These are explained in Chapter 5.) Duplication can also be accomplished by a card printer attached to a computer terminal. The master must be typed on a magnetic card, tape, or disk, either manually or by machine. The mechanism is then programmed to type out from the master a set of cards complete with headings.

3. **Card set purchased from outside; headings may be typed on in-house or the set may be purchased with headings already printed.**

The library selecting this method must have personnel to be responsible for ordering and checking in card sets and may also need personnel to type on headings if card sets are purchased without printed headings.

This method can use LC cataloging or cataloging done by a commercial firm. The library may arrange with a processing company to send sets of cards with items ordered from that company, or sets of cards may be ordered independently for the items that are acquired.

Under the system of ordering books and cards from a processing company, the items arrive in the library completely cataloged, with full sets of catalog cards, spines labeled with call numbers, and pockets and borrowers' cards, ready to use.

If sets of cards are ordered independently, the library usually orders card sets by card number, by author/title, or by a combination of these. Specified numbers of cards are received for each title, and these may or may not have printed headings.

The major drawback of the method of purchasing complete card sets from outside the library is that any local alteration of the descriptive cataloging must be made on every card of the set instead of on only the master before it is duplicated. Also, if the library chooses pre-printed headings and call numbers, it may need to change a heading to fit the local situation or to change a call number that duplicates one already used in the library. This happens because the outside cataloging source cannot check against the local catalog and shelflist.

Book and Microform Catalogs

For most book and microform catalogs, the master is created via computer. If the library is a member of one of the bibliographic utilities, the library's *archive tape* from that utility is sent periodically to the commercial firm that makes the catalog. The firm then integrates the new cataloging with the machine-readable version of the catalog saved from the previous update and creates a new update. In other cases, a library may be using a terminal that is connected to the commercial firm's computer. In this case, the firm collects the library's cataloging until time for a new update. In a very few cases, libraries have local facilities for creating their own COM catalogs from machine-readable files created in-house.

Online Catalogs

In some online catalogs, final approval and production of the master record enters it into the system and it is immediately available to the public. In other systems, index creation occurs only on an overnight basis—or for certain fields, less frequently. Thus, final approval enters the record into the system, but it will not be available to be called up by author, title, added entry, subject, etc., until a later time. Archive tapes are also used to interface with online catalogs to load master records, and availability can occur overnight.

CHECKING COPY AGAINST CATALOG

Libraries have traditionally considered that it is necessary to check in the local catalog all access points (i.e., main entry, added entries, and subject headings) that are suggested on outside cataloging, in order to determine whether the form of entry agrees or conflicts with entries already in the catalog and to determine whether references are needed. It has also been considered necessary to check the classification number in certain types of libraries to avoid duplication of the number and to keep editions, translations, etc., together.

With the advent of LC Copy Cataloging units and network cataloging systems using computer terminals, some libraries gave up checking the catalog before cards were made in the interest of speed. While information from the terminal screen can be printed, and the printout can be taken to the manual catalog for checking, such a procedure takes more time and much more paper than the same procedure once took. It is the belief of some librarians that the most important thing is to get the books cataloged and on the shelf as quickly as possible so that they will be accessible to the public. They have found that optimum use of outside cataloging is made only when the copy is used exactly as it is without change, except for correction of obvious typographical errors and perhaps local adaptation of series. Some feel that a title entry is the most useful access point and that, if such an entry is in the catalog, the item is retrievable. They find that many discrepancies in forms of entry and conflicts in classification can be caught in the filing process. Some believe that different forms of the same name are not a problem as long as *see also* references connect them. Those who use suggested call numbers without checking them say that the call number is only a location device and that patrons must learn to use the catalog to find items they want.

The preceding justifications have been made in order to make speedy use of copy from a computer system in a manual catalog. The increase in online catalogs is changing the landscape again. If an online catalog terminal is near, or integrated with, the terminal used for cataloging copy, the checking of headings may take little time, or may even be automatically carried out by the automated system as part of the cataloging process.

In libraries that continue to check the catalog, there are people who say that some discrepancies cannot be caught in filing. Except in a very small catalog, the filer will not determine that the author who is entered in the catalog under a common surname followed by initials (e.g., Taylor, T. H. C.) may be the same person as the new entry with forenames spelled out (e.g., Taylor, Thomas Hugh Colebrook). This kind of determination, they say, is made by a person who notices that a reference from the initial form may be necessary and, upon checking, finds the entry there. The filer who is filing an entry under "Midwest Prairie Conference (2nd : 1970 : University of Wisconsin, Madison and Parkside)" will not be able to determine that the first symposium was entered under "Symposium on Prairie and Prairie Restoration (1st : 1968 : Knox College)." Nor will filing an entry under "Bell Museum of Natural History" reveal that earlier entries for this museum appear in the catalog under "James Ford Bell Museum of Natural History." The filing of a subject heading under "Snake venom" will not show that earlier works on this topic were assigned the heading "Venom," unless the now-cancelled LC reference from "Snake poisons" to see "Venom" is in the catalog and the filer is suspicious enough not to file the new heading. (This subject heading would not be a problem in a library using a guide card method of authority, which is explained in Chapter 5.) Clues to determinations such as those mentioned above often cannot be found even on the cataloging copy itself but must be found in the item being cataloged. Some believe that since filers must concentrate on disregarding initial articles, filing abbreviations and/or numerals as if spelled out in the language (if older filing rules are still used), and many more complicated filing rules, it is asking a lot to expect them to resolve cataloging discrepancies as well. Also, it often happens in academic settings that students or other lower level staff are given responsibility for filing. These people lack the training for making catalog heading decisions. However, in some libraries, such staff members file *above the rod* after which someone with more training checks the filing and at the same time watches for heading discrepancies.

With the adoption of the *Anglo-American Cataloguing Rules*, second edition (AACR 2), in January 1981, some libraries, who had not had them previously, began authority files for names. In addition the LC authority file has been made available on microfiche from CDS, and is available online for many libraries through OCLC, RLIN, Utlas, WLN, and in some local systems. Access to authority files can help alleviate some of the types of problems noted above. The authority record for Eliot, T. S., for example, shows that the earlier authorized heading was Eliot, Thomas Stearns. The LC authority record, however, does not tell an individual library whether the earlier form of name appeared in that library's catalog, or whether original cataloging in that library appears under a form never authorized at LC. Only a local authority file can assist with such information, and most local authority files do not predate 1980. In addition local subject authority files are almost nonexistent, although this may change now that LC also distributes subject authority records on tape. Series authority files, however, are of long-standing existence, and are checked in most libraries before completion of cataloging.

In libraries that continue checking the catalog before completion of cataloging, there are those who wonder what value there is in increased cataloging speed if the result is that the catalog entries cannot be found once they have been entered into the catalog. In answer to those who suggest that a title entry is the most useful for retrieval, it is pointed out that patrons do not always know the exact wording of the title page title (otherwise called the title proper) and may need other access points.

Those who check the shelflist before accepting any outside call numbers believe that proper order is essential for shelf collocation as well as for an authoritative shelflist. Creation of duplicate call numbers is also a concern of some, considering the amount of work it takes to correct such errors. Also, the checking of call numbers against the shelflist or catalogs may better ensure keeping belles lettres authors together, as well as keeping translations and editions where a patron would expect to find them. Where class numbers are assigned to serials, it is often considered valuable to have successive titles stand with earlier titles. In some libraries with open stacks it is believed that carefully assigned call numbers provide a needed subject retrieval function.

As online catalogs become more sophisticated, much of the checking of new records against the existing catalog will be done automatically. Already there are systems that verify whether a particular new heading matches one already in the system or matches a reference. If there is no match, some systems return the heading for authority work. There are also systems that match author/title combinations so that two editions or a translation and original can be given successive call numbers, and at least one system brings up near-matches for the cataloger's inspection. The future may bring enhancements that will identify common variant spellings of names.

There is no easy way to prove whether or not checking the catalog for discrepancies before cataloging new items is essential to making a useful catalog. The patron who assumes that an item is not in the library because it was not found in the catalog may never know that it is there under other access points; and the library staff may never know that it was wanted and not found; although this, too, is being changed by the advent of online catalogs. Online catalog systems often keep what is called a transaction log — a record of the search terms input by a user and whether or not that request retrieved any *matches* in the catalog. In a study of such a log tape conducted by the author, one user searched for "Loti, Pierre," and got zero *hits*. In fact, the catalog contained a number of works of Pierre Loti, but they were under "Viaud, Julien," the author's real name, and there was, unfortunately, no reference.[2] This example is given to illustrate that we may soon be able to know much more about what users search for, and we may be able to make cataloging decisions accordingly. However, even in the libraries that use copy as it is, *see also* references are often added to resolve discrepancies in form of entry found during filing. The questions may then revolve around how much checking is essential and when it should be done.

AMOUNT AND TIME OF CHECKING

The amount of checking needed depends to a great extent on the size, purpose, and type of the catalog. In a small catalog whose main purpose is to provide the location symbol for items in the collection, it may not be vital that forms of entry be identical. It may even be advantageous for titles of certain authors to be entered under the name or form of name used on each work rather than all under the same form. But in this case the different names or forms of names ought at least to be connected by "see also" references.

In a large catalog whose patrons expect to use it for research purposes, there is increased need for all entries pertaining to a subject or to a name to be together or connected by references. Patrons of such a library often may be looking for everything the library has on a subject, or by and about an author. Even if the patron is looking for a specific item, the titles may be so complicated (e.g., proceedings of symposia) that the patron must know the *exact* form of entry in order to find the item.

A small card catalog offers a greater chance of discovering discrepancies during filing. In a catalog that has less than one drawer of entries beginning with the word "International," for example, an incorrect entry beginning with that word is not as lost as it would be if there were 10 drawers of "International" entries. The filing in book and microform catalogs, however, is seldom done manually. Therefore, discrepancies cannot be caught in filing but must be discovered before the cataloging process is completed.

In large card catalogs and in book and microform catalogs, the only way to be assured of catching discrepancies such as those mentioned above is to check access points in the local catalog *before* the cataloging process is *completed*. This does not necessarily mean before card sets are produced or before a bibliographic record is entered into the system. It may be considered that the cataloging process is not complete until authority work has been done, and authority work may be done six months after an item has been sent to the stacks (although this is certainly not ideal!). If book, microform, or online catalogs are used, checking may be done before cataloging or afterward in a proofreading process. However, when copy is contributed to a computer network, standards may require that authority work be complete before final production of a record. If a card set without headings is purchased, access points can be checked before headings are typed on; if a card set is purchased with preprinted headings, access points can be checked using the main entry or shelflist card, before or after the other cards are filed. How much of this checking can be done depends on the number, experience, and training of people available to do both the checking and the filing. In some libraries, every access point (i.e., main entry and all tracings that appear on the copy being used) is checked for form against the catalog as the first step in cataloging. Many of the access points will be new entries. Many will match what is in the catalog already. Others will differ only in lack of a birth or death date, for example, on the catalog entry. At some of the access points, the checker will find a reference from the form used on the copy to some other form. Such discrepancies can be discerned by people with only a small amount of training (e.g., those who have been taught filing rules and have had an explanation of tracings, such as the difference between subject headings and other added entries). Therefore, this kind of checking can be done by people who work only an hour or two a day (e.g., students). The checkers can indicate for the cataloger what was found.

Since the above kinds of discrepancies can also be discerned when filing into a card catalog, if the filer is trained to watch for them *and is allowed the time to do so*, some libraries elect not to do the preliminary checking. Instead, the cataloger must judge which entries present problems that may not be caught in filing. These usually are checked by the cataloger. This method, of course, takes a calculated risk. The cataloger must exercise judgment about the difficulties of entries, and such judgment usually requires a great deal of experience. This method also requires more of the cataloger's time. In addition, the filer must have more training and experience and must concentrate more when filing, or the filing must be done above the rod and then checked by an experienced reviser.

A certain amount of inconvenience results when filing reveals a discrepancy that involves a change on the card being filed. If it is a change in the main entry, the entire card set may have to be located and changed, and card sets may have to be recalled from other locations (e.g., reading rooms or branch libraries). If it is a change in a subject heading or added entry, the card(s) used for official tracings (i.e., main entry and/or shelflist) usually must be located and changed. Libraries that produce cards via computer and that care about the condition of their archive tape must call up the machine-readable record and update it. These inconveniences should be weighed against the time and effort spent before cataloging to check entries that turn out to be new to the catalog or identical to what is already there. A discrepancy that involves changing what is already in the catalog is no more inconvenient if found in filing than if found before cataloging. The proportion of discrepancies that will mean changing new cataloging copy versus those that mean changing entries already in the catalog depends on the library's cataloging policies. If the policy is to use one's own catalog as the authority, there will be more changing of new copy. If the authority of the outside cataloging source is accepted, there will be more changing of the entries in the catalog. Pros and cons of using one's own catalog as the authority versus using the outside source as the authority are discussed in Chapter 3.

When cataloging is going into an online catalog, much of what has just been said becomes moot. In some systems every access point that needs authority control on a new record entering the system is checked automatically against the authority file or index for the type of access point in question, and discrepancies are either identified immediately for the cataloger online, or they are printed out for later resolution. Such systems, of course, cannot identify such discrepancies as "Elizabeth A. Schwenn" and "Elizabeth Schwenn Ghatala" being two names for the same person, unless the authority file contains a reference from one to the other.

With or without preliminary checking of entries in the catalog, someone must be responsible for resolving conflicting entry forms when they are identified and for supplying needed references. Procedures used for processing materials for which copy is available will dictate the qualifications and training of staff.

KNOWLEDGE REQUIRED FOR PERSONNEL

In determining the personnel levels necessary to perform various functions, it is helpful to consider what knowledge is required in order to carry out specific assignments. Table 1.1 (pages 14 and 15) subdivides cataloging into its various components and indicates the knowledge required for carrying out different functions effectively. Not all of the items listed in the column under "knowledge required," of course, could be expected in every library. Searching of *National Union Catalog* (*NUC*) and *New Serial Titles* (*NST*) and use of authority files could not be required in libraries that do not have access to such tools. Knowledge of historical LC cataloging practices would not be extremely useful in a library that does not use Library of Congress cataloging. Foreign language requirements would probably not be expected in libraries that do not acquire a significant number of foreign language materials. Knowledge of computer system requirements would not be necessary for manual systems or for catalogers who never work at a terminal and whose work is MARC coded and input by others. One item of knowledge is so specialized that it has not been included in the table: knowledge of a specific subject usually would be required only in special libraries or for original catalogers in large libraries where work may be divided by subject.

Each of the functions given as headings of columns in Table 1.1 may involve various activities. Following is the interpretation of these activities as seen by the author:

Column 1. Filing only. For filing in the main catalog the filer would be expected to know the arrangement (i.e., dictionary or divided) of the catalog and to be able to place entries in the proper order. The filer might be expected to notice typing errors. For the shelflist the filer would be expected to arrange in numerical and/or in alpha/numeric order.

Column 2. Filing to catch discrepancies. In addition to the requirements for the filer in Column 1, this filer would be expected to notice such things as differences in form of entry and to know when such differences need correcting. This would require an understanding of forms used in the past (e.g., "Mrs." inserted before a married woman's forename) that are not now used and are not a conflict, as opposed to *different* forms of name, which do constitute a conflict. The filer would be expected to recognize references that conflict with a heading. Local tolerance levels for slightly different forms would have to be understood.

Column 3. Preliminary checking of access points given on outside cataloging. The person working in this capacity is asked to look up, in the local catalog, the access points found on outside cataloging to determine whether the entry form appears in the catalog and, if it does, whether or not it agrees in form. The person would require the same knowledge as the one expected to catch discrepancies in filing, except that a knowledge of filing rules should be applied for finding entries rather than for filing them. This assumes that the checker is asked to check every access point (i.e., main entry and all tracings) appearing on the copy. If less is required of the checker, then, of course, less knowledge is expected. The checker might also be asked to check authority files if the library has them.

Column 4. Locating best copy in computer system. A system searcher would need a thorough knowledge of the appropriate system commands. It would be important to know the most efficient ways of searching, but it would also be necessary to understand that duplicates may exist but may not show up under every access point. In addition to thorough knowledge of the relevant system manuals, the person in this position would need working knowledge of present and past rules for access points, some knowledge of foreign languages, and some exposure to local cataloging practice.

Column 5. Matching description between item and outside copy. The person performing this function would be asked to check the items given in the description on the copy to see if they are an exact match or a locally acceptable variation of the item in hand. No additional description is added. However, if the library accepts "shared cataloging" from LC, this person must be given an explanation of the variations in description used by some other countries (e.g., the practice by some of counting unnumbered pages in addition to the numbered ones; differences in use of brackets, etc.). (In shared cataloging the physical description was provided by the national library of the country where the item originated. Most of this description was accepted by LC, but the access points [i.e., main entry and all tracings] and their form were decided by LC. This practice occurred at LC from 1966 to 1982. LC may return to the practice of basing bibliographic description on cataloging prepared by the country of origin when computer tapes from such countries can be loaded into LC's automated system.) This person must also know something about older descriptive cataloging by LC, if retrospective LC copy is used. In addition this person would either be trained to perform the functions in Column 6, or would pass on items for which the descriptions did not match to a person who was trained for those functions.

Column 6. Making simple corrections on outside copy or completing CIP. This staff member would make, as required, minor corrections such as changes in paging, correction of typographical errors, or removal of notes not applicable to the item in hand. This person also could complete Cataloging-in-Publication (CIP) using either CIP found with the item or MARC CIP as a basis. The CIP record with the item requires addition of other title information, statement of responsibility, edition, publication details, physical description, and completion of some notes. MARC CIP requires addition of physical description, completion of some notes, and often requires changes of other parts of the description that have changed since the publisher sent prepublication information to LC. In addition to knowledge required by the person in Column 5, this column requires more knowledge of local descriptive policy so that variations desired locally (i.e., differences from standard practice) can be made. The staff members performing functions 5 and 6 would be working with *exact copy* only. That is, the outside source from which the copy came would have cataloged the same edition of the item, although not necessarily the same printing. If these corrections are to be made online, the person must know the system requirements for MARC coding the additional information and for editing system records.

Column 7. Making major changes on outside copy. This action would be required of someone working with *near copy* (i.e., copy that is for a different edition than the one in hand; also called *variant* or *kindred copy*). Besides major changes in description, authors or editors might have changed between editions; therefore, main and added entries would need attention. Subject headings might have to be changed or the terminology updated. This person might also work with

Table 1. Knowledge Required in Order to Perform Various Cataloging Functions

✓ = some exposure to the knowledge is required
✓✓ = working knowledge is required
✓✓✓ = thorough knowledge is required

KNOWLEDGE REQUIRED	1 filing only	2 filing to catch discrepancies	3 preliminary checking of access points given on outside cataloging	4 locating best copy in computer system	5 matching description only between item and outside copy
Filing rules (main catalog and/or shelflist)	✓✓✓	✓✓✓	✓✓✓		
Rules for description (AACR 2[1], Chaps. 1-13)					✓✓
Rules for main entry (AACR 2, Chap. 21)				✓	
Rules for additional access points (AACR 2, Chap. 21)				✓	
Rules for form of entry (AACR 2, Chaps. 22-25)		✓✓	✓	✓	
Rules for making refs. (AACR 2, Chap. 26)		✓	✓		
Procedure for searching NUC[2], and NST[3], etc. (i.e. variant filing rules and arrangements)					
Use of authority files			✓✓		
Use of subject heading tools					
Procedure for assigning new subject headings					
Procedure for completing suggested class numbers					
Use of classification schedules for assignment of class numbers					
Historical LC cataloging practices		✓✓	✓	✓✓	✓✓
Local cataloging variations and policy		✓✓	✓		✓
Foreign languages	✓	✓	✓	✓	✓
How procedures of other departments mesh with those of the Catalog Department					
Procedure for searching computer system			✓	✓✓✓	✓
System manuals				✓✓✓	
System requirements for input of new records					

[1]*Anglo-American Cataloguing Rules*, 2nd ed.   [2]*National Union Catalog.*   [3]*New Serial Titles.*   [4]Cataloging-in-Publication.

6	7	8	9	10	11	12	13	14	15	16	17	18
making simple corrections on copy or completing CIP[4]	making major changes on outside copy (e.g., near copy)	adding notes concerning contents, relation to other publications, etc., to outside copy	making references for names, series, or other added entries (not subjects)	resolving conflicts between copy and local entries; making additional added entries	adapting subject headings to local use	making subject references	determining if call number suggested can be used	adapting suggested classification numbers to local use	original descriptive cataloging (including main entry and added entries)	assigning original subject headings	assigning original call numbers	responsibility for correctness of MARC tags, indicators, subfield codes, and fixed field elements
		✓✓	✓✓	✓✓	✓✓	✓✓	✓✓	✓✓	✓✓✓	✓✓✓	✓✓✓	
✓✓	✓✓✓	✓							✓✓✓			✓
		✓	✓✓						✓✓✓			✓
	✓✓	✓✓✓	✓	✓✓✓					✓✓✓			✓
			✓✓✓	✓✓✓					✓✓✓			✓
			✓✓✓	✓✓✓					✓✓✓			
			✓✓✓	✓✓✓					✓✓✓			
	✓		✓✓✓	✓✓✓	✓✓✓	✓✓✓			✓✓✓	✓✓✓		
	✓				✓✓✓	✓✓✓				✓✓✓	✓	
	✓				✓					✓✓✓		✓
							✓✓	✓✓✓			✓✓✓	✓
	✓						✓	✓✓			✓✓✓	
✓✓	✓✓✓	✓✓	✓✓✓	✓✓✓	✓✓	✓	✓	✓✓	✓✓✓	✓✓✓	✓✓✓	✓
✓✓	✓✓✓	✓✓✓	✓✓✓	✓✓✓	✓✓✓	✓✓✓	✓✓✓	✓✓✓	✓✓✓	✓✓✓	✓✓✓	✓✓
✓	✓✓	✓✓	✓✓	✓✓	✓	✓✓			✓✓	✓✓✓	✓✓✓	✓
	✓	✓	✓✓	✓✓✓	✓✓	✓	✓	✓✓	✓✓✓	✓✓✓	✓✓✓	
✓	✓	✓	✓✓	✓	✓✓	✓✓	✓	✓	✓✓	✓✓	✓	✓
✓✓	✓✓✓	✓✓✓		✓✓				✓	✓✓✓	✓✓✓	✓✓	✓✓
	✓✓✓	✓		✓				✓	✓✓✓	✓✓✓	✓✓✓	✓✓

records from national agencies other than LC (e.g., records from the British Library, sometimes identified as *UKM* records). Such records often provide physical description in a different way from LC, omit codes for the "Contents" fixed field in MARC records, and have different standards for transcribing publication information and notes. They also usually provide only the LC classification number part in the LC call number field; and the forms of names in main and added entries can be very different from LC's because they are based on a different authority file. In an online environment, it would be mandatory for the person doing this job to be thoroughly familiar with the system requirements because editing major changes into copy would often require creating a new record in the system.

Column 8. Adds notes concerning contents, relation to other publications, etc., to outside copy. The person doing this job would be expected to add notes that pertain to the item in hand but that did not pertain to the item held by the source of the copy (e.g., label over imprint, autographed copy, numbered copy, etc.). Notes also may be added that have been missed by the cataloging source but that are deemed important to the individual library. In addition, notes would be added both to the copy being worked on and to entries already in the catalog if it were library policy to make connections in the catalog between editions with changed titles, between originals and translations, to draw together parts of a trilogy, or to explain bibliographical relationships of serials to one another. In order to do this, the filing rules of the catalog must be understood to facilitate the finding of related items. (The filing rules are considered necessary to functions 8 through 17 because of the need to find and relate items in the main catalog and/or shelflist to the item being cataloged.) This person may add notes that are felt necessary in order to justify an added entry wanted in the local library but not traced by the cataloging source. If working with an online system, this staff member would need a thorough understanding of MARC coding and editing and some knowledge of what changes or additions constitute new "editions" and therefore require new system records.

Column 9. Making references for names, series, or other added entries (not subjects). A staff member may be asked to determine what references are needed to guide users to the form used as the main entry or as any added entry on the copy. Since the outside copy does not come with suggested references, the staff member must know what is required both according to the rules and locally. If the library uses LC cataloging, the staff member may be required to find references made by LC either in depository reference files, in *NUC*, in LC authorities on microfiche, or in an online LC authority file. The staff member may also be asked to search the local catalog and authority files before making a reference in order to avoid references that would conflict with headings already in the catalog.

Column 10. Resolving conflicts between copy and local entry forms and making additional added entries. Whether conflicts are found before cataloging or during filing, someone will have to resolve them. This requires the same knowledge and skills as making added entries that may have been missed by the cataloging source or that may be required by local practice. Both activities require knowledge of rules for access points and form of entry and, if applicable, searching of bibliographical and biographical tools for verification of the access point and its form. The person carrying out these assignments must know how entries have been formed in the past and what differences have been applied locally. Since references are important to the process of resolving conflicts and for adding new access points, functions 9 and 10 require quite similar knowledge.

Column 11. Adapting subject headings to local use. Terminology in individual libraries sometimes differs from that used by the cataloging source. It also sometimes happens that the cataloging source changes terms. Conflicts with references may occur. The person asked to make these adaptations must be familiar with subject heading tools and historical and local cataloging practices with regard to subjects and should be able to use any online system available that will help in identifying current terminology. If the library uses LC cataloging, the staff member should be able to use LC subject authorities either in book form, on microfiche, or online.

Column 12. Making subject references. This function requires full understanding of the subject heading authority used in the library plus knowledge of how completely the local library will follow the suggested reference structure. An ability to sense present and future changes, by noting terminology changes in the literature and by an awareness of changes in the philosophy of the subject heading source, is helpful, as is an understanding of past practice. As with function 11, this person should be able to use whatever online system is available.

Column 13. Determining if the call number suggested can be used. There are often times when the suggested classification/call number on copy from an outside source cannot be used exactly as it is. The person who is asked to make this determination must thoroughly understand the local guidelines as to what may and may not be accepted. This requires a basic understanding of the call number system and a knowledge of past practices.

Column 14. Adapting suggested classification numbers to local use. If cataloging copy is not obtained from a processing firm that completes all call numbers, this must be done in the local library. Included in this category are all Dewey Decimal numbers suggested by the Library of Congress and the bracketed, incomplete, or alternative, LC classification numbers that often appear below completed LC call numbers. The person with this responsibility must have a thorough knowledge of call number structure and local applications, and should be able to make use of any available online system that might give assistance with assigning consistent numbers.

Column 15. Original descriptive cataloging (including choice and form of main entry and added entries). This activity is required when no copy is available from an outside source; also, it is done in some libraries when only cooperative copy is available. Cooperative copy is cataloging done by some source other than the official one usually used in that library (e.g., cataloging done by a library other than LC and printed in the *NUC* or copy input into one of the national databases by one of the member institutions). Original descriptive cataloging requires thorough knowledge of entry, description, referencing, searching, and historical cataloging practices, as well as an understanding of local cataloging practices. Where cataloging is completed online, it requires thorough knowledge of use of the system and of system requirements for input of new records.

Column 16. Assigning original subject headings. Original subject headings are assigned when no copy is available, when only cooperative copy is available and it either has no subjects or has subjects that cannot be accepted, or when copy available gives subjects not adequate for the item in hand. Thorough subject knowledge is required, along with an understanding of historical and local cataloging practice. Use of an online system requires knowledge of its use and requirements for input.

Column 17. Assigning original call numbers. Original call numbers are assigned when there is no copy, when only cooperative copy is available and cannot be accepted, when no suggested call number is given, or when the suggested number is not locally usable. In order to fulfill this function a person must have a complete understanding of the use of classification schedules, the shelflist, and knowledge of historical and local practice. Some knowledge of subject headings and their relationship to classification is also very helpful. Use of an online system requires knowledge of its use and requirements for input.

Column 18. Having responsibility for correctness of MARC tags, indicators, subfield codes, and fixed field elements. This activity is required when catalog records must be input into a system that uses the MARC format as a standard. The person carrying out this function may or may not be the same as the one responsible for the intellectual content of the record (i.e., physical description, access points, etc.). This function requires some knowledge of parts of a catalog record, some understanding of subject headings and call numbers (in order to decide, for example, where the classification part of an LC call number ends and where the specific work part begins), an exposure to historical cataloging practices of LC (in order to update older LC copy); and, the person may have to know how to search the system. If the library handles foreign materials, this person may need some understanding of these languages. A working knowledge of local policy is helpful. Finally, a working knowledge of system manuals and requirements for input is a necessity. Assigning of MARC tags is integrally related to many functions within the process of cataloging, and more often than not, tagging is a part of the entire process.

The most effective combination of functions into various positions depends on the type of cataloging system used, the local cataloging policies, and the goals of the individual library. Size plays a definite part, too, since a staff of two, for example, has relatively little freedom in the manner in which the functions may be divided. In each local situation, the trial and error method often determines which combinations work best. If there is unlimited staff, however, it is the author's opinion that functions 5, 6, 8, and 9 go well together for processing most material quickly and efficiently. Functions 11 and 13 work in well, too, if it is the library's policy to accept without change most subjects and call numbers given on the copy. Function 9 is included, even though it requires considerably more knowledge than the others, because needed references often can be determined only from the item in hand. It seems most efficient for the person who is matching the copy also to note potential references, such as corporate body hierarchies that appear prominently in the publication. If cataloging is done online, functions 4 and 18 need to be included with 5, 6, 8, 9, 11, and 13 for the most efficient processing of the majority of materials.

Before deciding on the basic qualifications of cataloging personnel, the library administration should decide which of the above functions will be required of whom. The more functions and/or the more complicated the functions, the higher will be the qualifications of the individual performing them and the longer will be the training period. The cataloger expected to perform only functions 5 and 6, for example, need not be as highly qualified nor as extensively trained as the one expected to perform functions 8 and 9 as well as 5 and 6. Addition of functions 4 and 18 (i.e., working in an online environment) would add yet another layer of required qualifications and training.

In the past, many large libraries restricted cataloging functions to librarians with master's degrees, or at least with undergraduate degrees in library science. In recent years, however, the trend has been to assign many of the cataloging functions to paraprofessionals (also called library technicians or library assistants), who often have bachelor's or associate degrees, two to four years relevant work experience, or a combination of college and work experience. The division of functions is usually made according to whether or not cataloging is available from an outside source. The professionals continue to catalog the items for which original cataloging is needed. In some libraries that use LC copy, the professionals also catalog with copy because it is felt that otherwise they will lose touch with what LC is doing and will not be aware of new cataloging practices. Most libraries, however, are finding that they cannot keep up with the materials waiting to be cataloged and that they must pursue more economical methods. Paraprofessionals are usually paid less than professionals. With enough time, however, paraprofessionals can be trained to perform most of the cataloging functions; and the more they are expected to do, the more they should be paid. With or without master's degrees, people should receive salaries commensurate with their contribution to the library.

Qualifications necessary for a person to perform each of the functions given in Table 1.1 cannot be dictated. Each library must deal with local realities (e.g., merit plans, unions, prevalence or dearth of highly qualified people, etc.) as well as library considerations. The qualifications considered necessary vary greatly from institution to institution. In one institution familiar to the author, copy catalogers who perform functions 4, 5, 6, 8, and 18 must have either a four-year college degree, or two years of experience in a library and some college education, or four years of library experience. In another institution the requirements are nothing more than a high school diploma.

The following chapters contain a discussion of the complexities that can arise when cataloging copy from an outside source is used. The people who catalog from such copy, whether professional or paraprofessional, are referred to throughout this book as *copy catalogers*.

SUMMARY

A library must grapple with certain basic considerations before undertaking any copy cataloging. The following questions must be answered:

1. What type of catalog is used?

2. What source(s) will be used for cataloging copy?

3. Is checking of cataloging against the local catalog and/or shelflist necessary?

4. If the answer to 3 is "yes," how much checking is essential and when?

5. What knowledge is required by personnel who file, check, or catalog with outside copy?

6. How will the work of filing, checking, and cataloging be divided among professionals, paraprofessionals, and/or clerks?

7. What qualifications are necessary for copy catalogers?

NOTES

[1]See, for example, Laura Salas-Tull and Jacque Halverson, "Subject Heading Revision: A Comparative Study," *Cataloging & Classification Quarterly* 7 (Spring 1987): 3-12, which discusses acceptance of subject headings found on member copy.

[2]Arlene G. Taylor, "Authority Files in Online Catalogs: An Investigation of Their Value," *Cataloging & Classification Quarterly* 4 (Spring 1984): 1-17.

2

DESCRIPTION

INTRODUCTION

The goals and objectives of a library that uses cataloging from an outside source must be examined in order to determine how much of the *description* will be accepted without change. Such philosophical considerations should help answer the question of what purpose is to be served by the descriptive cataloging on a catalog entry for the library. Just what is it that should be accomplished in that library? Should the description be an exact description of the item the library owns, or is it to be an identification device only? One determining factor may be the ease with which a patron can get to an item to examine it physically. If this is difficult because of closed stacks or because of outlying locations such as branch libraries, it may be more important for the description to be accurate. Another factor may be the type of library. It may be important that a research library describe the item accurately since minute differences can distinguish between editions. In a library whose main aim is to disseminate quickly the intellectual contents of its materials, however, it probably will be felt that it does not serve the library's purposes to spend an inordinate amount of time on minute detail in cataloging. A third factor may be the increased use of union catalogs and networks that serve persons at some distance from the item. Any library that is involved in these or that has even a remote possibility of being involved some day, must weigh its responsibilities to the distant as well as to the local clientele.

Basically, three types of outside copy may be available: *exact* copy, *near* copy, and *cooperative* (co-op) copy. Each of these types is called by different names in various places. Some of the alternate names are identified here, but after this the three types are identified as exact, near, and co-op, because these terms tend not to be specific to any one system.

Exact copy results when the usual outside source has cataloged the same edition of the item as the one the library has acquired (although it might be a different printing of that edition). *Edition* of a book is here defined as all the printings of a work done by one publisher in which there are no substantive changes in the work or its typesetting between printings. A different printing occurs whenever the same plates or settings of type are used to produce another *batch* of pages. Edition, in the case of items other than books, refers to all the copies of one master produced by one agency. Exact copy for a library that closely follows LC would be known as *LC exact copy*. In some network systems it is referred to as *DLC copy* or *DLC/DLC* in reference to the codes that appear in the MARC 040 field of such copy. Exact copy for a medical library might be that from the National Library of Medicine.

If the only copy found from the outside source is for some edition of the work other than the one owned by the local library, the result is near copy. This term, too, has its variants. It may be called *kindred* copy, *close* copy, or *variant* copy.

If copy is available from other than the usual source of outside cataloging, the result is co-op copy. Co-op copy may be called *member* copy or *member-contributed* copy in network systems. It is also sometimes called *090* copy because that is the MARC field where the local LC call number is input in such a record. (Copy created by LC has the LC call number in the 050 field.) Co-op copy can be exact in the sense that it may be cataloging for the edition the library has acquired, but it is seldom treated as exact copy. When such copy is not from the usual outside source, it often has to be altered in order to be integrated into the local catalog.

This chapter discusses the decisions required in order to use exact copy. Cataloging of near and co-op is discussed in Chapter 7.

Even when exact copy has been found, there is no guarantee that the description will match exactly the copy of the item that the individual library owns. Certain policy decisions need to be made about how completely the outside descriptive cataloging will be accepted, and the following factors should be given consideration. The discussion applies to both serial and monographic patterns of publication unless otherwise specified.

TYPOGRAPHICAL AND CATALOGING ERRORS

In a recent study conducted by the author and a colleague, 46.2 percent of the sample LC records had at least one error or discrepancy from current practice somewhere in the MARC record.[1] An additional 6.3 percent of records required change of at least one element of the record because the copy of the item received locally was different from LC's copy or because cataloging policy had changed since the copy was first created. Human errors occur with any cataloging source. The individual library must decide when these errors matter enough to make it worth the time required for word-by-word checking of the copy. In the aforementioned research, *significant* errors, defined as errors that would affect any kind of access point, were found in 19.6 percent of the records.[2] The difficulty was that there was no way to predict which records would fall into this group without examining every record.

Some of the errors found were in the main entry or tracings. Presumably in any library it would be absolutely necessary to correct these, since errors in these places would affect the filing of entries in card, book, or microform catalogs and would affect the creation of index entries in online catalogs. Correcting errors that occur in various descriptive elements, however, may be open to debate. If an error occurs in the transcription of the title proper or filing title, one assumes that it must be corrected. Because there is, in a majority of cases, a tracing for "Title" on manual records or an indicator calling for a title access point on MARC records, the spelling of the title as it appears in the description is used for this entry. There has been an increase in title main entries as well as title added entries made by cataloging agencies in the last few years. Correct spelling of the title in both cases is essential for correct filing or indexing. Many title errors are obvious just from looking at the cataloging, as in the case of a title "The Aztecs" which appears on the copy as "The Aztees." Others, however, are not apparent from looking at the copy (Examples 2.1 below and 2.2 on page 24) but are discovered in the process of comparing the copy with the title page of the book. These may change the sense of the title, as in Example 2.2.

```
OCLC: 6863466        Rec stat: c Entrd: 800930        Used: 820529
Type: a Bib lvl: m Govt pub:     Lang:  eng Source:     Illus: af
Repr:      Enc lvl:    Conf pub: O Ctry:  wb  Dat tp: c M/F/B: 10
Indx: 1 Mod rec:      Festschr: O Cont: b
Desc: a Int lvl:     Dates: 1981,1980
  1 010        80-24858
  2 040        DLC $c DLC
  3 050 0      ND653.B68 $b R63 1981
  4 082 0      759.9493 $2 19
  5 090        $b
  6 049        YCLM
  7 100 10     Roethlisberger, Marcel, $d 1929-
  8 245 00     Bartholemeus Breenbergh : $b the paintings / $c Marcel
Roethlisberger.
  9 260 0      Berlin ; $a New York : $b de Gruyter, $c 1981, c1980.
 10 300        v, 122 p., [170] p. of plates : $b ill. (some col.) ; $c 32
cm.
 11 504        Bibliography: p. 113-115.
 12 500        Includes index.
 13 600 10     Breenberch, Bartholomeus, $d 1599?-ca. 1659.
```

Example 2.1. First word of title proper should be spelled "Bartholomeus." (Note: "Breenberch" is the spelling of the painter's last name in the LC authority file, but the spelling of that name on the title page is "Breenbergh.")

```
OCLC: 7577465        Rec stat: p  Entrd: 810611          Used: 830223
Type: a Bib lvl: m  Govt pub:    Lang:  eng Source:      Illus: a
Repr:    Enc lvl:    Conf pub: 0  Ctry:  wau Dat tp: s  M/F/B: 10
Indx: 0 Mod rec:    Festschr: 0  Cont:
Desc: a Int lvl:    Dates: 1981,
   1 010        81-8378
   2 040        DLC $c DLC
   3 020        0914842595
   4 039 0      2 $b 3 $c 3 $d 3 $e 3
   5 043        n-us-wa
   6 050 0      F899.S443 $b P48 1981
   7 082 0      979.7/77 $2 19
   8 090        $b
   9 049        YCLM
  10 100 10     Peterson, Bob, $d 1941-
  11 245 14     The sight of Seattle, downtown : $b a photographic tour /
$c photographs by Bob Peterson ; text by Earl D. Layman ; with a
foreword by Mayor Charles Royer.
  12 250        1st ed.
  13 260 0      Seattle : $b Madrona Publishers, $c c1981.
  14 300        90 p. : $b ill. ; $c 28 cm.
  15 651 0      Seattle (Wash.) $x Description $x Views.
  16 650 0      Architecture $z Washington (State) $z Seattle $x Pictorial
works.
  17 700 10     Layman, Earl D.
```

Example 2.2. Title should be: The sights of Seattle, downtown.

Correct punctuation of a title can also be an issue. Example 2.3 shows two records from the OCLC system for the same work. Ideally the record from LC would have superseded the record input earlier, but the difference in title punctuation gave the two records different search keys and the appearance of being different works. It would also be possible to punctuate this as a title proper followed by a subtitle (i.e., "Contact : $b human communication and its history"). This, too, presents a problem. Some online catalogs index only titles proper, while others index other title information as well. In manual files, too, some libraries file through a subtitle, while others only file through a title proper, and then subfile by main entry, subtitle, or date if there are two or more identical titles proper.

An error may also occur in the subtitle, as in Example 2.4 (page 26). This element of the description usually does not affect filing except as noted above. However, it may affect retrieval in a system that allows keyword searching of entire titles. Whether to change this depends on the answer to several questions: What is the library's philosophy of descriptive cataloging? If it must describe the book in hand exactly, as discussed earlier in this chapter, or if keyword searching of titles and subtitles is allowed, the change must be made. Is it difficult to make such a change? If the error is noticed and if it is easily corrected on a master before duplication, or at a computer terminal, then it probably should be done. But if the library has acquired a whole set of cards with this error, the question will be: Is it really worthwhile to change it? The decision on whether to change may also be influenced by the extent to which students or lower level paraprofessionals are used. A simple rule with few exceptions will help make efficient use of the person's time and will simplify training.

Record (a)

```
OCLC: 8026597        Rec stat: c Entrd: 811229        Used: 830928
Type: a Bib lvl: m Govt pub:     Lang:  eng Source: d Illus: a
Repr:     Enc lvl: K Conf pub: 0 Ctry:  nyu Dat tp: s M/F/B: 10
Indx: 1 Mod rec:     Festschr: 0 Cont:
Desc: a Int lvl:     Dates: 1981,
  1 010        81-50663
  2 040        PBL $c PBL
  3 020        0500012393 : $c $27.50
  4 092        001.51
  5 090          $b
  6 049        YCLM
  7 245 00     Contact, human communication and its history / $c edited by
Raymond Williams.
  8 260 0      New York : $b Thames and Hudson, $c 1981.
  9 300        272 p. : $b ill. (some col.) ; $c 28 cm.
 10 504        Bibliography: p. 264-266.
 11 500        Includes index.
 12 650 0      Communication.
 13 700 10     Williams, Raymond.
 14 740 1      Human communication and its history.
```

Record (b)

```
OCLC: 8280692        Rec stat: n Entrd: 820223        Used: 840312
Type: a Bib lvl: m Govt pub:     Lang:  eng Source:     Illus: a
Repr:     Enc lvl:   Conf pub: 0 Ctry:  nyu Dat tp: s M/F/B: 00
Indx: 1 Mod rec:     Festschr: 0 Cont: b
Desc: a Int lvl:     Dates: 1981,
  1 010        81-50663
  2 040        DLC $c DLC
  3 020        0500012393 : $c $27.50
  4 039 0      2 $b 3 $c 3 $d 3 $e 3
  5 050 0      P90 $b .C66
  6 082 0      001.51 $2 19
  7 090          $b
  8 049        YCLM
  9 245 00     Contact--human communication and its history / $c Ferruccio
Rossi-Landi ... [et al.] ; edited by Raymond Williams.
 10 260 0      New York, N.Y. : $b Thames and Hudson, $c 1981.
 11 300        272 p. : $b ill. (some col.) ; $c 28 cm.
 12 504        Bibliography: p. 264-266.
 13 500        Includes index.
 14 650 0      Communication.
 15 700 20     Rossi-Landi, Ferruccio.
 16 700 10     Williams, Raymond.
```

Example 2.3. Punctuation of the title in Record (a) affected the search key used in OCLC at the time to locate records. This meant that Record (b) did not supersede Record (a) as it should have. [It will be noted also that the statements of responsibility differ, resulting in an additional access point on Record (b). This might also affect the superseding process.]

```
OCLC: 6707724      Rec stat: p Entrd: 800825         Used: 820417
Type: a Bib lvl: m Govt pub:    Lang:  eng Source:    Illus: a
Repr:    Enc lvl:    Conf pub: O Ctry:  nju Dat tp: s M/F/B: 10
Indx: 1 Mod rec:    Festschr: O Cont:
Desc: i Int lvl:    Dates: 1981,
  1 010        80-21596
  2 040        DLC $c DLC $d m.c.
  3 020        013275875X
  4 050  0     TK7874 $b .B77
  5 082  0     621.381/73 $2 19
  6 090         $b
  7 049        YCLM
  8 100  10    Buchsbaum, Walter H. $w cn
  9 245  10    Encyclopedia of integrated circuits : $b a practical
handbook of practical reference data / $c Walter H. Buchsbaum.
 10 260  0     Englewood Cliffs, N.J. : $b Prentice-Hall, $c c1981.
 11 300        xxii, 420 p. : $b ill. ; $c 26 cm.
 12 500        Includes index.
 13 650   0    Integrated circuits.
```

Example 2.4. Subtitle should be: A practical handbook of essential reference data.

The statement of author, editor, or other contributors can be considered in much the same light as the subtitle. In Example 2.5, probably the only harm done in a manual catalog by the misspelling of the forename in the statement of responsibility is that the cataloging reviser would call into question the correctness of the spelling of the main entry. Such an error in an online environment could be more serious in a system that allows keyword searching of

```
OCLC: 7274217      Rec stat: p Entrd: 810212         Used: 820819
Type: a Bib lvl: m Govt pub:    Lang:  eng Source:    Illus:
Repr:    Enc lvl:    Conf pub: O Ctry:  nyu Dat tp: s M/F/B: 10
Indx: 1 Mod rec:    Festschr: O Cont: b
Desc: a Int lvl:    Dates: 1981,
  1 010        80-29488
  2 040        DLC $c DLC
  3 020        0030590310
  4 039  0     2 $b 3 $c 3 $d 3 $e 3
  5 050  0     D16.9 $b .A77 1981
  6 082  0     335/.119 $2 19
  7 090         $b
  8 049        YCLM
  9 100  10    Aronowitz, Stanley.
 10 245  14    The crisis in historical materialism : $b class, politics,
and culture in Marxist theory / $c Standley Aronowitz.
 11 260  0     New York, N.Y. : $b Praeger, $c 1981.
 12 300        xxv, 345 p. ; $c 24 cm.
 13 500        "A J.F. Bergin Publishers book."
 14 504        Bibliography: p. 323-334.
 15 500        Includes index.
 16 650   0    Historical materialism.
 17 740  01    Class, politics, and culture in marxist theory.
```

Example 2.5. The name in the statement of responsibility is misspelled. "Stanley" is the correct spelling.

any selected field. In such a case the misspelled name might not be retrieved or might appear to be a different person. In Example 2.6 the misspelling in the statement of responsibility has affected the access point for that name. In most catalogs, the misspelled name would fall many entries away from the correctly spelled form, and the name would be lost. However, the decision may be to change only the tracing and not bother with changing the statement in the body of the description. As in Example 2.5, this could cause revising problems.

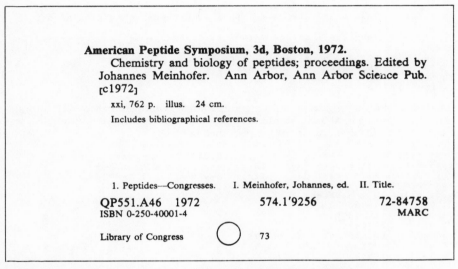

Example 2.6. The editor's surname should be spelled "Meienhofer."

Another kind of error in statements of responsibility occurs when information that was included in a MARC CIP record, created from prepublication information sent in by the publisher, is not changed to match the book when the record is updated to full MARC status. Two examples of this are shown in Examples 2.7 and 2.8 (page 28). In the first example, the form of the author's name was not changed to match the form on the title page. In the second example extra phrase words and a secondary statement of responsibility did not appear on the title page, but were not deleted from the full MARC copy (not to mention that the subtitle shown also did not appear on the title page). The error in Example 2.7 could affect the choice of AACR 2 form of name when *predominance* is being determined. The errors in Example 2.8 would be a problem mainly only in the case of someone trying to distinguish between editions. In the study by Taylor and Simpson mentioned earlier, it was found that the statement of responsibility was in error in this way in 4 percent of the CIP records, and the other title information had this kind of problem in 2.4 percent of the CIP records.[3] These are not high percentages, so procedures for their correction should follow the library's philosophy for descriptive cataloging.

```
OCLC: 6915050        Rec stat: p Entrd: 801009        Used: 840403
Type: a Bib lvl: m Govt pub:       Lang:  eng Source:    Illus: a
Repr:     Enc lvl:     Conf pub: O Ctry: enk Dat tp: s M/F/B: 10
Indx: 1 Mod rec:       Festschr: O Cont: b
Desc: i Int lvl:       Dates: 1981,
   1 010        80-25644
   2 040        DLC $c DLC $d m.c.
   3 020        0521235979
   4 050 0      HA30.3 $b .G67
   5 082 0      519.5/5/024301 $2 19
   6 090        $b
   7 049        YCLM
   8 100 10     Gottman, John Mordechai. $w cn
   9 245 10     Time-series analysis : $b a comprehensive introduction for
social scientists / $c John Mordechai Gottman.
  10 260 0      Cambridge ; $a New York : $b Cambridge University Press, $c
1981.
  11 300        xvi, 400 p. : $b ill. ; $c 24 cm.
  12 504        Bibliography: p. 393-396.
  13 500        Includes index.
  14 650 0      Time-series analysis.
```

Example 2.7. Title page shows author's name as John M. Gottman, but the CIP information had given the name as John Mordechai Gottman. The statement of responsibility was not corrected by LC upon receipt of the published book.

```
OCLC: 7553970        Rec stat: p Entrd: 810429        Used: 820525
Type: a Bib lvl: m Govt pub:       Lang:  eng Source:    Illus:
Repr:     Enc lvl:     Conf pub: O Ctry: nyu Dat tp: s M/F/B: 10
Indx: O Mod rec:       Festschr: O Cont:
Desc: a Int lvl:       Dates: 1981,
   1 010        81-7348
   2 040        DLC $c DLC
   3 019        8470626
   4 020        003059586X : $c $23.95
   5 039 0      2 $b 3 $c 3 $d 3 $e 3
   6 043        n-us---
   7 050 0      HC106.7 $b .N43
   8 082 0      338.973 $2 19
   9 090        $b
  10 049        YCLM
  11 100 10     Neal, Alfred Clarence.
  12 245 10     Business power and public policy : $b experiences of the
Committee for Economic Development / $c authored by Alfred C. Neal ;
foreword by Philip M. Klutznik.
  13 260 0      New York : $b Praeger, $c 1981.
  14 300        xiv, 163 p. ; $c 25 cm.
  15 610 20     Committee for Economic Development.
  16 651 0      United States $x Economic policy $y 1971-
  17 650 0      Industry and state $z United States.
  18 650 0      Industry $x Social aspects $z United States.
```

Example 2.8. Title page lacks subtitle, the phrase "authored by," and the author of the foreword. The 245 field *should* read:

   245 10   Business power and public policy / $c Alfred C. Neal.

Errors in the edition statement may consist of punctuation errors or misspellings. Punctuation errors should cause great concern only if it is considered extremely important to follow the specified punctuation of the International Standard Bibliographic Description (ISBD) for purposes of making the record machine-readable. It should be realized that if a great deal of time is spent on small details, the user will be deprived of access to the item for a longer time, the risk of duplicating an acquisition is increased, and the processing cost per title rises perhaps unnecessarily. Misspellings are subject to the questions raised regarding subtitles. However, the complete absence of an edition statement, as in Example 2.9, affects the identification of the item. The fact that this was the third edition was clearly indicated on the cover, spine, title page, and verso of the title page of the book; yet it was not noted on the copy, although the year in the imprint was recorded correctly. The patron looking specifically for the third edition might not realize that this is, in fact, that edition, or the library's acquisitions staff could possibly order an unneeded duplicate.

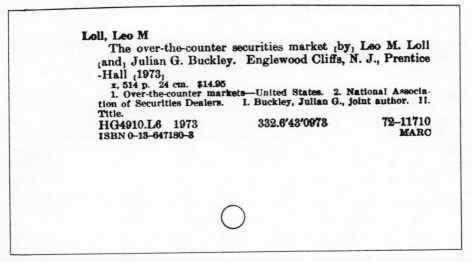

Example 2.9. Edition statement, "3d ed.," has been omitted. (The correct abbreviation in 1973 was "3d," not "3rd," as is currently used.)

As with the other areas of description, errors in the publication and distribution information may consist of punctuation errors or misspellings. The questions already identified should be addressed here. In addition, there can be differences in the form of name of the same publisher from record to record. In Example 2.8, the publisher is given as "Praeger," while in Example 2.10 (page 30) the same publisher is represented as "Praeger Publishers," even though the representations in the two books are identical (that is, the name "Praeger" appears in large type on the title page, and "Praeger Publishers" appears with the address on the verso of the title page). AACR 2 does not specify or require consistent transcription of publisher names. However, if it ever becomes desirable to search online systems by publisher, this could present problems.

Common errors in the physical description occur in transposition of numbers in the paging (e.g., 240 p. instead of 204 p.), omission of the number of preliminary pages, omission of the number of pages or leaves of plates, or

```
OCLC: 7572471        Rec stat: p Entrd: 810527        Used: 840327
Type: a Bib lvl: m Govt pub:    Lang:  eng Source:     Illus:
Repr:     Enc lvl:     Conf pub: 0 Ctry:  nyu Dat tp: s M/F/B: 10
Indx: 1 Mod rec:      Festschr: 0 Cont: b
Desc: a Int lvl:     Dates: 1981,
   1 010       81-8638
   2 040       DLC $c DLC
   3 020       0030595924 : $c $20.95
   4 039 0     2 $b 3 $c 3 $d 3 $e 3
   5 043       n-us---
   6 050 0     HV6791 $b .Z49
   7 082 0     364.1/62/088042 $2 19
   8 090        $b
   9 049       YCLM
  10 100 10    Zietz, Dorothy.
  11 245 10    Women who embezzle or defraud : $b a study of convicted
felons / $c Dorothy Zietz ; foreword by Vernon Fox.
  12 260 0     New York, N.Y. : $b Praeger Publishers, $c 1981.
  13 300       xii, 157 p. ; $c 24 cm.
  14 440 0     Praeger special studies in social welfare
  15 504       Includes bibliographical references and index.
  16 650 0     Female offenders $z United States.
  17 650 0     Fraud $z United States.
  18 650 0     Embezzlement $z United States.
```

Example 2.10. Form of name of publisher is different from the form given in Example 2.8, even though the forms given on the two title pages are identical.

describing *leaves* as *pages*. It must be decided at what point a discrepancy in the number of pages given becomes important to correct — 1 page? 5 pages? 50? 100? or not at all? Transposition of digits in the number of volumes takes on more significance, since this kind of discrepancy could be confusing both to acquisitions staff and to patrons who need to know if certain volumes are in the library. Errors may also occur in the statement of other physical details. The record may say "ill." when there are no illustrations, but the opposite case is the more common error. It should be considered how vital it is to a particular library's users to know whether or not an item is illustrated, and what kind(s) of illustrations it has.

In some cases where catalog cards are produced from MARC tapes, the physical description may not appear at all, as in Example 2.11. This is because incomplete Cataloging-in-Publication data have been used on the MARC tapes. It will need to be decided whether paging and the remainder of the physical description line are to be supplied.

The series statement should not be left with an error if it is to be used as a tracing, as shown in Example 2.12. Sometimes a series statement is omitted on the copy. This affects an access point if it is a series ordinarily traced by the library. The omission of the series tracing means that the patron looking for that number or all titles in a series may decide that the library does not own the title in question. This can also result in the purchase of duplicate titles from a series if a bibliographer is trying to fill gaps in a series by searching for the series title. A phenomenon that has occurred in conjunction with the CIP program is shown in Example 2.13 (page 32). A series may be included in the CIP MARC record and then not be removed from the updated MARC record if the book is not actually published as part of that series. Otherwise, the treatment of misspellings and other errors in the series statement should be similar to the treatment of misspellings mentioned above.

```
629.13  Dwiggins, Don.
D

        The sky is yours;; you and the world
     of flight.; Illustrated with photos.
     Childrens Press; [1973]
        p.
        Explores the many careers and hobbies
     open in general aviation and discusses
     the principles and challenges of
     building and/or flying a plane.




     1. Aeronautics as a profession.
     2. Flight.  3. Airplanes.  I. Title

                                         Follett Library Book Co.
              01900B
```

Example 2.11. There is no physical description information.

```
OCLC: 7278288        Rec stat: p Entrd: 810312        Used: 820520
Type: a Bib lvl: m Govt pub:   Lang:  eng Source:   Illus:
Repr:     Enc lvl:   Conf pub: 0 Ctry:  ilu Dat tp: s M/F/B: 00
Indx: 1 Mod rec:    Festschr: 0 Cont: b
Desc: a Int lvl:    Dates: 1981,
  1 010        81-2584
  2 040        DLC $c DLC
  3 020        0226709469 : $c $39.50 (est.)
  4 039 0      2 $b 3 $c 3 $d 3 $e 3
  5 043        n-us---
  6 050 0      Q125 $b .S43433
  7 082 0      500 $2 19
  8 090        $b
  9 049        YCLM
 10 245 00     Science in America, a documentary history, 1900-1939 / $c
edited, selected, and with an introduction by Nathan Reingold and Ida H.
Reingold.
 11 260 0      Chicago : $b University of Chicago Press, $c c1981.
 12 300        xii, 490 p. ; $c 24 cm.
 13 440     4  The Chicago history of sciences and medicine
 14 504        Includes bibliographical references and index.
 15 650     0  Science $x History.
 16 650     0  Science $z United States $x History.
 17 700 10     Reingold, Nathan, $d 1927-
 18 700 10     Reingold, Ida H.
```

Example 2.12. Series should read: The Chicago history of science and medicine.

```
OCLC: 7739808      Rec stat: p Entrd: 810810        Used: 820520
Type: a Bib lvl: m Govt pub:    Lang:  eng Source:    Illus: a
Repr:    Enc lvl:   Conf pub: 0 Ctry:  nyu Dat tp: s M/F/B: 10
Indx: 0 Mod rec:    Festschr: 0 Cont: b
Desc: a Int lvl:    Dates: 1982,
    1 010        81-13077
    2 040        DLC $c DLC
    3 020        0471097861
    4 039 0      2 $b 3 $c 3 $d 3 $e 3
    5 050 0      QA276.A1 $b C6
    6 082 0      519.5 $2 19
    7 090        $b
    8 049        YCLM
    9 100 10     Cochran, William Gemmell, $d 1909-
   10 245 10     Contributions to statistics / $c William G. Cochran.
   11 260 0      New York : $b Wiley, $c c1982.
   12 300        1 v. (various pagings) : $b ill. ; $c 26 cm.
   13 440 0      Wiley series in probability and mathematical statistics, $x
0271-6232. $p Probability and statistics section
   14 504        Includes bibliographical references.
   15 650 0      Mathematical statistics $x Collected works.
```

Example 2.13. Series statement is not in the book. It was included in CIP and was not removed from the updated copy.

Some notes are used as the basis for access points or for filing entries; for example, original titles of translations are given added entries in some libraries. Example 2.14 shows how far off the filing would be if the error in the "Title romanized" were not caught and corrected. This, of course, would affect filing both under the author's name and under the title entry. Another situation is shown in Example 2.15. The spine title and half title both differ from the title proper, but neither is mentioned in a note, and as a result, the record lacks an access point that may be the very title remembered by users, or even the one cited in bibliographies.

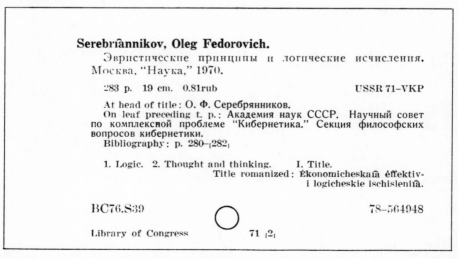

Example 2.14. Title romanized should be: Ėvristicheskie printŝipy i logicheskie ischisleniĭa.

```
OCLC: 8556792        Rec stat: n Entrd: 820622        Used: 840118
Type: a Bib lvl: m Govt pub:     Lang:  eng Source:    Illus: af
Repr:    Enc lvl:    Conf pub: 0 Ctry:  enk Dat tp: s M/F/B: 10
Indx: 1 Mod rec:     Festschr: 0 Cont: bc
Desc: a Int lvl:     Dates: 1981,
   1 010        81-66309
   2 040        DLC $c DLC
   3 020        0126729808
   4 039 0      2 $b 3 $c 3 $d 3 $e 3
   5 043        e-uk-en
   6 050 0      Z6611.T3 $b S77 1981 $a BX1970
   7 082 0      016.282 $2 19
   8 090        $b
   9 049        YCLM
  10 100 10     Stratford, Jenny.
  11 245 10     Catalogue of the Jackson Collection of manuscript fragments
in the Royal Library Windsor Castle : $b with a memoir of Canon J.E.
Jackson and a list of his works / $c by Jenny Stratford.
  12 260 0      London ; $a New York : $b Academic Press, $c 1981.
  13 300        xiii, 106 p., 10 p. of plates : $b ill. ; $c 24 cm.
  14 504        Includes bibliographical references and index.
  15 610 20     Catholic Church $x Liturgy $x Manuscripts $x Catalogs.
  16 650 0      Theology $x Manuscripts $x Catalogs.
  17 600 10     Jackson, John Edward, $d 1805-1891 $x Library $x Catalogs.
  18 600 10     Jackson, John Edward, $d 1805-1891 $x Bibliography.
  19 610 20     Windsor Castle. $b Royal Library $x Catalogs.
  20 710 20     Windsor Castle. $b Royal Library.
```

Example 2.15. The following notes are lacking on this copy:
    On spine: The Jackson Collection at Windsor Castle.
    Half title: The Jackson Collection of manuscript fragments at Windsor Castle.
Thus, the copy lacks an access point for "Jackson Collection ...," that would not file near any of the access points given.

Other notes have no relation to access points or filing but can be considered useful in relating the work to other works or in giving information about the item. Omission of bibliography notes is a common error. Decisions on including this note or on corrections of its misspelling, punctuation, incorrect listing of page numbers, or incorrect use of terminology must be based on the results of the philosophical discussion of the purpose of descriptive cataloging. Is the addition of a bibliography note worth the time required to look through each book to see if it has a bibliography? Are these notes worth the time necessary to add or correct them, especially if the library purchases card sets rather than working from a master? Should the pages, volume, etc., of the bibliography note be checked each time? If so, and the data are incorrect, is it worth the time to make such a correction?

In summary, it is the author's opinion that errors on outside cataloging copy fall into three groups: those that affect access points; those that affect identification of the item (i.e., differentiating between editions to the extent believed necessary by the library); and those that affect neither. At one time these three groups were easily distinguished. Access points were main entry, all tracings, and call number. Identification of the item, for the most part, came from the *body* of the entry (title through publication date), physical description, and series. Notes usually fell into the third group. However, in an online environment characterized by sophisticated searching capabilities, the lines are becoming quite blurred.

Virtually every linguistic or numeric element in a record becomes a potential access point. Notes, names of publishers, and statements of responsibility take on new relevance in the context of enhanced potential for retrieval of bibliographic information in an online system. Online capabilities will play an increasingly important role in determining copy cataloging policies. We may be headed toward a time when our technology no longer affords us the luxury of being less meticulous about certain bibliographic elements regardless of whether or not they appear in what once were traditional access points. To the extent, then, that the three groups mentioned above can be identified, the first two groups should be corrected if possible. Yet these errors will not be discovered unless the cataloging of each item is carefully compared word by word with the item. The extra time taken to find the errors will have to be weighed against the inconvenience to the patron of possibly not finding a desired item. The third group is in less urgent need of correction, and a decision on whether to correct will depend on the library's view of the purpose of its descriptive cataloging.

OUTDATED COPY

Any library that acquires material more than a few years old must decide how to deal with outdated cataloging copy. This problem formerly affected primarily those libraries using Library of Congress cataloging. Many other sources of cataloging copy, such as Baker & Taylor, for many years provided a kind of simplified cataloging that changed less than that done by LC. More recently, however, such companies have relied more and more on LC MARC records as the basis of the card sets they supply, and they, too, now face the problem of outdated copy.

The problem is that descriptive cataloging at LC and in the library profession has gone through periods of great change. Rules written in 1908 gave general guidance without many specific examples. By 1941 descriptive cataloging had become complete and definitive. Rules were written with the intention of covering every possible situation. By 1949 there was a revolt against this completeness in description. Ever since, there has been a trend toward being less definitive. Descriptive cataloging underwent another great change in the form of the adoption of ISBD for monographs in 1974, and for motion pictures and certain other graphic materials in 1975. In 1981 the adoption of AACR 2 meant the application of the ISBD standard to serials, sound recordings, and other formats that had previously been described quite differently. A library's decision to use or not use outdated copy may depend on several factors.

If the library's method of cataloging production is reproduction of master photocopies from book catalogs, or if card sets are ordered from an outside source, the library may want to use the copy as it is, with as little change as possible. If the library has decided to check copy against the items in hand to determine accuracy, the idiosyncrasies of outdated cataloging will have to be understood by the staff member who checks the copy. And decisions may need to be made about whether or not to add missing descriptive elements.

If the library's method of card production is such that the copy must be retyped (e.g., multilith or stencil), there may be a negative reaction to retyping outdated copy—especially a lengthy physical description. If cataloging is done online, there may be a temptation to fill in information on outdated copy that appears to be missing by today's standards, because it is relatively easy to do, especially on a dedicated terminal. *Modernizing* the copy, however, means that a person trained in current rules for description and familiar with the old techniques must examine all the outdated copy in order to make the changes necessary.

There are three major categories of outdated copy to be considered:

1. Pre-ISBD/pre-AACR 2 cataloging
2. Pre-1949 cataloging
3. Limited cataloging

Pre-ISBD/pre-AACR 2 Cataloging

Pre-ISBD cataloging includes almost all monographic cataloging done before September 1974, all audio-visual materials cataloging done before 1975, and all serials and sound recordings cataloged before January 1981. Examples of pre-ISBD monographic cataloging are found in Examples 2.6, 2.9, and 2.14. Many libraries using LC copy had some cataloging that followed ISBD principles prior to 1974 because LC's shared cataloging had been accepting ISBD from some other countries. Many of the differences are in punctuation (see Example 2.16). There are also some differences in abbreviation and in rules for how much information to include in the description and in what form. For example, the statement of responsibility was not always included as it is in ISBD; also, the original title, when given on pre-ISBD copy, always appeared in a note, but now it *may* appear in the title area. There are a number of other such changes.

Ringstad, Vidar, 1939-
    On the estimation of dynamic relations from combined cross section time series data = Om estimering av dynamiske relasjonar frå tverrsnitts-tidsrekkedata / by Vidar Ringstad. — Oslo : [H. Aschehoug], 1976.
    p. 27-37 ; 24 cm. — (Artikler frå Statistisk sentralbyrå ; nr. 87)
    Reprinted from the Scandinavian journal of economics, v. 78, 1976.
    Bibliography: p. 39.
    ISBN 8253706200 : kr5.00

    1. Labor supply—Norway—Mathematical models. 2. Econometrics. I. Scandinavian journal of economics. II. Title. III. Title: Om estimering av dynamiske relasjonar frå tverrsnitts-tidsrekkedata. IV. Series: Norway. Statistisk sentralbyrå. Artikler ; nr. 87.

HA1503.A45	Nr. 87	310'.8 s	79-301723
[HD5800.A6]		[330'.01'8]	MARC

Library of Congress   79

Example 2.16. Illustrated here are three kinds of punctuation that were not prescribed to appear on pre-ISBD copy: the equal sign before the parallel title, the slash before the author statement, and the period-space-dash-space between areas of the description. Other kinds of punctuation (e.g., colons and semi-colons) are prescribed for use in ways and places they were not used before.

One decision to make in accepting pre-ISBD copy concerns whether or not all copy should be changed according to ISBD practices. If it should not, copy catalogers have to make a distinction between those differences which result because information on the copy is inaccurate and those which result because ISBD requires that the information be presented in a different manner than was required by older rules. For example, the cataloger working with pre-ISBD copy has to know that for monographs the publisher was not given in the imprint when it appeared as the main entry; therefore, the lack of a publisher in such situations was not an oversight on the part of the outside cataloging source. The local library may choose to add the publisher when it is also the main entry, but it should not do so as an *error* correction. The cataloger also must know that the imprint date was given in brackets if it did not appear on the recto of the title page, that the number of leaves or pages of plates was not included in the pagination, that the index was not indicated in a note, that the statement of responsibility was not given in some instances, that the reprint imprint was given differently, etc.

In January 1981 LC adopted AACR 2. Although for description of monographs the changes were not drastic, the copy cataloger working with pre-AACR 2 copy must know, for example, that "second" and "third" were abbreviated "2d" and "3d" in edition statements; that abbreviations such as "with an introd. by" were allowed in the statement of responsibility area; that inclusive dates in the same century were shortened (i.e., 1973-76) in the publication area; that general material designations were capitalized; that a known country, state, or province where an item was published could not be given if the city or town were unknown; that subseries were usually given in a separate set of parentheses from the main series; that an ampersand rather than a plus sign introduced accompanying material; and a number of more minor details.

For pre-AACR 2 serials the cataloger must be aware that a statement of responsibility was almost never given; that the date of publication was usually given only in the *holdings* statement and not repeated in the publication area; that when the place of publication or name of publisher varied from issue to issue, one place or one name was given followed by "etc."; that the frequency was often given immediately following the physical description on the same line rather than as the first note; that some notes about title changes began with the words "superseded by" rather than always beginning with "continued by"; and many other such differences. Example 2.17 shows a card for a serial cataloged prior to use of ISBD format and one cataloged after adoption of ISBD format, which for serials coincided with adoption of AACR 2 in January 1981.

Catalogers of sound recordings also began using ISBD format with the adoption of AACR 2. Example 2.18 (page 38) shows cards for sound recordings cataloged before and after adoption of ISBD. Catalogers using pre-AACR 2 copy for sound recordings must know that there was no imprint as such. Instead, a label name and number was given followed by a date. Information about playing time was given in the notes. The general material designation (GMD) was capitalized (i.e., [Sound recording]), and prior to 1976 the term used was *Phonorecord* or *Phonodisc*. One major change from pre-AACR 2 cataloging has resulted from an LC policy decision. Prior to 1981, if there were two or three works on a sound recording, each was given a separate catalog record, and a "with" note gave the other work(s) that shared the same physical container, as illustrated by Record (a) in Example 2.18. With implementation of AACR 2, LC decided to create only

Record (a)

Contributions to music education. no. 1–

1972–
₍Columbus, Ohio₎ Ohio Music Education Association ₍etc.₎

    v. ill. 23 cm. annual.

Vols. for 1972–   issued by the OMEA Research Committee;
        by the Ohio Music Education Association.
Key title: Contributions to music education, ISSN 0190–4922.

1. Music—Instruction and study—Periodicals.   I. Ohio Music
Education Association. II. Ohio Music Education Association. Research Committee.

ML1.C9155   780′.72   79–640469
                                  MARC–S

Library of Congress   79   MN

Record (b)

Ceramic source / compiled by The American Ceramic Society. —
Vol. 1 ('86)- — ₍Columbus, Ohio₎ : The Society, ₍c1985₎-

    v. : ill. ; 28 cm.

Annual.
Title from cover.
ISSN 8756-8187 = Ceramic source.

1. Ceramics—Periodicals. 2. Ceramics—Directories. 3. Ceramics—Handbooks, manuals, etc. 4. Ceramic materials—Periodicals. 5. Ceramic materials—Directories—Periodicals. 6. Ceramic industries—Directories—Periodicals.
7. Ceramic materials—Handbooks, manuals, etc. I. American Ceramic Society.

TP785.C36   666′.05—dc19   86-641172
                                 AACR 2   MARC-S

Library of Congress   ₍8708₎

Example 2.17. Record (a) gives an example of cataloging for a serial prior to adoption of ISBD format; record (b) illustrates ISBD/AACR 2 serial cataloging.

one bibliographic record for each such collection, as illustrated by Record (b) in Example 2.18.

Record (a)

Szymanowski, Karol, 1882–1937.
　ₜMasques. Shéhérazadeₜ ₜSound recordingₜ
　Masques: Shéhérazade.　Royale ROY 2005.　p1977.
　on side 2 of 1 disc.　33⅓ rpm.　stereo.　12 in.

　With: Mozart, J. C. W. A.　Concerto, piano, K. 466, D minor.
　Peter Toperczer, piano.
　Duration: 9 min., 55 sec.
　Program notes by Anthony Hodgson on container.

　　　1. Piano music.　I. Toperczer, Petr.　II. Title.　III. Title: Shéhérazade.

　[M1010]　　　　　　　　○　　　　　　　　79–761043

　Library of Congress　　　　　　　　79　　　　　　　　R

Record (b)

Handel, George Frideric, 1685–1759.
　ₜWater music.　Selectionsₜ
　Water music ; Music for the royal fireworks ₜsound recordingₜ / George Frideric Handel. — Czechoslovakia :
Supraphon, p1974.
　1 sound disc : 33⅓ rpm, stereo. ; 12 in.

　Supraphon: 1110 1556.
　Ars Rediviva ; Milan Munclinger, conductor.
　Recorded Jan.-Mar. 1973 at the Supraphon Studio at the House of
Artists, Prague.
　Program notes by Milan Munclinger in English, French, and
German on container.
　The selections from the Water music include the Suite no. 1 in
F major and an additional Alla hornpipe.

　　　　　　　　　　　(Continued on next card)

　　　　　　　　　　　○　　　　　　83–752986
　　　　　　　　　　　　　　　　　　AACR 2
　　　　　　　　83　　　　　　　　　　R

---

　　　1. Suites (Orchestra)　　I. Munclinger, Milan.　II. Handel, George
Frideric, 1685–1759.　Music for the royal fireworks. 1974.　III. Ars
Rediviva.　IV. Title: Water music.　V. Title: Music for the royal
fireworks.

　[M1003]　　　　　　　　○　　　　　　83–752986
　　　　　　　　　　　　　　　　　　　AACR 2
　　　　　　　　　　　83
　Library of Congress　　　　　　　　　　R

Example 2.18. Record (a) illustrates pre-ISBD/AACR 2 cataloging of a sound recording; record (b) shows an example of cataloging for a sound recording according to ISBD/AACR 2 rules.

The cataloger using pre-ISBD and pre-AACR 2 copy should be aware that the differences outlined above are not errors. Whether changes are to be made in such instances must be a matter of local policy. However, changing all copy to ISBD/AACR 2 format would be a major project for any library that acquires retrospective materials.

If the decision is to change only what must be changed to make the copy match the items in hand, while leaving the rest of the copy as it is, then it must be decided whether ISBD/AACR 2 style or non-ISBD/pre-AACR 2 style is to be used in the changes made on pre-ISBD/pre-AACR 2 copy. The problem with using ISBD/AACR 2 style on non-ISBD copy is that the result is not aesthetically pleasing to some librarians. However, most users are not bothered by half an imprint in ISBD style. The problems with not using ISBD/AACR 2 style on everything are greater. The people who work with cataloging copy all down the line (i.e., catalogers, library assistants, and typists) cannot be expected to remember several different sets of rules and two styles of punctuation. The two soon become confused. It is especially difficult to teach new people several sets of rules and expect them to be able to remember which is which. Catalogers still have to recognize old-style cataloging, but it could be hoped that they do not have to remember in detail the previous rules governing description. Mixing cataloging styles is not allowed on new copy by the networks, but this author believes such a restraint does not have to be maintained at the local level.

At least one change called for by AACR 2 should be followed, in any case, on pre-AACR 2 copy because it affects the form of the title access point. On older copy numerals in foreign language titles were followed in brackets by the spelled out form. Now the title is transcribed and traced as it is, and an additional access point is made for the spelled-out form.

Pre-1949 Cataloging

The most common differences in pre-1949 LC cataloging fall in the area of detailed physical description. Ellipsis points (...) were used at all places in the body of the entry where information from the title page was not transcribed. Paging in the physical description area was given in detail and all unpaged leaves were accounted for (e.g., 3 p.l. was used to indicate preliminary leaves appearing before paged leaves). Types of illustrations were given in detail (through 1971, in fact), but the depth of detail varied with the years. Size was given to the nearest half centimeter. The first words in the series statement often were "Half-title" or "Added t.p." "At head of title" notes were often used, even though this information was often repetitious of items appearing elsewhere in the cataloging. Only the proper names or the first word in a corporate body name were capitalized, and the publisher's full name was given in the imprint including such terms as "& co.," "inc.," "ltd." Notes were much more extensive and numerous than they are now. There were many different forms of bibliography notes instead of the three relatively standard forms now used. These differences can be confusing if one is familiar only with current LC cataloging practices.

When working with pre-1949 copy, as with all pre-ISBD copy, a cataloger must distinguish between changes required because of inaccurate information, and changes resulting from differences in cataloging style. The latter should be made only if the library has decided to modernize the copy. Record (a) in Example 2.19 shows cataloging done in 1916. In order to modernize it, the changes in description listed on page 41 would have to be made.

Record (a)

Maitland, Frederic William, 1850–1906, *ed.*
... Select pleas in manorial and other seignorial courts. Volume I. Reigns of Henry III. and Edward I. Edited for the Selden society by F. W. Maitland   London. B Quaritch, 1889.

lxxvii, ₁1₁, 5, ₆6₁–188, ₆6₁–188, ₁185₁–212 p. 26½ᵐ.   (*Half-title:* The publications of the Selden society ... vol. II)

At head of title: Selden society.
Latin text and English translation on opposite pages, numbered in duplicate.
No more published.

1. Courts baron and courts leet.   2. Manors—Gt. Brit.   I. Title.

16—389

Library of Congress   ₁a41r8311₁

Record (b)

Wanklyn, Harriet Grace.
The eastern marchlands of Europe, by H. G. Wanklyn ... With a foreword by Alan G. Ogilvie ...   London, G. Philip & son, ltd.; ₁etc., etc.₁ 1941.

xxiii, ₁1₁, 356 p. illus. (maps) diagr. 22½ cm.

"Corrigenda" slip mounted on p. 1.
Bibliography at end of each chapter except the last.

CONTENTS. — General introduction. — **pt. I.** The Baltic group: Regional introduction. Finland. Estonia. Latvia. Lithuania.—**pt. II.** Poland and the city of Danzig.—**pt. III.** The Danube lands: Regional introduction. Czechoslovakia. Hungary. Yugoslavia.—Conclusion.

1. Baltic states.   2. Central Europe.   I. Title.

A 41—4520

Harvard Univ.   Library
for Library of Congress   D208.W35
                    ₁a500½₁†   940

Example 2.19. Cataloging done at the Library of Congress before 1949 was very detailed. If this copy is photocopied in order to produce card sets, it is not particularly a problem, but if a stencil is typed to be used in duplicating a set of cards, or if the record has to be MARC tagged and entered into a computer system, the amount of detail may be excessive.

Punctuation would be added to reflect ISBD.

Ellipsis points would be removed, before title and after series.

"Society" would be capitalized in editor statement and series note.

Physical description would read: lxxvii, 183, 212 p. ; 27 cm. --

Series note would read: (The Publications of the Selden Society ; v. 2)

At head of title note would be removed.

A sample of the detailed cataloging done between 1941 and 1949 is shown in Record (b) in Example 2.19. The following changes would modernize this copy:

Punctuation would be added to reflect ISBD.

Ellipsis points would be removed.

Imprint would be changed to: London : G. Philip, 1941.

Physical description would read: xxiii, 356 p. : ill. ; 23 cm.

First note would read: Errata slip inserted.

Second note would read: Includes bibliographies.

Contents note would probably be considered unnecessary.

These changes would have to be made by a cataloger, in many cases, although a typist could automatically make some changes without instructions. For example, half centimeters could always be rounded off to the next highest centimeter, and ellipsis points at the beginning, but not necessarily at the end, of titles and following names could be removed. But all of the internal manipulation of the descriptive elements would take the scrutiny of one trained in the varying descriptive rules.

Limited Cataloging

Limited cataloging was practiced at LC from 1951 to 1963 in order to cope with a large bulk of incoming materials. It is distinguished by a double dagger (‡) following the LC card [control] number (LCCN) on printed LC copy and by a "/L" following the LCCN in a MARC record. Most libraries will encounter very little of this cataloging unless they are cataloging large collections of older materials or are involved in retrospective conversion of manual records to machine-readable form. Limited cataloging was applied "on the basis of the relative value of the material to the library."[4] Cataloging was very much simplified. Title, edition, and imprint, but not author statement (as statement of responsibility was then called), were transcribed according to the rules. The author statement usually was transcribed only when necessary to show such a thing as joint authorship. The paging was reduced to the last numbered page of the volume or an indication of the number of volumes, with a few variations possible if the above did not apply. Preliminary pages were not given. "Illus." was used for all types of illustrations, a policy to which LC returned in 1971. Size was given according to the rules. Notes were reduced in length and only specified types of notes were to be used. For example, bibliographical history could be given for serials only if given on cover, title leaf, or end leaf. Search was allowed only if needed to discover the relationship of the piece being cataloged to earlier or later issues of the same publication. Bibliographic history of monographs could be given if discovered without special search. Bibliography notes were added only when of special importance, and then only as a general note: "Includes bibliography." Since added entries were, for the most part, limited to titles and sometimes joint authors, notes that would ordinarily be given to justify added entries were not used. Series notes were allowed even though *no series added entries were made*, even when a particular series had previously been traced.[5] The result was short, succinct cataloging, which may appear incomplete to the staff member trained in modern cataloging practice.

A library using this copy should decide whether it is willing to live with the limitations. One can probably do without the author statement, as long as needed references have been made. Example 2.20 is a sample of this situation. The copy has no author statement, but the author's name on the title page was Felix Youssoupoff. A cataloger adding this record to the catalog should be certain there is a reference from the title page form to ĪŪsupov. The physical description, too, may be sufficient, depending on one's philosophy of descriptive cataloging. The statement of illustrations, as mentioned earlier, is usually limited to "illus." or "ill." on copy since 1971 as well as on limited cataloging; so, if a library decides this is not sufficient, a great deal of changing will be required.

ĪŪsupov, Feliks Feliksovich, *kn͡iaz'*, 1887–
   En exil. Paris, Plon ₍1954₎
   253 p. Illus. 20 cm.

   ɪ. Title.

   DK254.I 7A33   56–86010 ‡

   Library of Congress   ₍8₎

Example 2.20. Cataloging done during limited cataloging did not include the author statement for single authorship. In this case the author's name on the title page was Felix Youssoupoff, and a reference would be required.

Since the addition of notes may affect the access points at which an item may be found, serious consideration should be given to whether these notes should be added. According to AACR 2 an access point should be justified by a note indicating the relationship of the access point to the work. If this practice is followed, notes may be needed to justify desirable access points to the cataloging in question. Furthermore, if it is believed important to indicate whether a work contains bibliographic references, these notes will have to be added. And if bibliographic history is deemed important, much of this must be added. Example 2.21 shows limited cataloging to which a library has added a bibliography note and an access point for the editor, which was felt to be important. Many libraries would also make a title added entry.

Example 2.21. On cataloging done during limited cataloging, bibliographic references were seldom noted. In this case the bibliography note has been added by the local cataloger.

MINIMAL LEVEL CATALOGING

Minimal level cataloging (MLC) is a program currently in use at LC that is reminiscent of limited cataloging. However, the treatment of descriptive information is quite different. MLC was begun in 1980 as a way to provide access to items that otherwise would not be accessible—i.e., items not considered to be worth the expense of full cataloging, and items from the arrearages that would otherwise not be brought out for cataloging.[6] A catalog record created according to MLC standards has an encoding level of "7" in a MARC record (see Example 2.22, page 44). MLC cataloging of monographs is also recognizable by a call number beginning with the letters "MLC." Shelf numbers for microforms and maps cataloged under MLC have different means of identification, and anyone working with these should consult the latest information from LC. Descriptive elements of MLC cataloging follow AACR 2 rules and format for title and statement of responsibility area, edition area, publication area, physical description area, and series area. Notes, however, are normally limited to those recording bibliographic history and those necessary to justify an access point. Other notes are made only in exceptional cases. Therefore, the library using this copy must be aware that notes are not made in accordance with full cataloging standards.

```
Type:  a  Bib lvl: m  Govt pub:     Lang:    spa Source:     Illus:
Repr:      Enc lvl: 7  Conf pub: 0 Ctry:    xx  Dat tp: s M/F/B: 10
Indx:  0  Mod rec:     Festschr: 0 Cont:
Desc:  a  Int lvl:     Dates: 1830,
   1 010        85-844633
   2 040        DLC $c DLC
   3 050 0      MLCS 86/1297 (F)
   4 049        YCLM
   5 100 10     Osejo, Rafael Francisco.
   6 245 10     Ynformi que el poder ejecutivo di'o al Consejo
Representativo sobre el decreto de 14 de noviembre de 1829 y su
refutaci'on compuesta / $c por Rafael Francisco Osejo.
   7 260 0      San Jos'e de Costarrica : $b Impr. de la Paz, $c 1830.
   8 300        36 p. ; $c 19 cm.
   9 490 0      Letras patrias ; $v 227
```

Example 2.22. MLC cataloging from LC is distinguished by an encoding level of "7" and by a call number in the 050 field beginning with the letters "MLC." Description is fairly complete through the series area, but fixed field information is sparse, there are few notes, and access points are severely limited. (In OCLC most of the fixed field elements have default settings. Those values appear in the above record even though not filled in by LC. The values may or may not apply to the record.)

The savings in MLC records are made, for the most part, in areas other than description: limitations on numbers of added entries, no subject headings or classification numbers, limited fixed field data. The implications of these practices are discussed in the chapters covering these concepts.

SHARED CATALOGING

Shared cataloging is the term applied to copy for which cataloging responsibility has been shared by the country of origin of the work and LC. The practice was begun in 1966 and ended in 1982. Originally it was intended that the description from the country of origin be accepted, while the form of the access points would be supplied by LC. However, LC found it necessary to adapt some of the description in order to supply statements of responsibility and/or publishers, and to conform with ISBD punctuation. Shared cataloging is recognizable by a symbol appearing at the end of the physical description line on records in card format or in the 015 field of a MARC record. The symbol consists of an abbreviation standing for the country of origin (e.g., It. for Italy) followed by either asterisks or a number from the country's national bibliography.

The acceptance of shared cataloging presents some of the same problems as the acceptance of outdated copy. If the copy is accepted, the idiosyncrasies of descriptive cataloging done by other countries must be explained to staff who check the copy. If the copy is not accepted, someone must be trained to make necessary changes. The distinction between differences due to style and differences due to inaccurate information should be made here as well as when working with outdated copy discussed earlier in the chapter.

The differences in description in shared cataloging fell mostly in the areas of punctuation, abbreviations, transcription of imprint, and collation. For example, use of brackets could differ, and parentheses were used instead of brackets in some cases. Some countries began use of ISBD before it was begun at LC. An example of the differences in abbreviation is that prior to AACR 2 "second" and "third" were abbreviated "2nd" and "3rd" by the British, but "2d" and "3d" in the United States. In the publication area, cities that were known in the country of origin were not followed, for identification purposes, by the larger jurisdiction as they would have been if cataloging had been done in the United States. The date was sometimes transcribed differently, as on copy from the Netherlands where the date could appear: 1972, [1973]. The appearance of two dates was not explained as it would have been if cataloging were done in the United States. Paging was often counted differently than in LC cataloging. For example, if the last numbered page was 351 but there was printing on another page, the paging was given by several countries as "352 p." Illustrations were accounted for in different ways, and wording of notes could be different. Example 2.23 shows shared cataloging from the Netherlands. The symbol "Ne79-1" in the 015 field identifies it as shared cataloging. The bracketed information in the publication area would not have been supplied if done originally at LC. The publication date would have been transcribed as "c1978," as this information appeared in the book, while "1979" did not. Also, Anglo-American practice does not include using "with" before "ill."

```
OCLC: 5405263        Rec stat: n Entrd: 790725        Used: 861128
Type: a Bib lvl: m  Govt pub:     Lang:  eng Source:   Illus: a
Repr:    Enc lvl:   Conf pub: 0 Ctry:  ne  Dat tp: s M/F/B: 10
Indx: 1 Mod rec:    Festschr: 0 Cont: b
Desc: p Int lvl:    Dates: 1979,
   1 010       79-309787
   2 040       DLC $c DLC $d m.c.
   3 015       Ne79-1
   4 020       9027976473 : $c fl 78.10
   5 043       e-fr---
   6 050 0     BF1434.F8 $b C6
   7 082       133/.092/4
   8 090       $b
   9 049       YCLM
  10 100 10    Copenhaver, Brian P. $w cn
  11 245 10    Symphorien Champier and the reception of the occultist
tradition in renaissance France / $c Brian P. Copenhaver.
  12 260 0     [2514 GC] The Hague (Noordeinde 41) ; $a New York : $b
Mouton, $c [1979]
  13 300       368 p. : $b with ill. ; $c 24 cm.
  14 500       A revision of the author's thesis, University of Kansas,
1970.
  15 504       Bibliography: p. [331]-351.
  16 500       Includes indexes.
  17 650  0    Occult sciences $z France $x History.
  18 600 10    Champier, Symphorien, $d 1472?-ca. 1535. $w cn
```

Example 2.23. This shared cataloging demonstrates one situation where other countries use different cataloging guidelines than are used in the United States. The date given in the book is "c1978." The bracketed information in the 260 field would be given differently or not at all in the United States. The word "with" in the 300 field would not be included.

One may notice that except for the difference between the date supplied and the copyright date, none of the differences mentioned above cause much problem in the identification of the item involved, nor do they have any influence on the access points. Therefore, if the differences are understood by the personnel who check the copy, there should be few real problems in accepting shared cataloging. However, a library may prefer to treat it just like any other copy cataloged by LC, so that the cataloging staff will not have another exception to remember.

DIFFERENCES BETWEEN PRINTINGS OF AN EDITION

Because an item acquired by the local library may be a later printing than the one that was cataloged by the outside source, there may be differences between the copy and the book, even when working with exact copy. For the most part, these differences occur in the publication area, series statement, and notes, but it is possible for them to appear elsewhere as well. Example 2.24 shows a case where the publisher has removed the "first edition" statement from the second printing.

Record

```
OCLC: 7541077      Rec stat: n Entrd: 810714      Used: 831019
Type: a Bib lvl: m Govt pub:    Lang:  eng Source:    Illus:
Repr:    Enc lvl:    Conf pub: 0 Ctry:  wiu Dat tp: s M/F/B: 10
Indx: 0 Mod rec:    Festschr: 0 Cont:
Desc: a Int lvl:    Dates: 1980,
   1 010      81-125141
   2 040      DLC $c DLC
   3 020        $c $4.00 (pbk.)
   4 039 0    2 $b 3 $c 3 $d 3 $e 3
   5 050 0    PS3553.U8 $b M3
   6 082 0    811/.54 $2 19
   7 090        $b
   8 049      YCLM
   9 100 10   Cutler, Bruce, $d 1930-
  10 245 14   The maker's name / $c by Bruce Cutler.
  11 250      1st ed.
  12 260 0    La Crosse, WI. : $b Juniper Press, $c 1980.
  13 300      23 p. ; $c 24 cm.
  14 440  0   William N. Judson series ; $v 14
```

Title Page

THE MAKER'S NAME

by Bruce Cutler

Juniper Press / La Crosse, WI.

Colophon

Acknowledgements:

The Canadian Forum, Kansas City Star, Kansas Quarterly, The New Salt Creek Reader, Prairie Schooner, The Smith, and Bookmark Press.

© 1980 by Bruce Cutler

Second Printing October 1981
Cover linocut by Speed Gold

Example 2.24. The bibliographic record is for a work that had a "first edition" statement in LC's copy. The title page and colophon show that the local library's copy bears a statement of "second printing" instead of "first edition."

Decisions on treatment of these differences affect not only the library's cataloging policy for the first copy acquired, but also its policy for additional copies. The decisions to be made are whether or not the differences between the printing cataloged by the outside source and the printing cataloged by the local library are to be recorded on the copy; and whether differences between the printing first received and the printing(s) received later in the local library are considered important enough either to be treated as different editions or to be recorded as differences on the cataloging for the first copy.

By far the most common of these differences occurs in the printing date. The rule in the pre-ISBD version of the *Anglo-American Cataloging Rules* for the recording of the imprint date called for recording the printing date followed by the copyright date if it was different. This rule was followed closely by the Library of Congress. Some of the other commercial card services minimized the problem considerably by recording the copyright date only, or the imprint date only in certain cases such as reprints. The ISBD version of the rule that was in effect prior to AACR 2 called for giving the date of the year of publication of the first impression of the edition, followed by the copyright date if different. There was also a provision for adding the date of a later impression if it was different and if it was important to identify a later impression as such. LC's interpretation of this provision was that they always included on the copy the date of a later impression as well as the date of the first. AACR 2, likewise, calls for giving the date of the edition being cataloged, and an option allows adding the latest copyright date if it is different. If the date of publication of the item in hand is unknown, the copyright date or the date of manufacture is to be used. LC applies the option and also follows a rule interpretation that calls for sometimes giving both copyright date and printing date when edition date is lacking.[7]

Again, the library's philosophy of descriptive cataloging should be considered. The printing date tells the age of the physical volume while the date of first impression and/or the copyright date tells the age of the intellectual contents. A decision must be made about the importance of these two dates, if any, to posterity.

When using pre-AACR 2 LC cataloging there are a number of situations in which differences in impression date(s) may occur. The most common occurs when LC cataloged an item the same year as its copyright date. Since the printing and copyright dates were the same, only the copyright date was used in the imprint (e.g., c1982). A local library may then acquire the title later, and it may contain a later printing date so that the imprint date should then read, for example, "c1982 (1984 printing)," instead of "c1982." Another situation occurs when LC has cataloged an item with an impression date four or more years later than the probable date of publication (e.g., 1985 printing, c1980). The local library may then acquire a different printing—either one with a later printing date (e.g., 1988 printing, c1980), or one with no printing date at all (e.g., c1980). Changing the LC copy which bears a printing date in addition to a copyright date may be a call number problem as well as a description problem for a library using LC call numbers, since a date used in the call number by LC is usually the date of the impression owned by LC. This is discussed further in Chapter 6.

The imprint date continues to be a problem when additional copies are acquired for a library, because any of the discrepancies mentioned that may occur between the LC cataloging and the item acquired by a local library can also occur between the acquisition of the first and second copies in that local library. And, in addition, an earlier printing may be acquired as a second or later copy. (This only rarely occurs with LC cataloging.) If the local library chooses not to supply a later printing date except when really important as the rule allows, the situation can be fairly easily remedied on new cataloging copy. LC's later printing date can be removed. The date of first impression and copyright date will usually match on first copies and added copies of the same edition, no matter how many different impressions are acquired. For bibliographic records already in the catalog, though, discrepancies must either be ignored, added as notes, dashed onto the cataloging for the first copy, or removed from the description in the catalog.

Although the printing date is the most common source of discrepancy between *book-in-hand* and cataloging copy, or between added copies in a library, place of publication in the publication area can also differ. LC or some other cataloging source may, for example, catalog the first printing of a book with New York on the title page. A local library may acquire a later printing with Los Angeles on the title page because the publisher is now headquartered there. Another situation is the publisher with headquarters in several cities or countries. Different printings of these may appear with the place names in a different order. AACR 2 calls for using the place named first (with certain exceptions). The first named place on the outside copy may differ from that on the publication acquired in a local library. The publisher's name may also change between printings. This may happen because the publisher changes its name, or it may happen as a result of merger of publishers (see Example 2.25, page 50).

Changes of place and/or changes of name of publisher are not, technically, new editions because nothing in the publication is changed except the title page, although LC treats most of these situations as different editions. When these situations occur, a library may decide to ignore them, change the copy, or make a note of the difference on the shelflist entry only. If changes occur between copies in the same library, the decision may be to ignore them, treat them as new editions (e.g., make a separate bibliographic record), make a note on the shelflist entry (e.g., Copy 2. New York : Van Nostrand Reinhold, 1973), or dash on the differences as a note. Again the decision made depends upon the library's philosophy of description. It should be pointed out, however, that if such changes are ignored, it is quite possible that in larger libraries a copy of the printing made after the change will be acquired because it may appear to be a different edition than the one described in the catalog. This could happen especially in the library's area of subject specialization, where it is important to collect all editions. Then, if the change continues to be ignored, this duplication could occur again and again.

Series statement is another part of the description that can change between printings. Occasionally a publisher may do a new printing of a work issued earlier in a series; and on the later printing, the series designation may be omitted in the book; or vice versa (e.g., A McGraw-Hill classic handbook reissue). More often, though, the series discrepancy occurs between the paperback and hardback editions. For example, the hardback may appear as (Praeger world of art series), while the paperback is designated (Praeger world of art paperbacks), yet this may be the only difference in the description on the copy. The same options exist here as for differences in imprint; although, again, following LC practice would mean treating such differences as new editions. A further consideration is whether that series is traced in the local library. Strictly speaking, paperback and hardback printings are different editions; but one cannot help observing that it seems wasteful to put an entirely new set of entries in a printed catalog when the only difference is a series that is not even traced. It is easier to enter multiple records into an online catalog, but it is just as frustrating for a user to retrieve multiple responses to a search, only to learn that two or more of the responses represent essentially the same item. A consideration, however, must be whether or not it is library practice to charge for lost books and, if so, on what basis. Would someone who lost a $4.95 paperback be charged for the hardbound edition? In some places the cost of processing and binding the paperback would equal the cost of a hardback, and so the charge should be the same. If not the same, some distinction might be necessary, at least in the shelflist.

Worrell, Estelle (Ansley) 1929–
  The dollhouse book. Basic house plans and photography
by Norman Worrell. Princeton, N. J., Van Nostrand ₁1964₁

  ix, 125 p. illus. (part col.) 29 cm.

  "Patterns for dolls' furniture, dollhouse plans, needlework and
accessories" : p. 53–118.
  Bibliography : p. 51–52.

  1. Doll-houses. 2. Furniture—Models. I. Title.

TT200.W6   745.5923   64–57228

Library of Congress   ₁4–1₁

The
Dollhouse
Book

ESTELLE ANSLEY WORRELL

Basic House Plans and Photography by

NORMAN WORRELL

 VAN NOSTRAND REINHOLD COMPANY
NEW YORK CINCINNATI TORONTO LONDON MELBOURNE

Example 2.25. The LC cataloging for this book was done from a printing of the book by Van Nostrand in 1964. The local library received a copy of a printing done after Van Nostrand and Reinhold merged.

Another difference that can occur between hardback and paperback editions is the International Standard Book Number (ISBN). A variant ISBN may be the only difference between the two, in which case the ISBN found on the local item may be added to the exact copy for the other binding.

The occasions when outside copy would contain a note that would be different because of a different printing are relatively rare and occur most often on old LC copy because of old cataloging practices that are no longer followed. An example is a note reading "Seventh printing, November 1944." The printing received in the local library may be the tenth, done in June 1946. Another example is a note reading "Ornamental green borders." A later printing may include no borders, or they may not be green! These will probably be ignored or removed. Changing would be wasteful since many of these types of notes would not be included if cataloging were done today. An example of a note that *would* need changing because of a new printing is shown in Example 2.26. The 1973 reprinting was bound with the entire title proper printed on the spine, making the "on spine" note incorrect.

```
OCLC: 52173        Rec stat: c Entrd: 700121        Used: 870603
Type: a Bib lvl: m Govt pub:     Lang:  eng Source:    Illus: c
Repr:     Enc lvl:   Conf pub: 0 Ctry:  nyu Dat tp: r M/F/B: 10
Indx: 1 Mod rec:     Festschr: 0 Cont: b
Desc:     Int lvl:   Dates: 1969,1937
    1 010        70-91261//r83
    2 040        DLC $c DLC $d m/c
    3 020        0837120586
    4 043        f-et---
    5 050 0      DT14 $b .H8 1969
    6 082        916/.03
    7 090        $b
    8 049        YCLM
    9 100 10     Huggins, Willis Nathaniel, $d 1886-1941.
   10 245 13     An introduction to African civilizations, $b with main
currents in Ethiopian history, $c by Willis N. Huggins and John G.
Jackson.
   11 260 0      New York, $b Negro Universities Press $c [1969]
   12 300        224 p. $b ports. $c 23 cm.
   13 500        Reprint of the 1937 ed.
   14 500        On spine: African civilizations.
   15 504        Includes bibliographies.
   16 651 0      Africa $x Civilization.
   17 651 0      Africa $x History.
   18 650 0      Black race.
   19 651 0      Ethiopia $x History.
   20 700 10     Jackson, John G. $e joint author. $w cn
   21 740 1      African civilizations.
```

Example 2.26. The 1973 reprinting of the work cataloged in this example has the entire title proper printed on the spine. Thus, the "On spine" note is incorrect for the 1973 printing.

NOTES RELATING TO PUBLICATION-IN-HAND
OR TO ENTRIES IN LOCAL CATALOG

Individual characteristics of an item cataloged by the outside source may not apply to the item received in the local library, and vice versa. These situations necessitate a look at the library's policy on note-making and, again, the decisions made should reflect the library's philosophy on the purpose of descriptive cataloging. Example 2.27 shows a situation where LC's copy of the book had a label on the title page while the local library's copy does not. Conversely, the local library may acquire a book with a label or stamp on the title page that did not appear on the copy cataloged by LC or other cataloging source. LC treats items with labels carrying imprint information as separate editions. However, LC is not likely to acquire both items. Therefore, the local library must either add or delete the label information when using LC exact copy. When using an online utility to catalog, it may be necessary to create a new record in this situation. Other such situations occur with numbered copies (e.g., "150 copies ... printed ... No. 27"), autographed or inscribed copies (e.g., Author's autographed presentation copy), imperfect copies (e.g., Pages 16-23 wanting), or copies with supplementary material (e.g., "Errata slip inserted," or "Folded map in pocket"). Such material could be present or absent in opposition to the copy, or it could be handled differently (e.g., tipped in rather than in pocket). Leaving imperfect copy notes that do not apply to the library's copy could be confusing. Leaving the other notes, however, would probably offend only the purist. Not adding such notes would cause problems in only two areas. The imperfect copy note might save someone a frustrating trip to the library's stacks, and other notes might be desired if, for example, the item was acquired mainly *because* it was a numbered or autographed copy.

Notes relating the publication-in-hand to bibliographic entries already in the catalog may also have to be added either to the copy-in-hand or to records already in the catalog. In the cataloging of monographs, these situations occur most often when a work is translated, or when it is published either simultaneously or later with a title different from that of the first edition acquired. For serials, notes must be added most often when a serial ceases, merges, divides, or changes its title. The addition of such notes depends to some extent on the library's policies concerning uniform titles and successive entry cataloging. But in any case, changed titles require that something be done in the catalog to relate these entries to each other. If LC copy is being used, it is little consolation that such notes are added to LC's own catalogs; each local library is responsible for adding such information itself.

It is especially important to relate different editions to each other when the main entry has changed. This can occur with title changes as discussed above, if the title is the main entry (e.g., *The Space Encyclopedia* is revised as the *New Space Encyclopaedia*). It can also occur when new editors or authors revise a work; sometimes when authors' names change order on the title page, indicating a shift in principal responsibility; or in any other situation when authorship responsibility changes. This is happening with increased frequency, and it usually results in main entries for the editions being separated by much more space in the catalog than they would be in the case of a title change. This makes it extremely important to relate the two, by notes, uniform titles, or name/title access points, which are discussed in Chapter 3. This same procedure may also be necessary for

Smith, Peter S
    50 photoelectric circuits and systems ₍by₎ P. S. Smith.   London, Iliffe Books ₍1972₎
        83 p.   illus.   23 cm.   B***

        Label mounted on t.p.: Transatlantic Arts, inc., New York, sole distributor for the U.S.A.

    1. Photoelectronic devices.   2. Electronic circuits.   I. Title.
    TK8304.S56   621.3815′42   73-161654
    ISBN 0-592-02817-8; 0-592-02879-8 (pbk.)   MARC

    Library of Congress   73

50 PHOTOELECTRIC CIRCUITS AND SYSTEMS

P. S. SMITH

Formerly
Technical Product Engineer
Mullard Ltd.

LONDON
ILIFFE BOOKS

Example 2.27. Note on copy is not applicable to book-in-hand.

supplements when the main entry has changed, or for such things as companion volumes.

Notes may be added to the catalog because a patron discovers bibliographic relationships. Such is the case in Example 2.28. The front matter of the two books bears no evidence of relationship, but a patron discovered that the texts are identical. They appear to be printed from the same plates.

Example 2.28. Title pages of two books with identical texts.

Record (a)

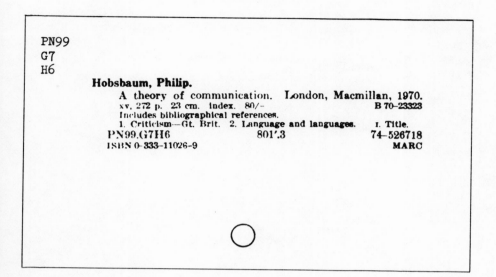

PN99
G7
H6

Hobsbaum, Philip.
    A theory of communication.   London, Macmillan, 1970.
    xv, 272 p. 23 cm. index. 80/-   B 70–23323
    Includes bibliographical references.
    1. Criticism—Gt. Brit. 2. Language and languages.   I. Title.
    PN99.G7H6   801'.3   74–526718
    ISBN 0–333–11026–9   MARC

Record (b)

PN99
G7
H6

Hobsbaum, Philip.
    A theory of communication.   London, Macmillan, 1970.
    xv, 272 p. 23 cm. index. 80/-   B 70–23323
    Includes bibliographical references.

American ed. published under title: Theory
of criticism.

    1. Criticism--Gt. Brit.   I. Title.

Example 2.28 *(continued)*. Records (a) (above) and (c) (page 56) show original LC cataloging for the two books with identical texts. Records (b) (above) and (d) (page 56) show revised cataloging done in a local library after discovery by a patron that the two are identical.

Record (c)

```
PN81
H52      Hobsbaum, Philip.
1970         Theory of criticism.   Bloomington, Indiana University Press
             [1970]

             xv, 272 p.   23 cm.   $8.50

             Includes bibliographical references.




             1. Criticism.    I. Title.

             PN81.H52   1970                   801'.95              74-108210
             ISBN 0-253-18850-4                                        MARC

             Library of Congress            ◯   71
```

Record (d)

```
PN99
G7
H6       Hobsbaum, Philip.
1970b        Theory of criticism.   Bloomington, Indiana University Press
             [1970]

             xv, 272 p.   23 cm.   $8.50

             Includes bibliographical references.
             British ed. published under title: A theory
          of communication.



             1. Criticism --Gt. Brit.  I. Title.

             PN81.H52   1970                   801'.95              74-108210
             ISBN 0-253-18850-4                                        MARC

             Library of Congress            ◯   71
```

Example 2.28 *(continued)*.

DIFFERENCES RELATING TO LOCAL HOLDINGS AND/OR BINDING

Multivolume sets and serials present each local library with situations that require descriptive cataloging decisions. Some method for indicating the parts that are held by the library must be chosen. In addition, local binding policies may create physical characteristics that should be identified in the descriptive cataloging.

For multipart items, the number of bibliographic parts and the number of physical parts, if different, are to be given in the physical description area, according to AACR 2. When outside copy is used, there are a number of situations where the physical description on the copy is not in agreement with what is held by the library. It may be that at the time of cataloging, only a partial set was held by the cataloging source. In this case the number of volumes or parts will be left blank in the physical description line of a printed record, or, in machine-readable copy from LC, the volumes held will be entered within angle brackets. It is necessary for the local library to devise some scheme for indicating which volumes are held locally. In a printed catalog, this scheme may be to write in pencil on each entry for the set, in the vicinity of the physical description, which volumes are held. This information is then updated as new volumes arrive until the set is complete. Another way may be to indicate holdings at the main entry only or, in a card catalog, on a *check-in* card behind the main entry and refer from other entries to the main entry. A third solution may be to have a central record of some sort where holdings of all incomplete entries (both monograph and serial) are shown on check-in cards. The catalog user must be referred from the catalog to this record. In an online catalog, ideally the catalog record would automatically reflect additional volumes as soon as they are checked in upon arrival in the library. Few online catalogs are so well integrated, however, and it is necessary to call up catalog records to add volume information to them. Calling up the records will be necessary even in a fully integrated environment when new volumes have new title information to be added to the record. Updating volume and title information for a microform catalog causes even greater delays in providing new volume information to patrons.

A second situation occurs when the cataloging source has cataloged a complete set. The local library may not have acquired a complete set, and it may or may not intend to complete it. It is quite misleading to the user if the extent of item is left as it is; yet it seems wasteful to remove the number of volumes only to replace it a few months later if and when the set is completed. One way of getting around this in a printed environment is to draw a pencil line through the number of volumes and indicate beside it which volumes are held or refer to the place where the holdings are given. It also occasionally happens that the cataloging source catalogs what it thinks is a complete set, but then more volumes are published. The copy first located for the set may reflect the earlier cataloging, but revised cataloging should appear when the cataloging source acquires the additional volumes. The local library may want to wait for revised copy, or, especially if the item is already in the catalog, adapt what it has.

A third situation requiring a decision occurs when, because of binding costs, two or more bibliographic volumes are subsequently bound together in one hard-bound volume. The rules call for giving the number of both bibliographic and physical volumes if they are different (e.g., 10 v. in 5). However, the outside copy, in this situation, will reflect only bibliographic volumes, and this information will be followed by the rest of the physical description with no space on a printed record for inserting the number of physical volumes. If this is left as it is, it can be confusing to users and to circulation personnel who may be searching for wanted items; it is often helpful to know how many physical volumes one is looking for. When using cards from an outside source, it is time-consuming to remove the remainder of the physical description, make the insertion, and then replace the information. One solution is to extend the volume information to the left margin — not aesthetically pleasing, but serviceable. Another solution is shown in Example 2.29. A third possibility is to add a note: e.g., Bound in 4 vols. This situation, of course, is no problem in an online environment. The number of physical volumes is simply inserted when the binding process is complete.

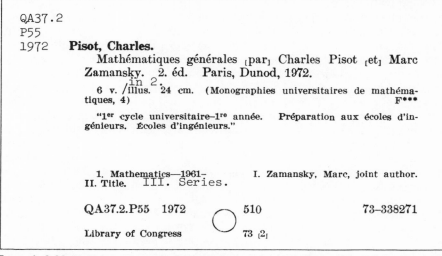

Example 2.29. Volumes 1 to 3 have been bound together as have 4-6. That there are only 2 physical volumes is shown by "in 2" above the collation line.

In addition to physical description problems, all the above situations may present problems with contents notes; the contents note on the copy may not agree with what is contained in the local library. For incomplete sets, the cataloging source may include in a contents note the titles of the volumes it has received. If these are not consecutive, space is left for filling in; often, however, not enough space is left. When cards are used in cataloging and there is not enough space, it is very time-consuming to remove the remainder of the note, only to put it back again, usually on a "card 2," or 3, or 4. This is particularly inefficient when it must be done on an entire set of cards. As a result, some libraries carry complete contents notes at the main entry only, and users are referred to the main entry for this information. For complete sets, all titles may be given in the contents note on the outside copy, but if the local library has not acquired all the volumes, it may consider the note to be misleading. For bibliographic volumes that are physically bound together by a local library, the contents note on the copy is given for different physical volumes, and the punctuation must be changed if it is considered necessary to show which volumes have been bound together. Contents notes more complete than the library's holdings or those that do not indicate physical entities, many catalogers believe, will not be confusing if the physical description explains the situation clearly. See Example 2.30 for a sample of additions made to copy when a multivolume set is involved. As with physical description, contents notes can be edited easily in an online environment.

Record (a)

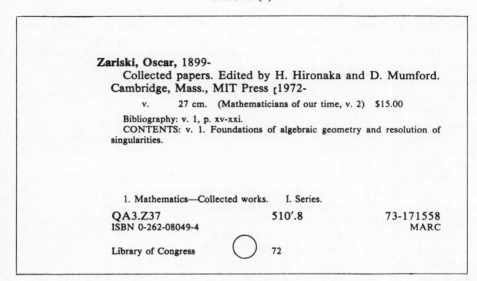

Record (b)

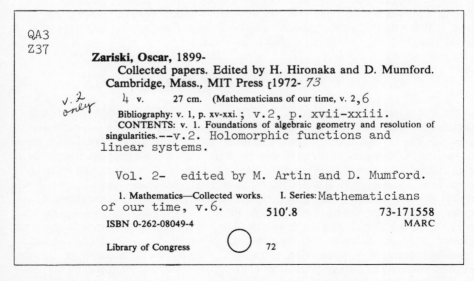

Example 2.30. Record (a) shows cataloging for a multivolume work. LC had only volume 1 when cataloging was done. Record (b) shows additions made to the copy by a local library, which received only volume 2.

Multivolume sets can also have local edition and/or publication area variations that require adjustment of the outside copy. The library must first differentiate between a mixed set and a set that has been transferred to a new publisher before publication of all volumes has been completed. A mixed set occurs when the library has acquired some volumes from one publisher's set and some volumes from another publisher's set; or it can occur when some volumes are from a different edition than the others. When a mixed set is received, a decision must be made whether to alter the copy and add notes to explain differences, catalog the volumes as two or more incomplete sets, or ignore the mixture. If the set is cataloged together, it may have to be recataloged in the future if other volumes of one set or the other are acquired as gifts or added copies, or if one of the editions is desired over the other. When a set has more than one publisher, notes are added to the catalog record(s) to explain the variation. Since the publisher may change after the outside source has cataloged the first volume, this information often has to be added locally. Another publication area variation occurs in the date of publication. In a printed catalog the library may wish to pencil in the date of the latest volume, add this information to a check-in record, or wait until the set is complete to fill in the last publication date.

For serials, AACR 2 calls for giving the description of the holdings of a *perfect* set in area 3 of the description, following the edition area, if there is one, while the extent of item in the physical description area will also describe the whole item when the serial ceases or changes title. The local library may not own the entire perfect set and will find it necessary to indicate somehow what is owned locally. In an online environment there is a MARC holdings format into which local holdings may be placed. The holdings record for each title can then be linked to the bibliographic record for that title for viewing online. The library with a card catalog might place this information in a note, which, if at all possible, should appear on card 1 rather than on cards 2, 3, or following cards. Another option would be to provide separate holdings cards following the serial title, which would indicate the exact local holdings. For any current serial title, an indication of what the library holds is important.

USE OF CATALOGING-IN-PUBLICATION

Cataloging-in-Publication (CIP) has been appearing in books published in the United States since 1971. (CIP for other materials is being attempted on a gradual basis, and CIP is also available in some books from some other countries.) Cataloging information is created from prepublication front matter and from data sheets publishers send to the Library of Congress. The cataloging data sent to the publisher to be published in the book lacks most of the description. The description given includes the title proper, series statement, and notes. In the notes paging is omitted. A library using manual cataloging methods may fill in the description from the book itself, in which case it should match exactly; any errors made will be the local library's own. There should be no outdated descriptive cataloging, although access points given may become outdated. However, the problems occurring between different copies of the book in the same library will not be solved. Since the CIP data found in the item usually are not in a standardized format, this information cannot be photocopied for use as a reproducible master. It may, however, be photocopied for use as a copy slip, or it may be hand-copied or typed from the book.

Cataloging-in-Publication in online format (MARC CIP) from LC contains much fuller bibliographic data. All cataloging information that can be gleaned from the front matter and data sheets is included in the MARC CIP record, leaving out only the physical description and page numbers in notes. An extra field (263) identifies the projected date of publication and is deleted when the record is changed to full MARC status by LC. MARC CIP often has descriptive data that differ from the finished publication. Publishers change their minds about the appearance of title pages, the use of series statements, and even about their own representation in a publication. In the study cited earlier (although not reported in the article "Accuracy of LC Copy"), Taylor and Simpson found that 92 percent of the records that began as CIP had some change made to the record (besides filling in the physical description and page numbers in notes) when the record was upgraded to full MARC. Example 2.31 (below and on pages 62-63) shows CIP as it appears in a particular book, as it appeared in MARC CIP before publication of that book, and as it appears as a full MARC record. A number of changes were required.

Record (a)

Library of Congress Cataloging in Publication Data

Droessler, Judith B. (Date)

Craniometry and biological distance.

(Research series / Center for American Archeology at Northwestern University; 1)
Bibliography: p.
Includes index.
    1.   Indians of North America—Illinois—Anthro-
pometry.   2.   Woodland Indians—Anthropometry.
3.   Mississippian culture.   4.   Craniology—Illinois.
I.   Title.   II.   Series: Research series (Center for American Archeology
at Northwestern University) (Evanston, Ill.); 1
[DNLM: 1.   Anthropology, Physical—
United States.   2.   Craniometry.   3.   Archaeology—
United States.   GN 75.A2 D783c]
E78.13D76   977.3'00497   81-11009
                            AACR2

Example 2.31. Record (a) shows CIP found in book; Record (b) (page 62) shows the MARC CIP for the same book; and Record (c) (page 63) shows the full updated MARC record for that book.

Record (b)

```
OCLC: 7574249       Rec stat: p Entrd: 810610        Used: 820701
Type: a Bib lvl: m Govt pub:     Lang:  eng Source:    Illus:
Repr:    Enc lvl: 8 Conf pub: 0 Ctry:   ilu Dat tp: s M/F/B: 10
Indx: 1 Mod rec:   Festschr: 0 Cont: b
Desc: a Int lvl:   Dates: 1981,
   1 010      81-11009
   2 040      DLC $c DLC
   3 020      0942118111
   4 020      094211812X (pbk.)
   5 039 0    2 $b 3 $c 3 $d 3 $e 3
   6 043      n-us-il
   7 050 0    E78.I3 $b D76
   8 060      GN 75.A2 D783c
   9 082 0    977.3/00497 $2 19
  10 090       $b
  11 049      YCLM
  12 100 10   Droessler, Judith B., $d 1947-
  13 245 10   Craniometry and biological distance : $b biocultural
continuity and change at the late-woodland - Mississippian interface /
$c Judith B. Droessler.
  14 260 0    Evanston, Ill. : $b Northwestern University Archeological
Program, $c [1981]
  15 263      8107
  16 300      p. cm.
  17 490 1    Scientific papers / Northwestern University Archeological
Program ; $v 6
  18 504      Bibliography: p.
  19 500      Includes index.
  20 650 0    Indians of North America $z Illinois $x Anthropometry.
  21 650 0    Woodland Indians $x Anthropometry.
  22 650 0    Mississippian culture.
  23 650 0    Craniology $z Illinois.
  24 650 2    Anthropology, Physical $z United States.
  25 650 2    Craniometry.
  26 650 2    Archaeology $z United States.
  27 830 0    Scientific papers (Northwestern University (Evanston, Ill.).
Archeological Program) ; $v 6.
```

Example 2.31 *(continued)*.

Record (c)

```
OCLC: 7574249        Rec stat:  c  Entrd:  810610          Used: 870512
Type: a Bib lvl: m  Govt pub:     Lang:  eng Source:    Illus: a
Repr:      Enc lvl:     Conf pub: 0 Ctry:  ilu Dat tp: s M/F/B: 10
Indx: 1 Mod rec:      Festschr: 0 Cont: b
Desc: a Int lvl:      Dates: 1981,
  1 010          81-11009//r85
  2 040          DLC $c DLC $d m/c
  3 020          0942118111
  4 020          094211812X (pbk.)
  5 039  0       2 $b 3 $c 3 $d 3 $e 3
  6 043          n-us-il
  7 050  0       E78.I3 $b D76 1981
  8 060          GN 75.A2 D783c
  9 082  0       977.3/00497 $2 19
 10 090          $b
 11 049          YCLM
 12 100 10       Droessler, Judith, $d 1947- $w cn
 13 245 10       Craniometry and biological distance : $b biocultural
continuity and change at the Late-Woodland - Mississippian interface /
$c Judith Droessler.
 14 260  0       Evanston, Ill. : $b Center for American Archeology at
Northwestern University, $c c1981.
 15 300          xvi, 253 p. : $b ill. ; $c 23 cm.
 16 490  1       Research series / Center for American Archeology ; $v v. 1
 17 500          Revised version of thesis (Ph.D.)--Indiana University,
1979.
 18 504          Bibliography: p. 231-246.
 19 500          Includes index.
 20 650  0       Indians of North America $z Illinois $x Anthropometry.
 21 650  0       Woodland Indians $x Anthropometry.
 22 650  0       Mississippian culture.
 23 650  0       Craniology $z Illinois.
 24 650  2       Anthropology, Physical $z United States.
 25 650  2       Craniometry.
 26 650  2       Archaeology $z United States.
 27 830  0       Research series (Center for American Archeology at
Northwestern University) ; $v v. 1.
```

Example 2.31 *(continued).*

A somewhat different kind of partial cataloging takes on two forms for serials. The National Serials Data Program (NSDP) is provided with the same type of information given LC for other CIP. However, the information provided is minimal, and because NSDP does not have a collection, neither subject headings nor call number is provided.

Library of Congress provides another type of incomplete copy that is called *Partial* (identifiable by the letters "PAR" in the 050 field of a MARC record). This cataloging is based on the published piece, but provides no subject analysis. In essence it is the exact opposite of CIP for books. Many books are published containing LC CIP data that include subject analysis, but incomplete description. Some serials are given the complete physical description, based on a published title, but no subject analysis.

SUMMARY

The possible discrepancies between the outside copy and the copy of the item held in the library have been mentioned here for the purpose of pointing out situations that can occur. This is not to say that all of these will occur frequently or that all possible kinds of discrepancies have been covered. But when they do occur, the cataloger should be prepared to deal with them; giving thought to the following questions is part of that preparation:

1. What is the philosophy of description in the library? Should there be exact description or enough for identification only?

2. By what process does cataloging arrive in the catalog, and how does this affect the philosophy of description? Are there entire card sets that have to be changed? Or a master only? Or is master copy on a computer terminal screen and thus easily corrected?

3. How much and what level staff is available to check copy against items and to make changes when needed?

4. How important is it that an item may not be found by a library user because of errors on copy or because the item is not bibliographically connected to a related work?

5. In the cataloging of outdated copy and/or shared cataloging, will a distinction be made between cataloging differences that result from different styles of cataloging and those that result from inaccurate information? When changes are made, what style of cataloging will be used?

6. How important are notes that may be lacking on minimal level cataloging (MLC) copy?

7. How important are the differences that occur between printings – both for the initial acquisition and for added copies?

8. How are local holdings of multivolume sets and serials to be indicated?

9. Will CIP copy be handled in the same manner as other exact copy?

NOTES

[1]Arlene G. Taylor and Charles W. Simpson, "Accuracy of LC Copy: A Comparison between Copy That Began as CIP and Other LC Cataloging," *Library Resources & Technical Services* 30 (October/December 1986): 375-87. *Error* is defined here as any information or punctuation mark appearing in a record that according to LC's own policies (as understood by the researchers) was incorrectly transcribed or placed.

[2]Ibid., 385.

[3]Ibid., 386.

[4]U.S. Library of Congress. *Cataloging Service*, bulletin 23 (May 1951): 1.

[5]Ibid., 2-3.

[6]*Cataloging Service Bulletin*, no. 36 (Spring 1987): 40-53.

[7]*Cataloging Service Bulletin*, no. 25 (Summer 1984): 30-32.

3

CHOICE OF NAME AND TITLE ACCESS POINTS

INTRODUCTION

In traditional cataloging practice, access points have been assigned to a bibliographic record to provide the means for locating the record in a catalog. Traditional access points include author, title, subject heading(s), series, and any names of persons or corporate bodies closely associated with a work. In a printed catalog (i.e., card, book, or microform) these access points are the places where copies of the bibliographic record are filed. In an online catalog it is possible for any set of characters in a record to be an access point. Typical access points in online files, in addition to the traditional ones, are LCCN, ISBN, and classification numbers. In addition many systems allow for keyword searching of every word in a title, subject phrase, or notes. This chapter discusses the *choice* of traditional access points for names and titles (including uniform titles and series titles). Chapter 4 covers the *form* of traditional access points for names and titles, and Chapter 5 covers traditional subject access points and names as subjects.

CHOICE OF MAIN ENTRY

Traditionally, one of the name or title access points has been chosen to be the *main entry*. In part this practice was necessary in order to have one entry in the catalog where all information about the work could be found (e.g., location of all copies, number of volumes held, contents information). It seemed that this information should be contained at the entry that was considered to be the most important one. Another lingering belief is that choosing a main entry is necessary for identifying an intellectual work (as opposed to identifying a particular physical object that contains the work). In addition the main entry is used in printed catalogs as the secondary filing element (e.g., all items under the subject heading "Psychology" are subarranged by main entry).

In the online environment the main entry concept has come under question. In an online catalog there is physically only one copy of a bibliographic record that is retrieved by any one of its access points. In many systems secondary filing arrangement is not by main entry: it may be by date of imprint, date of acquisition by the library, or title. Even in a printed file, if there are *unit records*, where all information appears at every access point, is it really necessary to choose one access point as the main one?

The one situation that still seems to call for choice of a main entry occurs when it is necessary to cite a work on the record for another work. This can happen when one work is the subject of another work, is contained in another work, or is part of a larger work. There are no current provisions for multiple access points for the cited work; however, this situation may occur in only about 6 percent of monographic records.[1]

Interpreting rules for choice of main entry requires greater expertise and training than is found in many copy cataloging units. Given the decline in need for one access point to be the main one, most copy catalogers refrain from changing the choice of main entry that appears on outside copy.

Altering Choice of Main Entry
on Outside Copy

Over the years many changes have occurred in rules for choice of main entry so that much older copy has a main entry that would not be correct under current rules. For example, in the original version of AACR 1, editors were chosen as main entry if they conceived a work and solicited the contributions to it. This rule was revised before the advent of AACR 2; therefore, copy from about 1975 to date should not have any editor as main entry, but copy prior to that date does have such entries (see Example 3.1). AACR 2 brought about major changes for selection of main entry for works that emanate from corporate bodies and for selection of main entry for serials. AACR 2 specifies certain categories of works that may have corporate body as main entry. All other categories must be given the main entry that would be chosen if a corporate body were not involved. The corporate body, however, is given an added entry. Example 3.2 (page 68) shows a record that was given a corporate body main entry in the past, but would be given

```
OCLC: 576804        Rec stat: n Entrd: 830322        Used: 870713
Type: a Bib lvl: m Govt pub:     Lang:  eng Source:   Illus:
Repr:      Enc lvl: 1 Conf pub: 0 Ctry:  nyu Dat tp: c M/F/B: 00
Indx: 0 Mod rec:      Festschr: 0 Cont: b
Desc:      Int lvl:    Dates: 1966,1958
    1 010         66-3776
    2 040         DLC $c DLC
    3 050  0      Z1006 $b .L3 1966a
    4 082  0      020.3
    5 090         $b
    6 049         YCLM
    7 100 10      Landau, Thomas, $e ed.
    8 245 10      Encyclopaedia of librarianship.
    9 250         3d rev. ed.
   10 260  0      New York, $b Hafner Pub. Co., $c 1966 [c1958]
   11 300         x, 484 p. $c 26 cm.
   12 504         Includes bibliographies.
   13 650  0      Library science $x Dictionaries.
```

Example 3.1. This record, created by LC in 1966 (although entered into OCLC in 1983) would have title rather than editor as main entry under AACR 2.

```
OCLC: 5355333        Rec stat: n Entrd: 790719           Used: 851101
Type: a Bib lvl: m Govt pub:     Lang:  eng Source:     Illus: a
Repr:     Enc lvl:    Conf pub: 0 Ctry:  enk Dat tp: s M/F/B: 10
Indx: 0 Mod rec:      Festschr: 0 Cont: bs
Desc: i Int lvl:    Dates: 1978,
   1 010        79-308835
   2 040        DLC $c DLC $d m.c.
   3 015        GB78-35123
   4 020        0902683055 (pbk.) : $c L9.50
   5 043        e-uk---
   6 050 0      HD5765.A6 $b U54 1978
   7 082        331.1/0941
   8 090          $b
   9 049        YCLM
  10 110 20     University of Warwick. $b Manpower Research Group.
  11 245 10     Britain's medium-term employment prospects / $c University
of Warwick Manpower Research Group ; by R. M. Lindley ... et al.
  12 260 0      [Coventry] : $b The Group, $c 1978.
  13 300        [1], v, 128 p. : $b ill. ; $c 30 cm.
  14 504        Bibliography: p. 127-128.
  15 650 0      Employment forecasting $z Great Britain.
  16 650 0      Manpower policy $z Great Britain.
  17 650 0      Labor supply $z Great Britain.
  18 700 10     Lindley, Robert M. $w cn
```

Example 3.2. Under AACR 2 this record would have title main entry because it does not fall into any of the categories allowed for corporate body main entry.

a title main entry under AACR 2. For serials there is no separate rule for main entry in AACR 2 as there was in AACR 1. Because most serials are created by corporate bodies, they are controlled by the aforementioned rule for corporate bodies and usually do not fall into the categories that call for a corporate body main entry. Serials not emanating from corporate bodies are controlled by rules for main entry under person or title. The result is that most serials are now given main entry under title, even those with generic titles like "Bulletin" that were formerly given main entry under the corporate body from which they emanated.

In almost all cases where main entry is not what it would have been using earlier rules, there is an added entry for the entity not chosen as main entry. Therefore, careful consideration should be given to whether the time required to recatalog is justified. Will a patron really be better served by this change, or simply served differently?

There are, however, three instances of main entry change that a local library might consider worthwhile. First, if the main entry begins with a term not ordinarily used as an entry in the local catalog (e.g., Proceedings of the ...) the entry may mislead the patron into thinking entries of this type are customarily made. It might then be assumed that the library has no other items with titles beginning with this word. An alternative to changing the main entry might be to make an explanatory reference.

The second change to consider is one where the name involved has many entries in a printed catalog and the filing rules call for filing added entries for a name following main entries for that name, so that the added entry is buried in an illogical place. If it is felt that the outside cataloging source's choice of entry was in error, it might be worth changing in this case. This would be a problem only in large card, book, or microform catalogs.

The third situation in which choice of main entry might be altered is one where a decision is made to enter all serials under title regardless of entry used on the copy. This would be especially important in a one-entry serials catalog. Many titles formerly entered under corporate body in serials cataloging are now entered under title due to AACR 2 restrictions. Thus, when a serial changes its name, the new record could be entered under title, and the preceding title(s) would be found under the corporate body. So as not to confuse patrons, a recataloging of all titles involved could be worthwhile.

It should be noted that in most libraries the part of the call number referred to as the cutter is based upon the main entry. Thus, if a decision is made to change the main entry in a library using LC call numbers from LC copy, a decision will also have to be made about whether to change the cutter number. This is discussed further in Chapter 6.

CHOICE OF ADDED ENTRIES

In traditional cataloging many names and titles associated with a work are chosen as access points. The ones not chosen as main entry are called added entries. In local catalogs there may be reasons not to accept access points provided by the outside source or to give access points in addition to those already provided.

Rejecting Added Entries That Appear
on Outside Copy

Added entries on outdated copy may be rejected because they would not be made if the cataloging were done today. Examples of such entries are those for translators and editors, which used to be made as a matter of course but which now are made only according to the guidelines in AACR 2. A patron who sees some entries for translators in the catalog may falsely assume that all translators are entered, and may therefore fail to look further for an item first searched under translator but not found there. Example 3.3 (page 70) shows a situation where added entries would not be made if LC cataloged the item today. Entries on lines 14 through 17 are translators, and entries on lines 18 through 21 would not be made since added title entries are not now made for contents, although name/title added entries may be made if there are not more than three items. Because in this example there are four items, not even name/title entries would be made.

The elimination of the eight outdated added entries from Example 3.3 not only would result in current practice entry-making but also would mean eight fewer entries to be added to the catalog. For a library with a crowded card catalog, this reduction in numbers of cards could be a necessity. Another possible elimination for space-saving purposes is found in Example 3.4 (page 70). The added entry is made for a corporate body, which appears on the copy as publisher. If the local library has no evidence that the body did more than publish the book, it may wish to eliminate the entry.

```
OCLC: 2794416        Rec stat: n Entrd: 770311          Used: 870611
Type: a Bib lvl: m Govt pub:    Lang:  eng Source:    Illus:
Repr:     Enc lvl: I Conf pub: 0 Ctry:  mnu Dat tp: s M/F/B: 00d
Indx: 0 Mod rec: m Festschr: 0 Cont:
Desc:     Int lvl:    Dates: 1934,
   1 010        34-39206
   2 040        DLC $c FNP $d m.c.
   3 082        839.8226
   4 050        PT8895 $b .E55
   5 090        $b
   6 049        YCLM
   7 100 10     Eikeland, Peter J       , $d 1852-1927.
   8 245 1      Ibsen studies, $c by P. J. Eikeland, edited by a committee
of the language group, St. Olaf college.
   9 260 0      Northfield, Minn., $b The St. Olaf College Press, $c 1934.
  10 300        177 p. $c 23 cm.
  11 505 0      Peer Gynt, tr. by A. C. Paulson.--The pretenders, tr. by
Nils Flaten.--Brand, tr. by M. M. M. Meyer.--The pillars of society, tr.
by Olav Lee.
  12 600 10     Ibsen, Henrik, $d 1828-1906. $w cn
  13 710 20     St. Olaf College $w cn
  14 700 10     Paulson, Arthur Christopher, $d 1896- $e tr.
  15 700 10     Flaten, Nils, $e tr.
  16 700 10     Meyer, Marie Malmin, $e tr.
  17 700 10     Lee, Olav, $e tr.
  18 740 1      Peer Gynt.
  19 740 1      The pretenders.
  20 740 1      Brand.
  21 740 1      The pillars of society.
  22 871 29      $j 710/1 $a St. Olaf College, Northfield, Minn.
```

Example 3.3. This outdated copy contains eight added entries (lines 14 through 21) that would not be made if the cataloging were done today.

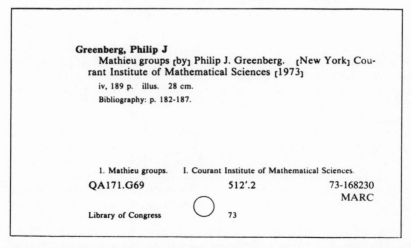

Example 3.4. On this copy there is an added entry for a corporate body which the local cataloger may believe had no responsibility for the work other than publishing it. Therefore, added entry no. I could be eliminated.

Another kind of local practice that affects acceptance of added entries involves whether to analyze individual issues of a serial. Ordinarily, on LC cataloging done before 1971, when latest entry cataloging was still being applied, added entries were made for earlier titles of a serial. But if the serial was analyzed, cross references were made from the earlier titles instead. This was necessary because the series added entry made for each analytic was filed only behind the main entry and not behind any title added entries for the serial. A library using such older copy may wish to reject added entries for the earlier serial titles in favor of providing catalog records for those titles with linking notes to the current title as is done in current practice. If the added entries are rejected, it will be necessary also to change the form of the series added entries on the affected analytics so that they will file with the serial title of which they are a part rather than with a later title.

A final situation where added entries may need to be rejected occurs when the outside source has given added entries in error. This sometimes occurs with LC copy when a final published work differs from the prepublication information used to create the MARC CIP record. Example 3.5 (pages 72 and 73) illustrates this problem. The two added entries in lines 19 and 20 of Record (b) were inadvertently left on the final copy, even though those names were removed from the statement of responsibility. Of course, the library user would not be harmed by these extra entries, but the inconsistency could be confusing.

Addition of Added Entries That Do Not Appear on Outside Copy

In a library with a card catalog, any decision to make more added entries than called for on the copy requires extra cards to complete a set. A library that orders completed card sets from outside and has no means of reproduction or no personnel available for retyping may not be able to consider these possibilities.

A divided catalog may be divided in one of several ways. If it is divided so that all *names* (both by and about) are in one catalog or online index while topical subjects are in another, the problem is the same as if the catalog were in a dictionary arrangement or had a single index. That is, the question becomes: do the filing rules arrange a name as subject following all main or added entries for that name, or are subjects, main entries, and added entries for a name interfiled? If separate, does the library want two entries for the same work filed at that name, or just one? If the catalog is divided so that *all* subject headings (including names) are in a separate catalog, or if the catalog is online but has separate indexes in which all subject access points coded with 6xx MARC tags are indexed separately from entries coded with 1xx and 7xx MARC tags, the library still must decide if two entries are needed for a work that is both by and about a person or a corporate body. The difference is that the separation of the two entries is much greater and two alphabets are involved. Example 3.6 (page 74) shows a situation where a library might wish to make an added entry for a name given only as a subject by LC.

Record (a)

```
OCLC: 7597629       Rec stat: n Entrd: 810625       Used: 821123
Type: a Bib lvl: m Govt pub:      Lang:  eng Source:   Illus:
Repr:     Enc lvl: 8 Conf pub: 0 Ctry:  nju Dat tp: s M/F/B: 10
Indx: 1 Mod rec:     Festschr: 0 Cont:
Desc: a Int lvl:     Dates: 1981,
   1 010       81-65018
   2 040       DLC $c DLC $d m/c
   3 020       0865980233 : $c $25.00
   4 039 0     2 $b 3 $c 3 $d 3 $e 3
   5 043       n-us---
   6 050 0     HV6791 $b .R87 1982
   7 082 0     364.1/0973 $2 19
   8 090        $b
   9 049       YCLM
  10 100 10    Carter, Timothy J.
  11 245 10    Rural crime : $b integrating research and prevention / $c
Timothy J. Carter, Joseph F. Donnermeyer, G. Howard Phillips.
  12 260 0     Totowa, N.J. : $b Allanheld, Osmun, $c [1981]
  13 263       8110
  14 300       p. cm.
  15 440 0     Studies in crime and deviance in American society
  16 500       Includes index.
  17 650 0     Rural crimes $z United States $x Addresses, essays,
lectures.
  18 650 0     Crime prevention $z United States $x Addresses, essays,
lectures.
  19 650 0     Juvenile delinquency $z United States $x Addresses, essays,
lectures.
  20 650 0     Offenses against property $z United States $x Addresses,
essays, lectures.
  21 700 10    Donnermeyer, Joseph F.
  22 700 10    Phillips, G. Howard $q (Garland Howard), $d 1926-
```

Example 3.5. Added entries in lines 21 and 22 were given on the MARC CIP record (Record a) because there were only three names in the statement of responsibility. When the book was published, a fourth name had been added. The statement of responsibility was changed in the finished MARC record (Record b), but the added entries were not removed.

Record (b)

```
OCLC: 7597629        Rec stat: p Entrd: 810625        Used: 870617
Type: a Bib lvl: m Govt pub:     Lang:  eng Source:     Illus: a
Repr:      Enc lvl:    Conf pub: 0 Ctry:  nju Dat tp: s M/F/B: 00
Indx: 1 Mod rec:      Festschr: 0 Cont: b
Desc: a Int lvl:      Dates: 1982,
   1 010        81-65018
   2 040        DLC $c DLC $d m/c
   3 020        0865980233 : $c $25.00
   4 039 0      2 $b 3 $c 3 $d 3 $e 3
   5 043        n-us---
   6 050 0      HV6791 $b .R87 1982
   7 082 0      364.1/0973 $2 19
   8 090         $b
   9 049        YCLM
  10 245 00     Rural crime : $b integrating research and prevention / $c
edited by Timothy J. Carter ... [et al.].
  11 260 0      Totowa, N.J. : $b Allanheld, Osmun, $c 1982.
  12 300        xvi, 265 p. : $b ill. ; $c 24 cm.
  13 504        Includes bibliographies and index.
  14 650  0     Rural crimes $z United States $x Addresses, essays,
lectures.
  15 650  0     Crime prevention $z United States $x Addresses, essays,
lectures.
  16 650  0     Juvenile delinquency $z United States $x Addresses, essays,
lectures.
  17 650  0     Offenses against property $z United States $x Addresses,
essays, lectures.
  18 700 10     Carter, Timothy J. $w cn
  19 700 10     Donnermeyer, Joseph F. $w cn
  20 700 10     Phillips, G. Howard $q (Garland Howard), $d 1926-
```

Example 3.5 *(continued).*

```
OCLC: 673371        Rec stat: c Entrd: 730711        Used: 851220
Type: a Bib lvl: m Govt pub:     Lang: eng Source:     Illus: c
Repr:     Enc lvl:   Conf pub: 0 Ctry: pau Dat tp: r M/F/B: 00b
Indx: 0 Mod rec:     Festschr: 0 Cont:
Desc:     Int lvl:   Dates: 1973,
   1 010        73-11301
   2 040        DLC $c DLC $d m.c.
   3 020        0841433828 (lib. bdg.)
   4 050 0      PS1981 $b .C7 1973
   5 082        818/.3/09
   6 090        $b
   7 049        YCLM
   8 100 10     Crothers, Samuel McChord, $d 1857-1927. $w cn
   9 245 00     Oliver Wendell Holmes; $b the autocrat and his fellow-
boarders. With selected poems.
  10 260 0      [Folcroft, Pa.] $b Folcroft Library Editions, $c 1973
[c1909]
  11 300        64 p. $b port. $c 24 cm.
  12 500        Reprint of the ed. published by Houghton Mifflin, Boston.
  13 600 10     Holmes, Oliver Wendell, $d 1809-1894. $w cn
  14 650 0      Authors, American $y 19th century $x Biography.
  15 650 0      Physicians $z United States $x Biography.
```

Example 3.6. A library with a divided catalog might wish to make an added entry for Holmes in addition to the subject heading since the section of Holmes's poems is nearly half the length of the book. This is also an example of the situation in which LC did not make a title added entry because the title is the name of a person given in direct order (the first indicator "0" in the 245 field indicates that no title added entry is to be made).

Another situation in which it might be desirable to add entries to copy would be when a larger work contains several smaller works. Name/title added entries could be given for the smaller works, which would be especially useful in smaller collections to help to avoid purchasing duplicates. Name/title added entries used in this way take the place of analytical entries, which are more time consuming to create if they have to be done with original cataloging.

Other additions to consider are joint authors, editors, corporate body sponsors, etc., which were left off the LC cataloging during the period of limited cataloging (see Example 3.7). Patrons may need these entries to locate desired materials. The more recent creation of Minimal Level Cataloging (MLC) copy at LC is reminiscent of limited cataloging in its paucity of added entries. MLC created from 1980 to 1984 had no added entries. From 1984 to 1986 one added entry was allowed when main entry was under title. Since 1986 MLC catalogers have been allowed to add two added entries when main entry is under title and one added entry with any other kind of main entry (see Example 3.8).[2]

Croft-Cooke, Rupert, 1903–
    The sawdust ring, by Rupert Croft-Cooke and W. S. Mead-
more. London, Odhams Press ₁1951₁

    159 p. Illus. 25 cm.

    1. Circus—Hist.   ɪ. Title.

GV1801.C7   ◯   791.3   52–19116 ‡

Library of Congress   ₁1₁

Example 3.7. LC made very few added entries under their limited cataloging policy. In this case the local library may want to add an entry for the joint author.

```
Type: a Bib lvl: m Govt pub:    Lang:  eng Source:   Illus:
Repr:     Enc lvl: 7 Conf pub: 0 Ctry:  xx  Dat tp: s M/F/B: 10
Indx: 0 Mod rec:     Festschr: 0 Cont:
Desc: a Int lvl:     Dates: 1963,
   1 010       85-844646
   2 040       DLC $c DLC
   3 050 0     MLCM 86/1284 (Q)
   4 049       YCLM
   5 100 10    Vargas, Jos'e Israel.
   6 245 14    The operation experience and the utilization of the Triga
reactor of the Instituto de Pesquisas Radioativas / $c J.I. Vargas, M.
Campos e O.C. Ferreira.
   7 260 0     Belo Horizonte, Brasil : $b Instituto de Pesquisas
Radioativas, Escola de Engenharia da Universidade de Minas Gerais, $c
1963.
   8 300       19 p. : $b ill. ; $c 23 cm.
   9 490 1     Publica₁c~ao ; $v IPR-44
  10 810 1     Belo Horizonte, Brazil. $b Universidade de Minas Gerais. $b
Instituto de Pesquisas Radioativas. $t Publica₁c~ao ; $v no. 44.
```

Example 3.8. In this MLC record, main entry is under the first author, but there are no added entries for the other two authors. The series, however, is traced, but in the form established prior to AACR 2.

It is also possible that a library may wish to make added entries for contributors that the outside source did not consider important enough, as in Example 3.9, or for which the rules do not allow. An example of the latter is the situation where four or more authors have collaborated on a work. Only the first named is given an added entry. A library may wish to make an added entry for one or more of the later named authors, especially if they are on the faculty (university or school library), or are prominent local citizens (public library), or are company employees (special library). Other additions that may be desired for patron access might include name/title of a related work and entry for a serial in which a work was first published.

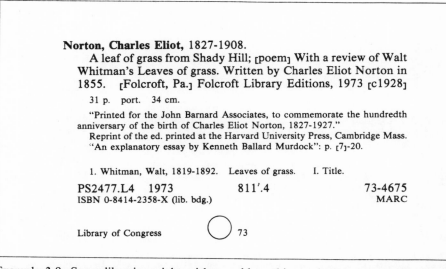

Norton, Charles Eliot, 1827-1908.
    A leaf of grass from Shady Hill; ₍poem₎ With a review of Walt Whitman's Leaves of grass. Written by Charles Eliot Norton in 1855. ₍Folcroft, Pa.₎ Folcroft Library Editions, 1973 ₍c1928₎

31 p.   port.   34 cm.

"Printed for the John Barnard Associates, to commemorate the hundredth anniversary of the birth of Charles Eliot Norton, 1827-1927."
Reprint of the ed. printed at the Harvard University Press, Cambridge Mass.
"An explanatory essay by Kenneth Ballard Murdock": p. ₍7₎-20.

1. Whitman, Walt, 1819-1892. Leaves of grass. I. Title.

PS2477.L4 1973   811'.4   73-4675
ISBN 0-8414-2358-X (lib. bdg.)   MARC

Library of Congress   73

Example 3.9. Some libraries might wish to add to this cataloging an added entry for Murdock, since his contribution to the book consists of 12 pages while Norton's contribution is only 7 pages long.

Most libraries would want to consider also adding entries that have been omitted from the copy in error. Example 3.10 shows that an author included in the statement of responsibility has not been given an added entry. The omission in Example 3.11 is not as obvious. The copy cataloger would have to notice that a prominent statement of corporate responsibility has been omitted from the notes and that the corporate added entry is needed.

```
OCLC: 5348012        Rec stat: n Entrd: 791121        Used: 870518
Type: a Bib lvl: m Govt pub:      Lang:  eng Source:      Illus: a
Repr:      Enc lvl:      Conf pub: 0 Ctry:  ohu Dat tp: s M/F/B: 00
Indx: 0 Mod rec:      Festschr: 0 Cont: bs
Desc: i Int lvl:      Dates: 1978,
  1 010        79-121955
  2 040        DLC $c DLC $d m.c.
  3 020        0933522010 : $c $2.95
  4 043        n-us---
  5 050 0      HN90.S6 $b A53 1978
  6 082        301.44/0973
  7 090        $b
  8 049        YCLM
  9 245 00     American class society in numbers / $c Beth Belton ... [et
al.] ; edited by Bob Howard and John Logue.
 10 250        Rev.
 11 260 0      Kent, Ohio : $b Kent Popular Press, $c c1978, 1979
printing.
 12 300        iv, 98 p. : $b ill. ; $c 21 cm.
 13 504        Bibliography: p. 88-90.
 14 650  0     Social classes $z United States.
 15 650  0     Income distribution $z United States.
 16 700 10     Howard, Bob, $d 1950- $w cn
 17 700 10     Logue, John, $d 1947- $w cn
```

Example 3.10. An added entry was inadvertently not made for the author in the statement of responsibility, even though added entries were made for the editors.

```
OCLC: 4654403        Rec stat: c Entrd: 800802        Used: 861031
Type: a Bib lvl: m Govt pub:      Lang:  eng Source:      Illus: a
Repr:      Enc lvl:      Conf pub: 1 Ctry:  wau Dat tp: s M/F/B: 00
Indx: 1 Mod rec: m Festschr: 0 Cont: b
Desc: i Int lvl:      Dates: 1978,
  1 010        80-122453//r85
  2 040        DLC $c DLC $d m.c.
  3 020        0892521821 (pbk.)
  4 050 0      TA1650 $b .I45
  5 082 0      621.3819/598 $2 19
  6 090        $b
  7 049        YCLM
  8 245 00     Image understanding systems and industrial applications :
$b [seminar], August 30-31, 1978, San Diego, California / $c Ramakant
Nevatia, editor.
  9 260 0      Bellingham, Wash. : $b Society of Photo-optical
Instrumentation Engineers, $c c1978.
 10 300        vi, 262 p. (p. 262 blank) : $b ill. ; $c 28 cm.
 11 490 1      Proceedings of the Society of Photo-optical Instrumentation
Engineers ; v. 155
 12 504        Includes bibliographical references and index.
 13 650  0     Optical pattern recognition $x Congresses.
 14 650  0     Image processing $x Congresses.
 15 700 10     Nevatia, Ramakant. $w cn
 16 710 20     Society of Photo-optical Instrumentation Engineers. $w cn
 17 830  0     Proceedings of the Society of Photo-optical Instrumentation
Engineers ; $v v. 155.
```

Example 3.11. This work bears the following statement prominently displayed: "Cooperating organization: American Meteorological Society." This should have been noted in the description and an added entry should have been made.

Uniform Titles

Although not strictly added entries, uniform titles need to be considered at this point because they are often used in name/title added entries, and when they occupy the 240 field of a MARC record, they can become additional access points. Uniform titles have been used by LC for many years, but before implementation of AACR 2, most uniform titles were not printed on LC's cards or in the *NUC*. On MARC records most uniform titles in the 240 field were coded with the first indicator "0" to indicate that they should not be printed (see Example 3.12). LC used these uniform titles in their own catalogs, in many cases writing them by hand in the upper right corner of the main entry card. This practice was followed because it was not deemed wise to have the uniform title appear on the cards for the added and subject entries for the set, as it would affect filing order. However, in order to have a card for a related work file immediately after the main entry and uniform title of the work to which it was related, added name/title entries contained the uniform title, not the title page title, as shown in Example 3.13 (page 80). Catalogers outside LC also encountered uniform titles when works given title main entry needed a uniform title (e.g., Mother Goose, or Bible).

In 1983 LC began updating 240 fields in MARC records so that the MARC record for Fehrenbach's critical edition of Shirley's *Politician* (shown in Example 3.12) now has a first indicator "1" in the 240 field, allowing the uniform title to print. However, most library catalogs, including the *NUC*, contain many records lacking uniform titles, both in printed catalogs and in online files. Catalogers using MLC copy need to be aware that MLC records created before 1986 have no uniform titles.

Name/title added entries often use uniform titles when translations or variant titles are involved. Such usage is an excellent way to avoid purchases of duplicate materials, as well as a means for bringing together editions and translations for users. However, if the copy cataloger or authority control person is not alert to the use of uniform title, there will be no access point for the title appearing on the piece (see Example 3.14, page 82). A library that does not file by uniform title may wish to substitute the title of the translation or other *title-in-hand* for the uniform title given. A reference from the author and uniform title may be made instead of the added entry. Most libraries, however, make a reference from the author and title page title to the added entry that uses the uniform title.

Record (a)

```
OCLC: 6278433        Rec stat: p Entrd: 800410        Used: 821110
Type: a Bib lvl: m Govt pub:        Lang:  eng Source:   Illus:
Repr:    Enc lvl:    Conf pub: 0 Ctry:  nyu Dat tp: s M/F/B: 10
Indx: 0 Mod rec:     Festschr: 0 Cont: b
Desc: i Int lvl:     Dates: 1980,
    1 010        79-54337
    2 040        DLC $c DLC $d m.c.
    3 020        082404455X : $c $32.00
    4 050 0      PR3144 $b .P6 1980
    5 082        822/.4
    6 090          $b
    7 049        IVEA
    8 100 10     Shirley, James, $d 1596-1666. $w cn
    9 240 04     The polititian
   10 245 12     A critical edition of The politician by James Shirley / $c
Robert J. Fehrenbach.
   11 260 0      New York : $b Garland Pub., $c 1980.
   12 300        cxxiv, 206 p. ; $c 24 cm.
   13 440 0      Renaissance drama
   14 500        A revision of the author's thesis.
   15 504        Bibliography: p. 195-206.
   16 700 10     Fehrenbach, Robert J., $d 1936- $w cn
```

Record (b)

Library of Congress Cataloging in Publication Data

Shirley, James, 1596–1666.
   A critical edition of The politician by James Shirley.

   (Renaissance drama)
   Bibliography: p.
   I. Fehrenbach, Robert J., 1936–   II. Title.
III. Series.
PR3144.P6   1980   822'.4   79-54337
ISBN 0-8240-4455-X

Example 3.12. Prior to AACR 2 implementation, uniform titles in MARC records were coded with a "0" in the first indicator position of the 240 field so that the uniform title would not print on cards, as shown in Record (a). The CIP paper version sent to publishers reflects the same practice, as shown in Record (b).

Record (a)

Rogers, Will, 1879–1935.
　　The writings of Will Rogers. Stillwater, Oklahoma
State University Press, 1973–

　　　v. illus. 24 cm.

　　1. American wit and humor.　　I. Title.

PN6161.R6644　　　　◯　　791'.092'4　　　73–163424
[PN6231.M4]　　　　　　　　　　　　　　　　　　MARC

Library of Congress　　　　73 [4]

Record (b)

Rogers, Will, 1879-1935.
　　There's not a bathing suit in Russia & other bare facts. Edited
with an introd. by Joseph A. Stout, Jr.　Stillwater, Oklahoma
State University Press, 1973.

　　95 p.　illus.　24 cm.　(The writings of Will Rogers, I, 2)　$6.95

　　I. Title.　II. Series: Rogers, Will, 1879-1935.　Works. 1973. I, 2.

PN6161.R6644　　ser. I, vol. 2　　　　　　　73-89307
　　　　　　　　◯　　791'.092'4
　　　　　　　　　　　　　　　　　　　　　MARC
Library of Congress　　　　74[74]

Example 3.13. The series added entry of the analytic (added entry number II on Record b) is constructed so that it will file with the uniform title of the set, which is not the title page title. Since the uniform title was not printed on the set copy, Record (a), it must be added, or the added entry of the analytic copy must be changed if the two are to file together. Record (c) shows the revised version of the MARC record for the set. The uniform title has been recoded so that it would now print on cards.

Record (c)

```
OCLC: 672607        Rec stat: c Entrd: 730703        Used: 870220
Type: a Bib lvl: m Govt pub: s Lang:  eng Source:    Illus: a
Repr:     Enc lvl:   Conf pub: 0 Ctry:  oku Dat tp: m M/F/B: 10a
Indx: 0 Mod rec:    Festschr: 0 Cont:
Desc: a Int lvl:    Dates: 1973,1983
   1 010      73-163424//r874
   2 040      DLC $c DLC
   3 050 0    PN6161 $b .R6644
   4 082 0    792.7/028/0924 $2 19
   5 090       $b
   6 049      YCLM
   7 100 10   Rogers, Will, $d 1879-1935.
   8 240 10   Works. $f 1973
   9 245 14   The writings of Will Rogers.
  10 260 0    Stillwater : $b Oklahoma State University Press, $c 1973-
1983.
  11 300      7 v. in 22 : $b ill. ; $c 24 cm.
  12 500      Vol. 22: Cumulative index / compiled and edited by Steven
K. Gragert ; Judy G. Buckholz, assistant editor.
  13 500      Sponsored by Oklahoma State University and the Will Rogers
Memorial Commission.
  14 650  0   American wit and humor.
  15 700 10   Gragert, Steven K.
  16 700 10   Buckholz, Judy G.
  17 710 20   Oklahoma State University.
  18 710 20   Will Rogers Memorial Commission.
```

Example 3.13 *(continued)*.

Record (a)

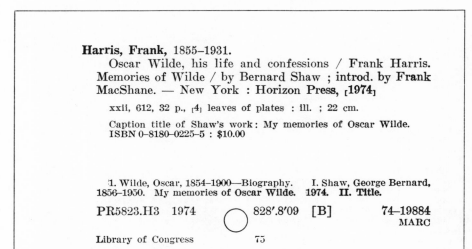

Harris, Frank, 1855–1931.
    Oscar Wilde, his life and confessions / Frank Harris.
Memories of Wilde / by Bernard Shaw ; introd. by Frank
MacShane. — New York : Horizon Press, ₁1974₁

    xxii, 612, 32 p., ₁4₁ leaves of plates : ill. ; 22 cm.

    Caption title of Shaw's work: My memories of Oscar Wilde.
    ISBN 0–8180–0225–5 : $10.00

    1. Wilde, Oscar, 1854–1900—Biography.   I. Shaw, George Bernard,
1856–1950. My memories of Oscar Wilde. **1974. II. Title.**

PR5823.H3   1974   828'.8'09 [B]   74–19884
                                              MARC

Library of Congress   75

Record (b)

Laguarda Trías, Rolando A
    El predescubrimiento del Río de la Plata por la expedi-
ción portuguesa de 1511–1512 / por Rolando A. Laguarda
Trías. — Lisboa : Junta de Investigações do Ultramar, 1973.
    xii, 220 p., ₁16₁ leaves of plates : ill., facsims., maps ; 30 cm. —
(₁Série de memórias₁ - Agrupamento de Estudos de Cartografia An-
tiga, Secção de Lisboa ; 13)
    "Nueva noticia de la Tierra del Brasil" (p. 136–139) is a trans-
lation of Copia der newen Zeytung auss Presillg Landt.
    Includes bibliographical references and index.
    150$00
    1. Rio de la Plata—Discovery and exploration—Portuguese. 2.
Fróis, Estêvão.   I. Copia der newen Zeytung auss Presillg Landt.
Spanish. 1973. II. Title: El predescubrimiento del Río de la Plata
por la expedición portuguesa ... III. Series: Agrupamento de Estudos de Cartografia An-   tiga. Série Memórias ; 13.

F2841.L27   75–558034
Library of Congress   75

Example 3.14. Record (a) shows cataloging for a book containing two works. The author/
title added entry for the second work gives the uniform title, not the title page title. Record
(b) also shows use of a uniform title. Added entry no. I represents the entry for the Spanish
translation of a work which has been published in the book being cataloged. The original
title, in an old form of German, followed by the language and publication date of the
translation, is used for the added entry.

Another situation related to uniform title is shown in Example 3.15. It is LC's practice to make an added entry for the part of a title that follows an author's name in the possessive form. In this example the title added entry (740 field) duplicates the uniform title. In a library that makes printed added entries for uniform titles, the two entries would file together. Many online systems also index the uniform title field, in which case the entry in the 740 field is superfluous.

```
OCLC: 7976674        Rec stat: p Entrd: 811104        Used: 870720
Type: a Bib lvl: m Govt pub:   Lang:  eng Source:   Illus:
Repr:    Enc lvl:   Conf pub: 0 Ctry:  nyu Dat tp: s M/F/B: 10
Indx: 0 Mod rec:     Festschr: 0 Cont: b
Desc: a Int lvl:   Dates: 1982,
  1 010        81-18815
  2 040        DLC $c DLC $d m/c
  3 020        0393952169 (pbk.)
  4 020        0393015998 (hard)
  5 039 0      2 $b 3 $c 3 $d 3 $e 3
  6 041 1      enggrc
  7 050 0      PN1040 $b .A513 1982
  8 082 0      808.2 $2 19
  9 090        $b
 10 049        YCLM
 11 100 00     Aristotle. $w cn
 12 240 10     Poetics. $l English
 13 245 10     Aristotle's Poetics / $c translated, with an introduction
and notes, by James Hutton ; preface by Gordon M. Kirkwood.
 14 250        1st ed.
 15 260 0      New York : $b Norton, $c c1982.
 16 300        x, 115 p. ; $c 21 cm.
 17 500        Translation of: Peri poietikes.
 18 504        Includes bibliographical references.
 19 650   0    Poetry $x Early works to 1800.
 20 650   0    Aesthetics $x Early works to 1800.
 21 700 10     Hutton, James, $d 1902- $w cn
 22 740 01     Poetics.
```

Example 3.15. LC makes title added entries for titles following authors' names in the possessive. They have purposely made the added entry in line 22 even though it duplicates the uniform title because uniform titles in a 240 field are not given added entries in LC's system.

Title Added Entries

The decision about how many title added entries to make must take into account their desirability, regardless of whether they were made by the outside source. The following are situations in which a title added entry may not have been made by the outside source, but may be wanted by a library using that copy:

1. Title added entries that are identical to the wording of the subject heading have traditionally not been made on outside copy. AACR 2 specifically states that such title added entries should not be made in catalogs where names, titles, and subjects are interfiled. LC, however, has stated that it would ignore this restriction and has done so since the implementation of AACR 2. There are still many records created earlier with no title added entries for titles that are identical to subject headings (see Example 3.16). The latter situation is probably best for a dictionary card catalog because it saves filing duplicates of the cataloging for a work in the same place. However, in a divided catalog or in an online catalog with separate title and subject indexes, both the title and the subject entries are needed, and a title entry needs to be added. Libraries with dictionary card catalogs, on the other hand, may wish to delete the title added entries for such items from the current records that now almost routinely have an added entry for the title proper.

```
OCLC: 1217433      Rec stat: n Entrd: 750214      Used: 811023
Type: a Bib lvl: m Govt pub:     Lang:  eng Source:    Illus: a
Repr:     Enc lvl:     Conf pub: O Ctry:  hiu Dat tp: s M/F/B: 10
Indx: O Mod rec:      Festschr: O Cont:
Desc: i Int lvl:      Dates: 1974,
  1 010        74-20271
  2 040        DLC $c DLC
  3 050  0     GV1469.B2 $b K36
  4 082        795/.1
  5 090        $b
  6 049        YCLM
  7 100 10     Kansil, Djoli, $c Prince, $d 1943-
  8 245 00     Backgammon! / $c Prince Djoli Kansil.
  9 260  0     Honolulu : $b Victoria Publishers, $c [1974]
 10 300        vi, 80 p. : $b ill. ; $c 23 cm.
 11 650  0     Backgammon.
```

Example 3.16. This record shows a situation where LC did not make a title added entry because the subject heading has the exact wording of the title (the first indicator "0" in the 245 field indicates that no title added entry is to be made).

2. Titles that consist solely of the name of a nonimaginary person given in direct order also have not traditionally been given added entries on outside cataloging. AACR 2 calls for omission of title added entries that are essentially the same as the main entry heading or a reference to it, as well as for titles identical to subject headings. This has been interpreted to include names in direct order, even though the headings are in inverted order. Again, LC currently ignores the restriction, but there are many older records of this type that lack the added entry (see Example 3.6, page 74). There is some evidence that library patrons look up titles word for word (even those that are names).

3. Titles that appear in the publication itself and that vary from the official title page may not appear as added entries on the outside copy (although some do). Such titles may appear on the cover or spine, or may be running titles, prominent subtitles, part of the title page title which stands out by reason of typography, or part of the title following the author's name in the possessive. Any of these may be the title remembered by the patron who has seen an item and wishes to return to it. Example 3.17 shows a case where part of a title shown in very large type on a title page was not given an added entry. This kind of omission may make less difference in the future as more libraries acquire online systems with keyword access to any word in a title, but the current form of the catalog should be the primary basis for access point decisions.

PRINCETON ALUMNI COLLECTIONS
WORKS ON PAPER

THE ART MUSEUM · PRINCETON UNIVERSITY

PUBLISHED IN ASSOCIATION WITH PRINCETON UNIVERSITY PRESS

```
OCLC: 7923918        Rec stat: n Entrd: 810926        Used: 870130
Type: a Bib lvl: m Govt pub:      Lang: eng Source:      Illus: a
Repr:    Enc lvl:    Conf pub: 0 Ctry: nju Dat tp: s M/F/B: 00
Indx: 1 Mod rec:    Festschr: 0 Cont: c
Desc: a Int lvl:    Dates: 1981,
  1 010        81-80640
  2 040        DLC $c DLC $d m/c
  3 020        0691039771 (Princeton Univ. Pr.)
  4 039 0      2 $b 3 $c 3 $d 3 $e 3
  5 043        n-us-nj
  6 050 0      NC15.P7 $b P76
  7 082 0      741.9/074/014967 $2 19
  8 090        $b
  9 049        YCLM
 10 245 00     Princeton alumni collections : $b works on paper.
 11 260 0      Princeton, N.J. : $b Published by the Art Museum, Princeton
University, in association with Princeton University Press, $c c1981.
 12 300        261 p. : $b ill. ; $c 25 x 28 cm.
 13 500        Catalogue of an exhibition held April 26-June21, 1981.
 14 500        Includes index.
 15 650 0      Drawing $x Exhibitions.
 16 610 20     Princeton University. $b Art Museum. $x Exhibitions. $w cn
 17 710 20     Princeton University. $b Art Museum. $w cn
```

Example 3.17. In this example a later part of the title was given greater prominence on the title page than the title proper, but an added entry was not made on the bibliographic record. (Note: Publication statement in 260 field was copied from the *verso* of the title page.)

4. Many titles contain abbreviations, numerals, or symbols that if heard rather than seen by a user could be thought to be either spelled out or not. Example 3.18 demonstrates such a case. LC currently makes title added entries in many such cases, but again, older copy did not have this treatment.

```
OCLC: 8039882        Rec stat: n Entrd: 811219        Used: 870629
Type: a Bib lvl: m Govt pub:      Lang: eng Source:    Illus: af
Repr:       Enc lvl:    Conf pub: 0 Ctry: ilu Dat tp: s M/F/B: 10
Indx: 0 Mod rec:        Festschr: 0 Cont:
Desc: a Int lvl:        Dates: 1981,
   1 010        80-54683
   2 040        DLC $c DLC $d m/c
   3 020        0895268892 (pbk.)
   4 039 0      2 $b 3 $c 3 $d 3 $e 3
   5 043        n-us---
   6 050 0      GV1061.2 $b .C85
   7 082 0      796.4/26 $2 19
   8 090         $b
   9 049        YCLM
  10 100 10     Cumming, John, $d 1915- $w cn
  11 245 10     Runners & walkers : $b a nineteenth century sports
chronicle / $c by John Cumming.
  12 260 0      Chicago : $b Regnery Gateway, $c c1981.
  13 300        177 p., [1] leaf of plates : $b ill. ; $c 28 cm.
  14 650  0     Running $z United States $x History $y 19th century.
  15 650  0     Walking $z United States $x History $y 19th century.
  16 650  0     Track-athletics $z United States $x History $y 19th
century.
```

Example 3.18. The ampersand in the title proper could logically be expected to be spelled out "and." Thus, an added entry for "Runners and walkers" could be very helpful. LC's rule interpretation calling for such title added entries was issued in 1982, after the creation of this record.

5. In the past *non-distinctive* titles were not given added entries on outside copy. In the 1970s, for example, LC omitted title added entries for such titles as "Poems," "Selections," "Journal," etc., and their equivalents in foreign languages. On older copy, even more categories of titles were considered non-distinctive, including those beginning with words such as "Introduction to ...," "Handbook of ...," etc. (see Example 3.19). When considering adding title added entries for non-distinctive titles, a library might also wish to consider the value of adding entries for parts of titles following prepositions when the first words of the title are generic and when the words following the prepositions are not repeated by subject headings (e.g., "An essay on the economics of detribalization"). Here again, however, the anticipated availability of keyword access may make such considerations moot.

6. As with any part of copy cataloging, there are cases when title added entries have been omitted in error. Example 3.20 demonstrates such a case.

BF81
B756ha

Brett, George Sidney, 1879–
History of psychology. Edited and abridged by R. S. Peters. London, Allen & Unwin; New York, Macmillan ₁1953₁

742 p. 22 cm. (The Muirhead library of philosophy)

Bibliography: p. ₍733₎-736.

1. Psychology — Hist.   2. Philosophy, Ancient.   3. Psychology, Patristic.

BF81.B7   1953   150.9   53–11596 ‡
Library of Congress   ₁15₁

Example 3.19. A title added entry was not made by LC because this title was considered to be too general at the time. This title would now be given an added entry.

```
OCLC: 8050601       Rec stat: p Entrd: 811210       Used: 860908
Type: a Bib lvl: m Govt pub:     Lang:  eng Source:    Illus:
Repr:     Enc lvl:   Conf pub: 0 Ctry:  nyu Dat tp: s M/F/B: 10
Indx: 0 Mod rec:     Festschr: 0 Cont: b
Desc: a Int lvl:     Dates: 1982,
  1 010       81-22389
  2 040       DLC $c DLC $d m/c
  3 020       0811208249
  4 020       0811208257 (pbk.)
  5 039 0     2 $b 3 $c 3 $d 3 $e 3
  6 041 1     engfre
  7 043       a-ii---
  8 050 0     BH221.I53 $b D38 1982
  9 082 0     700/.1 $2 19
 10 090       $b
 11 049       YCLM
 12 100 10    Daumal, Ren'e, $d 1908-1944. $w cn
 13 245 10    Rasa, or, Knowledge of the self : $b essays on Indian
aesthetics and selected Sanskrit studies / $c Ren'e Daumal ; translated
with an introduction by Louise Landes Levi.
 14 260 0     New York : $b New Directions, $c 1982.
 15 300       107 p. ; $c 21 cm.
 16 500       Essays selected and translated from the author's Les
pouvoirs de la parole, L''Evidence absurde, Bharata, and Les contre-
ciel.
 17 504       Includes bibliographical references.
 18 505 0     To approach the Hindu poetic art -- On Indian music --
Concerning Uday Shankar -- The origin of the theatre of Bharata --
Oriental book reviews -- The hymn of man -- To the liquid -- Knowledge
of the self -- Some Sanskrit texts on poetry.
 19 650  0    Aesthetics, Indic $x Addresses, essays, lectures.
 20 740 01    Rasa.
```

Example 3.20. Under current practice, LC makes a title added entry for the entire title proper when an alternative title is involved, for the alternative title alone, and for the part of the title preceding "or" (or its equivalent) if this part has three words or less. An added entry for "Knowledge of the self" should be added to this record.

At this time when title is becoming the most prominent means for searching for cataloging copy (e.g., paper *on order* and *in process* files are often arranged by title), when rules have been changed to have title as main entry in many more cases, when serials are being identified by title, and when *unit entry* (i.e., description of an item without assigning a main entry to it) is being seriously discussed, all libraries should give consideration to the adequacy of title access.

For whatever title added entries are made, there should be some way to indicate how far through the title the added entry should go. Otherwise, the arbitrary truncation of a lengthy title at the end of the second or third line by a computer or a typist could occur at an awkward spot. Occasionally at LC, lengthy titles have been printed in truncated form in the added entry position (see Example 3.21).

Allee, Virginia, 1923–
A family report of both genealogical and historical interest to loved ones and descendants, both now, and in the future generations / Virginia Allee. — [Boulder, Colo.] : Allee, [1974]

232 leaves in various foliations, [25] leaves of plates : ill. ; 29 cm.

1. Stevenson family. 2. Bogart family. 3. Alley family. I. Title: A family report of both genealogical and historical interest ...

CS71.S847   1974   929'.2'0973   75–304932
                                                   MARC

Library of Congress   75

Example 3.21. Because the title page title is lengthy, the title tracing shows how much of the title should be included as the added entry.

Serial titles present one other problem for title added entries because under AACR 2 even generic serial titles are being entered under title as main entry instead of under corporate body. This means that, if patrons are to be able consistently to find serial titles under title, title added entries must be added on all older copy for serials with generic titles cataloged under corporate bodies.

Series Added Entries

Discrepancies between Local Catalog and Outside Source

A library can use outside cataloging to the best advantage by tracing a series only if the copy has it traced, and by tracing it in the same form as found on the copy. However, this may not always be possible if the library wishes to be consistent in its treatment of a particular series. There will often be discrepancies between the copy and the local catalog, and there will sometimes be discrepancies in the treatment of a series by the outside source from one time to another.

The decision to make a series added entry will depend to a great extent on the individual library's past practice. To start making added entries for a series that has not previously been traced can be quite misleading because it would seem to indicate that earlier titles in that series are not in the library. A possible way around this would be to have an explanatory reference preceding the current series added entries explaining that the earlier volumes of the series must be found under their own authors or titles. Unless there is a series authority file or a check-in record for every series, however, it is difficult to tell whether an earlier decision was made not to trace the series, or whether the library actually has no other volumes of the series. An explanatory reference that says the volumes of the series in question will be found under their respective authors or titles can be useful to both patrons and catalogers. The presence of such a reference in the catalog shows that a definite decision has been made not to make added entries for the series. A series authority file, of course, gives this information for the cataloger, and in some libraries in which copy cataloging is done online, the series authority file (either one in card format or one in which the user has terminal access to an online file) is placed beside the cataloging terminals for immediate checking of local policy before completion of cataloging.

The decision to stop making added entries for a series that has been traced in the past is a little easier because added entries already made can be removed from the catalog. If this is done, the explanatory reference mentioned above would be especially helpful to the patron who previously found entries under the series but now finds that the entries have been removed.

Discrepancies in Copy from Outside Source

In addition to discrepancies between the library's own cataloging and that of the outside source, there are some discrepancies in cataloging from the source itself. If LC copy is used, the problem of limited cataloging surfaces again. Because no series were traced during limited cataloging, there are situations where a series was traced before 1951, not traced during limited cataloging, and then picked up again in 1963; or a series that started between 1951 and 1963 may have been traced after 1963 but not before. Another problem with LC tracings is that series were not traced on analytics before 1947. Therefore, retrospective analytic copy must have the entry for the serial added, or newer copy must have it removed or ignored, depending upon the policy of the individual library.

A third discrepancy occurring with the outside source is the situation where one title of a series is traced while another is not. It is difficult to know whether a change was made in the manner of tracing; whether an error was made; or whether the two items were cataloged at nearly the same time by two catalogers who made opposing decisions. Example 3.22 seems to illustrate the last possibility because the works in the series were cataloged the same year.

A fourth cause for discrepancy in series added entries in copy from LC results from the creation of MLC records. The MLC records created from 1980 to 1984 could only be tagged as 440 (the tag used to show tracing of a series in the form in which it appears on the piece). Beginning in 1984, series could be treated as in regular records; thus, series in MLC records created since that date reflect decisions already made on the treatment of those series. The series in Example 3.8 (page 75) is traced in its pre-AACR 2 form as previously established.

Record (a)

```
OCLC: 815831        Rec stat: n Entrd: 740208        Used: 870715
Type: a Bib lvl: m Govt pub:    Lang:  eng Source:    Illus: a
Repr:    Enc lvl:    Conf pub: O Ctry:  enk Dat tp: s M/F/B: 00a
Indx: 1 Mod rec:    Festschr: O Cont:
Desc:    Int lvl:    Dates: 1973,
   1 010        74-155296
   2 040        DLC $c DLC $d m/c
   3 015        GB***
   4 020        019255414X
   5 050 0      BX9225.C36 $b A29 1973
   6 082        914.1/03/7
   7 090        $b
   8 049        YCLM
   9 100 10     Carlyle, Alexander, $d 1722-1805. $w cn
  10 245 10     Anecdotes and characters of the times. $c Edited with an
introd. by James Kinsley.
  11 260 0      London, $a New York, $b Oxford University Press, $c 1973.
  12 300        xxiv, 318 p. $b illus. $c 24 cm.
  13 350        L4.50
  14 490 0      Oxford English memoirs and travels
  15 600 10     Carlyle, Alexander, $d 1722-1805. $w cn
```

Example 3.22. Records of two works from the same series are shown in this example. The series was not traced on Record (a) (indicated by the field tag 490 with a first indicator "0"). The series on Record (b) was traced (indicated by field tag 440).

Record (b)

```
OCLC: 1040359      Rec stat: n Entrd: 740213        Used: 870618
Type: a Bib lvl: m Govt pub:    Lang:  eng Source:   Illus: ach
Repr:     Enc lvl:  Conf pub: 0 Ctry:  enk Dat tp: s M/F/B: 10b
Indx: 1 Mod rec:    Festschr: 0 Cont: b
Desc:   Int lvl:    Dates: 1973,
   1 010       74-155348
   2 040       DLC $c DLC $d m/c
   3 015       GB73-30488
   4 020       0192554034
   5 043       e-uk---
   6 050 0     DA407.H9 $b H7 1973
   7 082       942.06/2/0924 $a B
   8 090        $b
   9 049       YCLM
  10 100 10    Hutchinson, Lucy (Apsley) $d b. 1620.
  11 245 10    Memoirs of the life of Colonel Hutchinson. $c Edited with
an introduction by James Sutherland; with the fragment of an
autobiography of Mrs. Hutchinson.
  12 260 0     London, $a New York, $b Oxford University Press, $c 1973.
  13 300       xxix, 347, (12) p. $b illus., facsims., ports. $c 24 cm.
  14 350       L4.50
  15 440 0     Oxford English memoirs and travels
  16 500       Memoirs based on the ms. now in the Nottingham Castle
Museum.
  17 500       Map on lining papers.
  18 504       Bibliography: p. xxvi-xxvii.
  19 500       Includes index.
  20 600 10    Hutchinson, John, $d 1615-1664. $w cn
  21 651 0     Great Britain $x History $y Puritan Revolution, 1642-1660.
```

Example 3.22 *(continued)*.

SUMMARY

The possible occasions for changing choice of main entry, for rejecting added entries that appear on outside copy, and for adding access points that do not appear on the copy have been mentioned to show the variety of situations that may require policy decisions. Each library should determine the needs of its clientele. Guidelines for catalogers should result from a consideration of the following questions:

1. Are there any situations where the choice of main entry on the outside copy will not be accepted?

2. Should outdated added entries be rejected in order to maintain consistency with current practices?

3. Is the card catalog so crowded that it is desirable to identify dispensable added entries that appear on outside copy?

4. Are additional access points required because of the arrangement (e.g., dictionary or divided) of the local catalog, or because of the type of indexes maintained for an online catalog?

5. Are there occasions requiring addition of access points that were omitted from the outside copy because it was not the policy of the outside source to make such access points?

6. Are uniform titles used? What adjustments to LC copy are necessary to implement the local policy?

7. What is the local library's policy for title added entries? What title added entries will be made because it was not the policy of the outside source to make them?

8. Is consistency in the tracing of series considered necessary? If so, how will discrepancies between copy and catalog, or in the copy itself, be handled?

NOTES

[1]Lisa Hall Jacob, "A Descriptive Study of the Occurrence of Bibliographic Relationships as Found in Notes and Subject and Added Entries in the Library Catalog," Master's paper, Graduate Library School, University of Chicago, 1987, 12-13.

[2]*Cataloging Service Bulletin*, no. 36 (Spring 1987): 40-42.

4

FORM OF NAME AND TITLE ACCESS POINTS

INTRODUCTION

Most library catalogs contain at least three types of entry forms: *old* LC entries (i.e., those for which the form of entry was constructed according to one of several previous sets of rules); *new* LC entries (i.e., those constructed according to AACR 2; and local entries (i.e., those constructed at the local level, using whatever set of rules was in force at the time, and based on information possibly different from that available to LC). There may also be differences of form within these types (e.g., some entries with death dates, some without). Small catalogs are likely to have the above range of entry forms plus *simplified* forms of entry from one of the services designed to organize smaller collections. These forms coexist in a catalog, but they do not necessarily mesh. Therefore, most libraries must make constant changes so that the catalog can remain a usable tool for finding materials in the library's collection.

If the library is to make use of any kind of outside cataloging, a basic question concerning form of entry must be decided upon before the copy can be integrated into the catalog: is it necessary that headings for the same person, place, or thing be uniform? If the answer to this question is "yes," what will be the authority for the form used?

The answer to the first question may lie in the purposes of the library and in the functions it would like its catalog to serve. Paul Dunkin discusses in *Cataloging U.S.A.* the *rigid* versus the *relaxed* approach. He suggests that the rigid approach of having a uniform heading is more useful in the large research library where it is desirable to list all works of an author together. The relaxed approach of using the name the author uses, he says, may be more useful in the public or school library.[1] From the point of view of the user of outside cataloging copy, the question is not only which name to use, but also the form and fullness of the name that is used. Does it matter if some materials of an author appear under "Jones, A. J.," while others appear under "Jones, Alan James"? Can some publications of the Hogg Foundation for Mental Health appear under that form of name while others are entered under "Texas. University. Hogg Foundation for Mental Health"? To answer these questions the following points should be considered:

1. What do the users expect from the catalog? Do they need to find all works associated with a particular person or body together?

2. Can the library afford the duplication of material that may occur if headings are not uniform?

3. Is the library a member of a network or union catalog or does it have future plans to join one? If so, what would be the effects, if any, of non-uniform headings?

AUTHORITY CONTROL

If the library decides that headings need not be uniform, the question of authority for form is eliminated. The library simply accepts whatever heading appears on the copy and leaves in the catalog whatever forms appear there. References may be made to direct the user to other names or forms of names that do not file together.

If it is decided that uniform headings are important, the question of authority must be faced. The form of headings that appear on outside copy can vary greatly depending on the physical source of the copy. The version of LC copy for an item as it appears in print in *NUC* may not be the same as that appearing online. Copy found online from a MARC record source (e.g., one of the CD-ROM distributors of MARC records) may vary from that found online through a utility.

The headings that appear in *NUC* are frozen in time in print. It is commonly believed that they reflect the rules that were in effect at the time the cataloging was done. This is not entirely true, however, because of *superimposition*, a policy followed at LC from 1967 to 1981, whereby a heading, once established, continued to be used in that form on the cataloging for new works, regardless of what might have been called for by the rules then in use. During this time, supposedly, only new headings were established according to the rules in use although in reality, old headings were sometimes revised and reprinted. The reprinted versions were printed in later cumulations of *NUC* so that sometimes several successive versions of the same record can be found in *NUC*. With the implementation of AACR 2 the policy of superimposition was dropped. When a new work using a name established under earlier rules is cataloged, the form of name is established according to AACR 2, and older records in MARC format using that name are revised and reissued. Pre-MARC records are not revised, however, nor are pre-AACR 2 headings revised, if no new works associated with those names are cataloged.

Bibliographic records from LC that are available on CD-ROM or in microform are usually cumulated so that only LC's latest version would be present. In cumulations of bibliographic records created or revised since January 1981, all headings should be in AACR 2 form. But cumulations containing older records will have headings representing a mixture of rules.

Records from the utilities also represent a mixture, but of a different sort. Here again, a revised LC record replaces the earlier one so that both do not appear. In addition, use of authority control, either in real time or in the form of batch processing, has been used in some utilities to compare headings in bibliographic records with those in authority records and to change obsolete heading forms to current forms.

Even when a name has been originally established according to AACR 2, there will still be revised headings. The name established according to the rules in the first year of AACR 2 may not necessarily still be in the correct form in subsequent years. An author may regularly begin using a different name or a different form of name. Or the appearance of a new author with a name like one already in the catalog may require that the previously established name be changed. But even when LC has reissued records for a revised heading, *it does not revise the entries already appearing under the old heading in local catalogs* across the land. Those headings remain until someone discovers the revision and decides to make the change, or until an online authority record triggers the change in an automated system. The latter case is still a relatively rare possibility, but it will become more common in the future. If the local changes are not made, any new copy received for a particular heading will not file with the old unless the new copy itself is changed. Also, there may be many headings in the catalog established by local original cataloging, sometimes using information not available to the cataloging source. New copy for material associated with these names will not necessarily bear the same form of heading as in the catalog. For this reason a decision on authority must be made. There are basically three options:

1. The local catalog or local authority file will be the authority (i.e., the form of heading already used locally will continue to be used).

2. The outside source's latest form of heading will be the authority.

3. Every attempt will be made to set up headings according to the latest rules, regardless of form used by local catalog or outside source.

There are advantages and disadvantages to each of these.

Local Catalog or Authority File as Authority

Advantages:

1. Entries already in the catalog and authority file, if applicable, will not have to be retrieved and revised.

2. When adding new cataloging in a master copy system, the heading can be corrected before card production if the library checks entries before completion of cataloging.

3. It is not necessary to search to determine the *latest* form used by the cataloging source.

Disadvantages:

1. If an established heading does not agree with the outside source, every piece of new copy added later for that name will have to be changed.

2. The catalog becomes further removed from the optimum future use of network systems because entries will not mesh with those of other libraries.

3. The catalog entry becomes less likely to correspond to the way the name is cited in other bibliographic sources.

4. When the library decides to change to an online catalog, online authority control will be more difficult because the local heading may not match either the authorized heading or a reference in any existing MARC-format authority file. The library would have to create its own online authority file.

Latest Form of Heading Used by
Outside Source as Authority

Advantages:

1. For users of LC copy, use of any network system based on LC will be enhanced because all libraries that have followed this method will have entries that mesh with each other.

2. Once the catalog entries have been made to agree with the form used by the outside source, new copy can be used without change.

3. The MARC LC authority file can be loaded online and be programmed to interface with the bibliographic file so that many changes can be made automatically.

Disadvantages:

1. Many entries already in the catalog and local authority file, if applicable, may require changing, often more than once.

2. When cataloging with copy done several years earlier by the outside source, the form in the catalog may actually be a later form than that on the copy; research must be undertaken to determine this.

3. LC copy that uses a non-AACR 2 name form is assured of needing attention (e.g., changing, having references made, etc.) as soon as LC begins making entries for that name under AACR 2.

4. The LC authority file does not yet contain every heading used by LC, and in addition, LC often has not established the name in question at all. Therefore, to determine the latest heading or the heading considered to be correct may require research.

Latest Rules as Authority

Advantages:

1. Because the rules tend to use the title page form, the form is more likely to conform to the way the name will be cited in bibliographies.

2. It is not necessary to search for latest form of name used by the outside source.

3. Most LC copy created since 1981 can be used without changing heading forms.

4. Quality standards in most utilities require following the most current cataloging rules when creating new records.

Disadvantages:

1. Both entries in the catalog and copy new to the catalog sometimes must be changed.

2. Network participation is jeopardized because headings on older records in the network's database may not mesh with headings created according to the latest rules.

It is, of course, also possible to have a combination of the above options. One possibility would be a combination of using the local catalog and the latest form of the outside source as authorities. Such a policy usually is carried out only in a card catalog. Headings in catalogs produced by computer in printed or online form are much more easily changed and refiled than in a card catalog. This policy is often accomplished by specifying a number of entries under a particular heading for determining which authority will be used. If the catalog contains more than this number of entries for a heading, the new copy may be changed to agree with the local catalog; or the headings in the catalog may be left as they are, the new copy left as it is, and *see also* references made to connect the two; or the old and new forms may be interfiled, with an explanatory guide card filed before the interfiled forms. If there are fewer than this number of entries for a heading in the catalog, the entries in the catalog may be changed to agree with the latest form of the outside source. (See Chapter 9 for further discussion of catalog changes.)

Local Authority Control Procedures

Whether or not the authoritative form is kept in an authority file separate from the catalog is a local policy matter that is independent of the use of outside copy. However, the way in which copy from a computer-based network is handled may be determined partially by whether or not there is an authority file. If a card catalog is used as the authority file, names cannot be checked against it before completion of the cataloging process unless copy is printed out to be taken to the catalog. It would be possible occasionally to check an authority file near the terminal. The ideal is an online authority file to be checked as needed during the cataloging process.

Another matter of local policy concerns which personnel will decide on form of entry. If either the local catalog or the latest form used by the outside source is the authority, the decision can be automatic, unless there is a conflict. If the latest rules dictate form of entry, however, or if there is a conflict, or if a combination from among the three options is used for determining form of entry, someone must be responsible for interpreting rules and local policy. There has to be a decision whether this will be the responsibility of professional catalogers or whether time will be taken to train paraprofessionals to carry out this function.

If the library has decided that the headings should be uniform and has then decided what to use as the entry authority, the next step is to consider some of the situations that may require changes when using outside cataloging copy. Example 4.1 demonstrates the complexity of the problem by showing an entry for a name that has had five forms since it was first established by LC.

Record (a)

White, Margaret Bourke, 1905–

... Eyes on Russia; with a preface by Maurice Hindus. New York, Simon and Schuster, 1931.

135 p. front., plates, ports. 28½ᶜᵐ.

At head of title: Margaret Bourke-White.
"This book records, partly in words, partly in photographs, my experiences in the soviet union during the summer of 1930."—Author's note.

1. Russia—Descr. & trav.—1917–   2. Photography.   3. Industry—Pictorial works.   ɪ. Title.

31—28578

Library of Congress   ◯   DK267.W43

Record (b)

Bourke-White, Margaret, 1905–

Eyes on Russia; with a pref. by Maurice Hindus. New York, Simon and Schuster, 1931.

135 p. plates, ports. 29 cm.

"Records, partly in words, partly in photographs ... ₍the author's₎ experiences in the Soviet Union during the summer of 1930."

1. Russia—Descr. & trav.—1917–   2. Photography.   3. Industry—Pictorial works.   4. Russia—Indus.   ɪ. Title.

DK267.B63   ◯   914.7   31–28578 rev*

Example 4.1. Record (a) shows earliest form of entry of this author's name under the second part of the compound surname. Record (b) shows a revision of Record (a) with entry under compound surname. Record (c) shows addition of a death date, while Record (d) is another revision, which changes the birthdate from 1905 to 1906. Record (e) (page 100), the current authority record, shows that the birthdate has been changed again — this time to 1904.

Record (c)

Bourke-White, Margaret, 1905–1971.
    Eyes on Russia. With a pref. by Maurice Hindus. New
York, Simon and Schuster, 1931. ₍New York, **AMS Press,**
1971₎
    135 p. illus. 27 cm. $27.50
    1. Russia—Description and travel—1917-   I. Title.
  DK267.B63 1971   914.7′04′842   79–39515

Record (d)

Bourke-White, Margaret, 1906–1971.
    Eyes on Russia; with a pref. by Maurice Hindus. New
York, Simon and Schuster, 1931.
    135 p. plates, ports. 29 cm.
    "Records, partly in words, partly in photographs ... ₍the author's₎
experiences in the Soviet Union during the summer of 1930."
    1. Russia—Description and travel—1917-   2. Russia—Indus-
try—Pictorial works.   I. Title.
  DK267.B63   914.7   31–28578
                  rev 2

Example 4.1 *(continued)*.

Record (e)

```
ARN: 1502012    Rec stat: c      Entrd: 860309        Used: 870311
Type: z         Geo subd: n      Govt agn: _ Lang:    Source:
Roman: _        Subj: a          Series: n _ Ser num: n Head: aab
Ref status: a   Upd status: a    Auth status: a       Name: a
Enc lvl: n      Auth/Ref: a      Mod rec:             Rules: c
```

```
 1 010      n  85208699 $z n  79065986
 2 040      DLC $c DLC $d DLC
 3 100 20   Bourke-White, Margaret, $d 1904-1971.
 4 400 10   White, Margaret Bourke-, $d 1904-1971
 5 400 10   Caldwell, Margaret Bourke-White, $d 1904-1971
 6 667      Includes old catalog heading: Bourke-White, Margaret, 1906-
1971
 7 670      Goldberg, V. Margaret Bourke-White, c1986: $b CIP t.p.
(Margaret Bourke-White) pub. info. sheet (b. 1904; d. 1971;
photojournalist)
 8 670      LC data base, 11-4-85 $b (hdgs.: Bourke-White, Maragaret,
1904-1971; Bourke-White, Margaret, 1906-1971) LC manual auth. cd. (b.
June 1904; author contacted)
```

Example 4.1 *(continued)*.

A cautionary note should be mentioned: the outside copy may have errors in the entry points just as it has errors in the description. If the library has decided to use the outside source as its authority, it will undoubtedly wish to use the correct form when an error is discovered. LC revises records when errors are discovered in access points but local libraries that have already used the copy with the error must correct these themselves. In Example 4.2, the author's second forename has been misspelled in the heading. This is especially interesting because the cataloger at LC went to the trouble to add "[sic]" following the name in the statement of responsibility, which is really the correct spelling! This would lead most catalogers to accept LC's heading as especially authoritative. The form of this name was corrected by LC, and the records were reissued in the mid-1970s with the form "Lancaster, Frederick Wilfrid, 1933- ," but libraries that used the record in the late 1960s and early 1970s may still have the incorrect form in their catalogs. Evidently the incorrect spelling of the name in a local catalog influenced the cataloger who created Record (b) in Example 4.2. LC's form of entry was changed in 1984 to the AACR 2 form: "Lancaster, F. Wilfrid (Frederick Wilfrid), 1933- ." So libraries that did make the spelling correction, as well as those that did not, now need to change to the AACR 2 form. Example 4.3 (page 102) shows a misspelled name in an added entry—in this case recognizable by the correct form in the description. In most printed catalogs Petersen and Peterson would file far enough apart that this misspelled entry would be lost, and in an online catalog without a *spelling checker*, no match would be found. In this case a corrected record has not been issued by LC, although in the OCLC system, the library that input the record, creating a MARC format for it, also made the correction for the spelling of Petersen.

Record (a)

Lancaster, Frederick Wilfred, 1933–
Information retrieval systems; characteristics, testing,
and evaluation ₍by₎ F. Wilfrid ₍sic₎ Lancaster. New York,
Wiley ₍1968₎
xiv, 222 p. illus. 23 cm. (Information sciences series)
SBN 471-51240-0
Includes bibliographical references.
1. Information storage and retrieval systems.   I. Title.
Z699.L35   029.7   68-31645

Record (b)

```
OCLC: 7082333      Rec stat: c Entrd: 810126        Used: 860304
Type: a Bib lvl: m Govt pub:    Lang:  eng Source: d Illus:
Repr:     Enc lvl: I Conf pub: 0 Ctry:  inu Dat tp: s M/F/B: 10
Indx: 0 Mod rec:    Festschr: 0 Cont:
Desc: a Int lvl:    Dates: 1980,
   1 010
   2 040      CAS $c CAS $d OCL $d m/c
   3 090      $b
   4 049      YCLM
   5 100 10   Lancaster, F. Wilfred $q (Frederick Wilfred), $d 1933-
   6 245 14   The Impact of a paperless society on the research library
of the future / $c F. W. Lancaster, Laura Drasgow and Ellen Marks.
   7 260 0    [Champaign-Urbana] : $b Library Research Center, Graduate
School of Library Science, University of Illinois, $c 1980.
   8 300      218 p. ; $c 28 cm.
   9 500      "A report to the National Science Foundation, Division of
Information Science and Technology"
  10 500      Loose-leaf.
  11 500      "NSF Grant no. DSI 78-04768"
  12 504      Bibliography: p. 143-164.
  13 650  0   Communication of technical information.
  14 700 10   Drasgow, Laura. $w cn
  15 700 10   Marks, Ellen L. $w cn
  16 710 20   University of Illinois. $b Library Research Center.
  17 710 20   National Science Foundation (U.S.). $b Division of
Information Science and Technology. $w cn
  18 870 19    $j 700/2 $a Marks, Ellen.
```

Example 4.2. The spelling of the author's second forename is actually correct in the author
statement of Record (a), not in the main entry. Even though the form of Lancaster's name
in Record (b) is AACR 2, the spelling error has been perpetuated.

Farmers' Northwestern almanac; 1864. **A facsim. reproduc-tion, slightly enl., of an 1864 almanac. Reprinted with an introd. by William J. Petersen for members of the State Historical Society of Iowa. Iowa City, 1963.**

36 p. illus. 21 cm.

Cover title. Editor's historical introd. on p. [2–4] of cover.
Original t. p. reads: 1864 farmers' Northwestern almanac. Pub-lished by Wm. C. Chamberlain, Dubuque, Iowa.

1. Almanacs, American—Iowa.   I. Chamberlain, William C.,
b. 1834. II. Peterson, William John, 1901–   ed. III. Iowa. State
Historical Society.

AY171.I 6F3   1864a ( )   64–63541

Example 4.3. The spelling of the editor's surname is correct in the description, not in the added entry.

Name and title access points fall into four principal categories: personal names, corporate names, titles, and series. A discussion of possible changes required in these categories follows.

PERSONAL NAMES

Dates of Birth and Death

Birth and death dates attached to personal names are sometimes the only distinction between two people who have the same name, so they cannot be considered inconsequential. In other cases, the dates have been added because they were conveniently available when the form of name was established; they may some day be a distinguishing factor, but they are not yet. Without searching, one cannot be sure when the dates are essential.

Situations that may require date resolution are the presence (or absence) of dates on a local entry for a name for which outside copy has no dates (or does have dates), or the presence of dates on the entry in the catalog which conflict with the dates from the outside source.

Addition of death dates presents a slightly different problem. This date does not often distinguish between persons but is usually added upon the person's death. LC reissues records to add death dates only when the date is needed to differentiate between two people or when a death date has been found to be inaccurate. LC does not reissue records just to add the death date, but any new records for that author will have the date recorded on them. The decision to be made locally is whether records with the date can interfile with ones without the date, or whether the date should be added to all entries for the name in question.

Example 4.1 amply demonstrates two of the above situations. For a different kind of problem, see Example 4.4. In this example, the cataloger cataloging *Expectation States Theory* finds in the catalog two identical names, but one with a date and one without. The birth date seems to distinguish between two people on the two pieces of LC copy; but is the local original cataloging that lacks a date the same as the one being entered, or is a third person represented? Some sort of verification work is necessary.

Record (a)

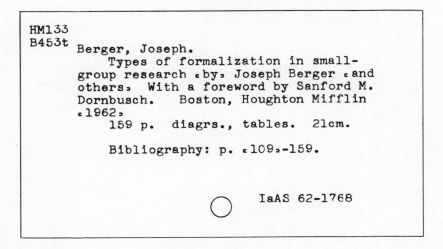

```
HM133
B453t  Berger, Joseph.
          Types of formalization in small-
       group research ₍by₎ Joseph Berger ₍and
       others₎  With a foreword by Sanford M.
       Dornbusch.    Boston, Houghton Mifflin
       ₍1962₎
          159 p.  diagrs., tables.  21cm.

       Bibliography: p. ₍109₎-159.



              ◯        IaAS 62-1768
```

Record (b)

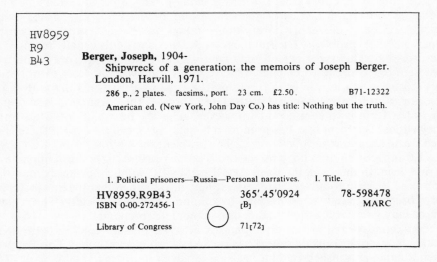

```
HV8959
R9
B43    Berger, Joseph, 1904-
          Shipwreck of a generation; the memoirs of Joseph Berger.
       London, Harvill, 1971.
          286 p., 2 plates.  facsims., port.  23 cm.  £2.50.        B71-12322
          American ed. (New York, John Day Co.) has title: Nothing but the truth.




          1. Political prisoners—Russia—Personal narratives.   I. Title.
          HV8959.R9B43              365'.45'0924          78-598478
          ISBN 0-00-272456-1      ◯  ₍B₎                      MARC

          Library of Congress          71₍72₎
```

Example 4.4. In this example Record (a) and Record (b) are already in the catalog, while Record (c) (page 104) is just being cataloged. It seems possible that the authors on Records (a) and (c) are the same person.

Record (c)

Berger, Joseph, 1924–
    Expectation states theory : a theoretical research program,
edited by Joseph Berger, Thomas L. Conner ₍and₎ M. Hamit
Fisek. Cambridge, Mass., Winthrop Publishers ₍1974₎

    viii, 248 p. illus. 24 cm.

    Bibliography : p. 244–248.

    1. Social psychology — Research.   2. Expectation (Psychology)
I. Conner, Thomas L., 1939–   joint author.   II. Fisek, M. Hamit,
1941–   joint author.   III. Title.

HM251.B455   301.1′01′8   73–4667
ISBN 0–87626–253–1   MARC
Library of Congress   73 ₍4₎

Example 4.4 *(continued)*.

Fullness of Name

The fullness of name also can be the distinguishing factor between two
names (e.g., Smith, James R. is not the same person as Smith, James Raymond).
As with dates, there are situations where the fullness found on the outside copy is
not the same as that appearing in the local catalog. This sometimes happens when
the name was established by original cataloging before being established by the
outside source. A university library that catalogs the theses written locally often
experiences this problem. The full name of the thesis writer is usually required on
the title page; this same person may later author a book using only initials to
represent one or more forenames. If AACR 2 is followed, the later form should
be used because the rule calls for using the predominant form the author has
used, or if no form predominates, the latest form. If the latest form is in doubt,
the fullest form is to be used. LC, however, skips the possibility of *latest* form.
They choose the form that has been used 80 percent of the time, or if there is no
such form, they use the fullest form.[2] The problem for a library using LC copy is
that LC most often does not own the thesis or have access to the form of name on
its title page. In this case, the form established by LC will be the later form rather
than the full form found on the thesis. It may also happen that a name including
only forename initials is established by original cataloging locally. The outside
source may later establish the name using complete forenames.

A second occasion for discrepancies between outside copy and the local
catalog is when the outside source has revised its established entry. This happens
when a name established by older rules is changed in order to follow AACR 2,
and also when a name established using forename initials is revised to fill in the
forenames because the author begins writing with full names rather than initials,
or vice versa. The third situation in which fullness on copy and in catalog may not

agree occurs when more fullness is needed in order to differentiate between a name established by the outside source and a name being added locally by original cataloging.

Changes of Name

For various reasons, some authors change their names, either permanently or temporarily; as a result, a catalog entry under one of the names used may not be the same as the entry from the outside source. AACR 2 gives many situations in which a person may use a different name: marriage, titles of nobility, use of pseudonyms, etc. Rules are given for when to use which name. But this does not automatically resolve the problem of integrating copy into an existing catalog. The entries for the same person using different names will remain in the catalog until an alert cataloger discovers the discrepancy and changes either the catalog entries or the new copy. The name on the outside copy may or may not be the latest name used, depending on the age of the copy. As a result, the name on the outside copy cannot automatically be assumed to be the one that should be used.

As already mentioned, it takes an *alert cataloger* to resolve this particular problem because usually the different names do not file together. An especially difficult example is when a woman who formerly wrote under her birth name begins to use her married name, or vice versa. If she uses her birth name as a middle name, this may lead one to earlier entries under that name; if she does not, however, there may be no clue, and her writings may remain entered under different names. Names established under rules earlier than the 1967 AACR gave a little help in this area since birth names were included and enclosed in parentheses. But now under the philosophy of using, whenever possible, the form of name the author has used, birth names are not as obvious. Example 4.5 (page 106) shows a situation where a woman has used her birth name as a middle name after having written under her birth name.

Another kind of name variance may occur when an author's name appears in different language forms or with different spellings. These, too, may appear differently in the local catalog than on the outside copy received, for the reasons previously enumerated.

Changes in Form of Entry
Due to Rule Changes

In January 1981 LC began to use AACR 2 and abandoned the policy of superimposition. Some names that had been established under AACR 1 or prior rules were changed to the form called for by AACR 2. Research showed that somewhere between 14 percent and 20 percent of headings dealt with during the first year would be different under AACR 2, but only 7 percent to 13 percent of all headings would cause conflict the first year in a catalog (depending upon the size of that catalog). The percentages of personal names to cause conflict were projected to be between 5 percent and 8 percent the first year, with the percentages dropping in subsequent years.[3] However, those percentages assumed that every heading on all cataloging would be made to conform to AACR 2. In actual practice most libraries waited for LC to change headings on copy first. Thus, the percentage of headings to trigger changes in existing catalogs was around 3 percent the first year.

Record (a)

```
OCLC: 790224        Rec stat: c Entrd: 731206      Used: 870701
Type: a Bib lvl: m Govt pub:      Lang:  eng Source:     Illus: a
Repr:      Enc lvl:    Conf pub: 0 Ctry:  nyu Dat tp: s M/F/B: 10
Indx: 1 Mod rec: m Festschr: 0 Cont: b
Desc:      Int lvl:    Dates: 1974,
   1 010        73-9431//r84
   2 040        DLC $c DLC $d m.c.
   3 020        0124113605
   4 050 0      LB1051 $b .K668 1974
   5 060        BF441 K63c 1973
   6 082        370.15/2
   7 090         $b
   8 049        YCLM
   9 100 10     Klausmeier, Herbert J. $q (Herbert John), $d 1915- $w cn
  10 245 10     Conceptual learning and development: $b a cognitive view $c
[by] Herbert J. Klausmeier, Elizabeth Schwenn Ghatala [and] Dorothy A.
Frayer.
  11 260 0      New York, $b Academic Press, $c 1974.
  12 300        xi, 283 p. $b illus. $c 24 cm.
  13 504        Includes bibliographies.
  14 650  0     Learning, Psychology of.
  15 650  0     Concept learning.
  16 650  2     Child development.
  17 650  2     Concept formation.
  18 700 10     Ghatala, Elizabeth Schwenn. $e joint author. $w dn
  19 700 10     Frayer, Dorothy Ann. $e joint author. $w dn
```

Record (b)

```
OCLC: 3256084       Rec stat: c Entrd: 740206      Used: 870529
Type: a Bib lvl: m Govt pub:      Lang:  eng Source:     Illus:
Repr:      Enc lvl:    Conf pub: 0 Ctry:  wiu Dat tp: s M/F/B: 10
Indx: 0 Mod rec: m Festschr: 0 Cont:
Desc:      Int lvl:    Dates: 1970,
   1 010        73-633398//r84
   2 040        DLC $c DLC $d m.c.
   3 050 0      LB1065 $b .K53
   4 082        370.15/4
   5 090         $b
   6 049        YCLM
   7 100 10     Klausmeier, Herbert J. $q (Herbert John), $d 1915- $w cn
   8 245 12     A system of individually guided motivation, $c by Herbert
J. Klausmeier, Elizabeth A. Schwenn, and Peter A. Lamal. Report from the
Situational Variables and Efficiency of Concept Learning Project.
   9 260 0      Madison, $b Wisconsin Research and Development Center for
Cognitive Learning, $c 1970.
  10 300        ix, 28 p. $c 28 cm.
  11 410 20     Wisconsin Research and Development Center for Cognitive
Learning. $t Practical paper $v no. 9 $w cn
  12 500        Supported in part by funds from the U.S. Office of
Education under contract OE 5-10-154.
  13 650  0     Motivation in education.
  14 650  0     Individualized instruction.
  15 700 10     Schwenn, Elizabeth A., $e joint author.
  16 700 10     Lamal, Peter A., $e joint author.
```

Example 4.5. The cataloger working with Record (a) suspected that "Schwenn" might have been the birth name of the author in line 18. This was found to be true, and also it was discovered that she had written under her birth name, as shown in Record (b).

AACR 2 headings are still triggering conflict in catalogs, although the percentages are much smaller than they were at first. The problem for integrating AACR 2 headings into existing catalogs comes from two sources:

1. LC may have changed a name to AACR 2 form, in which case the name on all associated records in *MARC format* would be changed, but *pre-MARC records* would *not* have been reissued. If the local library adds many older materials, copy may be found with both forms of name. And even though LC has changed its MARC records, the many records already copied by local libraries before the change cannot be changed by LC.

2. A local library may have changed a name to AACR 2 form because it was triggered by original cataloging. The name may still be in pre-AACR 2 form on LC records.

Several major changes account for most changes to personal names under AACR 2. Authors with varying fullness of name are now entered under the form most commonly found rather than the fullest form. If an author uses more than one name (e.g., a real name and a pseudonym) and none is predominant, multiple headings are made rather than one name being chosen. If a person uses initials, the entry form uses initials, but LC adds the names the initials stand for in parentheses, if known. Titles of nobility are included only if they appear commonly in association with the name. Nonroman names that have well-established English forms are entered under those forms rather than under their systematically romanized forms, although most nonroman names are now systematically romanized. Example 4.6 shows a record in which the form of one personal name was changed from the fullest form known to the initials followed by fuller names in parentheses.

```
OCLC: 5950737       Rec stat: n Entrd: 800204       Used: 870815
Type: a Bib lvl: m Govt pub:     Lang:  eng Source: d Illus: a
Repr:     Enc lvl: I Conf pub: 0 Ctry:   enk Dat tp: s M/F/B: 10
Indx: 0 Mod rec:     Festschr: 0 Cont:
Desc: i Int lvl:     Dates: 1979,
  1 010        79-51901
  2 040        BUF $c BUF $d m.c.
  3 020        0529056801
  4 090        BR125 $b .L67 1979b
  5 090        $b
  6 049        YCLM
  7 100 10     Lewis, C. S. $q (Clive Staples), $d 1898-1963 $w cn
  8 245 14     The Screwtape letters / $c by C. S. Lewis ; illustrated by
Papas.
  9 260 0      London : $b Collins, $c 1979.
 10 300        133 p. : $b ill. ; $c 25 cm.
 11 500        "Reprinted with some alterations by ... permission of 'The
Guardian'."
 12 500        "First published by Geoffrey Bles 1942."
 13 650 0      Christianity $y 20th century.
 14 870 19      $j 100/1 $a Lewis, Clive Staples, $d 1898-1963.
```

Example 4.6. The name in line 7 has been changed to AACR 2 form. In the OCLC system, when a name was changed by machine comparison with the LC Name Authority File, the form originally used in the record was placed in an 870 field. Thus, the pre-AACR 2 form for Lewis's name is shown in line 14.

Assistance in determining the form LC is currently using for a name can be found in *Name Authorities*, published in microform by LC. It is issued quarterly and is cumulated annually. It contains personal and corporate names, uniform titles, and series for which LC authority records are in machine-readable form. These authority records give the form currently in use at LC, identify whether it is in AACR 2 form or not, and often include in the references and notes information about old forms of heading when a change has been made. Libraries that are tied to a network, such as RLIN or OCLC, have access to these authority records online. A major benefit of this access is that the file is updated more frequently than is the microform version. Neither the online nor the microform version gives a record of every name ever used by LC or even of all names used in MARC bibliographic records, and the names that are included are not yet all in AACR 2 form. However, the size of the file is growing steadily, making it more and more helpful.

CIP Entries

As mentioned in Chapter 3, the access points chosen can change between the time the CIP data is sent to the publisher and the time the cataloging is updated to finished form. In addition to this, the form of name used can also differ — sometimes deliberately and sometimes not. The deliberate differences in personal names can result from the publisher's agreeing not to publish in the book personal information the author wishes not to appear there, such as birthdate or real name of an author writing under a pseudonym. When it is desired that a birthdate not be printed in the CIP that appears in the item, the name is followed by the word "date," to alert the cataloger that the name has been established with the date. When it is desired not to reveal the author's real name in a book written under a pseudonym, if the author is still living, and if AACR 2 would still establish the author under real name, the CIP data contains a dash where the main entry would be. This alerts the cataloger to search for a form of entry not found on the title page.

As outlined in *Cataloging Service Bulletin*, no. 29 (Summer 1985), page 15, in 1985 LC began entering pseudonymous works of contemporary authors under the pseudonym unless the name was covered by a heading already coded "AACR 2." This has been done even when the name would be under the real name if AACR 2 rule 22.2C2 were applied. According to a rule revision concerning pseudonyms published in the revised edition of AACR 2 in 1988, living authors' pseudonymous works are always entered under pseudonym rather than real name. However, CIP data printed before implementation of the revised rule will continue to exhibit occasional dashes in place of main entry.

The nondeliberate differences in personal names between CIP printed in an item and finished copy are of two sorts: printing errors, and the procedure of printing the name as it is established at one point in time only to have the name revised at a future time. As CIP ages, such occurrences will increase in number since new printings of an item are not sent in for new CIP data. CIP entries in books, like the local catalogs across the country, cannot be reprinted by LC every time an entry is revised.

There are also differences between forms of name on MARC CIP and the finished MARC records. This often occurs because the CIP data sheet sent in by a publisher gives a name in one form, but the item when published gives the name in another form. Example 4.7 (below and page 110) shows such a case.

Record (a)

```
OCLC: 8283163        Rec stat: n Entrd: 820209        Used: 830106
Type: a Bib lvl: m Govt pub: s Lang:  eng Source:  Illus:
Repr:    Enc lvl: 8 Conf pub: 0 Ctry:  onc Dat tp: s M/F/B: 10a
Indx: 0 Mod rec: m Festschr: 0 Cont:
Desc: a Int lvl:    Dates: 1982,
  1 010        82-2823
  2 040        DLC $c DLC
  3 020        0295959304
  4 039 0      2 $b 3 $c 3 $d 3 $e 3
  5 043        n-us--- $a n-cn---
  6 050 0      F851.5 $b .W16
  7 082 0      979.5/02 $2 19
  8 090        $b
  9 049        YCLM
 10 100 10     Walker, Alexander, $d 1764-1831.
 11 245 13     An account of a voyage to the north west coast of North
America in 1785 and 1786 / $c by Alexander Walker ; edited by R.A.
Fisher and J.M. Bumsted.
 12 260 0      Toronto : $b Douglas & McIntyre ; $a Seattle : $b
University of Washington Press, $c 1982.
 13 263        8209
 14 300        p. cm.
 15 500        Reproduced from the unpublished manuscript in the National
Library of Scotland (Ms 13780)
 16 651 0      Northwest coast of North America $x Description and travel.
 17 650 0      Nootka Indians $x Social life and customs.
 18 650 0      Indians of North America $z Northwest coast of North
America $x Social life and customs.
 19 600 10     Walker, Alexander, $d 1764-1831.
 20 700 10     Fisher, R. A. $q (Robin A.), $d 1946-
 21 700 10     Bumsted, J. M.
 22 740 01     Voyage to the north west coast of North America in 1785
and 1786.
```

Example 4.7. Record (a), the MARC CIP version of the record, shows that the form of name for Fisher (shown in line 20) was established in accordance with data in the CIP statement of responsibility. Record (b) (page 110), the finished MARC record, shows the form of name that appeared in the finished publication.

Record (b)

```
OCLC: 8283163        Rec stat:  c Entrd:  820209        Used:  870806
Type: a Bib lvl:  m Govt pub:  s Lang:   eng Source:      Illus:  a
Repr:    Enc lvl:    Conf pub:  0 Ctry:   bcc Dat tp: s M/F/B:  10a
Indx: 1 Mod rec:  m Festschr:  0 Cont:  b
Desc: a Int lvl:    Dates:  1982,
   1 010       82-2823//r842
   2 040       DLC $c DLC $d m/c
   3 019       9533738
   4 020       0295959304
   5 043       n-us--- $a n-cn---
   6 050 0     F851.5 $b .W16 1982
   7 082 0     979.5/02 $2 19
   8 090       $b
   9 049       YCLM
  10 100 10    Walker, Alexander, $d 1764-1831. $w cn
  11 245 13    An account of a voyage to the north west coast of America
in 1785 & 1786 / $c by Alexander Walker ; edited by Robin Fisher and
J.M. Bumsted.
  12 260 0     Vancouver : $b Douglas & McIntyre ; $a Seattle : $b
University of Washington Press, $c 1982.
  13 300       319 p. : $b ill. ; $c 24 cm.
  14 504       Bibliography: p. 304-313.
  15 500       Includes index.
  16 500       Reproduced from the unpublished manuscript in the National
Library of Scotland (Ms 13780)
  17 651 0     Northwest coast of North America $x Description and travel.
  18 650 0     Nootka Indians $x Social life and customs.
  19 650 0     Indians of North America $z Northwest coast of North
America $x Social life and customs.
  20 600 10    Walker, Alexander, $d 1764-1831. $w cn
  21 700 10    Fisher, Robin, $d 1946- $w cn
  22 700 10    Bumsted, J. M. $w cn
  23 740 01    Voyage to the north west coast of America in 1785 and 1786.
  24 870 19     $j 700/1 $a Fisher, R. A. $q (Robin A.), $d 1946-
```

Example 4.7 *(continued)*.

A further area of CIP entries requiring attention is the CIP produced by other countries for their publications. These are identified in the same way that American publications identify LC's data with the legend "Library of Congress Cataloging-in-Publication Data." The form of name access points in these entries, of course, may or may not agree with the form that is or would be used by the Library of Congress. Therefore, libraries using LC as their authority need to be alert to identify CIP from other countries (especially English-speaking ones).

References for Personal Names

It has already been mentioned that catalog cards do not arrive with suggested references for names. Therefore, this has been one of the more difficult aspects of training new catalogers—either professional or paraprofessional. The afore-mentioned cataloging tool *Name Authorities*, as well as the online LC Authority File (LCAF), has been helpful in this task. (This file is often referred to as the "LC Name Authority File," or "LCNAF." However, because it also includes series and uniform titles, the "Name" part is misleading. "LCAF" can also be misleading because LC's new list of subjects in MARC format is also an authority file. The terminology will no doubt become established in the next few years. In the meantime this book will use "LCAF" to refer to the file that contains names, series, and uniform titles.) References to be made to a name are listed on its authority record along with information about the forms of name that may have been used on records in the past. Record (e) in Example 4.1 (page 100) shows such an authority record. These records can be of tremendous advantage in suggesting possible references to make, although a library should use from these records only the references needed for the size of its catalog and also may wish to add local references of its own.

For libraries without access to the LCAF, or for names not in the LCAF, some help can be found in the LC/NUC book and microform catalogs, but these are not as complete as authority records. In any case, a library should have a list of the kinds of references that are thought useful and necessary in that catalog. This should include those required because of local filing rules.

CORPORATE ENTRIES

Corporate entries can be more complicated than personal name entries because, unlike a person, the corporate body does not necessarily remain one entity until it dies. Not only can it change its name, as a person can, but it may also merge, be absorbed, or subdivide. Also, the hierarchical structure may change or the name of the higher body may change. The mutation of cataloging rules through the years has further complicated the handling of corporate entries.

In working with outside copy, one of the most difficult aspects of corporate body names is to identify relevant entries already in the catalog. Once these have been identified, it must then be decided whether form-of-entry changes or name changes are involved. Do the differing forms of entry result from different catalogers' interpretations of how the name should be entered, do they result from a change in the rules for form of corporate names, or do they result from an actual name change of the body? Example 4.8 (pages 112-13) demonstrates this problem. The cataloger making an entry for the British Library of Political and Economic Science, London, intuits that a cross reference may be needed from London. Upon checking there, an entry is found—in this case, one established years earlier by local original cataloging. In addition it is discovered that the AACR 2 form of name provides a third variation.

Record (a)

```
Z710        London. British library of political
L846r           and economic science.
          London school of economics and political
             science.
             A reader's guide to the British
          library of political and economic science.
          London, London school of economics and
          political science, 1934.
             97, ₍1₎ p. plans. 24cm.


          1. London. British library of political
          and economic science. I. London. British
          library of political and economic science.


                    ◯        IaAS 36-1669
```

Record (b)

```
          A London bibliography of the social sciences. v. 1–
          1929–
          London, Mansell Information/Publishing Ltd. ₍etc.₎
               v. 29 cm.
            Vols. 1–14 issued as Studies in economics and political science.
          Bibliographies, no. 8.
            Vols. 1–4 include material to June 1, 1929.
            Vols. 5–      called also supplement 1–
            Vols. 1–5 issued by the London School of Economics and Political
          Science; v. 6–      by the British Library of Political and Economic
          Science, London.
            1. Social sciences—Bibliography—Union lists.    I. London School
          of Economics and Political Science.    II. British Library of Political
          and Economic Science, London.    (Series: Studies in economics
          and political science. Bibliographies, no. 8)


          Z7161.L84                 016.3                 31–9970

          Library of Congress    ◯  ₍r70k²2₎  rev 3
```

Example 4.8. The cataloger working with added entry II on Record (b) found Record (a) in the catalog with a variant form of entry when checking to see if a reference had already been made from "London ..." to *see* "British ..." The authority record, Record (c), shows a third form. In this record, the form used in Record (b) is given as a *see from* reference (i.e., tagged 410 in line 7), but it is coded for the reference not to be made (i.e., "nnaa" in $w). The form used in Record (a) does not appear at all in the authority record because it was never used at LC.

Record (c)

```
ARN: 422235        Rec stat: c       Entrd: 840819             Used: 851029
Type: z            Geo subd: n       Govt agn: _ Lang:         Source:
Roman: _           Subj: a           Series: n   Ser num: n Head: aab
Ref status: a      Upd status: a     Auth status: a           Name: n
Enc lvl: n         Auth/Ref: a       Mod rec:                 Rules: c

  1 010       n  80040165
  2 040       DLC $c DLC $d DLC
  3 110 20    British Library of Political and Economic Science.
  4 410 20    British Library of Political Science
  5 410 20    London School of Economics and Political Science Library
  6 410 20    London School of Economics and Political Science. $b
British Library of Political and Economic Science
  7 410 20    British Library of Political and Economic Science, London.
$w nnaa
```

Example 4.8 *(continued)*.

Changes of Name

Before the advent of AACR 1 at LC, corporate name changes were handled by recataloging items published under the old name and entering under the new name everything previously published by that body. This was time consuming and costly. Some felt it was also a disservice to the patron who approached the catalog with a citation to the old name. AACR 1 called for entry of items under the name the body had at the time of publication, as does AACR 2. However, because of superimposition, many items remain entered on LC copy under a newer name than the one held by the body at the time of publication. This means that the older names are not official entry points in LC catalogs. LC has revised some of these situations so that each name is now an official entry, but many superimposed forms remain. Example 4.9 (page 114) is an authority record demonstrating this phenomenon. This can be very difficult to explain to persons who work with outside copy.

The situation can be further complicated locally because of the presence of local entries under those older names, which were official at the time they were cataloged but were not locally revised when revised at LC because no materials with the new name were acquired locally. It is also possible that both the new and old names are in the local catalog with no connecting references because the relationship of the new entry to the old entry was not discovered. The difficulty in explaining this situation is that a patron cannot safely be told to look for a work under the name the body had at the time of publication. Instead, the librarian must say something like this (after taking a deep breath): "You will find the work under the name it had at the time of publication unless works by this body were cataloged by LC before 1967, in which case it may be under the latest name it had before 1967 unless, in this library, none of the publications of that name were acquired!" A well-written explanatory reference is essential. It is a temptation to suggest, at this point, that a library would best serve the patron by choosing to set up headings according to the latest rules, regardless of form used by the local catalog or the outside source. Unfortunately, many large catalogs already have so many entries following older rules that this would be a massive project. It would also mean changing many of the entries on retrospective copy.

```
ARN: 37829        Rec stat: n     Entrd: 840817          Used: 840817
Type: z           Geo subd: n     Govt agn: _ Lang:      Source:
Roman: _          Subj: a         Series: n   Ser num: n Head: aab
Ref status: b     Upd status: a   Auth status: a         Name: n
Enc lvl: n        Auth/Ref: a     Mod rec:               Rules: c

  1 010        n  50002171
  2 040           DLC $c DLC
  3 110 20        Arizona Pioneers' Historical Society.
  4 410 20        Society of Arizona Pioneers
  5 410 20        Pioneer Historical Society of Arizona
  6 410 20        Arizona Pioneer Historical Society
  7 410 20        State Historical Society of Arizona
  8 510 20        Arizona Historical Society $w nnnd
  9 551  0        Arizona $x History $x Societies, etc. $w nb
 10 665           The Society of Arizona Pioneers was founded in 1884. In
1897 its name was changed to Arizona Pioneers' Historical Society and in
1971, to Arizona Historical Society. $a Works by this body published
before the change of name in 1971 are found under $a Arizona Pioneers'
Historical Society. $a Works published after that change of name are
found under $a Arizona Historical Society. $a SUBJECT ENTRY: Works about
this body are entered under the name used during the latest period
covered. In the case where the required name is represented in this
catalog only under a later form of the name, entry is made under the
later form.
 11 670           De Long, S. R. $b The history of Arizona, 1905.
```

Example 4.9. This authority record explains that the corporate body has had three names. Only the last two of those names are used as official entry points. The original name is entered only as a "see from" reference.

Of course, not all corporate name changes are this complicated. Some have changed only once, requiring simple references explaining that earlier works are found under the earlier name while later works are under the later name. However, it usually cannot be discovered from the cataloging copy that these references are needed. Some clue may be found in the work being cataloged or simply through the cataloger's suspicion that two similar names may be related. In Example 4.10 (pages 115-16) the work in hand and copy both provided clues. The other title information refers to "Northeast conference," and the prefatory matter calls the conference the "8th Annual Northeast Bioengineering Conference," and is followed by a roster of the first seven "Northeast (New England) Bioengineering Conferences." This made the local copy cataloger wonder about the main entry beginning with the words "New England." Three authority records were found that explained the situation. The item being cataloged (i.e., the 8th conference) should have been given the entry "Northeast Bioengineering Conference." Symposia, conferences, etc., have a tendency to change names and continue numbering as if nothing had happened. The researcher looks for new proceedings under the name by which a conference has always been known and finds nothing. It takes an alert copy cataloger to note the clues that signal a name change so that connecting references can be made.

Record (a)

```
OCLC: 6943555        Rec stat: c Entrd: 801021        Used: 860924
Type: a Bib lvl: m Govt pub:     Lang:  eng Source:    Illus: a
Repr:   Enc lvl:   Conf pub: 1 Ctry:  nyu Dat tp: s M/F/B: 10
Indx: 0 Mod rec: m Festschr: 0 Cont: b
Desc: i Int lvl:     Dates: 1980,
   1 010        80-81642
   2 040        DLC $c DLC $d m.c. $d CUX
   3 020        0080260004 (pbk.)
   4 050 0      R856.A2 $b N49 1980
   5 060        QT 34 B559 1980
   6 082 0      610/.28 $2 19
   7 090        $b
   8 049        YCLM
   9 111 20     New England (Northeast) Bioengineering Conference $n (8th :
$d 1980 : $c Massachusetts Institute of Technology) $w mn
  10 245 10     Bioengineering : $b proceedings of eighth Northeast
conference, March 27-28, 1980, Massachusetts Institute of Technology,
Cambridge, Massachusetts / $c edited by Igor Paul.
  11 260 0      New York : $b Pergamon Press, $c c1980.
  12 300        xiv, 533 p. : $b ill. ; $c 28 cm.
  13 504        Includes bibliographical references.
  14 650 0      Biomedical engineering $x Congresses.
  15 650 2      Biomechanics $x congresses
  16 650 2      Biomedical Engineering $x congresses
  17 700 10     Paul, Igor. $w cn
  18 872 29     $j 111/1 $a New England (Northeast) Bioengineering
Conference, $b 8th, $c Massachusetts Institute of Technology, $d 1980.
```

Record (b)

```
ARN: 314270     Rec stat: n   Entrd: 840819       Used: 840819
Type: z         Geo subd: n   Govt agn: _ Lang:   Source:
Roman: _        Subj: a       Series: n   Ser num: n Head: aab
Ref status: a   Upd status: a Auth status: a      Name: n
Enc lvl: n      Auth/Ref: a   Mod rec:            Rules: c

   1 010        n 79081740  $z n  5060612
   2 040        DLC $c DLC
   3 111 20     New England Bioengineering Conference.
   4 411 20     Bioengineering Conference, New England
   5 511 20     New England (Northeast) Bioengineering Conference $w b
   6 670        Its 4th, Yale University, 1976. Proceedings ... c1976.
```

Example 4.10. Record (a) shows the name of a conference given in a form not supported by the subtitle or by the prefatory matter, which calls it the "8th Annual Northeast Bioengineering Conference." Authority records (b), (c) (page 116), and (d) (page 116) give three names for this annual conference. The third name actually began with the 8th conference, as shown in the subtitle of Record (a), and further supported by the book's prefatory matter, rather than with the 9th conference as indicated in Record (d).

Record (c)

```
ARN: 314930      Rec stat: n     Entrd: 840819      Used: 840819
Type: z          Geo subd: n     Govt agn: _ Lang:  Source:
Roman: _         Subj: a         Series: n  Ser num: n Head: aab
Ref status: a    Upd status: a   Auth status: a     Name: n
Enc lvl: n       Auth/Ref: a     Mod rec:           Rules: c
```

```
1 010       n  79082406
2 040       DLC $c DLC
3 111 20    New England (Northeast) Bioengineering Conference.
4 411 20    Bioengineering Conference, New England (Northeast)
5 511 20    New England Bioengineering Conference $w a
6 511 20    Northeast Bioengineering Conference $w b
7 670       Its 7th, Rensselaer Polytechnic Institute, 1979.
Proceedings ... c1979: $b t.p. (Seventh New England (Northeast)
Bioengineering Conference, 3/22-3/23/79, Rensselaer Polytechnic
Institute) p. iii (Seventh Annual New England Bioengineering Conference)
8 670       Phone call to Rensselaer $b (New England (Northeast)
Bioengineering Conference is transitional name; formerly New England
Bioengineering Conference; will eventually be Northeast Bioengineering
Conference)
```

Record (d)

```
ARN: 636485      Rec stat: n     Entrd: 840821      Used: 840821
Type: z          Geo subd: n     Govt agn: _ Lang:  Source:
Roman: _         Subj: a         Series: n  Ser num: n Head: aab
Ref status: a    Upd status: a   Auth status: a     Name: n
Enc lvl: n       Auth/Ref: a     Mod rec:           Rules: c
```

```
1 010       n  81091291
2 040       DLC $c DLC
3 111 20    Northeast Bioengineering Conference.
4 411 20    Bioengineering Conference, Northeast
5 511 20    New England (Northeast) Bioengineering Conference $w a
6 670       Bioengineering, c1981 (a.e.) $b t.p. (March 19-20, 1981,
Rutgers Univ.) p. v (Ninth Annual Northeast Bioengineering Conference)
7 670       Phone call to Rensselaer Pol. Inst. 6/22/79 $b (New England
(Northeast) Bioengineering Conference is transitional name; will
eventually change to Northeast Bioengineering Conference)
```

Example 4.10 *(continued)*.

The most complex corporate name changes are those that involve mergers, subdivisions, and absorptions. Because any of the individual bodies involved in these transactions can also have had individual name changes, the resulting relationships can become very complicated indeed. See Example 4.11 (pages 117-20) for such a case, found as the result of retrieving the LC copy shown. This example also illustrates another serious problem encountered when using retrospective LC copy. LC has not been able to change the headings for subdivisions of a corporate body at the same time they change the name of the parent body. Instead, they wait for a work issued by the subordinate body to trigger full evaluation of the heading under AACR 2 standards. Many subdivisions previously entered subordinately are now entered independently. Thus, changing the name of the parent body would not necessarily make the heading AACR 2 in form. However, the headings shown in Records (a) and (g) (page 119) in Example 4.11 are properly subordinate, but need the form of the parent body to be changed to AACR 2 form.

Record (a)

```
OCLC: 4857237        Rec stat: c  Entrd: 790322        Used: 870202
Type: a Bib lvl: m  Govt pub:     Lang:  eng Source:    Illus:
Repr:    Enc lvl:    Conf pub: 0  Ctry:   enk Dat tp: s M/F/B: 10
Indx: 0 Mod rec:    Festschr: 0  Cont: b
Desc: i Int lvl:    Dates: 1978,
   1 010      79-300134//r862
   2 040      DLC $c DLC $d m.c.
   3 015      GB***
   4 020      0905984072 : $c L2.50 ($5.00 U.S.)
   5 043      e-uk---
   6 050  0   QC5.3 $b .S55
   7 082      530/.07
   8 090       $b
   9 049      YCLM
  10 100 10   Singleton, Alan. $w cn
  11 245 14   The communication system of physics : $b final report of
the Physics Information Review Committee / $c A. K. J. Singleton.
  12 260  0   London : $b British Library, Research and Development
Dept., $c 1978.
  13 300      iv, 45 p. ; $c 30 cm.
  14 490  1   Reports - British Library, Research & Development ; $v no.
5386 $x 0308-2385
  15 500      "Appendix": 4 sheets (microfiche) in pocket.
  16 504      Bibliography: p. 32-37.
  17 650  0   Communication in physics $z Great Britain.
  18 710 20   Institute of Physics (1971- ). $b Physics Information
Review Committee.
  19 810  2   British Library. $b Research and Development Dept. $t
Reports - British Library, Research and Development ; $v no. 5386. $w cn
```

Record (b)

```
ARN: 466494        Rec stat: c    Entrd: 840820        Used: 861008
Type: z            Geo subd: n    Govt agn: _ Lang:    Source:
Roman: _           Subj: a        Series: n   Ser num: n Head: aab
Ref status: a      Upd status: a  Auth status: a       Name: n
Enc lvl: n         Auth/Ref: a    Mod rec:             Rules: c

   1 010      n 80085293 $z n 8085292
   2 040      DLC $c DLC $d DLC
   3 110 20   Institute of Physics (Great Britain)
   4 410 20   British Institute of Physics
   5 410 20   Institute of Physics (1971- ) $w nnaa
   6 510 20   Institute of Physics and the Physical Society
   7 667      In 1960 the Physical Society and the Institute of Physics
merged to form the Institute of Physics and the Physical Society. In
1971 the name changed to Institute of Physics.
   8 670      Journal of Physics ... Feb. 1970-
```

Example 4.11. Record (a) was retrieved for a work being cataloged locally. Upon checking the authority record for the added entry in line 18, it was discovered that the form for the parent body had been changed to AACR 2 form, shown in Record (b). (Headings for subordinate bodies are not changed by LC when there has been a change in the heading for a parent body to AACR 2 form, because the subordinate body might be entered independently under AACR 2.) Following up on the name change given in Record (b), the cataloger was led to Records (c), (d), (e) (page 118), and (f) (page 119), showing name changes, an absorption, and a merger. In the catalog, among others, were Records (g) (page 119) and (h) (page 120). Record (g) used a now unused form of one name, and Record (h) used an earlier name on a record that followed a name change. Resolution of the complications required considerable time.

Record (c)

```
ARN: 466495      Rec stat: c      Entrd: 840820       Used: 861008
Type: z          Geo subd: n      Govt agn: _ Lang:   Source:
Roman: _         Subj: a          Series: n  Ser num: n Head: aab
Ref status: a    Upd status: a    Auth status: a      Name: n
Enc lvl: n       Auth/Ref: a      Mod rec:            Rules: c
```

```
 1 010        n  80085294
 2 040           DLC $c DLC $d DLC
 3 110 20        Institute of Physics and the Physical Society.
 4 410 20        Institute of Physics and Physical Society
 5 510 20        Institute of Physics (Great Britain)
 6 510 20        Physical Society (Great Britain) $w a
 7 550  0        Physics $x Societies, etc. $w nb
 8 667           Unused subdivision: Institute of Physics and the Physical
Society. Council
 9 667           In 1960 the Physical Society and the Institute of Physics
merged to form the Institute of Physics and the Physical Society. In
1971 the name changed the the Institute of Physics.
10 670           Its Report of the Council, 1961-
```

Record (d)

```
ARN: 466497      Rec stat: c      Entrd: 840820       Used: 861008
Type: z          Geo subd: n      Govt agn: _ Lang:   Source:
Roman: _         Subj: a          Series: n  Ser num: n Head: aab
Ref status: a    Upd status: a    Auth status: a      Name: n
Enc lvl: n       Auth/Ref: a      Mod rec:            Rules: c
```

```
 1 010        n  80085296
 2 040           DLC $c DLC $d DLC
 3 110 20        Physical Society (Great Britain)
 4 410 20        Physical Society, London $w nnaa
 5 510 20        Optical Society (Great Britain)
 6 510 20        Institute of Physics and the Physical Society $w b
 7 510 20        Physical Society of London $w a
 8 667           Physical Society absorbed Optical Society in 1933. In 1960
Physical Society merged with the Institute of Physics to form Institute
of Physics and Physical Society.
 9 670           Science abstracts. Section A, Physics, Dec. 25, 1940, $b
t.p. (Physical Society; London)
10 675           Science abstracts, 1898: Vol. t.p. (Physical Society of
London)
```

Record (e)

```
ARN: 466496      Rec stat: c      Entrd: 840820       Used: 861008
Type: z          Geo subd: n      Govt agn: _ Lang:   Source:
Roman: _         Subj: a          Series: n  Ser num: n Head: aab
Ref status: a    Upd status: a    Auth status: a      Name: n
Enc lvl: n       Auth/Ref: a      Mod rec:            Rules: c
```

```
 1 010        n  80085295
 2 040           DLC $c DLC $d DLC
 3 110 20        Optical Society (Great Britain)
 4 410 20        Optical Society, London. $w nnaa
 5 510 20        Physical Society (Great Britain)
 6 667           In 1933 the Optical Society was absorbed by the Physical
Society.
```

Example 4.11 *(continued)*.

Record (f)

```
ARN: 1698371    Rec stat: n     Entrd: 861113      Used: 861113
Type: z         Geo subd: n     Govt agn: _ Lang:   Source: c
Roman: _        Subj: a         Series: n   Ser num: n Head: aab
Ref status: a   Upd status: a   Auth status: a      Name: a
Enc lvl: n      Auth/Ref: a     Mod rec:            Rules: c
```

```
 1 010      n  85261912
 2 040      MH $c DLC
 3 110 20   Physical Society of London.
 4 510 20   Physical Society (Great Britain) $w b
 5 667      Old catalog heading: Physical Society, London
 6 670      Science abstracts, 1898: $b t.p. (Physical Society of
London)
 7 675      Science abstracts. Section A, Physics, Dec. 25, 1940: t.p.
(Physical Society; London)
```

Record (g)

```
TD891
P48
1949    Physical Society, London. Acoustics Group.
            Noise and sound transmission : report of the 1948 summer
        symposium of the Acoustics Group. — London : Physical So-
        ciety, 1949.
            200 p., ₁3₁ leaves of plates : ill. ; 26 cm.
            Includes bibliographical references.


            1. Noise control—Congresses.  2. Noise—Measurement—Congresses.  3.
        Sound—Transmission—Congresses.   4. Acoustical materials—Congresses.
        I. Title.
        TD891.P48   1949            620.2'3              79-302220
                                                         MARC
        Library of Congress    ◯    79
```

Example 4.11. *(continued)*

Record (h)

```
QH212      Institute of Physics and the Physical Society.
E4           Electron Microscopy and Analysis Group.
E38        Electron microscopy and analysis: proceedings of the 25th Anni-
             versary Meeting of the Electron Microscopy and Analysis
             Group of the Institute of Physics held at Cambridge, England,
             29 June - 1 July, 1971.  London, Institute of Physics, 1971.

               ix, 343 p.  illus.  26 cm.  (Institute of Physics and the Physical Society.
             Conference series ; no. 10)   £10.00                              B71-19195

             Includes bibliographical references.
             ISBN 0-85498-100-4


               1. Electron microscopy—Congresses.    I. Institute of Physics and the Physi-
             cal Society.  Electron Microscopy and Analysis Group.  II. Series: Conference
             series (Institute of Physics and the Physical Society) ; no. 10.

             QH212.E4E38                    535'.3325                    72-180476
                                                                          MARC

             Library of Congress        ◯        72
```

Example 4.11 *(continued)*.

Again, when using outside copy, the headings for corporate bodies come established without references. The publication mentioned earlier, *Name Authorities* in microform, or the LCAF online, can help with many corporate body name changes, mergers, splits, etc. (if, indeed, LC discovers the relationships; LC's catalogers are, like us, only people!). The *Encyclopedia of Associations* (Gale, 1956-) also can prove very helpful in cases where LC has not established some, or any, of the headings.

When the cataloging of on-going serials is involved, corporate name changes mean that one of three courses of action must be followed:

1. If the body is the main entry and if successive entry cataloging is *not* followed, the serial must be completely recataloged under the new name. (See a discussion of successive entry cataloging and use of outside copy under section headed "Serial Titles" later in this chapter [see page 129]).

2. If the body is the main entry and if successive entry cataloging *is* followed, the old entry has to be withdrawn from the catalog, closed, and notes added, and a new entry has to be created.

3. If the body is an added entry, an additional added entry must be made for the new name.

On-going traced monographic series entered under corporate body names are affected in a similar manner, except that recataloging of items already in the catalog is required only if successive entry cataloging is not followed. If it is followed, series added entries can be made for the new copy under the new name, but references must be made that explain at each point where the earlier or later series titles may be found.

Changes of Form of Entry

Form of entry, like corporate name change, has been handled in various ways through the several cataloging codes. At one time a distinction was made between societies and institutions—the former being entered under name and the latter under place. Later, the distinction was dropped in favor of entering all bodies under name, except that certain institutions (e.g., schools and churches with nondistinctive names) were to continue to be entered under place. In 1974 that exception also was dropped. The general philosophy now is to enter a body under its own name unless that name is not unique or cannot stand alone, in which case something is added to it, or it is given a hierarchical entry including its parent body.

AACR 2 has brought a number of changes to corporate names. Geographic names now have all additions made by a cataloger placed in parentheses, e.g., "Springfield (Ill.)," not "Springfield, Ill." Thus, corporate names beginning with geographic names also have this form. LC's practice in implementing AACR 2 is to provide qualifiers even for famous city names, e.g., "Paris (France)," not "Paris." Corporate names are no longer inverted, amplified, or otherwise modified, e.g., "Stephen Bosustow Productions," not "Bosustow (Stephen) Productions." Form of qualifiers for corporate names has changed, and the format and punctuation has been standardized, e.g., "Conference on Static Electrification (3rd : 1971 : London)," not "Conference on Static Electrification, 3d, London, 1971."

Most libraries using LC copy have in their catalogs representations of all of the above forms of heading, plus local headings, and revised LC headings. The problem lies in identifying headings in the catalog that are for the same body as the one on the copy, but that are entered in a different form. If the library has done a good job of making references in the past, these should lead to the form used in the local catalog. Example 4.12 (pages 122-25) illustrates how this can work.

There are also examples of changes made by LC in which the place formerly used as the entry point has been dropped or placed at the end. An example of this is the change from "United States. Educational Resources Information Center" to entry under "Educational Resources Information Center (U.S.)." This, of course, is one of the most common results of abandoning the policy of superimposition.

Record (a)

```
OCLC: 806363        Rec stat: c Entrd: 740126        Used: 870618
Type: a Bib lvl: m Govt pub:     Lang:  eng Source:    Illus:
Repr:    Enc lvl:    Conf pub: 0 Ctry:  mau Dat tp: s M/F/B: 10
Indx: 0 Mod rec:     Festschr: 0 Cont: bc
Desc:    Int lvl:    Dates: 1972,
   1 010        74-152760
   2 040        DLC $c DLC $d m.c.
   3 020        0816109702
   4 041 0      engmul
   5 043        e------- $a n-cn-on
   6 050 0      Z6203 $b .P64 1972
   7 082        019/.1
   8 090         $b
   9 049        YCLM
  10 110 20     Pontifical Institute of Mediaeval Studies. $b Library. $w
cn
  11 245 10     Dictionary catalogue of the Library of the Pontifical
Institute of Mediaeval Studies, Toronto, Canada.
  12 260 0      Boston, $b G. K. Hall, $c 1972.
  13 300        5 v. $c 37 cm.
  14 505 0      v. 1. A-Church F.--v. 2. Church G-Gou.--v. 3. Gov-Mant.--v.
4. Manu-Rob.--v. 5. Roc-Z. Manuscript microfilm catalogue, authors A-Z.
  15 650  0     Middle Ages $x Bibliography $x Catalogs.
  16 650  0     Church history $y Middle Ages, 600-1500 $x Bibliography $x
Catalogs.
  17 610 20     Pontifical Institute of Mediaeval Studies. $b Library. $w
cn
```

Example 4.12. The cataloger working with the main entry on Record (a) finds a cross reference from that form, Record (b), and upon finding the heading referred to, Record (c), learns that this was the official LC entry in 1972 (see tracing III), and that it was a change from the official entry of 1961, Record (d) (page 124), which lacked the word "Pontifical" (see tracing I). Upon checking out the conflict, the cataloger finds Record (e) (page 124), an authority record for the parent body with a "not made" reference from the form used in Records (c) and (d). Also found is Record (f) (page 125), an authority record for the institute under its own name with a reference from the current form of name of the parent body followed by the institute's name. It may be noted that the earlier name without the word "Pontifical" is given on Record (f) only as a "see from" reference. This is another example of the earlier policy of using latest name for all works of a corporate body.

Record (b)

Pontifical Institute of Mediaeval Studies

see

Toronto. University. St. Michael's College.
Pontifical Institute of Mediaeval Studies.

Record (c)

KBG
R63x

Toronto. University. St. Michael's College.
Pontifical Institute of Mediaeval Studies.

Robert of Flamborough.
Liber poenitentialis; a critical edition with introduction and notes, edited by J. J. Francis Firth. Toronto, Pontifical Institute of Mediaeval Studies, 1971.

xxviii, 364 p. 26 cm. (Pontifical Institute of Mediaeval Studies. Studies and texts, 18)
O•••

An abridgement of the editor's thesis, Pontifical Institute of Mediaeval Studies in Toronto.
Latin text with English notes.
Bibliography: p. [ix]–xxiv.
1. Penitentials.   I. Firth, J. J. Francis, ed. II. Title. III. Series: Toronto. University. St. Michael's College. Pontifical Institute of Mediaeval Studies. Studies and texts, 18.

72–196985
MARC

ISBN 0-88844-018-0

Library of Congress   72 [4]

Example 4.12 *(continued)*.

Record (d)

D111
M44

Toronto. University. St. Michael's College.
    Pontifical Institute of Mediaeval Studies.
  Mediaeval studies. **v. 1–**
  New York, London, Pub. for the Institute of mediaeval
  studies by Sheed & Ward, 1939–

  v. 25½ cm.

    I. Toronto. University. St. Michael's college. Institute of medi-
  aeval studies.

  D111.M44   940.104   40—1003

  Library of Congress   ◯   61j1

Record (e)

```
ARN: 817099    Rec stat: n    Entrd: 840822        Used: 840822
Type: z        Geo subd: n    Govt agn: _ Lang:    Source:
Roman: _       Subj: a        Series: n  Ser num: n Head: aab
Ref status: a  Upd status: a  Auth status: a       Name: n
Enc lvl: n     Auth/Ref: a    Mod rec:             Rules: c

 1 010      n  82120741
 2 040      DLC $c DLC
 3 110 20   St. Michael's College (Toronto, Ont.)
 4 410 10   Toronto. $b University. $b St. Michael's College $w nnaa
 5 410 20   Saint Michael's College (Toronto, Ont.)
 6 410 20   University of Toronto. $b St. Michael's College
 7 510 20   University of St. Michael's College $w b
 8 670      Its St. Basil's hymnal, 1889.
 9 670      NLC 5/14/82 $b (AACR 2: St. Michael's College (Toronto,
Ont.); name chgd. to University of St. Michael's College 1958)
```

Example 4.12 *(continued)*.

Record (f)

```
ARN: 56852      Rec stat: c     Entrd: 840817      Used: 851018
Type: z         Geo subd: n     Govt agn: _ Lang:  Source:
Roman: _        Subj: a         Series: n _ Ser num: n Head: aab
Ref status: a   Upd status: a   Auth status: a     Name: n
Enc lvl: n      Auth/Ref: a     Mod rec:           Rules: c
```

```
   1 010       n  50021428
   2 040       DLC $c DLC $d DLC
   3 110 20    Pontifical Institute of Mediaeval Studies.
   4 410 20    Institut pontifical d''etudes m'edi'evales
   5 410 20    Institute of Mediaeval Studies
   6 410 20    University of St. Michael's College. $b Pontifical
Institute of Mediaeval Studies
   7 410 20    PIMS
   8 670       Scollard, R. J. $b A list of photographic reproductions,
1943.
   9 670       Arch'eologie du signe, c1983: $b t.p. (Pontifical Institute
of Mediaeval Studies, Institut pontifical d''etudes m'edi'evales)
  10 670       Mundy, J.H. The repression of Catharism at Toulouse, c1985:
$b t.p. (Pontifical Institute of Mediaeval Studies) spine (PIMS)
```

Example 4.12 *(continued)*.

Another common occurrence for change of form of entry on LC copy has been the changing of entries in English to entries in the vernacular of the country where they are located (e.g., Japanese, Egyptian). Example 4.13 (pages 126-27) shows a case where the form was changed from English to the vernacular and then the vernacular form was changed to move the name of the country from the beginning to the end.

Changes of form that involve change of punctuation or insertion of parenthetical terms affect the cataloging if the filing rules call for regarding such items. For example, if punctuation is not regarded in filing, then "Iowa. State University" and "Iowa State University" can be interfiled with no problem. But if punctuation is regarded in filing, the second entry could be filed a considerable distance from the first. A reference from the form not used is desirable when punctuation is regarded in filing (e.g., "Iowa. State University *see* Iowa State University"). An example of a parenthetical term that may cause filing differences is in the changing of the order of conference dates from the end of the qualifier to just before the place. These kinds of differences often occur between the outside copy received and the cataloging already in the catalog as well as sometimes appearing as discrepancies between new and old outside copy.

Record (a)

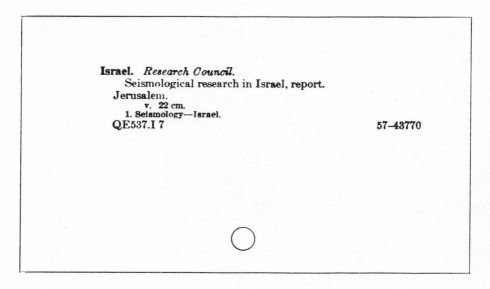

Record (b)

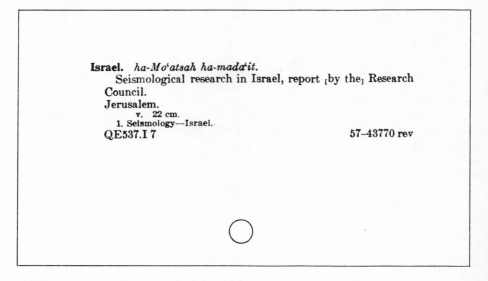

Example 4.13. Record (b) is revised cataloging of Record (a), changing the form of entry from English to Hebrew. Record (c) is the current authority record for the corporate body, showing that the form has been changed again to enter the body under its name rather than as a subdivision under the name of the government.

Record (c)

```
ARN: 851223     Rec stat: n     Entrd: 840823      Used: 840823
Type: z         Geo subd: n     Govt agn: _ Lang:  Source:
Roman: _        Subj: a         Series: n ⁻ Ser num: n Head: aab
Ref status: a   Upd status: a   Auth status: a     Name: n
Enc lvl: n      Auth/Ref: a     Mod rec:           Rules: c

    1 010       n 82155229
    2 040       DLC $c DLC
    3 110 20    Motatsah ha-madatit le-Yi'srael.
    4 410 20    Research Council of Israel
    5 410 10    Israel. $b Motatsah ha-madatit
    6 410 10    Israel. $b Research Council
    7 510 20    Motatsah ha-leumit le-mehkar ule-fituah (Israel) $w b
    8 510 10    Palestine. $b Board for Scientific and Industrial Research
    9 670       Israel. Motatsah ha-leumit le-mehkar ule-fituah.
Bulletin. Section G: Geo-sciences, May 1962 surrogate (a.e.) $b t.p.
(Research Council of Israel)
```

Example 4.13 *(continued)*.

References for Corporate Names

It has already been mentioned, but cannot be overemphasized, that a well-developed system of references is essential in a library that intends to help the user find corporate body publications. In order to ensure that these references are made when outside copy is used, copy catalogers must be trained to examine the item being cataloged for clues to the identity of the organization. They must also know what kinds of references are needed and they must have an understanding of past cataloging practice.

TITLES

As discussed in Chapter 3, title main entries occur regularly when AACR 2 is used, and added entries for titles are made in almost all other cases. The form of title main and added entries often takes the form of the title proper as transcribed in the description. In some cases, however, it becomes necessary to be concerned about the form of titles. Any time there is more than one manifestation of a work (e.g., multiple editions, translations, adaptations, various physical formats), catalogers must be certain that the title access point on each manifestation is in the same form so that the different forms can be found together in the catalog. In addition, when a work appears in more than one part (e.g., series), it is necessary to be concerned about the form of the access point for the larger work on the bibliographic record for each part so that the parts can be found together. This is also true if a work that was originally part of a larger work is published in a different form (e.g., an offprint from a serial). Likewise, when a work originally published alone is later published as part of a larger work, the form of the title of the smaller work is of concern as an access point on the bibliographic record for the larger work.

Uniform Titles

The library using outside copy will find that most problems in the title area are related to the library's use of or lack of uniform titles. The decision to use uniform titles is related to the library's decision about whether the headings for names should be uniform, and both of these decisions depend on the purpose the catalog is to serve. Use of outside copy is related because LC uses uniform titles; if a library wishes to use that copy unchanged, it must follow this practice with certain title main entries, such as in the case of anonymous works or sacred scriptures, as well as with added entries that are made using the uniform title form rather than the form found in the item, as discussed in Chapter 3 (see Example 3.14 on page 82).

Form of Uniform Titles

Uniform titles, like names, can be changed in form, and when this happens, the same kind of resolution is needed that is required with names. Example 4.14 shows a title that has been changed from English language form to the transliterated form of the original language. There have been a number of other kinds of changes in form of uniform title due to rule and policy changes. Collections previously labeled "Selected works" are now given the form "Selections." Prior to AACR 2, a separately cataloged part of a work with a title of its own was entered as a subheading under the title of the whole work; now, such a part is given a uniform title that consists of its own title (unless the work is sacred scripture or is a musical composition). Legal materials previously were entered under what was called *form subdivision*; that is, the main entry consisted of the name of the jurisdiction followed by "Laws, statutes, etc." Now an item that is legal material is given a uniform title that for a single law is its title, for a group of laws on the same subject is a subject name, and for a collection not on a particular subject is "Laws, etc." Uniform titles for music titles consisting solely of the name of one type of composition are now always given in the plural (e.g., Symphonies). Formerly, such titles were sometimes singular and sometimes plural. In addition, uniform titles for special collections derived from a composer's complete works are given in direct order rather than inverted order (e.g., "Piano works," not "Works, piano").

References for Uniform Titles

Because patrons may approach the catalog with a citation to the title used in a particular edition of a work, rather than its uniform title, the copy cataloger must be responsible for identifying titles that are used in the item in hand so that references can be made from them. It is also important with uniform titles for separately published parts of a work to make references from the titles of such parts constructed as subheadings under the uniform title for the whole work (e.g., "Chaucer, Geoffrey, d. 1400. Canterbury tales. Pardoner's tale *see* Chaucer, Geoffrey, d. 1400. Pardoner's tale."). Conversely, if a separately published part is given a uniform title as a subheading under the whole work (e.g., "Bible. O.T. Exodus"), a reference should be made from the title of the part, e.g., "Exodus (Book of the Bible) *see* Bible. O.T. Exodus." It is also important when collective titles are used (e.g., "Selections. English") to make certain there is access from any distinctive title associated with the work.

Novgorod chronicle.
    The chronicle of Novgorod, 1016–1471. Tr. from the Russian by Robert Michell and Nevill Forbes ... With an introduction by C. Raymond Beazley ... and an account of the text by A. A. Shakhmatov ... London, Offices of the Society; 1914.

xliii p., 1 l., 237 p., 1 l. 22 x 17ᶜᵐ. (₍Royal historical society. Publications₎ Camden third series. vol. xxv)

1. Novgorod, Russia (City)—History.   i. Michell, Robert, tr.
ii. Forbes, Nevill, 1883–   tr

A 15–2256

    DA20.R91 3d ser., vol. 25

Novgorodskaia letopis'.
    The chronicle of Novgorod, 1016–1471. Translated from the Russian by Robert Michell and Nevill Forbes. With an introd. by C. Raymond Beazley, and an account of the text by A. A. Shakhmatov. London, Offices of the Society, 1914.
xliii, 237 p. 22 cm. (₍Royal Historical Society, London. Publications₎ Camden third series, v. 25)
Bibliography: p. ₍223₎–224.
1. Novgorod, Russia (City)—Hist.   i. Michell, Robert, tr.
(Series)
DA20.R91 3d ser., vol. 25   A 15–2256 rev 2*

Example 4.14. The form of the uniform title of this anonymous classic has been changed from English to the vernacular.

Serial Titles

    One major decision affecting use of outside copy for serial cataloging is whether or not to accept successive entry cataloging (i.e., a policy stating that if the title or main entry of a serial or monographic series changes, a separate entry will be made for the issues appearing after the change). Although AACR 1 prescribed successive entry cataloging for serials, LC continued to follow the practice of latest entry cataloging (i.e., the policy by which a serial was held together as one bibliographic entity under the last title or corporate author entry with added entries for prior titles or entry forms). In 1971, however, LC went to successive entry, and AACR 2 continues to call for successive entry cataloging; although some librarians would prefer to keep a serial together. A recent article argued for either earliest or latest entry cataloging rather than successive entry.[4] With earliest entry cataloging, a title change would only entail adding a note and an added entry to the already existing bibliographic record. With latest entry cataloging in an online system, the penultimate title could easily be moved to note position, and the new title inserted in its place. If a library does *not* follow the policy of successive entry cataloging, however, it would be necessary to change the numeric and chronological designation, notes, and often the publication and physical description areas when using LC's copy for the new title. Also, notes would have to be added and added entries would vary. In other words, it would almost require original cataloging. Because the primary source of serials cataloging is through LC's conversion of serials (CONSER) Program, which adheres to successive entry cataloging, much work is required if local policies differ.

Involved, too, in the successive entry decision is the cut-off date for applying successive entry when cataloging retrospective materials. If the local library does not have the same cut-off date as LC but wants to catalog older titles by successive entry, then use of older LC copy will bring the same problems faced by the library that does not follow the policy at all.

It should be mentioned that even with a decision to use successive entry with the same cut-off date as LC, much of the copy found is incomplete. LC does not uniformly reissue its cataloging in order to close entries or to add notes when a new successive entry record is created. Each library often must complete this for itself.

Form of Series Tracing

The form in which a serial title is traced on the records for individual titles from that series can also be a source of difficulty in using outside copy. A series may have been traced previously by a local cataloger in a form different from that eventually established by the outside source. For example, the local cataloger may have entered the series under the responsible corporate body while the outside source entered it under title, or vice versa. Over time there have been several different ways of treating form for series with generic titles. Prior to 1974 they were generally entered under the name of the corporate body—see line 11, Record (b) of Example 4.5 on page 106. In May 1974, LC began establishing series with generic titles under corporate body followed by the *distinctive title* (i.e., generic title and corporate body). For example, a series previously would have been established as "Northern Illinois Cooperative in Education. Occasional paper." Because that series was established after May 1974, however, it was established as: "Northern Illinois Cooperative in Education. Occasional paper — Northern Illinois Cooperative in Education." This form was abandoned in 1981 with the implementation of AACR 2, but copy created between 1974 and 1981 can still be found with this form of series tracing—see line 19 of Record (a) in Example 4.11 on page 117. Beginning in 1981 the new method of tracing generic series created a title entry, adding to the generic title the name of the corporate body or the place in parentheses, e.g., "Occasional paper (Northern Illinois Cooperative in Education)."

Form of series can also vary depending upon whether the local library follows successive entry cataloging. All the variations that occur with form of serial entries that are discussed above apply also to the tracing of monographic series.

For series entered under corporate body, all variations discussed earlier in this chapter that can occur with corporate names can also affect the form of entry of series. A change in form of entry of the type that means changing all entries that appear under the old form (e.g., change from entry under place to entry under name of body) can mean changing many, many entries if a series is involved.

As with any part of cataloging with copy, errors may be found in the form of series added entries found on outside copy. In Example 4.15 (page 132) a generic title has been left unqualified. In this case checking LC's series authority record would identify the error. Many libraries have a policy of checking their series authority file during copy cataloging, even when they check no other entries, because the local tracing so often differs from LC's.

References for Series

Since so many discrepancies are possible in the tracing of series, the copy cataloger must be especially alert to identify references that may be needed to guide the patron to a desired series. If entry is under corporate body, a reference from nongeneric title is necessary and possibly one from generic title, if a particular library makes added entries for *all* titles. If entry is under a title closely associated with a corporate body or personal name, a reference is needed from the name, especially for a series with a generic title. Corporate body name changes or title changes that require successive entry cataloging call for references at each form of entry explaining where earlier or later volumes of the series are found (unless the series added entries follow a bibliographic record for the whole serial that has "continues" and/or "continued by" notes). If latest form of entry is used, instead of successive entry, a reference is required from each earlier form to the later form.

Record (a)

```
OCLC: 8055995       Rec stat: c Entrd: 820303        Used: 870619
Type: a Bib lvl: m Govt pub: s Lang:  eng Source:    Illus: a
Repr:     Enc lvl:    Conf pub: 1 Ctry:  txu Dat tp: s M/F/B: 10
Indx: 0 Mod rec:     Festschr: 0 Cont: b
Desc: a Int lvl:     Dates: 1981,
   1 010       81-214601//r87
   2 040       DLC $c DLC
   3 020       0896720748 (pbk.) : $c $50.00
   4 020       0896720756 : $c $75.00
   5 041 0     engger
   6 050 0     B945.P44 $b C16 1976
   7 082 0     191 $2 19
   8 090       $b
   9 049       YCLM
  10 111 20    C.S. Peirce Bicentennial International Congress $d (1976 :
$c Amsterdam, Netherlands, etc.)
  11 245 10    Proceedings of the C.S. Peirce Bicentennial International
Congress / $c edited by Kenneth L. Ketner ... [et al.].
  12 260 0     Lubbock, Tex. : $b Texas Tech Press, $c 1981.
  13 300       399 p. : $b ill. ; $c 26 cm.
  14 490 1     Graduate studies / Texas Tech University, $x 0082-3198 ; $v
no. 23
  15 500       Two papers in German.
  16 504       Includes bibliographical references.
  17 600 10    Peirce, Charles S. $q (Charles Sanders), $d 1839-1914 $x
Congresses.
  18 700 10    Peirce, Charles S. $q (Charles Sanders), $d 1839-1914.
  19 700 10    Ketner, Kenneth Laine.
  20 830 0     Graduate studies ; $v no. 23.
```

Record (b)

```
ARN: 32424        Rec stat: n     Entrd: 840817        Used: 840817
Type: z           Geo subd: n     Govt agn: _ Lang:    Source:
Roman: _          Subj: a         Series: a   Ser num: a Head: aaa
Ref status: a     Upd status: a   Auth status: a       Name: n
Enc lvl: n        Auth/Ref: a     Mod rec:             Rules: c

   1 010       n  42034748
   2 040       DLC $c DLC
   3 130 0     Graduate studies (Texas Tech University)
   4 410 20    Texas Tech University. $t Graduate studies $w nna
   5 642       no. 22 $5 DLC
   6 643       Lubbock, Tex $b Texas Tech Press
   7 644       f $5 DLC
   8 645       t $5 DLC
   9 646       s $5 DLC
  10 670       Oberhelman, H.D. The presence of Faulkner in the writings
of Garc'ia M'arquez, 1980.
```

Example 4.15. The qualifier authorized in authority Record (b) has been omitted from the series added entry in line 20 of Record (a).

SUMMARY

The possible discrepancies between outside copy and the local catalog or between different pieces of outside copy have been mentioned here in order to point out the problems that may occur. They will not necessarily all occur in great quantities. They do occur frequently enough, however, that, during the preparation of the first edition of this book, when a particular kind of example was needed for this chapter, it usually showed up within a week in the LC copy unit supervised by the author. Because these situations do occur, the cataloger should be prepared to handle them by having answered the following questions:

1. Is it necessary that headings for the same person, place, or thing be uniform?

    a. How important is it to the library's patrons and staff to find all works of an author together?

    b. How much staff is available to check copy against the catalog and to make changes in the catalog or on the copy so that entry forms will agree?

2. If the answer to 1 is "yes," what is the authority for the form used?

3. What references are required for the users of the local library?

4. Are there any occasions when the form of entry of personal name may vary? (For example, may death dates be left open on some entries? May fullness of name vary? May entry be under the name the author used at the time of publication even though different on various publications? May a form used under an earlier set of rules be left as it is, with the new form being used on new copy?)

5. Are all corporate body publications entered under the name used at the time of publication, or are they entered under the latest name, or is a combination of these practices used?

6. Are there any occasions when the form of entry of a corporate name may vary?

7. Are there any occasions when the form of entry of a uniform title may vary?

8. Is successive entry cataloging practiced? If so, is it applied completely or only from a certain cut-off date?

9. Are there any occasions when the form of entry of a series tracing may vary?

NOTES

[1]Paul S. Dunkin, *Cataloging U.S.A.* (Chicago: American Library Association, 1969), 28-32.

[2]*Cataloging Service Bulletin*, no. 37 (Summer 1987): 11.

[3]Arlene Taylor Dowell, *AACR 2 Headings* (Littleton, Colo.: Libraries Unlimited, 1982), 22-35.

[4]Sue C. Lim, "Successive Entry Serials Cataloging: A Reevaluation," *Technicalities* 6 (September 1986): 14-15.

5

SUBJECT HEADINGS

INTRODUCTION

Most libraries attempt to maintain consistency in use of terms for subject headings by following a standardized list. Usually references are provided in the list to link unused synonyms to the valid forms. Whenever changes or additions occur in the list, a library must react in some way. Subject cataloging can be more effective if the problems are anticipated and procedures clearly defined for handling. To make best use of copy cataloging, it is mandatory that such decisions be made in advance, although many of the same decisions are needed for local subject work.

The two main authorities for nonspecialized subjects found on outside cataloging copy are the *Library of Congress Subject Headings* (*LCSH*) and the *Sears List of Subject Headings* (*Sears*). These lists have been made up for different clientele and with different purposes in mind; therefore, they do not mesh with each other. A term used as a heading in *Sears* (e.g., Fossils) may be a term from which a reference is made in *LCSH* (e.g., Fossils, *see* Paleontology). A library that intends to use outside cataloging copy must select copy that makes available the subject headings accepted by the library and used for its catalog.

LCSH includes a separate list of subject headings intended for use in a children's catalog. On LC printed cards these appear as a second set of subject headings in brackets in the tracings (see Example 5.1 on page 136). On MARC records, the second indicator in the line for a children's subject heading is coded "1" rather than the "0" that is used for regular *LCSH* headings (see Record (b) in Example 5.1). Sometimes these headings repeat the terms used as regular headings, but often they do not. Like *Sears* headings, they do not necessarily mesh with the regular LC headings. A library using LC copy should decide which of these sets of headings will be used.

Companies that sell catalog cards identify their subject authority, and some offer a choice. Catalog Card Corporation of America, for example, offers cataloging using either *LCSH* or *Sears*. Libraries using utilities have a choice of *LCSH* or National Library of Medicine (NLM) subject headings for many items.

Record (a)

Educational Research Council of America. Social Science Staff.
  American communities, a military community, Fort Bragg, North Carolina / prepared by the Social Science Staff of the Educational Research Council of America. — Learner-verified ed. 2. — Boston : Allyn and Bacon, ₁1974₁
    66 p. : ill. (some col.) ; 26 cm. — (Concepts and inquiry, the Educational Research Council social science program)
    SUMMARY: Using Fort Bragg, North Carolina, as an example, defines a military community, describes what life is like on a post, and explains the work the soldiers do there.
    1. Fort Bragg, N. C.—Juvenile literature. ₁1. Fort Bragg, N. C. 2. Military posts₁ I. Title. II. Title: A military community, Fort Bragg, North Carolina. III. Series.

U294.5.B8E38 1974   355.7′09756′373   73–80552
                                                        MARC
    Library of Congress   74 ₁4₁   A C

Record (b)

```
OCLC: 1205812        Rec stat: c Entrd: 741231        Used: 850725
Type: a Bib lvl: m Govt pub:     Lang:  eng Source:    Illus: a
Repr:      Enc lvl:    Conf pub: 0 Ctry: mau Dat tp: s M/F/B: 10
Indx: 0 Mod rec: m Festschr: 0 Cont:
Desc: i Int lvl: j Dates: 1974,
  1 010        73-80552/AC/r84
  2 040        DLC $c DLC $d m.c.
  3 050 0      U294.5.B8 $b E38 1974
  4 082        355.7/09756/373
  5 090        $b
  6 049        YCLM
  7 110 20     Educational Research Council of America. $b Social Science
Staff. $w cn
  8 245 10     American communities, a military community, Fort Bragg,
North Carolina / $c prepared by the Social Science Staff of the
Educational Research Council of America.
  9 250        Learner-verified ed. 2.
 10 260 0      Boston : $b Allyn and Bacon, $c [1974]
 11 300        66 p. : $b ill. (some col.) ; $c 26 cm.
 12 490 1      Concepts and inquiry, the Educational Research Council
social science program
 13 520        Using Fort Bragg, North Carolina, as an example, defines a
military community, describes what life is like on a post, and explains
the work the soldiers do there.
 14 610 20     Fort Bragg (N.C.) $x Juvenile literature.
 15 610 21     Fort Bragg (N.C.)
 16 650 1      Military posts.
 17 740 1      A military community, Fort Bragg, North Carolina.
 18 830 0      Concepts and understanding.
```

Example 5.1. The annotated cataloging series for children's materials from the Library of Congress offers two sets of headings – one set for an adult catalog using regular headings from *LCSH*, and a second set using headings designed for a children's catalog. On printed cards the children's headings appear in brackets, as shown on Record (a). On MARC records, they are coded with a "1" in second indicator position, as shown on Record (b). These records are also recognizable by the LCCN, which bears an "AC" qualifier.

NLM headings appear on some copy from LC as an alternative to LC's headings (see Example 5.2) and they also accompany cataloging available on CATLINE (Cataloging on-Line) and SERLINE (Serials on-Line), both services available from the National Library of Medicine. In more recent times records from NLM

Record (a)

**Institut national de la santé et de la recherche médicale (France).
Section Cancer.**
Code histopathologique des tumeurs humaines / INSERM, Section Cancer. — Paris : INSERM, 1971.

138 p. ; 30 cm.   F***

50.00F

1. Tumors—Classification.   I. Title.
ₜDNLM: 1. Neoplasms—Classification.   QZ15 I59c 1972ₜ

ₜRC258.I43   1971ₜ   616.9'92'0012   74-594757
                                                             MARC

Shared Cataloging with
DNLM   O
Library of Congress   75ₜr86ₜrev2

Record (b)

```
OCLC: 1254656        Rec stat: c Entrd: 750107        Used: 861018
Type: a Bib lvl: m Govt pub:    Lang: fre Source: b Illus:
Repr:     Enc lvl:    Conf pub: 0 Ctry: fr  Dat tp: s M/F/B: 10
Indx: 0 Mod rec: m Festschr: 0 Cont:
Desc: i Int lvl:    Dates: 1971,
  1 010      74-594757//r862
  2 040      DLC $c DLC $d m.c.
  3 015      F***
  4 020       $c 50.00F
  5 050 1    RC258 $b .I43 1971
  6 060      QZ15 I59c 1972
  7 082      616.9/92/0012
  8 090       $b
  9 049      YCLM
 10 110 20   Institut national de la sant'e et de la recherche m'edicale
(France). $b Section Cancer. $w cn
 11 245 10   Code histopathologique des tumeurs humaines / $c INSERM,
Section Cancer.
 12 260 0    Paris : $b INSERM, $c 1971.
 13 300      138 p. ; $c 30 cm.
 14 650 0    Tumors $x Classification.
 15 650 2    Neoplasms $x Classification.
```

Example 5.2. Some LC records have both LC and NLM subject information. On such printed cards subjects and call numbers assigned by the National Library of Medicine appear in brackets below the tracings of the Library of Congress, as shown on Record (a). Record (b) shows the code "2" in the second indicator position of line 15 to indicate that the subject is from NLM. The NLM classification of this record is given a field tag of "060" and appears in line 6.

have been loaded into the utilities, resulting sometimes in the choice between an LC record or an NLM record for the same item. Other choices available from the utilities are offered by records from the National Library of Canada (NLC), with NLC subject headings in English and French, and records from the British Library, with PRECIS (Preserved Context Indexing System) subject strings. These are discussed further in Chapter 7. Other specialized subject areas have lists of headings, but these are not readily available on outside cataloging. They must be applied internally in a local specialized collection.

LCSH evolved in order to organize a particular collection, that of the Library of Congress, and it remains tied to that collection. New headings are added whenever new material being cataloged is not covered by existing headings. New headings can be added at any time and can begin appearing on copy as soon as established. Outdated terminology can also be changed at any time. Additions and changes appear in weekly lists, which can be purchased from LC's Cataloging Distribution Service, although most *LCSH* libraries purchase the *LCSH in Microform*, which appears as a completely new edition each quarter, cumulating the additions and changes made that quarter into the entire list. Each weekly list is a separate, noncumulated list, and therefore time-consuming to use. These weekly lists, which are actually LC's working tool, include headings that are under study. They may change before the quarterly cumulation.

Changing terminology has, in the past, been considered a serious matter at LC because of the groups of cards bearing old headings in their catalogs. In more recent times LC has been changing out-of-date terminology quite rapidly. With the completion of their subject authority file, now available in machine-readable format, changes are made easily and quickly. They are also able to revise every MARC record that used an old form of a heading, and then reissue it with the new form. The reissued records replace the out-of-date records in the databases of the utilities, but they do not replace the local versions of those records maintained by RLIN and Utlas, nor do they replace the records on archival tapes or in local catalogs.

Sears is not associated with a particular collection. When new editions are published every four or five years, new headings can be anticipated without actual existence of materials on a subject, and terminology can be changed as the editors see the need. Local libraries that use *Sears*, like those using *LCSH*, have catalogs that must be adjusted when changes are made. No library that uses outside copy can avoid decisions involving additions and changes of terminology used in subject headings.

Important considerations in choice of a list should be size and purpose of the library. A larger and/or specialized library will find its needs better served by *LCSH*, which uses more specific terminology and gives more subdivisions to allow closer subject analysis. Small general libraries will find that the *Sears* headings are more general, less subdivided, and consist of more commonplace terminology. There is also more freedom in the creation of headings than in other lists. However, before deciding on *Sears*, a library should consider two points about *LCSH*. If there is any possibility of significant growth, it may be necessary later to switch to *LCSH* even though the two would not mesh. The second point is that CIP uses *LCSH*. CIP has the potential of being quite useful to small libraries, and it can be used most efficiently if the subject headings are acceptable. A small library could consider using the headings without LC's subdivision to avoid too-deep subject analysis, but this would not solve the problem of specialized rather than commonplace terminology.

SUBJECT HEADING SYSTEMS
USED IN PUBLIC CATALOGS

Decisions about how to handle subject headings are affected by the type of public catalog one has. Subject headings are much easier to add to, change, or correct in online systems than in printed form. In some online systems they are also easier to manipulate—that is, sometimes searching can be by keyword using Boolean operators rather than having to find each subject starting with the left-most word and continuing character by character to the end of the string.

Printed Catalogs

There are three basic methods for entering subject headings in a printed catalog, each with infinite variations: *over-printing, highlighting,* and *guide term.* Over-printed headings occur when each card or entry has the heading typed or printed above the main entry. Highlighting uses the principle of underlining in the tracing the heading to be used to file the entry. The guide term method follows the principle that the heading appears once, either on a guide card as in a card catalog or at the head of a listing as in a book catalog. The guide term is followed by as many entries as there are items in the library requiring that heading. Over-printing and highlighting can be used in card catalogs with either a dictionary or divided catalog arrangement. The guide term principle is usually the one used in book or microform catalogs. Either a dictionary or a divided arrangement of book catalog may follow this method. In a card catalog, the guide term method requires a *guide card* for each subject and for each subject-with-subdivision used in the catalog. It works best in a divided card catalog. It is extremely difficult to use in a card catalog with a dictionary arrangement, because many entries interspersed among the subject entries are not subjects. As a result, not all the cards between two guide cards are subject entries pertaining to the preceding guide card. There would have to be a guide card for every author or other contributor, every title, every series, and every reference.

The three systems differ in the ease with which changes may be made. Over-printed headings must be erased or lined-through and retyped, or new card sets must be ordered or created. With highlighting the proper heading in the *tracing* must be given the same treatment, and there often is not enough room to do this. Also, in some libraries the tracings (or some of them) may not appear on the front of the card. With the guide term method, the heading must be changed on the guide card or at the head of the list of entries and then the guide term and the following block of entries are refiled into the new alphabetical place in the catalog. In such a case, the library may decide not to change all tracings on the corresponding main entry, shelf list, or other official location of tracings. In such a library, the belief is that if there is a reference, the person looking for the heading as it was before the change will find the reference and then proceed to the new form. Because the alteration of over-printed and highlighted headings is quite time consuming, libraries may wish to consider interfiling some minor types of heading changes, in order to have them appear together, using explanatory references to explain the arrangement. (See later in this chapter the section on Interfiling.) They also may wish to consider leaving old headings where they are, entering new copy under new headings, and using *see also* references to connect the two.

Online Catalogs

Subject systems in online catalogs are so varied at this point in time that they almost defy group description. In online catalogs where the searching can be done only from left to right, character by character, to the end of the heading, they strongly resemble the guide term method described above. That is, the term searched is given at the top of the screen followed by (usually) brief listings of any items owned by the library that are indexed with that heading. Or, in some cases, the subject headings are accessible through a browsable index from which selections may be made. Upon selection of an entry from the index listing, the resulting display may be either brief listings, as above, or displayed records.

In systems that have keyword access to subject headings, the terms requested are usually listed at the top of the screen followed by a listing of titles that have one or more of the terms (depending on the Boolean operators used in the request) given in a subject heading. Some systems also include keyword search of titles in subject requests. Title words, however, consist of uncontrolled vocabulary so that a search in an *LCSH* system for "fossils" could retrieve titles with the term used in the title as well as the reference "Fossils, *see* Paleontology." In some systems the reference would be given, while in others the items with subject heading "Paleontology" would be listed.

Changes to subject headings in online catalogs are usually fairly easy. When subject character strings are stored in each record, a command can be given to find all occurrences of, say, "East" as a subject heading and to change them to "Orient." The index entry would also have to be changed in the internal system index. Changes are even easier in systems where the character string is stored only in the authority file, with an authority record reference number stored in each bibliographic record that has the character string in question as a subject. A change in terminology must be made only in the authority record. Unlike the printed catalog where a decision has to be made about whether to change the tracing in addition to the heading, the tracing and heading are the same in an online system where only one copy of a record is stored and is retrieved in response to the searching of any one of its access points. Theoretically, references could be created automatically from the term used before the change. However, reference structure for catalogs is so complicated that it has been the last feature to be added in online systems, and many do not yet have it. *LCSH* in MARC format is beginning to be loaded into some local online systems and is currently available on OCLC. With *LCSH* online, more online catalogs should be able to display references from unused and related terms, as well as to be able to keep up with new and changing terminology.

PROBLEMS OF USING OUTSIDE COPY

No matter which subject authority is used and which subject heading system is used in the public catalog, the problems of integrating outside cataloging into an existing catalog are similar. These fall broadly into five groups: headings changed by the authority, newly composed headings, out-of-date or inadequate headings, headings to be rejected, and references.

Headings That Have Been Changed
by the Authority

Subject heading lists do not remain stable. As accepted terminology changes, some headings are revised to reflect new concepts; new headings are added; old ones are deleted. The problem for users of outside cataloging copy is that, except for copy which has been updated, the copy reflects the headings that were in use at the time of cataloging. The copy cataloger deals with copy reflecting obsolete headings, copy with valid headings, and the local catalog, which contains cataloging, both original and outside copy, to which old-style, as well as still current, headings have been assigned.

Several factors are involved in deciding how to handle subject heading changes. One is the library's philosophy on keeping materials dealing with the same subject concept together in the catalog. If it is believed to be unnecessary, and if it is also found to be unnecessary to connect the various terms used for a concept with a reference structure, then the outside copy may be used with whatever form of heading appears, and whatever terms appear in the catalog may be left as they are. This means, of course, that if it is important to find everything held by the library on a given subject, the catalog user must be able to think of all possible terms that could have been used for the concept, even outdated words that now have different meanings than they once did. It also means that editions of the same work that have not changed in subject content may be separated because of a terminology change by the subject authority (see Example 5.3, page 142). This is closely related to the library's philosophy about whether the call number serves mainly as a location device, discussed in the next chapter. If the call number is accepted as a location device and if subject headings on outside copy are left as they appear, materials on the same subject may be separated in both places. Even when the call number is supposed to serve a collocating function, material out on loan or housed in an outlying location will not be available with other material on the subject. It can be drawn together only by maintaining good retrieval in the subject catalog.

If the choice is either to use the same heading for all materials on a subject, or to connect the various headings with a reference structure, methods and procedures for handling changes must be devised. These may be determined partially by the amount of staff available.

One question to be answered concerns whether the library should maintain a subject authority file. This is a matter of total cataloging policy, which must be decided whether or not outside copy is used. Use of outside copy may affect the decision, however. New and changed headings often appear on copy before they appear in the printed subject heading lists; although for *LCSH* libraries, access to LC's subject authority file through utilities remedies this. A local authority file offers one way of keeping track of such headings and allowing them to be sent on to the catalog. If these headings are flagged in the authority file, a reference structure can then be provided when the heading appears in the new printed list or the online file with its suggested reference structure. Authority files provide a means of knowing when to update old copy, and they can also help in maintaining consistency and providing a reference structure. In addition, because many public catalogs are at a distance from the technical processing areas, an authority file makes checking easier. In a system where cataloging is done centrally for several scattered catalogs and there is no central catalog, an authority file or its equivalent is probably a necessity. Even with a central catalog, the authority file is necessary if references are to be provided for scattered catalogs.

Record (a)

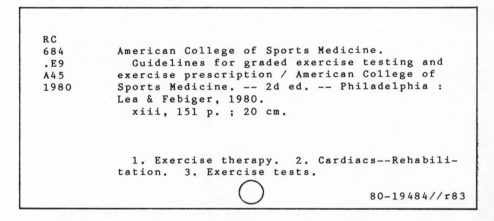

```
R C
684      American College of Sports Medicine.
.E9        Guidelines for graded exercise testing and
A45      exercise prescription / American College of
1975     Sports Medicine. -- Philadelphia : Lea &
         Febiger, 1975.
           xii, 116 p. ; 20 cm.



           1. Gymnastics, Medical.  2. Cardiovascular
         patient--Rehabilitation.  3. Exercise tests.

                                              75-5894
```

Record (b)

```
R C
684      American College of Sports Medicine.
.E9        Guidelines for graded exercise testing and
A45      exercise prescription / American College of
1980     Sports Medicine. -- 2d ed. -- Philadelphia :
         Lea & Febiger, 1980.
           xiii, 151 p. ; 20 cm.



           1. Exercise therapy.  2. Cardiacs--Rehabili-
         tation.  3. Exercise tests.

                                          80-19484//r83
```

Example 5.3. These three editions of one work have been published and cataloged during the course of the use of three sets of terminology in *LCSH* to represent the same concept. Record (a) shows that subject number 2 used the term "Cardiovascular patient" when the first edition was first cataloged. A revised version of the cataloging for the second edition, Record (b), uses the term "Cardiacs" for the concept. In 1987 the terminology was changed again to "Heart--Diseases--Patients." Record (c) shows the revised record for the third edition using the new terminology for subject number 2. It will also be noted that subject number 1 had a terminology change between the first and second editions. If the outside copy in these cases were simply used with the forms of heading that appeared at the time of cataloging, a reader looking under "Cardiac patients" would find only the second edition in a card catalog (and nothing in an online catalog), instead of a reference to the current heading where all editions should be found.

Record (c)

```
RC
684      Guidelines for exercise testing and prescription /
.E9         American College of Sports Medicine. -- 3rd
G85         ed. -- Philadelphia : Lea & Febiger, 1986.
1986        xii, 179 p. ; 22 cm.
            Rev. ed. of: Guidelines for graded exercise test-
         ing and exercise prescription / American College of
         Sports Medicine. 1975.
            Includes bibliographical references and index.
            ISBN 0-8121-1022-6 (pbk.)
            1. Exercise therapy.  2. Heart--Diseases--Patients--
         Rehabilitation.  I. American College of Sports
         Medicine.  II. American College of Sports Medicine.
         Guidelines for graded exercise testing and exercise
         prescription.                      MTTRme 85-24030r87
```

Example 5.3 *(continued)*.

Another question is, should the subject heading lists be checked against the catalog or authority file whenever new lists appear, or should the changes be made only after the new form has appeared on copy going into the catalog? If we mean by *new lists* new editions of the authorized heading lists, either in book form or in microform, checking them is out of the question. New editions do not identify which headings are new to the list, and checking every heading would be impossible. Beginning in 1982 *Cataloging Service Bulletin* (*CSB*) has listed "Subject Headings of Current Interest," a short list of some new subjects and a few changes (although the old heading for such changes was not identified). In the Spring 1986 issue of *CSB*, LC discontinued listing changed headings in "Subject Headings of Current Interest" and began "Revised LC Subject Headings," which lists changed or cancelled subject headings with their replacement headings or explanations of cancellations. This replaced a selective list of significant changes that had been previously given in the printed annual supplements to *LCSH*, which are no longer published. It is possible to check the changed or cancelled headings listed in *CSB* each quarter in a catalog using *LCSH*, if personnel are available. Some changes appear on outside copy before these revised lists appear (see Example 5.4, page 144). These often must be dealt with as they occur, because there already may be a reference in the catalog from the form on the new copy to the form that has been used in the past. On the other hand, there may *not* be such a reference, and this is a disadvantage of just letting changes be discovered when they appear on new copy. With no reference from the new form, it is not evident that the heading is a *change*. If, however, a record of new headings going into the catalog is kept until a revised list appears, the change will likely be discovered when authority determination for the new heading is done.

If the decision on the question of when to make changes is to let new copy determine when changes will be made, there must be a procedure for determining when a heading *is* new to the catalog. It may be decided to check the headings

Record (a)

```
OCLC: 965528        Rec stat: c Entrd: 740710        Used: 870725
Type: a Bib lvl: m Govt pub:     Lang: eng Source:      Illus: a
Repr:    Enc lvl:    Conf pub: 0 Ctry: enk Dat tp: s M/F/B: 00
Indx: 1 Mod rec:    Festschr: 0 Cont: b
Desc:    Int lvl:    Dates: 1973,
   1 010        73-10635//r83
   2 040        DLC $c DLC $d m.c.
   3 015        GB74-03175
   4 019        991652
   5 020        0347010210
   6 041 1      engdan
   7 043        e-dk---
   8 050 0      HV861.D4 $b S513
   9 082        155.4
  10 090        $b
  11 049        YCLM
  12 100 10     Sjolund, Arne. $w cn
  13 240 10     Bornehavens og vuggestuens betydning for barnets udvikling.
$1 English
  14 245 10     Daycare institutions and children's development, $c
translated from the Danish by W. Glyn Jones.
  15 260 0      Farnborough, $b Saxon House; $a Lexington, Mass., $b
Lexington Books, $c 1973.
  16 300        viii, 308 p. $b illus. $c 24 cm.
  17 350        L5.75
  18 500        Translation of Bornehavens og vuggestuens betydning for
barnets udvikling.
  19 504        Bibliography: p. 267-297.
  20 500        Includes index.
  21 650 0    Day care centers $z Denmark.
  22 650 0    Child study.
```

Record (b)

Day care

see

DAY NURSERIES

Example 5.4. Record (a) above appeared in the local library before the arrival of the "additions and changes," which authorized "Day care centers" as the official heading. The authorized reference in the catalog, Record (b), made it necessary to decide whether the new copy should be changed to "Day nurseries," or the old entries changed to "Day care centers," or the reference changed to a *see also* (or removed from the catalog) and both forms filed without change. (It will be noted that the second subject on Record (a) is no longer authorized. Two headings, "Child development" and "Child psychology," are used instead. However, records using the heading "Child study" have not been revised. This policy is discussed later in this chapter.)

against the catalog or authority file before cataloging. This has an advantage in a library which catalogs much retrospective material. It means that heading changes, which have been made since the outside source cataloged the older item, can be made on the copy before it goes into the catalog. It is also an advantage for libraries that make their own changes in headings. (See the section in this chapter on "Out-of-date or inadequate headings.") Another common method for handling subject heading authority is to let the existence of the heading in the catalog at filing time determine whether authority work has already been done. If the heading is not present in the catalog, the item is returned to cataloging for authority work. This is especially workable with the guide term method. In a card catalog, the guide cards themselves can serve as an authority file because they can bear a record of the references made.

Just as with description, and main and added entries, there may be typographical and/or cataloging errors in subject headings. So the appearance of a term as heading when it has formerly appeared only as a term referred *from* in a reference should not necessarily send the staff flying to the catalog to change all cards. Singular and plural forms are sometimes inadvertently interchanged on copy, punctuation can be misprinted, words or letters can be omitted, or the wrong words can be used, e.g., "Molecules (Algebra)." Therefore, any heading new to the catalog should be verified individually before wholesale catalog changes result. As pointed out earlier, however, this is not always possible since changes on copy may appear before the additions and changes to *LCSH*. Therefore, it may be necessary to make some arbitrary decisions.

One other cautionary note might be mentioned at this time, concerning CIP subjects. CIP at LC is prepared from what the publisher provides before publication. This is usually front matter (i.e., a mock-up of the proposed title page, a preface or introduction, and perhaps a table of contents) and a data sheet filled out by the publisher. With only this information in hand, the cataloger may misunderstand the content to be included in the publication. Upon receiving the published work, the LC cataloging may then be changed (see Example 5.5, pages 146-47). This is a change of perception of the material being cataloged rather than a change of the terminology used to identify and draw together all material on a concept. In addition, as shown in Example 5.5, the headings decided upon after publication of a work may undergo change in terminology at a later date.

As has been mentioned already, the library that wishes to keep all entries for a topic together in the catalog has at least three options: interfiling, making references to connect old and new, or actually changing the old headings to the new form. Each of these is discussed below. It should be kept in mind that much of what is said below concerning these three options has to do with physical limitations that apply only in a printed catalog. The decisions that involve intellectual preferences, however, are equally valid in online catalogs.

1. Interfiling

Some types of headings lend themselves relatively easily to interfiling. This applies only to over-printed or highlighted headings in card catalogs because under the guide term method all entries after the guide term would automatically reflect the heading appearing as the guide term, and in online catalogs, it is not feasible to program a computer for interfiling. In order to interfile easily, the heading must begin with the same word or words and have only minor differences. One example of such a situation is the one where a subject is subdivided by time periods. When the time period is a recent one, it may be left *open* with space left to fill in a closing date (see Example 5.6, page 147). Periodically, such subdivisions are *closed* officially by the subject heading authority, either because a specific incident, such as a war, has ended, or because an era has come to a close. In the latter case, the closing is often accompanied by the beginning of a new open time division. On copy appearing after the change, the closing date is filled in, while copy from before the change continues to

Record (a)

Published by R. R. Bowker Co. (A Xerox Education Company)
1180 Avenue of the Americas, New York, N.Y. 10036
Copyright © 1974 by Diane Gersoni-Stavn
All rights reserved
Printed and bound in the United States of America

Library of Congress Cataloging in Publication Data

Gersoni-Stavn, Diane, comp.
    Sexism and youth.

      1. Sex instruction—Addresses, essays, lectures.
2. Sex role—Addresses, essays, lectures. I. Title.
[DNLM: 1. Adolescence. 2. Sex behavior—In
adolescence. HQ35 G38s 1973]
HQ56.G46   301.41   73-21651
ISBN 0-8352-0710-2

Record (b)

Gersoni-Stavn, Diane, comp.
    Sexism and youth. New York, Bowker, 1974.
    xxviii, 468 p. 23 cm.
    Includes bibliographies.

    1. Adolescence. 2. Sex role—Addresses, essays, lectures. 3. Youth—Sexual behavior—Addresses, essays, lectures. I. Title.
    [DNLM: 1. Adolescence. 2. Sex behavior—In adolescence. HQ35 G382s 1973]

HQ796.G418   301.41   73-21651
ISBN 0-8352-0710-2   MARC

Library of Congress   73

Example 5.5. Record (a) shows CIP from the verso of the title page of a book. Subject number 1 was not a correct representation of the content of the work. Record (b) shows that when the cataloging was completed upon receipt of the book, subject number 1 was changed and number 3 was added. The LC call number was also changed. A later version of the record, shown as Record (c), changes the terminology of subject number 2, so that neither of the subjects given in the CIP is now the LC authorized heading for this work. In addition LC no longer assigns the subdivision "Addresses, essays, lectures." (It may also be noted that the form of name of the author has been changed.)

Record (c)

```
OCLC: 790325        Rec stat: c  Entrd: 731204        Used: 870727
Type: a  Bib lvl: m  Govt pub:      Lang:  eng Source:      Illus:
Repr:       Enc lvl:    Conf pub: 0 Ctry:  nyu Dat tp: s M/F/B: 10
Indx: 1  Mod rec:      Festschr: 0 Cont: b
Desc:       Int lvl:    Dates: 1974,
   1 010        73-21651//r80
   2 040        DLC $c DLC $d m.c. $d OCL
   3 020        0835207102
   4 050  0     HQ796 $b .G418
   5 060        HQ35 G382s 1973
   6 082        301.41
   7 090         $b
   8 049        YCLM
   9 100 20     Gersoni-Edelman, Diane, $d 1947- $w cn
  10 245 10     Sexism and youth $c [by] Diane Gersoni-Stavn.
  11 260  0     New York, $b Bowker, $c 1974.
  12 300        xxviii, 468 p. $c 23 cm.
  13 504        Includes bibliographies.
  14 650  0     Adolescence.
  15 650  0     Sexism $x Addresses, essays, lectures.
  16 650  0     Youth $x Sexual behavior $x Addresses, essays, lectures.
  17 650  2     Adolescence.
  18 650  2     Sex behavior $x In adolescence.
```

Example 5.5 *(continued)*.

```
OCLC: 1615546       Rec stat: n  Entrd: 750910        Used: 870717
Type: a  Bib lvl: m  Govt pub:      Lang:  eng Source:      Illus:
Repr:       Enc lvl: I Conf pub: 0 Ctry:  ___ Dat tp: s M/F/B: 10
Indx: 0  Mod rec: m  Festschr: 0 Cont:
Desc:       Int lvl:    Dates: 1943,____
   1 010        43-4105
   2 040        DLC $c DZM $d m/c
   3 050  0     Z315.U42 $b U4
   4 082        655.443
   5 090         $b
   6 049        YCLM
   7 100 10     Ullstein, Hermann, $d 1877-
   8 245  1     The rise and fall of the house of Ullstein, $c by Herman
Ullstein.
   9 260  0     New York, $b Simon and Schuster, $c 1943.
  10 300        5 p. l., 3-308 p. $c 22 cm.
  11 610 20     Ullstein GmbH. $w cn
  12 651  0     Germany $x Pol. & govt. $y 1918-
  13 651  0     Germany $x Pol. & govt. $y 1933-
  14 871 19      $j 610/1 $a Ullstein, firm, publishers, Berlin.
```

Example 5.6. Subjects in lines 12 and 13 have open time period dates that have been closed by *LCSH*. The dates in line 12 should be 1918-1933, and the dates in line 13 should be 1933-1945. If a heading is used without the closing date, however, it could interfile with headings using the closing date and not cause any filing problem. The abbreviation "Pol. & govt." is another example of older practice that could be interfiled with the current spelled out form in a manual catalog (but not so easily in an online catalog).

appear with the open date. These present no filing problem if interfiled. Another example of such a situation is the decision made by LC in 1974 to accompany all verbal time period subdivisions with numerical time designations (see Example 5.7). Because these were already supposed to be filed in chronological order, interfiling should be relatively easy. A third example is the change of the form of place names as subject that occurred with the implementation of AACR 2. Some of these changes consist of little more than punctuation differences. For example, the former heading "Boco Mountain, Colo." is now punctuated "Boco Mountain (Colo.)."

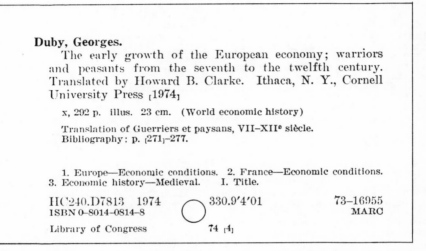

Duby, Georges.
The early growth of the European economy; warriors and peasants from the seventh to the twelfth century. Translated by Howard B. Clarke. Ithaca, N. Y., Cornell University Press [1974]

x, 292 p. illus. 23 cm. (World economic history)

Translation of Guerriers et paysans, VII–XIIᵉ siècle.
Bibliography: p. [271]–277.

1. Europe—Economic conditions. 2. France—Economic conditions. 3. Economic history—Medieval. I. Title.

HC240.D7813   1974   330.9'4'01   73–16955
ISBN 0–8014–0814–8   MARC

Library of Congress   74 [4]

Example 5.7. Subject number 3 would now appear as "Economic history — Medieval, 500-1500." However, it might be possible to interfile headings with and those without the dates.

Another type of subdivision that may be considered for interfiling is represented by the change from "Collections" to "Collected works" made by LC in 1973 for all but a few headings. Since the eighth letter of the word is the first letter to make a difference in spelling, these headings could be interfiled, or "Collections" could follow immediately after "Collected works" with little chance of anything falling between. (In 1988 LC discontinued assigning the subdivision "Collected works." Thus, another option here would be to draw lines through these subdivisions and ignore them completely.)

One more situation where interfiling might be considered is the one where two words have been changed to one word or vice versa. An example of this is when the change was made from the heading "Air lines" to "Airlines." Since this type of change would require a reference from the form not used, in any case, it would be simple to have the reference read:

AIR LINES

Headings in this form are interfiled with those spelled as one word: AIRLINES

In card catalogs, it is useful to have explanatory references on raised cards at the beginning of interfiled sequences. Raised cards reduce the possibility of the explanation going unnoticed; the explanation aids the patron who may be confused by the mixed sequence. In larger files multiple explanatory cards are helpful (e.g., one at the beginning, one or more in the middle, and perhaps one at the end) in case a user does not start at the beginning of the file, or the file extends beyond one drawer.

2. References connecting old and new headings

Sometimes the official subject heading source itself keeps an old heading and makes references to the new form instead of making a wholesale change from the old to the new. An example is the heading "Buddha and Buddhism." This heading was cancelled and two headings were established in its place: "Buddhism" and "Gautama Buddha." Records with the old heading have not been changed. Another example is the heading "Child study," shown in Example 5.4 on page 144. There are situations where it would be useful to make such references locally. Then some retrospective copy could be used without changing the subject tracings, and some entries already in the catalog would not have to be changed. An example of this is the old LC heading "Lantern slides," which has been changed to "Slides (Photography)." There are older materials for which "Slides (Photography)" is an inappropriate heading while "Lantern slides" fits much better. Yet the subject heading list has dropped the older heading. If a library decides in such a case to keep both headings, it should be noted that by the time the more modern heading was established, many newer materials had been assigned the old inappropriate heading. A decision would have to be made about whether someone should go through the items under the old heading and pull out the ones that should be changed.

Another example is in the area of headings for political jurisdictions. Whenever a country, state, etc., changes its name without changing its territorial boundaries, LC has a policy of making subject entries under the new name and changing all entries under the old name to the new name. If a library follows this policy, some of the same entries could be changed several times over a period of years. The amount of work involved in changing depends on the number of entries in the catalog about the country, state, etc. Non-MARC copy for materials cataloged by the outside source before the change of name bears the earlier name as subject. These also have to be changed if the *latest name* policy is followed. References in a dictionary catalog have to specify that *subject* entries appear under the latest name, since main and added entries use the name used at the time of publication. Some libraries may find it desirable to use *see also* references or history cards for subject entries, as well as author entries, in such cases.

Although many heading changes may be handled in this way, there are some headings that, because they are prejudicial against people (e.g., Women as lawyers), can serve to alienate people if they continue to be used after the heading has been changed to a less prejudicial form (e.g., Women lawyers).

3. Changing old headings to a new form

There are some kinds of subject changes made by the subject authority that may seem illogical to leave in both forms, but because of wording cannot be interfiled. Some libraries, too, find it desirable to make the headings match in all cases, regardless of the kind of change made. In both instances a decision must be made either to continue using the form already in the catalog and change all new copy to that form, or to change the headings in the catalog to the new form. The latter is easiest to accomplish either in online catalogs, or with the guide term method in printed catalogs — the entire change can be accomplished by changing the guide term and, in most instances, making a reference from the old form. With the other methods in printed catalogs, each entry must be changed individually. Some libraries would also find it necessary to change the tracings at the main entry, shelflist, or other official record of tracings for each title involved, no matter which method is used to change the headings themselves.

One situation in which many libraries would prefer to change the heading to the new form has already been mentioned — i.e., headings that are prejudicial against people. Another situation is the outdated heading, in which case the terminology has changed so much that the heading is no longer understood to have the meaning it once was intended to have, or it has actually come to mean something else. "Physics — Early works to 1800" replacing the old heading "Natural philosophy" is an example of this (see also Example 5.8).

```
OCLC: 279503        Rec stat: c Entrd: 720410        Used: 870729
Type: a Bib lvl: m Govt pub:    Lang:  eng Source:     Illus: a
Repr:    Enc lvl: I Conf pub: 0 Ctry:  nyu Dat tp: s M/F/B: 00
Indx: 0 Mod rec:   Festschr: 0 Cont:
Desc:    Int lvl:  Dates: 1963,
  1 010        63-13674/L
  2 040        DLC $c MSC $d OCL $d SER
  3 050 0      HV1780.S4 $b P45
  4 082        636.74
  5 090        $b
  6 049        YCLM
  7 100 10     Pfaffenberger, Clarence J.
  8 245 14     The new knowledge of dog behavior. $c Foreword by J. P.
Scott. Consultant on genetics: Benson E. Ginsburg.
  9 260 0      New York, $b Howell Book House, $c 1963.
 10 300        206 p. $b illus. $c 23 cm.
 11 650 0      Seeing eye dogs.
 12 650 0      Dogs $x Training.
```

Example 5.8. The subject "Seeing eye dogs" was changed a number of years ago to "Guide dogs." Although it would probably still be understood to have the meaning it was intended to have, "Seeing eye dogs" seems archaic because that is not the terminology now used.

An example of a case where it may seem illogical to leave the old headings while using the new form at the same time is the case of headings made up of two or more words for which the order of the words has been rearranged in some fashion. Even with *see also* references, few patrons would be sympathetic to having entries under both "Musicians, Women" (old form) and "Women musicians" (new form) or under both "American literature (Irish)" (old form) and "Irish-American literature" (new form). As another example, sometimes common names in *LCSH* are replaced by systematic names of family, genus, or species in botany and zoology. Even with references, it would be easy for a nonscientist to overlook the reference to "Simuliidae" when finding some titles under "Black-flies" and for the scientist to do the same thing when finding titles under "Simuliidae." A third example of illogical separation is the case where a noun followed by nationality has been changed to the form of noun subdivided by name of country. What patron would understand use of both "Educators, German" and "Educators—Germany"? Granted, there is a subtle difference in meaning, but prior to the change, LC used "Educators, German" for both meanings. In many catalogs these would be filed in separate sequences. If punctuation is disregarded in filing, however, these could possibly be considered for interfiling. It would not be as easy, though, to interfile "Educators, American" and "Educators—United States." They might be candidates for *see also* references, however, if changing them is not possible. An explanatory reference could be devised, e.g.:

EDUCATORS

Many groups have been divided by nationality in adjective form and also by place name. Both forms may appear in this catalog, and both should be consulted, e.g.

EDUCATORS, AMERICAN
EDUCATORS—UNITED STATES

Such references should be on raised cards in a card catalog for the reason already given.

Related to the situation of nationality in adjective form and in noun form is the policy for subdivision of a subject geographically. Until 1976 *LCSH* subdivision could be either *direct* or *indirect*. Direct subdivision meant that the place name was written as it would be written to address a letter (e.g., "Theater audiences—Lake Placid, N.Y."). In indirect subdivision the elements of the geographic name are arranged hierarchically, with a broader place name preceding the local name (e.g., "Theater audiences—New York—Lake Placid"). Late in 1976 *direct* subdivision was abandoned, and all headings formerly subdivided *direct* began to be subdivided *indirect*, but earlier records that had *direct* subdivision were not revised. These could be considered for interfiling, but this would require much more concentration on the part of the filer than is usually expected. They could be considered for *see also* references, but provide another example of a situation where patrons would find the two locations very illogical.

Many more examples could be cited of different types of subject changes. The point is that when a library is using outside copy that begins to appear with variant headings from those in the catalog, a decision must have been made in that library about whether there is to be an overall policy or whether each change is to be handled on an individual basis. Even if the catalog is online and heading changes can be made relatively easily from a physical viewpoint, the intellectual decisions concerning what to change and when to make those changes still have to be made.

Newly Composed Headings That Have Been
Added by the Authority

The headings that are completely new to the list each time it appears present a problem slightly different from the changes. The appearance of a completely new heading usually means that previously cataloged materials on the subject are buried under some other heading, which was the most closely related heading available at the time, as can be seen from the following discussion.

There are several situations where the appearance of outside copy using a new subject heading requires the library to make a decision. One is the case where a specific topic, which has in the past been incorporated into a more general topic, is now assigned its own heading. This may involve a case where the more specific topic did not have enough material on it to warrant its own heading or else, as in Example 5.9, it was once thought undesirable to separate it from the more general material on the subject. There is often a reference from the specific, unused term to the more general one. One problem to be resolved is that if the new term is adopted it may leave older material on the topic hidden among materials that have been given a broader heading. They are *hidden* if local subject heading practice follows the practice in the subject heading lists that do not allow for *see also* references from the specific to the general, but only the other way around. Thus, a person looking first under "Human reproduction," for example, would not be directed to the older materials to be found under "Reproduction." This can be resolved by deciding not to use the new heading and changing all new copy; by going through all the entries under the broader heading to pull out the ones that seem to deal only with the specific topic; or by deciding to make a *see also* from specific to general even though not authorized. Instead of a simple *see also*, an explanatory reference might be devised to read:

HUMAN REPRODUCTION

Materials on this subject cataloged before 1974 are interfiled in this catalog with other materials under the heading:
REPRODUCTION

This reference would file with the new specific heading. At the broader heading the authorized *see also* reference to the narrower heading would appear.

Record (a)

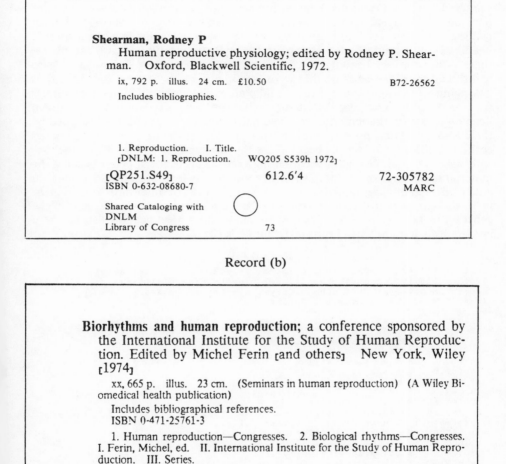

Shearman, Rodney P
 Human reproductive physiology; edited by Rodney P. Shearman.   Oxford, Blackwell Scientific, 1972.

 ix, 792 p.   illus.   24 cm.   £10.50   B72-26562
 Includes bibliographies.

 1. Reproduction.   I. Title.
 [DNLM: 1. Reproduction.   WQ205 S539h 1972]

 [QP251.S49]   612.6'4   72-305782
 ISBN 0-632-08680-7   MARC

 Shared Cataloging with
 DNLM
 Library of Congress   73

Record (b)

Biorhythms and human reproduction; a conference sponsored by the International Institute for the Study of Human Reproduction. Edited by Michel Ferin [and others]   New York, Wiley [1974]

 xx, 665 p.   illus.   23 cm.   (Seminars in human reproduction)   (A Wiley Biomedical health publication)

 Includes bibliographical references.
 ISBN 0-471-25761-3

 1. Human reproduction—Congresses.   2. Biological rhythms—Congresses. I. Ferin, Michel, ed.   II. International Institute for the Study of Human Reproduction.   III. Series.
 [DNLM: 1. Biological clocks—Congresses.   2. Reproduction—Congresses. QT167 B616 1973]

 QP251.B568   612.6   73-14700
                                                              MARC

 Library of Congress   73[8010]

Example 5.9. Until 1973 materials on reproduction in plants and animals (including humans) were given the heading "Reproduction." In 1973 LC began using "Human reproduction." This leaves older materials on the subject in the more general heading interfiled with other kinds of material on the subject, unless the entries under the more general heading are gone through to pull out the ones specifically dealing with the more specific subject. Also, if Record (a) were received in the local library *after* the change, it would be difficult to identify the fact that it should now be given a more specific subject heading, since there is not a *see* reference from Reproduction to Human reproduction but only a *see also* to this heading in a list with several others.

A second type of new heading is the heading for a completely new concept. The problem is that before such a new heading is coined, several pieces of cataloging copy for materials on the topic may have appeared. These may be scattered among several headings in the catalog because the cataloger used the heading that seemed to be most closely related — a concept that varied from cataloger to cataloger (see Example 5.10). The options available when a specific heading is pulled out of a larger one are not really options in this case because (a) there is no one old heading to continue using; (b) it may not be possible to identify all the older headings that were used in order either to pull out the entries belonging to the new concept or to make an explanatory reference that directs users to the older headings. This assumes that the library has not invented its own heading to use on the materials received before the new heading was assigned by the authority. (For a discussion of this possibility, see the next section.) In many cases, the library must simply begin to use the new heading and hope that the user will somehow stumble upon the earlier materials. This is not hopeless because the material under the newer, more specific concept may lead back to older material either through bibliographies or through earlier works of an author. It is of great help, though, if patrons are instructed in the use of subject headings and in the general theory of subject headings. Browsing in the subject heading lists can help in situations like the one shown in Example 5.10.

Record (a)

```
OCLC: 11113642        Rec stat: c Entrd: 840803         Used: 861018
Type: a Bib lvl: m  Govt pub:     Lang: eng Source:    Illus: a
Repr:     Enc lvl:  Conf pub: 0 Ctry: nyu Dat tp: s M/F/B: 10
Indx: 1 Mod rec:    Festschr: 0 Cont: b
Desc: a Int lvl:    Dates: 1985,
  1 010         84-17528
  2 040         DLC $c DLC
  3 020         0231059485 (alk. paper)
  4 043         n-us---
  5 050 0       HQ734 $b .W7645 1985
  6 082 0       306.8/1 $2 19
  7 090         $b
  8 049         YCLM
  9 100 10      Winfield, Fairlee E.
 10 245 10      Commuter marriage : $b living together, apart / $c Fairlee
E. Winfield ; illustrations by Louise Waller.
 11 260 0       New York : $b Columbia University Press, $c 1985.
 12 300         xvi, 186 p. : $b ill. ; $c 24 cm.
 13 504         Bibliography: p. [179]-181.
 14 500         Includes index.
 15 650 0       Marriage $z United States.
 16 650 0       Married people $x Employment $z United States.
 17 650 0       Married people $z United States $x Social conditions.
```

Example 5.10. Before establishment of the heading "Commuter marriage" in 1987, materials on this topic could be assigned one or more of several different headings, as shown by Records (a), (b), and (c). Record (c) shows member-input cataloging, but uses LC subject headings. In mid-1986 LC established the heading "Dual-career families." Record (d) (page 156) shows how Record (a) was revised to use this new heading. In early 1987 LC established the heading "Commuter marriage." Record (e) (page 156) shows that Record (b) was revised to use this new heading. Thus, these two books with identical titles proper now do not have any subject headings in common.

Record (b)

```
OCLC: 10912259      Rec stat: c Entrd: 840611        Used: 870123
Type: a Bib lvl: m Govt pub:     Lang:  eng Source:     Illus:
Repr:     Enc lvl:    Conf pub: 0 Ctry:  nyu Dat tp: s M/F/B: 10
Indx: 1 Mod rec:     Festschr: 0 Cont: b
Desc: a Int lvl:     Dates: 1984,
   1 010       84-12829
   2 040       DLC $c DLC
   3 020       0898620767
   4 043       n-us---
   5 050 0     HQ734 $b .G425 1984
   6 082 0     306.8/1/0973 $2 19
   7 090       $b
   8 049       YCLM
   9 100 10    Gerstel, Naomi.
  10 245 10    Commuter marriage : $b a study of work and family / $c
Naomi Gerstel, Harriet Gross ; foreword by Bert N. Adams.
  11 260 0     New York : $b Guilford Press, $c c1984.
  12 300       x, 228 p. ; $c 24 cm.
  13 440 0     Perspectives on marriage and the family
  14 504       Bibliography: p. 215-222.
  15 500       Includes indexes.
  16 650 0     Marriage $z United States.
  17 650 0     Work and family $z United States.
  18 700 10    Gross, Harriet.
```

Record (c)

```
OCLC: 12719792      Rec stat: n Entrd: 851025        Used: 851106
Type: a Bib lvl: m Govt pub:     Lang:  eng Source: d Illus:
Repr:     Enc lvl: I Conf pub: 0 Ctry:  xx  Dat tp: s M/F/B: 10
Indx: 0 Mod rec:     Festschr: 0 Cont: b
Desc: a Int lvl:     Dates: 1985,
   1 010
   2 040       SNN $c SNN $d OCL
   3 090       $b
   4 049       YCLM
   5 100 10    Greenbaum, Iris.
   6 245 10    Commuter marriage : $b the experience of intimacy and
separation : a project based upon an independent investigation / $c Iris
Greenbaum.
   7 260 1     $c 1985.
   8 300       iii, 85 leaves ; $c 28 cm.
   9 500       Typescript.
  10 502       Thesis (M.S.)--Smith College School for Social Work, 1985.
  11 504       Bibliography: leaves 64-67.
  12 650 0     Marriage.
  13 650 0     Intimacy (Psychology)
  14 650 0     Separation (Psychology)
```

Example 5.10 *(continued).*

Record (d)

```
OCLC: 11113642       Rec stat: c Entrd: 840803        Used: 870805
Type: a Bib lvl: m Govt pub:    Lang:  eng Source:     Illus: a
Repr:    Enc lvl:    Conf pub: 0 Ctry:  nyu Dat tp: s M/F/B: 10
Indx: 1 Mod rec:     Festschr: 0 Cont: b
Desc: a Int lvl:     Dates: 1985,
  1 010        84-17528//r87
  2 040        DLC $c DLC $d m/c
  3 020        0231059485 (alk. paper)
  4 043        n-us---
  5 050 0      HQ734 $b .W7645 1985
  6 082 0   ·  306.8/1 $2 19
  7 090          $b
  8 049        YCLM
  9 100 10     Winfield, Fairlee E. $w cn
 10 245 10     Commuter marriage : $b living together, apart / $c Fairlee
E. Winfield ; illustrations by Louise Waller.
 11 260 0      New York : $b Columbia University Press, $c 1985.
 12 300        xvi, 186 p. : $b ill. ; $c 24 cm.
 13 504        Bibliography: p. [179]-181.
 14 500        Includes index.
 15 650 0      Marriage $z United States.
 16 650 0      Married people $x Employment $z United States.
 17 650 0      Dual-career families $z United States.
```

Record (e)

```
OCLC: 10912259       Rec stat: c Entrd: 840611        Used: 870811
Type: a Bib lvl: m Govt pub:    Lang:  eng Source:     Illus:
Repr:    Enc lvl:    Conf pub: 0 Ctry:  nyu Dat tp: s M/F/B: 10
Indx: 1 Mod rec:     Festschr: 0 Cont: b
Desc: a Int lvl:     Dates: 1984,
  1 010        84-12829//r87
  2 040        DLC $c DLC
  3 020        0898620767
  4 043        n-us---
  5 050 0      HQ734 $b .G425 1984
  6 082 0      306.8/1/0973 $2 19
  7 090          $b
  8 049        YCLM
  9 100 10     Gerstel, Naomi.
 10 245 10     Commuter marriage : $b a study of work and family / $c
Naomi Gerstel, Harriet Gross ; foreword by Bert N. Adams.
 11 260 0      New York : $b Guilford Press, $c c1984.
 12 300        x, 228 p. ; $c 24 cm.
 13 440 0      Perspectives on marriage and the family
 14 504        Bibliography: p. 215-222.
 15 500        Includes indexes.
 16 650 0      Commuter marriage $z United States.
 17 650 0      Work and family $z United States.
 18 700 10     Gross, Harriet.
```

Example 5.10 *(continued)*.

A third situation using new headings occurs when new subdivisions are established for subjects already in existence. Subdivisions can be added to subdivide a subject about which materials have increased dramatically, or they can simply result from the application of the expanded lists of *free-floating* and *pattern* heading subdivisions available for use with LC subject headings.[1] New time period divisions can be started. New concepts can evolve within a subject area. These present some of the same problems as completely new headings, but one difference is that if older materials on shrines in Bangkok, for example, are entered under "Bangkok, Thailand" and newer materials are entered under "Bangkok (Thailand) — Shrines," they are at least near each other so that there is some hope that the user will find all materials on the subject.

Geographic subdivision can be authorized at any time, and is occurring with greater frequency. This can drastically split up material on the same subject. For example, before authorization for geographic subdivision of "Science — Information services," material on the subject of United States information sources was assigned "Science — United States — Information services." After authorization, such material has been assigned "Science — Information services — United States." These would be widely separated in most catalogs. This is an example of illogical separation that should be a candidate for change. When only the main heading, and not the subdivision, is authorized for geographic division, it may be wise in many catalogs to make two headings — one with the topical subdivision and another with geographic followed by topical subdivision (e.g., "Botany — Ecology" and "Botany — United States — Ecology"). This, of course, is much less a problem in online catalogs with keyword searching.

Out-of-Date or Inadequate Headings

That the subject heading lists have had a number of out-of-date, prejudicial, and inadequate headings has been brought to the attention of the library world quite eloquently by Sanford Berman[2] and others, and need not be reiterated here. The problem for users of outside cataloging copy is that the process of substituting one's own headings for those on the copy is time consuming and costly. It requires that someone locally make decisions about which headings to reject and what terminology to substitute or add. There is some help in this decision making in the form of an authority file available from the Hennepin County Library (HCL).[3] Additions and revisions to this file are published bimonthly.[4] Supervised by Sanford Berman, HCL catalogers establish new headings and references not yet used by LC and suggest replacements for out-of-date and prejudicial headings. For example, early in 1987, HCL added the subject heading "Homeless families," a heading not yet used by LC at the time of writing this book. However, if a library decides to follow HCL's authority, someone locally must examine all copy to decide when to apply the supplementary headings. Records of the changes must be kept, so that the same headings will be changed in the same way in the future. If card sets with preprinted headings are used, someone must erase the rejected headings and retype the local substitution. If additional headings are made to compensate for the inadequate ones, extra cards must be made for the set. Then if the outdated or prejudicial term is changed by the authority at a later date or when adequate new terms are added, the wording may be slightly different from the local wording. For example, in 1981 HCL established "Cervical cap (birth control)." Early in 1987 LC established "Cervical caps." When this happens, the cards already in the catalog must be changed to the form used by the authority, interfiled with use of a guide term, or all new copy must continue to be changed to the local form if cards for the subject are to file together. On the other hand, if a new term is not supplied for the inadequate, it may be impossible to locate materials later when an adequate heading is established by the authority (as discussed in the preceding section). It should be pointed out that the majority of headings established by HCL, and later established by LC, are given identical forms by the two agencies. (LC, in fact, checks HCL's list when establishing new headings.) Therefore, even with the added expense, many libraries decide that in order to help their patrons find the materials they need, these changes and/or additions will be made.

To deal with out-of-date or prejudicial headings, some libraries have a list of terms that are used by their subject authority and that appear on the outside copy they receive, but that they believe cannot be tolerated in the local situation. If the list is not too long, it can be referred to easily by the copy cataloger, and changes can be made without the need for reviewing all headings for suitability.

In their own cataloging HCL catalogers do much more than replace out-of-date headings or add new terms. They consider LC's cataloging to be inadequate in the number and coverage of subject headings assigned. Example 5.11 shows the cataloging done at HCL for the work shown in Example 5.5 (page 146). Many libraries cannot afford this depth of subject analysis. However, there are some cases where coverage in LC cataloging is not adequate even according to LC policy. Examples 5.12 and 5.13 show two such records. The first example is more or less obvious from the title, but the other requires a cursory look at something in the book other than the title page. Yet most libraries do not train or encourage their copy catalogers to question LC's subject analysis. The study of errors on LC copy mentioned in an earlier chapter showed that subject headings were in error 3 percent of the time.[5] (This did not include identification of terminology changes, subdivision changes, or new headings that would have showed up if the authority file had been checked.) Perhaps this small percentage is not considered worth the training time and effort. However, much of our past failure to train copy

```
301.41      Gersoni-Stavn, Diane, comp.
G                Sexism and youth.   Bowker, 1974.

            468p.

            Includes material on non-sexist children's
       literature, socialization, men's liberation,
       and sexism in education, media, and games.

            1. Sex role and children. 2. Sexism in
       children's literature. 3. Sexism in education.
       4. Sex role and toys. 5. Men's liberation.
       6. Socialization. 7. Sexism in mass media.
       8. Nonsexist      O      children's literature.
       I. Title.                73-21651
```

Example 5.11. The cataloging shown in this example is cataloging of the title shown in Example 5.5 done at the Hennepin County Library when the book was published. Eight subject headings were assigned. (Courtesy of Sanford Berman.)

```
OCLC: 7151148          Rec stat: c Entrd: 810707          Used: 861201
Type: a Bib lvl: m Govt pub: s Lang:   eng Source:    Illus:
Repr:     Enc lvl:    Conf pub: 0 Ctry:   inu Dat tp: s M/F/B: 00
Indx: 0 Mod rec:      Festschr: 0 Cont: b
Desc: a Int lvl:      Dates: 1980,
  1 010          81-620733//r83
  2 040          DLC $c DLC $d m/c
  3 020            $c $4.95 (pbk.)
  4 039 0        2 $b 3 $c 3 $d 3 $e 3
  5 050 0        LB41 $b .0576
  6 082 0        371.1/02 $2 19
  7 090            $b
  8 049          YCLM
  9 245 00       On teaching philosophy / $c George S. Maccia, guest editor.
 10 260 0        Bloomington, Ind. : $b School of Education, Indiana
University, $c 1980.
 11 300          v. 93 p. ; $c 23 cm.
 12 440   0      Viewpoints in teaching and learning, $x 0160-8398 ; $v v.
56, no. 4
 13 504          Includes bibliographies.
 14 505 0        Can moral education be divorced from philosophical inquiry?
/ Matthew Lipman and Ann Margaret Sharp -- The teaching of philosophy in
social studies / James P. Shaver -- Philosophy and the high school
curriculum / Grant Wiggins -- Teaching philosophy in a two-year college
/ James F. Perry -- Teaching moral criticism in the sciences / Elizabeth
Steiner and Ruth Hitchcock -- Forum / Christine I. Bennett -- Media
exchange / Gary J. Anglin -- Legislation / David H. Florio.
 15 650   0      Teaching $x Addresses, essays, lectures.
 16 700 10       Maccia, George S. $w cn
```

Example 5.12. It can be seen from the title and contents note that this book is not just about "Teaching." A subject heading "Philosophy—Study and teaching" is needed.

```
OCLC: 7977678          Rec stat: n Entrd: 811104          Used: 851119
Type: a Bib lvl: m Govt pub: s Lang:   eng Source:    Illus:
Repr:     Enc lvl:    Conf pub: 0 Ctry:   onc Dat tp: s M/F/B: 00
Indx: 0 Mod rec:      Festschr: 0 Cont: b
Desc: a Int lvl:      Dates: 1980,
  1 010          81-481381
  2 040          DLC $c DLC $d m/c
  3 015          C***
  4 020          0774349247 (pbk.)
  5 039 0        2 $b 3 $c 3 $d 3 $e 3
  6 043          n-cn-on
  7 050 0        LB1140.25.C2 $b E37
  8 082 0        371/.21/09713 $2 19
  9 090            $b
 10 049          YCLM
 11 245 00       Early childhood education : $b perceptions of programs and
children's characteristics / $c M.W. Wahlstrom ... [et al.].
 12 260 0        Toronto, Ont. : $b Ontario Ministry of Colleges and
Universities, $c c1980.
 13 300          ix, 254 p. ; $c 29 cm.
 14 504          Bibliography: p. 171-174.
 15 650   0      Education, Preschool $z Ontario.
 16 700 10       Wahlstrom, Merlin W. $w cn
 17 710 10       Ontario. $b Ministry of Colleges and Universities. $w cn
```

Example 5.13. It is not clear from the title, but a quick look at the book shows that kindergarten through third grade are included. Thus, there should also be a subject "Education, Primary—Ontario."

catalogers in subject analysis was based on past card catalog use studies that showed that most users conducted known-item searches, not subject searches. Newer online catalog use studies show that users want more and better subject searching. Perhaps copy cataloging policies need reevaluation in this area.

There are also situations where it is not LC policy to make a subject heading, but where a local library might wish to identify the subject aspect. Examples 5.14 and 5.15 show two such situations.

```
OCLC: 8112119        Rec stat: n Entrd: 811219        Used: 861209
Type: a Bib lvl: m Govt pub:      Lang:  eng Source:      Illus: a
Repr:     Enc lvl:    Conf pub: 0 Ctry:  nyu Dat tp: r M/F/B: 00
Indx: 0 Mod rec:      Festschr: 0 Cont:
Desc: a Int lvl:      Dates: 1981,
    1 010        81-82531
    2 040        DLC $c DLC $d m/c
    3 020        0394523261
    4 039 0      2 $b 3 $c 3 $d 3 $e 3
    5 050 0      TR670.5 $b .H86 1981
    6 082 0      779/.9623822 $2 19
    7 090          $b
    8 049        YCLM
    9 245 02     A Hundred years of sail / $c Beken of Cowes.
   10 250        1st American ed.
   11 260 0      New York : $b Knopf : $b Distributed by Random House, $c
1981.
   12 300          ca. 200 p. : $b ill. ; $c 37 cm.
   13 650   0    Photography of sailing ships.
   14 710 20     Beken of Cowes Ltd. $w cn
```

Example 5.14. This book contains descriptions of the ships that are pictured; so it could be quite useful to a user looking for works on "Sailing" and its history. Yet that subject would only be found in an online catalog with keyword searching. A local library might wish to add the heading "Sailing — History."

```
OCLC: 5678258        Rec stat: c Entrd: 791019        Used: 870729
Type: a Bib lvl: m Govt pub:      Lang:  eng Source:      Illus:
Repr:     Enc lvl:    Conf pub: 0 Ctry:  nyu Dat tp: s M/F/B: 10
Indx: 0 Mod rec:      Festschr: 0 Cont: b
Desc: i Int lvl:      Dates: 1980,
    1 010        79-54329//r83
    2 040        DLC $c DLC $d m.c.
    3 020        0824044770 : $c $23.00
    4 050 0      PR2574 $b .F29 1980
    5 082        822/.3
    6 090          $b
    7 049        YCLM
    8 100 10     Heywood, Thomas, $d d. 1641. $w cn
    9 240 10     Fayre mayde of the Exchange
   10 245 12     A critical edition of The faire maide of the Exchange / $c
by Thomas Heywood ; [edited by] Karl E. Snyder.
   11 260 0      New York : $b Garland Pub., $c 1980.
   12 300        224 p. ; $c 24 cm.
   13 440   0    Renaissance drama
   14 504        Bibliography: p. 221-224.
   15 700 10     Snyder, Karl E. $w cn
   16 740 01     Faire maide of the Exchange.
```

Example 5.15. This work has sixty pages of commentary on the work, "The faire maide...." That is not considered enough for a subject entry for the work by LC. However, in a smaller library subject approach could be important, especially in a divided catalog where *all* subjects are in the subject catalog, or in an online catalog with a separate subject index.

Inadequate subject headings may also be apparent on older copy due to changes of LC policy. That is, at some point LC starts to add certain kinds of headings, but does not add them to retrospective copy. For example, in 1973 LC began adding as subject headings names of certain kinds that had previously only been used on copy as main or added entries. Included are autobiographies, correspondence, corporate histories, corporate reports, general laws, and artistic reproductions with commentary. In libraries with divided catalogs, or with online catalogs with separate subject indexes, copy catalogers must identify older copy that lacks such names as subjects, if subject access is to be consistent (see Example 5.16).

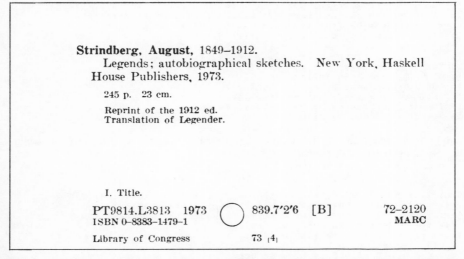

Strindberg, August, 1849–1912.
    Legends; autobiographical sketches. New York, Haskell House Publishers, 1973.

    245 p. 23 cm.

    Reprint of the 1912 ed.
    Translation of Legender.

    I. Title.

PT9814.L3813 1973   839.7′2′6 [B]   72–2120
ISBN 0–8383–1479–1   MARC

Library of Congress   73 ₍4₎

Example 5.16. This cataloging was done before LC began adding a name as subject heading to printed cards for which the main entry or an added entry is that name. In libraries with all subject headings in a separate catalog or subject index, or in very large catalogs, it might be desirable to add Strindberg as a subject to this cataloging.

LC has also begun at different times in the last decade to *double* certain kinds of subjects. For example, when a work is about a particular group of Indians, LC now adds a subject heading for the major group to which the tribe belongs in addition to a heading for the individual tribe (see Example 5.17, page 162). When a work is an individual biography, a subject heading is now added that represents the class of persons to which the biographee belongs, in addition to a subject heading for the name of the person (see Example 5.18, page 162). Other instances in which LC now follows a *doubling policy* include: specific topics, bridges, streets, buildings, etc., in cities (e.g., "War memorials — France — Paris" and "Paris (France) — Monuments"); local history; folk music; and names of species in zoology.

Minimal Level Cataloging (MLC) records have no subject headings at all. If these are to be handled through copy cataloging, original subject analysis training is required.

```
OCLC: 6387870      Rec stat: c Entrd: 810826       Used: 870128
Type: a Bib lvl: m Govt pub:    Lang:  eng Source:    Illus: a
Repr:    Enc lvl:    Conf pub: 0 Ctry:  cau Dat tp: c M/F/B: 10a
Indx: 0 Mod rec:    Festschr: 0 Cont: b
Desc: a Int lvl:    Dates: 1979,1980
   1 010      79-89978
   2 040      DLC $c DLC $d m/c
   3 039 0    2 $b 3 $c 3 $d 3 $e 3
   4 043      n-us-ca
   5 050 0    E99.C815 $b L518 1980
   6 082 0    970.004/97 $a B $2 19
   7 090      $b
   8 049      YCLM
   9 100 10   Librado, Fernando, $d 1804?-1915. $w cn
  10 245 10   Breath of the sun : $b life in early California / $c as
told by a Chumash Indian, Fernando Librado, to John P. Harrington ;
edited with notes by Travis Hudson ; illustrated by Georgia Lee.
  11 260 0    Banning, Calif. : $b Malki Museum Press ; $a [S.l.] : $b
Ventura County Historical Society, $c 1979, c1980.
  12 300      xv, 178 p. : $b ill. ; $c 24 cm.
  13 504      Bibliography: p. 175-178.
  14 650 0    Chumashan Indians.
  15 600 10   Librado, Fernando, $d 1804?-1915. $w cn
  16 650 0    Chumashan Indians $x Biography.
  17 700 10   Harrington, John Peabody. $w dn
  18 700 10   Hudson, Travis. $w cn
```

Example 5.17. Under current LC policy, this record would also have a subject heading under "Indians of North America."

```
OCLC: 113884       Rec stat: c Entrd: 701012       Used: 870723
Type: a Bib lvl: m Govt pub: _ Lang:  eng Source:    Illus: c
Repr:    Enc lvl:    Conf pub: 0 Ctry:  nyu Dat tp: c M/F/B: 10b
Indx: 1 Mod rec: m Festschr: 0 Cont: b
Desc:    Int lvl:    Dates: 1970,1908
   1 010      78-106990
   2 040      DLC $c DLC $d m.c. $d OCL
   3 020      306718774
   4 050 0    E340.B2 $b H8 1970
   5 082      973/.072/024 $a B
   6 090      $b
   7 049      YCLM
   8 100 10   Howe, M. A. De Wolfe $q (Mark Antony De Wolfe), $d 1864-
1960. $w 1n
   9 245 0    The life and letters of George Bancroft.
  10 260 0    New York, $b Da Capo Press, $c 1970 [c1908]
  11 300      2 v. in 1. $b ports. $c 23 cm.
  12 504      "A bibliography of books and pamphlets by George Bancroft,"
compiled by Henry C. Strippel: v. 2, p. [329]-341.
  13 600 10   Bancroft, George, $d 1800-1891. $w cn
  14 870 19   $j 100/1 $a Howe, Mark Antony De Wolfe, $d 1864-1960.
```

Example 5.18. Under current LC policy, this record would also have a subject heading under "Historians – United States – Biography."

Inadequate headings, in particular, are problems in highly specialized collections. A community college, for example, that offers a course for Licensed Practical Nurses may find that the general headings for nursing materials found on LC copy are inadequate to represent effectively the material in its collection. Catalogers in such libraries often make their own subject authority file for the subject area involved and regularly assign their own subjects, ignoring the headings on the outside copy.

Local libraries may also wish to add headings to copy for items that include chapters or articles of particular local interest. Examples of added headings of local interest could include parks, museums, or other institutions, and prominent local citizens.

Rejection of Headings Assigned to Copy

We have already mentioned some situations where a library may find it desirable to reject subject headings on outside copy. One is the situation where, for satisfaction of local needs, the library wishes to use headings of its own instead of the ones on the copy. Another possible situation is the one in which a subject heading appears with an error. It is assumed that most libraries would find it necessary to reject these headings in favor of the correct form.

There are also times when the subject that has been assigned by LC or other outside source is incorrect. Most libraries would want to reject such headings and replace them with correct ones. However, in order to find such errors, it is necessary to train copy catalogers to give the work being cataloged at least a cursory perusal for subject content (see Examples 5.19, and 5.20 and 5.21 on page 164). Example 5.21 shows an incorrect form subdivision. Such errors are of little consequence in printed catalogs. However, in online catalogs with keyword searching, form can be used as a limiting factor, and thus an error could cause a work not to be included in a list of responses.

```
OCLC: 7836638        Rec stat: p Entrd:  810922         Used: 870507
Type: a Bib lvl: m Govt pub:      Lang:  eng Source:     Illus:
Repr:     Enc lvl:     Conf pub: 0 Ctry:  nju Dat tp: s M/F/B: 10
Indx: 1 Mod rec:      Festschr: 0 Cont:  b
Desc: a Int lvl:     Dates: 1981,
    1 010        81-14969
    2 040        DLC $c DLC $d m/c
    3 020        0893910821 : $c $15.00
    4 039 0      2 $b 3 $c 3 $d 3 $e 3
    5 043        n-us---
    6 050 0      Z668 $b .S52 1981
    7 082 0      020/.7/11 $2 19
    8 090        $b
    9 049        YCLM
   10 100 10     Shiflett, Orvin Lee. $w cn
   11 245 10     Origins of American academic librarianship / $c by Orvin
Lee Shiflett.
   12 260 0      Norwood, N.J. : $b Ablex Pub. Corp., $c c1981.
   13 300        xxii, 308 p. ; $c 24 cm.
   14 440 0      Libraries and librarianship
   15 504        Bibliography: p. 279-300.
   16 500        Includes index.
   17 650 0      Library science $x Vocational guidance $z United States.
   18 650 0      College librarians $z United States.
   19 650 0      Library education $z United States.
```

Example 5.19. This work is not about choosing a career in or education for librarianship as implied by the first and third subject headings. It should have instead a heading: "Libraries, University and college—United States—History."

```
OCLC: 7073023        Rec stat: n Entrd: 810113         Used: 870414
Type: a Bib lvl: m Govt pub:       Lang:  eng Source:     Illus: a
Repr:    Enc lvl:   Conf pub: 0 Ctry: enk Dat tp: s M/F/B: 10
Indx: 1 Mod rec:    Festschr: 0 Cont: b
Desc: i Int lvl:    Dates: 1980,
  1 010        80-515888
  2 040        DLC $c DLC $d m.c.
  3 015        GB***
  4 020        0002113791 : $c L12.95
  5 050 0      NK5104 $b .V67 1980
  6 082 0      748.2 $2 19
  7 090        $b
  8 049        YCLM
  9 100 10     Vose, Ruth Hurst. $w cn
 10 245 10     Glass / $c Ruth Hurst Vose.
 11 260 0      London : $b Collins, $c 1980.
 12 300        221 p. : $b ill. ; $c 23 cm.
 13 440 0      Collins archaeology
 14 504        Bibliography: p. 204-212.
 15 500        Includes index.
 16 650 0      Glassware $x Collectors and collecting.
```

Example 5.20. This is not a work on glassware collecting. It is instead a history of glassmaking, including archaeological evidence found in Britain. It includes photographs of, among other things, archaeological excavations.

```
OCLC: 5845076        Rec stat: n Entrd: 810327         Used: 870706
Type: a Bib lvl: m Govt pub:       Lang:  eng Source:     Illus:
Repr:    Enc lvl:   Conf pub: 0 Ctry: ke  Dat tp: s M/F/B: 00
Indx: 0 Mod rec:    Festschr: 0 Cont: b
Desc: i Int lvl:    Dates: 1979,
  1 010        79-980849
  2 040        DLC $c DLC $d m.c.
  3 043        f-tz---
  4 050 0      HC885 $b .P36
  5 082 0      330.9678/04 $2 19
  6 090        $b
  7 049        YCLM
  8 245 00     Papers on the political economy of Tanzania / $c editors,
Kwan S. Kim, Robert B. Mabele, and Michael J. Schultheis.
  9 260 0      Nairobi : $b Heinemann Educational Books, $c 1979.
 10 300        294 p. ; $c 25 cm.
 11 490 1      Studies in the economics of Africa
 12 504        Includes bibliographical references.
 13 651 0      Tanzania $x Economic conditions $y 1964-  $x Periodicals.
 14 700 10     Kim, Kwan S. $w cn
 15 700 10     Mabele, Robert B. $w cn
 16 700 10     Schultheis, Michael J. $w cn
 17 830 0      Studies in the economics of Africa (Nairobi)
```

Example 5.21. The use of the subdivision "Periodicals" with the subject heading is incorrect. It should be used on items that are themselves periodicals.

If the library has a dictionary catalog or if the catalog is divided in such a way that names are all in the same catalog, the copy from LC created since 1973 may have too many entries for such items as autobiographies (see Example 5.22). Especially if the catalog is not a very large one, two headings on the same copy could conceivably be the only headings in the catalog for that name, and they would file one after the other. Also, in an online catalog in which names, titles, and subjects are combined in the same index, two such headings are an unnecessary duplication. In another case, a heading might be rejected if there are

Record (a)

Banco Nacional da Habitação.
    Banco Nacional da Habitação : documenta. — ₍Rio de
Janeiro : Secretaria de Divulgação, Banco Nacional da
Habitação, Ministério do Interior, 1974₎

    184 p. : ill. ; 27 cm.

    1. Banco Nacional da Habitação.   I. Title.
    HG2888.H3B34   1974   75-557424

    ◯

Record (b)

Allderidge, Patricia.
    Richard Dadd / by Patricia Allderidge. — London :
Academy Editions ; New York : St. Martin's Press, 1974.

    109, ₍2₎ p. : chiefly ill. (some col.) ; 30 cm.   GB***
    Bibliography: p. ₍111₎
    $8.95 (U.S.)

    1. Dadd, Richard, 1817-1886.   I. Dadd, Richard, 1817-1886, illus.
    N6797.D32A79   760'.092'4   74-78121
                                      ◯   MARC
    Library of Congress   74 ₍4₎

Example 5.22. Record (a) shows a situation where both main and subject entries are made
for the same name. Record (b) shows both subject and added entry for the same name.
This duplication might be unnecessary in small or dictionary catalogs, or in online catalogs
with combined indexes.

two or more headings beginning with the same term, which is then subdivided in one or more of the headings (see Example 5.23). In a small catalog, they could file too closely together to provide any real value as secondary headings. Crowded catalogs could perhaps make better use of space. In instances where there are many entries for the same name or subject, however, it could be useful to have more than one heading for the same cataloging. It is also difficult to foresee which subjects may have sudden growth and then need the specific subdivision. The library should decide on the relative importance of being able to use headings as they appear, as opposed to being able to discard unnecessary headings.

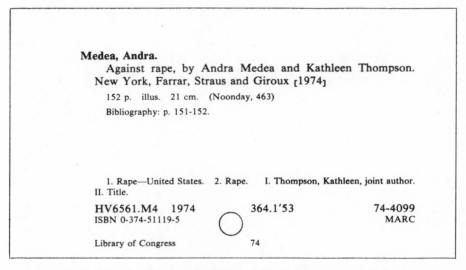

Example 5.23. Subjects 1 and 2 could possibly file so closely to each other in a small catalog that they would not add anything. One or the other would be enough in many catalogs.

Decisions to reject headings, like those to change or add, must be based on knowledge of the users' needs, the ease with which changes can be made, the staff available to make changes in copy, and the effects of the physical arrangement of the catalog.

It should be reiterated here that LC copy is created for use in its own collection and is based on the needs of LC's catalog and users. Therefore, those using this copy need to evaluate it in this light.

Providing Subject References

References that are made to names, both personal and corporate, usually arise from alternative usages of the names in the works being cataloged or from possible alternative constructions of the names. Suggestions for references for names used as subjects may be found in LC's *Name Authorities* in microform, or the online LC Authority File. These references can be handled in the same way as references for main and added entries.

Topical subject heading references are suggested by the subject authority, although these may be supplemented with references that are needed locally. If copy catalogers are responsible for subject references, all must learn the reference structure and how to deal with the relationships of a hierarchy of general to specific and the relationships of terms on the same level of specificity. This kind of responsibility for subject references means that headings must be checked against the catalog or authority file before cataloging to see if they have previously been used.

It may be desirable to have one or several specified people responsible for all subject reference work instead of having each cataloger do it before an item can leave the cataloging process. With this system, headings may be checked either before cataloging or at the time of entering the copy into the catalog. If they are checked beforehand, a system should be devised for notifying the proper person when a new heading appears on copy or when a conflicting heading indicates a possible change by the authority. If checked at the time of entering the copy into the catalog, new or conflicting headings can be brought to the attention of the proper person for the subject authority work. In a manual system, however, it must be remembered that if filers are expected to do this, they require more training and they must spend more time and pay more attention when filing.

SUMMARY

There are a variety of situations in which a library may choose to change or reject headings given on outside copy or may wish to add headings not given. In order to determine which of these may be applied in a particular library, the following questions should be considered:

1. Does the outside copy used provide a choice of headings (e.g., are there two sets of headings, one set in brackets); and if so, which set of headings will the library use?

2. What effect does the size, type, and/or arrangement of catalog have upon the kind of subject heading system (e.g., over-printing, highlighting, guide term) used in the public catalog; and what effect does the system used have upon making changes in the catalog or on copy?

3. Is it important to keep materials dealing with the same subject concept together in the catalog or at least to relate similar headings with a reference structure?

4. Is a subject authority file needed to help keep up with changes that appear on outside copy?

5. Should new subject heading lists be checked against the catalog or authority file when they appear, or should changes be dealt with only after the new form has appeared on new copy?

6. Should headings on outside copy be checked against the catalog or authority file before cataloging, or against the catalog at filing time, or through postproduction catalog maintenance?

7. If the library has a policy of matching headings to the newest form used by the authority, should all headings always be made to match or are there times when there are other solutions?

   a. Are there cases in which the library would allow interfiling of different forms of the same heading?

   b. Are there situations where old forms of headings could be left as they are while new copy is given new forms of headings, with references connecting the two?

8. When a completely new heading is authorized in the subject heading list or appears on new copy and begins to be used in the library, will any attempt be made to locate items on the subject that have been assigned one of the related headings available at an earlier date, so that the new heading can be assigned to these items?

9. Will copy catalogers be asked to evaluate the appropriateness of headings assigned to copy?

10. Will any attempt be made in the library to change, locally, headings regarded as out-of-date or prejudicial, even though the subject heading authority still uses them?

11. Do local needs require the use of headings in addition to or instead of those that appear on the outside copy?

12. What effect does the size, type, and/or arrangement of the catalog have on rejecting or adding to the headings that appear on outside copy?

13. What method will be used in the library for maintaining the reference structure used for subject headings?

14. Will any attempt be made to add references from terms not suggested by the authority?

NOTES

[1]The most up-to-date listing of these subdivisions is given in Library of Congress, Subject Cataloging Division, *Subject Cataloging Manual: Subject Headings.* Rev. ed. (Washington, D.C.: Library of Congress, 1985).

[2]Sanford Berman, *Prejudices and Antipathies* (Metuchen, N.J.: Scarecrow Press, 1971); "Cataloging Philosophy," *Library Journal* (September 1, 1974): 2033-2035; *Joy of Cataloging* (Phoenix, Ariz.: Oryx Press, 1981); "Reference, Readers and Fiction: New Approaches," *Reference Librarian*, nos. 1-2 (Fall/Winter 1981): 45-53; and numerous other publications.

[3]*Hennepin County Library Authority File*, cumulated annually (Edina, Minn.: Hennepin County Library, Technical Services Division).

[4]*HCL Cataloging Bulletin*, no. 1- (Edina, Minn.: Hennepin County Library, Technical Services Division, 1973-).

[5]Arlene G. Taylor and Charles W. Simpson, "Accuracy of LC Copy: A Comparison between Copy That Began as CIP and Other LC Cataloging," *Library Resources & Technical Services* 30 (October/December 1986): 386.

6

CLASSIFICATION AND CALL NUMBERS

INTRODUCTION

The two major classification schemes that appear on outside copy are Library of Congress Classification (LC) and Dewey Decimal Classification (Dewey). An offshoot of Dewey that is available for small general libraries is the Abridged Dewey Classification. An example of a choice available to specialized libraries is that assigned by the National Library of Medicine (see Example 5.2 in the preceding chapter). Other specialized classification schemes exist, but these are not as readily available on outside cataloging.

Companies that sell catalog cards identify the classification they use, and some offer a choice. Some companies also offer options on how the call number is printed and on whether certain types of material (e.g., fiction) will be assigned classification numbers or other designations. Libraries using LC cards or copy direct from LC, from book catalogs, from microform systems, or from computerized services must decide locally what call number is to be printed on the cataloging, using LC's suggestions as a guide. All of these situations require that certain basic policy decisions be made.

CLASSIFICATION SCHEMES USED

Only a new library will be selecting a classification scheme for the first time, but some established libraries occasionally must decide whether to reclassify or to start using a new scheme with newly cataloged materials. Much has been written on the relative merits of the various available schemes.[1]

Like the two major subject heading lists, the Dewey and LC classification systems have, to some extent, come to serve different types of libraries. With its specific assignment of numbers to subjects and its combination of letters and numbers that shorten classification numbers, LC best serves larger and/or specialized collections. Dewey has more general numbers, which can better serve less specialized collections. Dewey numbers can be built upon to be quite specific, but this process can result in unreasonably long numbers.

Revision occurs regularly with both schemes. LC *adds* numbers to its classification scheme whenever new materials appear needing new classification. These numbers can be inserted wherever needed. There are many unused letters and numbers; but if a new concept needs to be inserted where no unused numbers fall, decimals may be used. A decimal number is not required to be a conceptual subdivision of the subject represented by the number without the decimal. LC also occasionally *revises* a number or section of numbers; but this is done only when the need is very great, since it necessitates the reclassification of LC's collections. An example of revision of a section was in 1973 when PR9080-9899 (for English Literature outside of Great Britain) was reworked and new numbers were developed for most countries of the world. More often when a section of numbers is inadequate, completely new schedules are constructed using letters and/or numbers not previously used as occurred when BQ was developed for Buddhism and the numbers in BL for Buddhism were abandoned. Additions and changes to LC classification are published quarterly.

Dewey schedules also are revised on an irregular basis, and approximately once a year revisions are printed in *Dewey Decimal Classification, Additions, Notes, and Decisions.* The publishers of Dewey have followed a policy of *continuous revision* since 1985. This means that major revisions are published as separates between editions, and new editions serve as cumulations. New editions appear less frequently than the approximately five-year intervals at which they appeared before 1985. Changes in Dewey are often reworkings of sections of numbers that were previously used with other meanings. This is necessary because of Dewey's hierarchical structure. New concepts cannot just be inserted in their logical place between numbers, as in LC, unless there happens to be an unused number at that spot, or unless numbers that once stood for other concepts are reused. When reworking of a section is done immediately from one edition to the next without allowing the numbers to go unused for an edition or two, the new section of the schedule is called a *Phoenix* schedule.

There is, of course, merit in the periodic updating of classification schemes. If they were not updated, local libraries would have to invent many more numbers for new topics than they now do. However, these variations have definite implications for the library that uses outside cataloging, especially if the intention is to mix new and retrospective copy. The class numbers suggested on copy at any point in time may not have the same meaning in the latest edition of the classification schemes being used, nor will they necessarily be the most current class numbers available for the subject being covered.

A difference faced by users of LC copy is that most suggested LC numbers are complete call numbers, while suggested Dewey numbers are classification numbers only. Also, the percentage of copy lacking a suggested Dewey number is much higher than the percentage lacking an assigned LC number. These differences suggest a higher efficiency in classifying with LC because less time must be spent completing call numbers and assigning original classification. In one library where the author supervised copy catalogers, LC classification is used without prechecking the shelflist. Alternatives are sometimes used, and there are some local exceptions to the LC classification scheme. An attempt is made to keep editions and translations together. Even with these changes, an informal survey showed that 85 percent of the exact copy had LC call numbers that were being used without change. Because many of the 15 percent changes were made in the cutter numbers, an even higher percentage of the classification part of the numbers was acceptable. (The second part of the Library of Congress call number is called a *cutter*, with a small "c" in this book because the traditional terminology, *author notation*, is not applicable in many cases. The first filing word of the main entry usually provides the letter for this part of the call number, and in many instances the main entry is a title, not an author. *Book number* is not appropriate either, since such numbers are also assigned to serials, sheet music, sound recordings, tapes, films, etc. A capital "C" will continue to be used when actually referring to numbers from the Cutter or Cutter-Sanborn tables.) In a large Dewey library, such a percentage is not possible because it is unlikely that a Dewey number will be suggested for 85 percent of the copy. However, if one is using cards from a commercial service such as Catalog Card Corporation of America, the service will, of course, provide Dewey classification for everything.

Dewey classification from LC is also affected by the fact that the numbers are not assigned against a shelflist, as is LC classification. More is said about this in the section on Dewey classification.

CALL NUMBER: LOCATION OR SUBJECT COLLOCATION DEVICE

A very basic decision concerns the importance of subject collocation in the library and whether the classification should reflect this importance. Each library should have a policy about whether the call number assigned to an item is strictly a location device or whether there is to be an attempt to put related materials together in such a way that a searcher can find materials on or related to a particular subject by knowing certain classification numbers.

The latter is virtually impossible to achieve completely. Interdisciplinary subjects have proliferated recently, and supporting materials must be placed in one discipline or the other in Dewey or LC unless separate copies of an item are classified separately. Items that are parts of a serial or set classified in a general number can be related to very specific materials on a topic but cannot be classified with them. There are also topics that fit equally well in two or more places in the schedules, depending on which aspect of the subject is emphasized. It is possible, therefore, for two copies of the same book to be classified in different places by different catalogers or by the same cataloger at different times! (See Examples 6.1, 2.28 on pages 54-56, and 7.7 on page 259.) Classification schemes are revised, but the suggested numbers on the copy reflect the edition of the scheme in use at the time of cataloging (see Example 6.2 on page 174). Thus, the cataloger deals with old copy reflecting some abandoned classification numbers, new copy with some new numbers, and the local shelflist, which contains all classification used during the library's existence. These and other problems have led a number of libraries to consider the call number a location device only and to rely on subject headings to serve the collocating function. They leave older materials in old classifications while putting new materials in the current classification number. Other libraries have decided not to use new editions of the schemes or revised numbers as they appear. Instead, they continue to use the earlier classification for new materials; this means that many suggested numbers on new copy cannot be used. Still other libraries make a decision to reclassify materials from an out-of-date classification into the revised classification, so that new copy can be used and all materials on the subject will appear together in the new classification. The latter practice requires that

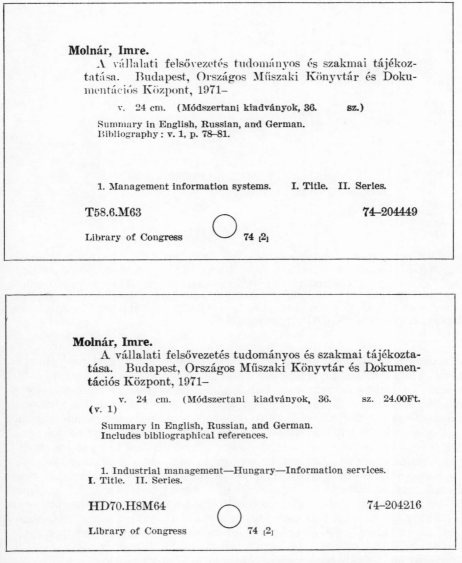

Molnár, Imre.
A vállalati felsővezetés tudományos és szakmai tájékoztatása. Budapest, Országos Műszaki Könyvtár és Dokumentációs Központ, 1971–

    v. 24 cm. (Módszertani kiadványok, 36.   **sz.**)
Summary in English, Russian, and German.
Bibliography : v. 1, p. 78–81.

    1. Management information systems.   I. Title. II. Series.

T58.6.M63   74–204449

Library of Congress   74 [2]

Molnár, Imre.
A vállalati felsővezetés tudományos és szakmai tájékoztatása. Budapest, Országos Műszaki Könyvtár és Dokumentációs Központ, 1971–

    v. 24 cm. (Módszertani kiadványok, 36.   sz. 24.00Ft.
(v. 1)

    Summary in English, Russian, and German.
Includes bibliographical references.

    1. Industrial management—Hungary—Information services.
I. Title. II. Series.

HD70.H8M64   74–204216

Library of Congress   74 [2]

Example 6.1. These two cards show cataloging for two copies of the same book. They were given different call numbers and subject headings.

```
OCLC: 2527373      Rec stat: c Entrd: 770421          Used: 870530
Type: a Bib lvl: m Govt pub:    Lang:  eng Source:    Illus:
Repr:      Enc lvl:    Conf pub: 0 Ctry:  onc Dat tp: s M/F/B: 10
Indx: 1 Mod rec: m Festschr: 0 Cont: b
Desc: i Int lvl:    Dates: 1976,
   1 010       77-354563//r85
   2 040       DLC $c DLC $d m.c.
   3 015       C76-017038-X
   4 020       0773600442 : $c $12.95. $a 0773610197 $b pbk.
   5 043       n-cn---
   6 050 0     NX513.A1 $b C68
   7 082       301.5
   8 090          $b
   9 049       YCLM
  10 100 10    Crean, S. M., $d 1945- $w cn
  11 245 10    Who's afraid of Canadian culture? / $c S. M. Crean.
  12 260 0     Don Mills, Ont. : $b General Pub. Co., $c c1976.
  13 300       296 p. ; $c 22 cm.
  14 504       Bibliography: p. 279-286.
  15 500       Includes index.
  16 650 0     Arts, Canadian.
  17 651 0     Canada $x Culture.
  18 650 0     Art patronage $z Canada.
```

Example 6.2. The Dewey number assigned to this work, "301.5," was a satisfactory number in the 18th edition of Dewey, used at the time of cataloging this work. It covered sociology in institutions and was concerned with patterns governing behavior in recurring organized situations. There is no "301.5" in the 19th edition. "301" in the 19th edition is for comprehensive works on society and on anthropology. The number for this work in the 19th edition should be "700.971" or "306.40971."

sufficient personnel be available to do the reclassification each time changes appear. This is particularly a financial burden for large collections when Phoenix revisions of Dewey occur. Since Phoenix schedules reassign all values for a particular area of the scheme, every item already in a collection in that area must be reclassified if a decision is made to reclassify completely into a new edition.

A slightly different but related decision concerns whether later editions of a work should be shelved next to earlier editions and whether translations should appear beside originals. This can be a problem with any classification scheme. One cause of variation is the occasion when the classification scheme has been changed between editions or translations of a work (see Example 6.3 on pages 175-76). In such a case, the suggested classification numbers reflect the edition of the schedule in use at the time each edition of the work was cataloged. In the case of LC classification, cataloging for an earlier edition published less than three years earlier is revised if the classification changes, but that does not change the record that has already been entered into a local library's catalog.

Record (a)

```
OCLC: 2503065        Rec stat: n Entrd: 761014        Used: 871008
Type: a Bib lvl: m Govt pub:      Lang:  eng Source:      Illus:
Repr:     Enc lvl: I Conf pub: O Ctry:  xx  Dat tp: s M/F/B: 00
Indx: O Mod rec:       Festschr: O Cont:
Desc:     Int lvl:       Dates: 1960,
   1 010        60-8491
   2 040        DLC $c TOL
   3 050  0     HF5548 $b .G73
   4 082        651.26
   5 090          $b
   6 049        YCLM
   7 100 10     Gregory, Robert Henry.
   8 245  1     Automatic data-processing systems: $b principles and
procedures $c [by] Robert H. Gregory [and] Richard L. Van Horn.
   9 260  0     San Francisco, $b Wadsworth Pub. Co. $c [c1960]
  10 300        705 p. $b illus. $c 24 cm.
  11 650   0    Electronic data processing.
  12 700 10     Van Horn, Richard L., $e joint author.
```

Record (b)

```
OCLC: 1175453        Rec stat: c Entrd: 711228        Used: 871005
Type: a Bib lvl: m Govt pub:      Lang:  eng Source:      Illus: a
Repr:     Enc lvl: 1 Conf pub: O Ctry:  cau Dat tp: s M/F/B: 10
Indx: O Mod rec:       Festschr: O Cont: b
Desc:     Int lvl:       Dates: 1963,
   1 010        63-15504//r84
   2 040        DLC $c DLC
   3 050  0     HF5548.2 $b .G68 1963
   4 082        651.26
   5 090          $b
   6 049        YCLM
   7 100 10     Gregory, Robert Henry.
   8 245 10     Automatic data-processing systems; $b principles and
procedures $c [by] Robert H. Gregory [and] Richard L. Van Horn.
   9 250        2d ed.
  10 260  0     Belmont, Calif., $b Wadsworth Pub. Co. $c [1963]
  11 300        xi, 816 p. $b illus. $c 24 cm.
  12 490  0     Wadsworth accounting and data processing series
  13 504        "Guide to the literature": p. 780-788.
  14 650   0    Business $x Data processing.
  15 700 10     Van Horn, Richard L., $e joint author.
```

Example 6.3. These examples show LC classification changes between editions due to changes in the LC classification schedules. Record (b) shows the second edition of the book represented by Record (a). In this case "HF5548.2" was added to the schedule between 1960 and 1963. This is a much less drastic change than that shown by Records (c) and (d) (page 176), where the change was the addition of a whole new classification for Buddhism, "BQ," in 1972. In the latter case the editions will be more greatly separated than in the former case if call numbers are used just as they are without change.

Record (c)

```
OCLC: 1936211        Rec stat: c Entrd: 760120        Used: 871006
Type: a Bib lvl: m Govt pub:      Lang:  eng Source:   Illus: b
Repr:    Enc lvl: I Conf pub: 0 Ctry:   ne Dat tp: s M/F/B: 00
Indx: 0 Mod rec: e Festschr: 0 Cont: bi
Desc:    Int lvl:    Dates: 1959,
  1 010        59-16762
  2 040        DLC $c CIN $d SER
  3 050 0      BL1430 $b .Z8
  4 082        294.30951
  5 090          $b
  6 049        YCLM
  7 100 10     Zurcher, Erik.
  8 245 14     The Buddhist conquest of China; $b the spread and
adaptation of Buddhism in early medieval China.
  9 260 0      Leiden, $b E. J. Brill, $c 1959.
 10 300        2 v. (ix, 468 p.) $b maps. $c 25 cm.
 11 440  0     Sinica Leidensia, $v v. 11
 12 500        Errata slip inserted.
 13 504        Bibliography: p. [441]-447.
 14 502        Proefschrift--Leyden.
 15 505 0      1. Text.--2. Notes. Bibliography. Indexes.
 16 500        "Stellingen" slip inserted: p.1.
 17 650  0     Buddha and Buddhism $z China.
```

Record (d)

```
OCLC: 386028         Rec stat: c Entrd: 721101        Used: 870929
Type: a Bib lvl: m Govt pub:      Lang:  eng Source:   Illus:
Repr:    Enc lvl:    Conf pub: 0 Ctry:   ne Dat tp: r M/F/B: 10
Indx: 1 Mod rec:    Festschr: 0 Cont:
Desc:    Int lvl:    Dates: 1972,1959
  1 010        72-192783
  2 040        DLC $c DLC
  3 015        Ne72-28
  4 019        408179 $a 861947
  5 043        a-cc---
  6 050 0      BQ636 $b .Z84 1972
  7 082        294.3/0951
  8 090          $b
  9 049        YCLM
 10 100 10     Zurcher, Erik.
 11 245 14     The Buddhist conquest of China. $b The spread and
adaptation of Buddhism in early medieval China. $c By E. Zurcher.
 12 250        Reprint, with additions and corrections.
 13 260 0      Leiden, $b Brill, $c 1972.
 14 300        2 v. $c 25 cm.
 15 350        f1128.00
 16 440  0     Sinica Leidensia, $v v. 11
 17 500        "First published 1959."
 18 505 0      v. 1. Text.--v. 2. Notes, bibliography, indexes.
 19 650  0     Buddhism $z China $x History.
```

Example 6.3 *(continued).*

In some cases the classification may differ because the classifier did not know of the existence of the other edition at the time of cataloging (see Example 6.4).

Record (a)

Simon, Gerhard.
    Church, state, and opposition in the U. S. S. R. Translated by Kathleen Matchett in collaboration with the Centre for the Study of Religion and Communism. Berkeley, University of California Press ₁1974₁
      x, 248 p. 23 cm. $12.00
      Translation of Die Kirchen in Russland.
      Bibliography: p. 242–244.
      1. Church and state in Russia.   I. Title.

BR933.S5413   261.7'0947   73–87754
ISBN 0-520-02612-8   MARC

Record (b)

Simon, Gerhard.
    Church, state and opposition in the USSR / ₁by₁ Gerhard Simon ; translated ₁from the German₁ by Kathleen Matchett in collaboration with the Centre for the Study of Religion and Communism. — London : C. Hurst, 1974.

      x, 248 p. ; 23 cm.   GB 74–05031

      Translation of Die Kirchen in Russland.
      Bibliography: p. 242–244.
      Includes index.
      ISBN 0–903983–10–9 : £4.20

      1. Church and state in Russia.   I. Title.

BR933.S5413 1974b   322'.1'0947   75–302834
                                                      MARC

Library of Congress   75

Example 6.4. These two copies of the same book were published as editions—one in the United States and one in England—in the same year. The Dewey classification numbers, however, are different—one in the social theology area of Christianity and civil government, and the other in the political science area of relations of state to social groups (religious groups, in this case).

In another situation, one edition may have been classified locally before appearance of outside cataloging, and thus the number may differ from the number assigned to another edition by the outside source (see Example 6.5).

Record (a)

```
HC68
07x
        Organization for Economic Co-operation and
            Development.  Information Service.
            OECD at work for environment.    [Paris]
        1971.
            30, [2] p.  illus.  21cm.

            1. Organization for Economic Cooperation
        and Development. Environment Committee.  2.
        Pollution.  3. Man--Influence on nature.  I.
        Title.


                         ◯
```

Record (b)

```
OCLC: 613414        Rec stat: c Entrd: 730302        Used: 870919
Type: a Bib lvl: m Govt pub:     Lang:  eng Source:    Illus:
Repr:     Enc lvl:    Conf pub: 0 Ctry:  fr  Dat tp: s M/F/B: 10
Indx: 0 Mod rec:    Festschr: 0 Cont:
Desc:     Int lvl:    Dates: 1971,
   1 010        73-150209//r86
   2 040        DLC $c DLC $d m.c.
   3 015        F***
   4 019        1018415
   5 050 0      TD177 $b .073
   6 082        363.6
   7 090          $b
   8 049        YCLM
   9 110 20     Organisation for Economic Co-operation and Development. $b
Information Service. $w cn
  10 245 10     OECD at work for environment.
  11 260 1      [Paris, $c 1971]
  12 300        30 p. $c 21 cm.
  13 650  0     Pollution $x International cooperation.
```

Example 6.5. Record (a) shows local cataloging done before appearance of LC cataloging. Record (b) shows that the cataloger at LC gave it a classification number different from that given by the local cataloger. Record (c) shows two interesting phenomena. The first is that the classifiers of the second edition evidently did not know about the existence of the first. Both LC and Dewey numbers are different. The second is that the LC number (HC79.E5) assigned to the second edition in 1974 did not exist as a classification number in 1971 when the local cataloger assigned HC68, and by 1973, when the first edition was cataloged at LC, HC68 had been canceled.

Record (c)

```
OCLC: 3207628        Rec stat:  c  Entrd:  740909          Used:  870917
Type:  a  Bib  lvl:  m  Govt pub:  i  Lang:   eng Source:     Illus:
Repr:      Enc  lvl:     Conf pub:  0  Ctry:   fr  Dat tp:  s  M/F/B:  10
Indx:  0  Mod  rec:      Festschr:  0  Cont:
Desc:      Int  lvl:     Dates:  1973,
   1 010        74-171829//r862
   2 040        DLC $c DLC $d m.c.
   3 015        F***
   4 019        1098245 $a 1106100 $a 1180625
   5 050  0     HC79.E5 $b 074 1973
   6 082        301.31/094
   7 090         $b
   8 049        YCLM
   9 110 20     Organisation for Economic Co-operation and Development. $b
Information Service. $w cn
  10 245 10     OECD at work for environment.
  11 250        2nd ed.
  12 260  0     [Paris] $b Organisation for Economic Co-operation and
Development, Information Service, $c 1973.
  13 300        56 p. $c 21 cm.
  14 650  0     Environmental policy $z Organization for Economic
Cooperation and Development countries.
  15 650  0     Environmental protection $z Organization for Economic
Cooperation and Development countries.
```

Example 6.5 *(continued)*.

Still another situation involves a serial that has changed its title and at the same time has changed its subject matter coverage in some way. Both Dewey and LC classification numbers can differ on cataloging for the new title, meaning that the volumes of the old and new parts of the serial are shelved in different places if the library arranges them by classification number (see Example 6.6, page 180). Monographs also can change in content between editions, with the same resulting differences in classification numbers. This, too, usually accompanies a change in title (see Example 6.7, page 181). Similar problems occur in a library that has changed classification schemes (e.g., from Dewey to LC) but has not reclassified materials that had been classified under the old scheme.

In a library with closed stacks, the separation of editions or translations probably will not affect their being found unless the shelflist is available for public browsing. Then the problem is the same as for open stacks. Patrons in a closed stack library without the shelflist available will learn that they must find what they want through the catalog and then make a request by call number (essentially a location device). Patrons also learn to find wanted items through the catalog in libraries that have changed from one classification scheme to another but have not reclassified.

In a library with open stacks, however, where patrons enjoy browsing and expect to find subject materials together, there may be some expectation that editions and translations will be shelved together. In some universities, for example, researchers may expect new editions about which they have received prepublication notices to appear beside older ones. They may not even check the cataloging to determine whether classification has changed.

Record (a)

Home builders monthly.

[Washington] Home Builders Association of Metropolitan Washington.

v. illus. 28 cm.

1. Construction Industry—Period. 2. Construction Industry—Washington, D. C. 3. Dwellings. I. Home Builders Association of Metropolitan Washington.

TH1.H74   ◯   690.5   52–16473 ‡

Library of Congress   [1]

Record (b)

Metropolitan area home builder. v. 19, no. 11–v. 27; Nov. 1962–Dec. 1970. [Washington, Home Builders Association of Metropolitan Washington]

v. illus. 28 cm. monthly.

Continues Home builders monthly.
Running title: Home builder.
Continued by Metropolitan Washington builders.

1. Construction industry—Washington metropolitan area—Periodicals. I. Home Builders Association of Metropolitan Washington. II. Title: Home builder.

HD9715.U53W34   ◯   338.4'7'690809753   79–618036

Library of Congress   72 [2]

Example 6.6. This shows a situation where the cataloging for the second title of a serial bears different classification numbers from the cataloging of the first title. This is done when the subject matter is considered to have changed with a title change.

Record (a)

```
OCLC: 1374704       Rec stat: n Entrd: 750605        Used: 870918
Type: a Bib lvl: m Govt pub:      Lang:  eng Source: u Illus:
Repr:       Enc lvl: I Conf pub: 0 Ctry:  xx  Dat tp: _ M/F/B: 10
Indx: 0 Mod rec:        Festschr: 0 Cont:
Desc:       Int lvl:    Dates: 1960,____
  1 010       59-8559
  2 040       DLC $c RIU
  3 050 0     NA6230 $b .R53
  4 082       725.23
  5 092       AM 725.2 $b R592o
  6 090         $b
  7 049       YCLM
  8 100 10    Ripnen, Kenneth H
  9 245 0     Office building and office layout planning.
 10 260 0     New York, $b McGraw-Hill, $c 1960.
 11 300       ix, 182 p. $b illus., plans. $c 26 cm.
 12 650  0    Office buildings.
```

Record (b)

```
OCLC: 662142        Rec stat: p Entrd: 730613        Used: 870926
Type: a Bib lvl: m Govt pub:      Lang:  eng Source:   Illus: a
Repr:       Enc lvl:   Conf pub: 0 Ctry:  nyu Dat tp: r M/F/B: 10
Indx: 1 Mod rec:        Festschr: 0 Cont:
Desc:       Int lvl:    Dates: 1974,1960
  1 010       73-9801
  2 040       DLC $c DLC
  3 020       0070529361
  4 050 0     HF5547 $b .R55 1974
  5 082       651/.32
  6 090         $b
  7 049       YCLM
  8 100 10    Ripnen, Kenneth H.
  9 245 10    Office space administration $c [by] Kenneth H. Ripnen.
 10 260 0     New York, $b McGraw-Hill $c [1974]
 11 300       viii, 216 p. $b illus. $c 24 cm.
 12 350       $14.95
 13 500       Published in 1960 under title: Office building and office
layout planning.
 14 650  0    Office layout.
```

Example 6.7. Title and classification changed with the later edition of this work. Examination of these two publications shows that in the later edition, represented by Record (b), the author has rearranged material found in the first and has added some new material, but content really has not changed. LC may have reclassified its earlier edition in such a case, but each local library that has a copy of both editions and that wants to have editions together must deal locally with the class change. For the first edition, both LC and Dewey numbers reflect architecture of office buildings. For the later edition they reflect office management.

If the library decides that editions and translations should be shelved together, there must be some mechanism for advising catalogers of the call numbers of other editions or of originals owned by the library. If catalogers have done their own searching, they will have found this information themselves. However, if searching is done by others, there must be some method for giving the cataloger this information. There must also be a decision on how to go about getting the editions and translations together. There are basically two options — reclassify the old with an adjusted form of the new number, or use an adjusted form of the old number on the new. Most libraries will probably use a combination. If the items already in the library are always reclassified, this does not satisfy the needs of the patron who is looking for the new edition to appear beside the old. On the other hand, if the old classification number is an outdated, inadequate one, placing a new edition in that classification does a disservice to other patrons. The library must also consider the cost of reclassification, especially if multiple copies, sometimes from many locations in the library system, and/or several editions are involved.

The question of whether call numbers will serve a collocation function or a location function has definite implications for use of outside copy. Suggested classification numbers can be used as they appear on the copy, without change, only if the call number is to be a location device and if editions and translations do not have to be together. Most libraries seem to take a stand somewhere between the extremes. An attempt is made to get similar subjects near each other where possible, but it is understood that only one classification number can be affixed to any one piece of material; thus, there will necessarily be a certain amount of scattering of materials on a given subject.

UNIQUE CALL NUMBERS

Regardless of whether the classification is used for collocation or location, a library must decide whether each item must have a call number that is not duplicated by any other call number in the system. Use of cataloging from an outside source is directly affected by the answer to this question. Most of the commercial firms that sell cards with preprinted call numbers cannot attempt to provide unique call numbers for each item because each local shelflist is not available to them for checking to see if they are duplicating call numbers already used for other items. Only with the use of LC call numbers printed on the cards can unique call numbers be approached by an outside source. Even those cannot be assured of being different from some number already assigned locally, and because companies must sometimes supply the call numbers for items that for some reason do not have LC numbers, the company-supplied number may later conflict with an LC-assigned number. Some libraries affix a letter "x" to the cutter of locally assigned LC call numbers to help avoid conflict with numbers assigned by LC. With Dewey numbers it is virtually impossible for an outside source to supply unique call numbers. This must be done at the local level.

Libraries need to consider whether their circulation systems, for example, require unique call numbers for satisfactory operation. Perhaps an accession number or other device, such as barcoding, would more economically serve this purpose. The cost of local assignment of numbers should be considered, especially in situations where checking the shelflist is required before any number can be assigned. Another factor to be considered is whether there is so much material in a classification that it cannot be kept shelved in meaningful order without unique call numbers.

REQUIREMENT FOR
CLASSIFICATION OF ALL ITEMS

A third basic decision concerns whether all kinds of materials require classification numbers, or whether they simply require some code as a shelving device. Each library has its own list of types of material that it will not classify. Recordings, for example, may simply be numbered in order of receipt; periodicals may be shelved in alphabetical order by title; maps may be marked with the drawer number of the case in which they are housed. It is possible, too, that some libraries will choose not to classify even the monographs, but this chapter is predicated on the assumption that at least some items in the library require classification/call numbers.

The alphabetical versus classified arrangement of serials question is still of concern in many libraries. Classified arrangement places serials in proximity with other kinds of material on the subject. One argument against classified arrangement is that people who want a serial have a citation to a title that they would prefer to find alphabetically rather than having to look up a call number. However, this only works if serials with title changes are split up—that is, if a patron has a citation to *Journal of Library Automation* and looks in the "*J*s" only to find that the *Journal* is now shelved with its new title, *Information Technology and Libraries* in the "*I*s," a second look-up is still required and the patron might as well have had to look up a call number. The value of the classified approach is questioned in a specialized library where almost all serials are on the same general subject in any case; but an alphabetical arrangement can be difficult to administer in large collections because of the massive shifting necessary when more space is needed in the "*A*s." So the answer to this problem lies, in part, in the type and size of library involved.

Another situation that calls classification into question and that has become more common in recent years is compact storage. Storage of little-used items is much more efficient if it can be by size of materials rather than by classification. In any case, whatever items are not to be classified must be identified so that copy catalogers will know when to substitute some other location device.

VARIATION IN CLASSIFICATION
WITHIN A LIBRARY

Related to the question of whether or not certain types of material will be classified is the question of whether there are certain groups of materials that will be handled with a different type of classification or call number device than that used for the majority of the collection. For example, many libraries classify current fiction separately from the literature section. Biographies may be pulled out to be classified or shelved together rather than with the subject area with which the biographee is associated. Juvenile collections for children and/or young people are often given separate treatment. Superintendent of Documents classification numbers are used to classify government documents in some libraries. There are also situations where the classification schemes suggest inclusion of a kind of subject matter in one area of the scheme, but the local library prefers to use another area or areas of the scheme. An example is bibliographies, which Dewey and LC both prefer to bring together in one part of the scheme, but which many libraries prefer to classify with the subject area covered by each bibliography. All of these special handlings mean that the person cataloging with outside copy must be fully aware of local classification policy so that the suggested classification numbers can be adapted when necessary. Libraries that receive preprinted cards must select a company that will cater to these special handlings. Then the library should be willing to accept the judgment of the company, in most instances, if optimum use of the outside copy is to be made.

The questions raised in the preceding paragraphs and sections represent decisions that must be made regardless of the classification scheme used. The direction these decisions take, however, may be affected by the particular scheme in use. There are also specific decisions to be made that relate *only* to the scheme being used. Each of the major schemes is discussed below, therefore, in order to point out decisions required when using a particular one.

LIBRARY OF CONGRESS
CLASSIFICATION AND CALL NUMBERS

The library that uses LC classification should try to accept, unaltered, as many LC-assigned call numbers as possible, if greatest efficiency is to be achieved. But there are situations where accepting the LC call number may not be desirable. Some of these situations include cases where items on the same subject, editions, or translations will be separated; items that are classified by LC only as analyzed parts of serials or sets while the local library wishes to classify them as separate titles; and situations where the printing date has been used as part of the call number, but the local library has a different printing. There is also copy that has no LC-assigned call number at all, and other copy with only a suggested *classification* number, not a complete call number. The following sections discuss decisions to be made when LC cataloging is used.

Acceptance of LC's Choice of
Classification Number

A primary early decision concerns whether to accept the classification part of an LC call number. This decision is related to the library's philosophy about whether the call number is to serve a collocating function or to act purely as a location device. If it is to be mainly a location device, a library may decide to accept LC's number without checking it in the classification schedules. It may be decided that the small percentage of error inevitable in printing, as well as errors made by the classifier, can be tolerated since the item should be retrievable as long as the number in the catalog matches that on the item.

In the study of LC cataloging mentioned in earlier chapters, LC classification numbers were checked against the outline of LC class numbers produced by the CDS Alert Service. Granted, this method would not have found some inversion typographical errors (e.g., PN2278 instead of PN2287), but it was designed to identify class numbers that were completely out of place. It was found that 98.8 percent of the LC class numbers were logically placed in the scheme.[2] Examples 6.8 and 6.9 show two of the 1.2 percent that were completely out of place.

```
OCLC: 7734300        Rec stat: c Entrd: 810814        Used: 830420
Type: a Bib lvl: m Govt pub:      Lang:  eng Source:       Illus:
Repr:      Enc lvl:      Conf pub: 0 Ctry:  enk Dat tp: s M/F/B: 10
Indx: 1 Mod rec:      Festschr: 0 Cont: b
Desc: a Int lvl:      Dates: 1982,
     1 010        81-13909
     2 040        DLC $c DLC
     3 020        0080286283 (pbk.) : $c L6.50 ($12.50 U.S.)
     4 039 0      2 $b 3 $c 3 $d 3 $e 3
     5 050 0      PS3 $b .K73 1982
     6 082 0      407 $2 19
     7 090        $b
     8 049        IVEA
     9 100 10     Krashen, Stephen D.
    10 245 10     Principles and practice in second language acquisition / $c
Stephen D. Krashen.
    11 250        1st ed.
    12 260 0      Oxford ; $a New York : $b Pergamon, $c 1982.
    13 300        ix, 202 p. ; $c 21 cm.
    14 440 0      Language teaching methodology series
    15 504        Bibliography: p. 191-200.
    16 500        Includes index.
    17 650 0      Language and languages $x Study and teaching.
    18 650 0      Language acquisition.
```

Example 6.8. This example shows a typographical error in the LC classification number. "PS3" is for yearbooks in American literature, while P53, the number that should have been used, is for study and teaching of linguistics.

```
OCLC: 7089308        Rec stat: n Entrd: 810521        Used: 870915
Type: a Bib lvl: m Govt pub:      Lang:  eng Source:       Illus:
Repr:      Enc lvl:      Conf pub: 1 Ctry:  nyu Dat tp: s M/F/B: 00
Indx: 0 Mod rec:      Festschr: 0 Cont: b
Desc: a Int lvl:      Dates: 1980,
     1 010        80-52791
     2 040        DLC $c DLC $d m/c
     3 043        n-us---
     4 050 0      LB2336 $b .C62
     5 082 0      379.1/54 $2 19
     6 090        $b
     7 049        YCLM
     8 245 00     Conducting evaluations : $b three perspectives.
     9 260 0      [New York, N.Y. (888 Seventh Ave., New York, N.Y. 10106)] :
$b Foundation Center, $c c1980.
    10 300        vii, 60 p. ; $c 28 cm.
    11 500        Papers from a workshop held in Feb. 1980, sponsored by the
Exxon Education Foundation, the International Paper Company Foundation,
and the Levi Strauss Foundation.
    12 504        Bibliography: p. [55]-60.
    13 650 0      Endowments $z United States $x Evaluation $x Congresses.
    14 710 20     Exxon Education Foundation. $w cn
    15 710 20     International Paper Company Foundation. $w cn
    16 710 20     Levi Strauss Foundation. $w cn
```

Example 6.9. The book represented here is about how to evaluate all grants that have been given out—not just the ones to higher education. There is a section in LC classification, "AZ191-193," for general evaluation.

It may also be decided that differences of opinion about which classification number is best suited to the item are just that — differences of opinion — and time spent searching for a better number will result only in another difference of opinion (see Examples 6.10 and 6.11). It should also be noted that it would require the highest level of copy cataloger, or even a professional, to make evaluations of this sort. Libraries that accept LC's classification also find merit in the idea that acceptance of the number will have value in networks and union catalogs. If many libraries wish to share an online catalog, the system would be much less complicated if all the libraries were to have the same call number for any one item.

```
OCLC: 574990        Rec stat:  c  Entrd:  730308        Used:  870828
Type: a  Bib lvl: m  Govt pub:     Lang:  fre Source:    Illus:
Repr:    Enc lvl: I  Conf pub: O  Ctry:  fr  Dat tp: s  M/F/B: 10b
Indx: O  Mod rec:  m  Festschr: O  Cont:
Desc:    Int lvl:     Dates: 1972,
   1 010        72-322515
   2 040        DLC $c CIN $d SER $d m.c. $d SER $d m/c
   3 015        F***
   4 050  0     PQ2605.L2 $b Z578
   5 090        $b
   6 049        YCLM
   7 100 10     Bibescu, Martha, $d ca. 1887-1973. $w cn
   8 245 10     'Echanges avec Paul Claudel; $b nos lettres in'edites $c
[par la] princesse Bibesco.
   9 260  0     [Paris] $b Mercure de France, $c 1972.
  10 300        210 p. $c 21 cm.
  11 350        26.00F
  12 600 10     Claudel, Paul, $d 1868-1955. $w cn
  13 700 10     Claudel, Paul, $d 1868-1955. $w cn
  14 870 19     $j 100/1 $a Bibesco, Marthe Lucie (Lahovary), $c
princesse, $d 1887-
```

Example 6.10. This item has been given the LC classification number for Paul Claudel. Because literature is usually classified according to author, some catalogers might decide that the classification for Bibescu, "PQ2603.I24," should be used instead. Other catalogers would find the class number given to be completely acceptable.

```
OCLC: 8130405       Rec stat:  n  Entrd:  820422        Used:  870924
Type: a  Bib lvl: m  Govt pub:     Lang:  eng Source:    Illus:
Repr:    Enc lvl:    Conf pub: O  Ctry:  enk Dat tp: s  M/F/B: 10
Indx: 1  Mod rec:     Festschr: O  Cont:  b
Desc: a  Int lvl:     Dates: 1981,
   1 010        81-194715
   2 040        DLC $c DLC $d m/c
   3 015        GB***
   4 020        0416726402 : $c $47.50 (U.S.)
   5 050  0     RC504 $b .K56 1981
   6 082  0     150.19/52 $2 19
   7 090        $b
   8 049        YCLM
   9 100 10     Kline, Paul. $w cn
  10 245 10     Fact and fantasy in Freudian theory / $c Paul Kline.
  11 250        2nd ed.
  12 260  0     London ; $a New York : $b Methuen, $c 1981.
  13 300        xi, 510 p. ; $c 25 cm.
  14 504        Bibliography: p. 448-493.
  15 500        Includes indexes.
  16 650   0    Psychoanalysis.
  17 600 10     Freud, Sigmund, $d 1856-1939. $w cn
```

Example 6.11. This item has been classed as a work of medicine in LC class "RC." Some classifiers would consider it to be psychoanalytic theory and place it in class "BF."

Other libraries, however, have the philosophy that the call number serves to draw together materials on a subject and these materials should be drawn together in the best way to serve the local user. Such a library may believe that an item that is assigned a "TX" number when it should have had a "JX" number is lost to certain types of users. It may be decided that there are certain areas in which it is better to classify materials reflecting the needs of the local clientele. For example, a book of religious poems would serve some users best if classified with religion, although others would be better served by finding it with other poetry in the literature section.

Along with the user-service consideration, a library needs to consider the length of time it takes to verify correctness of every suggested class number and to change those deemed unsuitable. The value of such change to the local user should be balanced against the extra time required to make materials available to the public.

Use of Copy That Lacks
LC Classification Numbers

Whichever philosophy is followed, there are certain cases where there is no class number to accept or where it is necessary to choose among alternatives offered by LC. The largest group lacking class numbers has been items in the field of law. As law schedules appeared beginning in 1969, LC began classifying new materials with the new schedules. Libraries will find much retrospective copy, however, that lacks the classification, and for these items it must be supplied locally (see Example 6.12, page 188). Another group that lacks classification is recordings, which are not classified by LC; since 1972, however, a classification number only has been offered for these items. It appears in brackets on cards, and on MARC records it appears in the 050 field with no subfield "b." Titles that LC does not wish to retain also sometimes have classification numbers only. These also appear in brackets on cards but are identified by a first indicator "1" in the 050 field in a MARC record. If any of these suggested classification numbers are accepted, a library is obliged to determine whether the call number is complete and to add its own cuttering if not (see Example 6.13, page 189).

Record (a)

Baz, Jean.
  Étude sur la nationalité libanaise / par Jean Baz. — 2.
éd., entièrement refondue avec reproduction en annexe des
textes législatifs en vigueur. — ₁Beyrouth? : s. n.₁, 1969.

  vi, 15–271 p. ; 25 cm.

  Bibliography: p. 263–264.

  1. Citizenship—Lebanon.   I. Title.
                                            323.6′095692   75–500875
                                                                      MARC

      Library of Congress   75 ₁2₁

Record (b)

```
OCLC: 8784920       Rec stat: n Entrd: 820828        Used: 870605
Type: a Bib lvl: m Govt pub:     Lang:  eng Source:    Illus:
Repr:     Enc lvl:   Conf pub: 0 Ctry:  mau Dat tp: s M/F/B: 10
Indx: 1 Mod rec:     Festschr: 0 Cont: b
Desc: a Int lvl:    Dates: 1982,
   1 010        78-70247
   2 040        DLC $c DLC $d m/c
   3 020        0910956723
   4 043        e-fr---
   5 050 0      LAW
   6 082 0      944/.84 $2 19
   7 090         $b
   8 049        YCLM
   9 100 10     Rogozi'nski, Jan. $w cn
  10 245 10     Power, caste, and law : $b social conflict in fourteenth-
century Montpellier / $c Jan Rogozi'nski ; foreword by Joseph R.
Strayer.
  11 260 0      Cambridge, Mass. : $b Medieval Academy of America, $c 1982.
  12 300        xxii, 200 p. ; $c 24 cm.
  13 440 0      Medieval academy books ; $v no. 91
  14 504        Bibliography: p. 179-194.
  15 500        Includes index.
  16 650 0      Law $z France $z Montpellier $x History and criticism.
  17 650 0      Taxation $x Law and legislation $z France $z Montpellier.
  18 651 0      Montpellier (France) $x History.
```

Example 6.12. There is much retrospective LC copy in the field of law that lacks any kind
of LC classification. Local libraries must supply their own call numbers for such items.
Record (a) shows that on cards from LC there is a blank space where the LC class number
would ordinarily be. Record (b) shows that on MARC records, the word "LAW" is entered
in the 050 field.

Record (a)

Chaĭkovskiĭ, Petr Il'ich, 1840–1893.
₍The nutcracker₎ Phonodisc.
Casse-noisette. ₍The nutcracker₎; ballet in 2 acts, op. 71.
London CSA 2239 (CS 6686–6687). ₍1974₎
4 s. 12 in. 33⅓ rpm. stereophonic.

National Philharmonic Orchestra; Sydney Sax, leader; Richard
Bonynge, conductor.
Durations: 24 min., 19 sec.; 17 min., 9 sec.
Automatic sequence.
Program notes (₍3₎ p.) by M. Williamson laid in container.

1. Ballets.   I. Bonynge, Richard.   II. National Philharmonic
Orchestra, London.   III. Title.   IV. Title: The nutcracker.

[M1520]   74–750562

Library of Congress   75   R

Record (b)

Harich-Schneider, Eta.
The harpsichord; an introduction to technique, style, and
the historical sources. 2d ed. **Kassel, New York, Baren-
reiter,** 1960 ₍ᶜ1954₎

70 p. illus., music. 23 cm.

Translation of Kleine Schule des Cembalospiels.
"Musical examples" (22 p.) in pocket.
Bibliography: p. 68–70.

1. Harpsichord—Instruction and study.   ɪ. Title.

[MT252]   786.3   65–8168/MN/CD

Printed for Card Div.
Library of Congress   ₍4–1₎

Example 6.13. LC classification numbers only, not complete call numbers, are given in
some cases. These are usually given in situations where LC does not classify the type of
item involved, as shown in Record (a), or where LC does not retain the item, as shown in
Record (b). In order to be used as a call number in a local library, a cutter must be added to
this classification. (It will be noted that the main entry and uniform title of Record (a) are
not in AACR 2 form. This is because records not in LC's MARC file have not been
changed to reflect current authorized forms for headings that have changed since the
creation of the record.)

There also are items that receive a call number that is based not on LC classification but on a unique LC arrangement for that type of item. An example is incunabula (i.e., books printed before 1501). LC arranges these under the abbreviation "Incun." followed by the year of printing. LC began in the mid-1970s, however, to supply suggested alternative classification numbers for these items, as discussed below. Other examples are microfilm call numbers that include the word "Microfilm" followed by a sequencing number, and call numbers for Minimal Level Cataloging (MLC) records that begin with the letters "MLC" (see Example 6.14). MLC records *do*, however, give in parentheses following the MLC call number the first letter of the LC classification into which the item would be placed if it were to be classified.

```
Type: a Bib lvl: m Govt pub:    Lang:  por Source:    Illus:
Repr:     Enc lvl: 7 Conf pub: 0 Ctry:  xx  Dat tp: s M/F/B: 10
Indx: 0 Mod rec:     Festschr: 0 Cont:
Desc: a Int lvl:     Dates: 1961,
  1 010        85-844643
  2 040        DLC $c DLC
  3 050 0      MLCM 86/1264 (B)
  4 049        YCLM
  5 100 10     Grande, Humberto.
  6 245 10     Trabalho, cultura e esp'irito / $c Humberto Grande.
  7 260 0      [Rio de Janeiro], Brasil : $b Servi,co de Documenta,c~ao,
MTPS, $c 1961.
  8 300        84 p. ; $c 23 cm.
  9 440 0      Cole,c~ao Lindolfo Collor
```

Example 6.14. Minimal level cataloging (MLC) records for monographs from LC have a call number that begins with the letters "MLC" followed by a letter for size (in this case "M" for "medium"). The four letters are followed by the year of cataloging and an accession number. The first letter of the classification into which the item would be placed (in this case "B") is given in parentheses after the call number.

Alternative Suggested Classification Numbers

In addition to copy with only a suggested classification number, there is copy that offers numbers as alternatives to the classification given in the complete call number used by LC. The first situation for which LC gave alternative numbers was for fiction beginning in 1968. They were still classifying English language fiction in PZ3 and PZ4. Beginning in November 1968, LC provided a bracketed classification number from the literature schedules for the benefit of libraries that wanted to place English language adult fiction with other literature (see Example 6.15). On July 1, 1980, LC abandoned use of PZ3 and PZ4, meaning that other libraries that used PZ3 and PZ4 were faced with either changing policy or creating their own call numbers. The advantage of using LC's literature numbers, particularly in a research library, is that an author's fiction is not separated from that author's other literary works and biographical material. In addition English translations of fiction in other languages are not separated from the originals. For other libraries, however, there is merit in placing all English language fiction together in order to provide in one place a leisure reading section. Whichever policy is followed, copy cataloging is affected, unless numbers are simply accepted as LC assigned them. For those libraries that follow LC's current policy, retrospective copy prior to July 1980 requires choosing the alternative number and making it a complete call number. For libraries wishing to use PZ3 and PZ4, copy for fiction after June 1980 must be identified and a local call number must be supplied.

Record (a)

Wodehouse, Pelham Grenville, 1881–
    French leave / by P. G. Wodehouse ; ₁with a new preface by the author₁. — London : Barrie & Jenkins, 1974.

206 p. ; 19 cm.   **GB 74–09347**

Originally published in 1955.
ISBN 0–257–65831–9 : £2.25

I. Title.

PZ3.W817Fr 5   823′.9′12   74–192909
[PR6045.O53]   MARC

Library of Congress   74 ₁4₁

Record (b)

```
OCLC: 3242072      Rec stat: c Entrd: 741223      Used: 870720
Type: a Bib lvl: m Govt pub:    Lang:  eng Source:    Illus:
Repr:    Enc lvl:   Conf pub: 0 Ctry:  enk Dat tp: r M/F/B: 11
Indx: 0 Mod rec: m Festschr: 0 Cont:
Desc: i Int lvl:    Dates: 1974,1955
   1 010      74-192909//r86
   2 040      DLC $c DLC $d m.c.
   3 015      GB74-09347
   4 020      0257658319 : $c L2.25
   5 050 0    PZ3.W817 $b Fr5 $a PR6045.053
   6 082      823/.9/12
   7 090      $b
   8 049      YCLM
   9 100 10   Wodehouse, P. G. $q (Pelham Grenville), $d 1881-1975. $w cn
  10 245 10   French leave / $c by P. G. Wodehouse ; [with a new preface
by the author].
  11 260 0    London : $b Barrie & Jenkins, $c 1974.
  12 300      206 p. ; $c 19 cm.
  13 500      Originally published in 1955.
```

Example 6.15. A suggested literature classification number was provided by LC between 1968 and 1980 as an alternative to the English language fiction numbers "PZ3" and "PZ4." The alternative is a class number only, not a complete call number. On cards these numbers appear in brackets under the full LC classification number, as shown in Record (a). In MARC records they appear in a second subfield "a" of the 050 field, as shown in Record (b).

In 1970, LC began supplying the secondary numbers that it used in its classed catalog of music score holdings.[3] These numbers represent aspects of the works not covered by the call numbers assigned. (As with other suggested alternative classification numbers, these appear in brackets on cards and in subsequent "a" subfields of the 050 field of a MARC record.) The Music Division's classified catalog was closed with the adoption of AACR 2; so these secondary numbers have not been supplied since 1981.[4] A library using copy produced between 1970 and 1981 could choose to use any one of these classification numbers as the basis for its call number, since it might be better for local patrons if the item is placed at one of the alternative numbers instead of at the one used by LC (see Example 6.16).

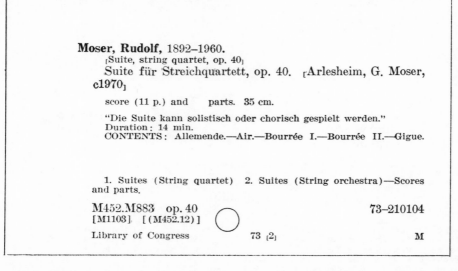

Example 6.16. Some music scores cataloged by LC between 1970 and 1981 are given classification numbers in addition to the one used as a basis for the call number. Numbers within brackets represent different aspects of the work. The number in this example that is enclosed in parentheses within the brackets is a number that is not part of the regular classification schedule.

Alternative numbers for monographic titles of items that LC classifies as collected sets began to appear on LC copy in 1972.[5] However, they usually are supplied only when the number covering the content of the individual title would be different from the number for the collected set (see Example 6.17). These are useful in a library that prefers to shelve each title of a set in the specific classification with other works that have the same content. The collected set number is usually a much more general one. Classifying all volumes of a series together is helpful to the patron who expects every volume of that series to be of value and who, therefore, appreciates finding the parts of that series together. Usually, an individual decision is made for each series or set, instead of having an overall policy that all items in series will be classified together or all will be classified separately. If each case is decided on its own merit, the copy cataloger,

Record (a)

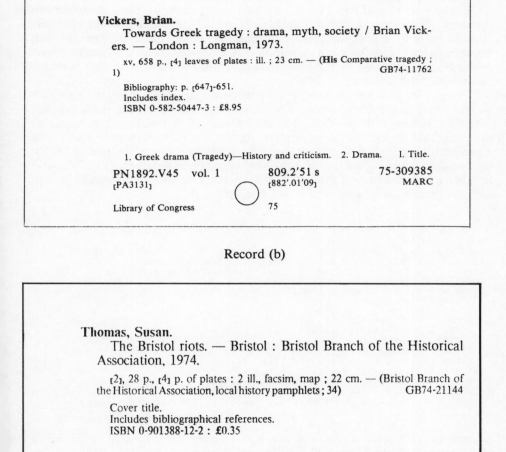

Vickers, Brian.
  Towards Greek tragedy : drama, myth, society / Brian Vickers. — London : Longman, 1973.
  xv, 658 p., [4] leaves of plates : ill. ; 23 cm. — (**His** Comparative tragedy ; 1)   GB74-11762

  Bibliography: p. [647]-651.
  Includes index.
  ISBN 0-582-50447-3 : £8.95

  1. Greek drama (Tragedy)—History and criticism.   2. Drama.   I. Title.

PN1892.V45   vol. 1   809.2'51 s   75-309385
[PA3131]   [882'.01'09]   MARC

Library of Congress   75

Record (b)

Thomas, Susan.
  The Bristol riots. — Bristol : Bristol Branch of the Historical Association, 1974.
  [2], 28 p., [4] p. of plates : 2 ill., facsim, map ; 22 cm. — (Bristol Branch of the Historical Association, local history pamphlets ; 34)   GB74-21144

  Cover title.
  Includes bibliographical references.
  ISBN 0-901388-12-2 : £0.35

  1. Bristol (Avon)—History.   2. Riots—England—Bristol (Avon)   I. Title.
  II. Series: Historical Association. Bristol Branch. Local history pamphlets ; 34.

DA690.B8H5   no. 34   942.4'1   75-301523
                                        MARC

Library of Congress   75[r86]rev2

Example 6.17. For both LC and Dewey classification numbers, LC supplies an alternative classification number for the individual title that they classify as part of a collected set, Record (a). These numbers may not appear when the individual number would be the same as the set number, Record (b), nor do they appear on copy cataloged before 1972.

or perhaps someone else before copy is sent to the cataloger, must be able to recognize an *analytic* call number (i.e., call number for the collected set plus an individual volume or identification number) so that a decision can be made on how to handle any series new to the library. If collected set numbers are not accepted, local classification must be supplied for items cataloged by LC before 1972, and cutters and dates must be added in all cases to make complete call numbers. Most of the commercial producers of catalog card sets routinely classify parts of monographic series separately. They supply a complete call number on older copy or add a notation to the suggested classification number on newer copy. This must be taken into consideration when choosing to purchase cards with preprinted call numbers.

Two other situations for which alternatives began appearing in the 1970s are *Bound withs* and bibliographies. For the second and following titles that are issued or bound with another title, the classification number that would be assigned that title follows the call number for the first title, either in brackets or in a second subfield "a". The call number for the first title is the one used at LC for the physical volume when two or more works are bound together. The alternative number allows the library that receives the second or later title bound alone to assign a proper classification to it (see Example 6.18).

Record (a)

```
OCLC: 12975339      Rec stat: n Entrd: 851107        Used: 860104
Type: a Bib lvl: m Govt pub:      Lang:  hun Source:     Illus:
Repr:       Enc lvl:    Cont pub: 0 Ctry:  hu  Dat tp: s M/F/B: 11
Indx: 0 Mod rec:       Festschr: 0 Cont:
Desc: a Int lvl:    Dates: 1982,
    1 010        83-132923
    2 040        DLC $c DLC $d m/c
    3 020        963326796X : $c 12.00Ft
    4 050 0      PH3213.B512 $b S95 1982
    5 090        $b
    6 049        YCLM
    7 100 10     Bistey, Andr'as, $d 1942- $w cn
    8 245 10     Szib'eria melege / $c Bistey Andr'as.
    9 260 0      Budapest : $b Zr'inyi Katonai Kiad'o, $c 1982.
   10 300        99 p. ; $c 19 cm.
   11 501        Issued with: A repulosz'azad / L. P'eczely. Budapest,
1982.
```

Example 6.18. When two or more works are bound together, the cataloging for the second or following work bears a second classification number for that specific title. In this example Record (a) represents the first of two works bound together. The LC call number in the 050 field is for that work and for the physical item containing both works. Record (b) is the MARC record for the second work contained in the volume. The call number given first in the 050 field is for the complete volume and is identical to that in Record (a). The alternative classification given in a second subfield "a", however, is for the work being cataloged and could be used by a library that acquires this work issued separately.

Record (b)

```
OCLC: 12973146        Rec stat: n Entrd: 851107         Used: 860104
Type: a Bib lvl: m Govt pub:      Lang:  hun Source:      Illus:
Repr:     Enc lvl:    Conf pub: 0 Ctry:  hu  Dat tp: s M/F/B: 11
Indx: 0 Mod rec:      Festschr: 0 Cont:
Desc: a Int lvl:      Dates: 1982,
  1 010        85-119705
  2 040        DLC $c DLC $d m/c
  3 020          $c 12.00Ft
  4 050 0      PH3213.B512 $b S95 1982 $a PH3291.P394
  5 090          $b
  6 049        YCLM
  7 100 10     P'eczely, L'aszl'o. $w cn
  8 245 12     A repulosz'azad / $c P'eczely L'aszl'o.
  9 260 0      Budapest : $b Zr'inyi Katonai Kiad'o, $c 1982.
 10 300        161 p. ; $c 19 cm.
 11 501        Issued with: Szib'eria melege / A. Bistey. Budapest, 1982.
 12 651 0      Hungary $x History $y Revolution, 1918-1919 $x Fiction.
```

Example 6.18 *(continued)*.

Requests from libraries for alternative classification numbers for bibliographies, which LC puts in Class Z, finally brought results in late 1974. LC now suggests a number to be used by libraries that prefer to classify bibliographies of a subject with other items on that subject, instead of all together as a group of bibliographies[6] (see Example 6.19).

```
OCLC: 1054269        Rec stat: p Entrd: 740904         Used: 870727
Type: a Bib lvl: m Govt pub:      Lang:  eng Source:      Illus:
Repr:     Enc lvl:    Conf pub: 0 Ctry:  nyu Dat tp: s M/F/B: 10
Indx: 0 Mod rec:      Festschr: 0 Cont: b
Desc:     Int lvl:    Dates: 1975,
   1 010        74-19226
   2 040        DLC $c DLC $d m/c
   3 020        0824010566
   4 043        a-ii---
   5 050 0      Z7165.I6 $b C5 $a HN683.5
   6 082        016.3091/54/04
   7 090          $b
   8 049        YCLM
   9 100 10     Chekki, Danesh A. $w cn
  10 245 14     The social system and culture of modern India: $b a
research bibliography, $c edited with an introd. by Danesh A. Chekki.
  11 260 0      New York, $b Garland, $c 1975.
  12 300        xxxv, 843 p. $c 22 cm.
  13 651 0      India $x Social conditions $y 1947-  $x Bibliography.
```

Example 6.19. Since late 1974 LC has provided an alternative number for each bibliography classified in LC Class Z. This number is the most general number for the subject covered by the bibliography.

Whenever a library chooses to use the alternative classification numbers provided by LC, it must be remembered that cutters have to be added to them to make complete call numbers and that retrospective copy before a certain period of time does not provide the alternatives. Yet many libraries believe that these choices serve their patrons better than the classification used at LC.

A final choice that LC sometimes "offers," although inadvertently, is provided when they revise copy to correct a classification number that was in error the first time (see Example 6.20). A library that has used the initial version may wish to change it. Unfortunately, there is no way to know when classification for an item already in the local catalog has been revised by LC. It is discovered either by accident or because of the acquisition of another edition.

Record (a)

U. S. President, 1969–   (Nixon)
U. S. foreign policy for the 1970's: building for peace;
a report to the Congress by Richard Nixon, President of
the United States, February 25, 1971. ₁Washington; For
sale by the Supt. of Docs., U. S. Govt. Print. Off., 1971₁
      vii, 235 p. port. 24 cm. $1.00
      "Second annual Presidential review of United States foreign
policy."
      1. U. S.—Foreign relations—1969–   I. Title.
JX1417.A59   327.73   79–611236
                                                  MARC

Example 6.20. There have been at least two editions of this work—one printed by the U.S. Government Printing Office, Record (a), and one printed by Harper & Row, Record (b). A library that acquired one or both editions may have discovered that LC assigned JX1417 to one and E840 to the other, which may have necessitated a decision as to which number to use. Later, however, both records were revised, Records (c) and (d) (page 198), to appear with E855 classification numbers. Whichever number had been decided on in the first place then became obsolete, and local libraries that received foreign policy speeches for other years (which bear the same title proper) faced the decision of whether to use JX1417 or E840 on the new works or to reclassify the older one to E855 so that the works would stand together.

Record (b)

U. S. President, 1969–   (Nixon)
   United States foreign policy for the 1970s; building for
peace. A report by President Richard Nixon to the Con-
gress, February 25, 1971. New York, Harper & Row ₁1971₎
      xiii, 198 p.   22 cm. $5.95
      1. U. S.—Foreign relations—1969-   I. Title.
   E840.A55   1971   327.73   70–157503
   ISBN 0–06–013210–8   MARC

○

Record (c)

United States. President, 1969-   (Nixon)
   U.S. foreign policy for the 1970's: building for peace; a report
to the Congress by Richard Nixon, President of the United
States, February 25, 1971. ₍Washington; For sale by the Supt.
of Docs., U.S. Govt. Print. Off., 1971₎

   vii, 235 p. port. 24 cm. $1.00

   "Second annual Presidential review of United States foreign policy."

   1. United States—Foreign relations—1969-1974.   I. Title.

   E855.A484   1971b   327.73   79-611236
                                                          MARC
                                  ○
   Library of Congress   71₍74r72₎rev2

Example 6.20 *(continued)*.

Record (d)

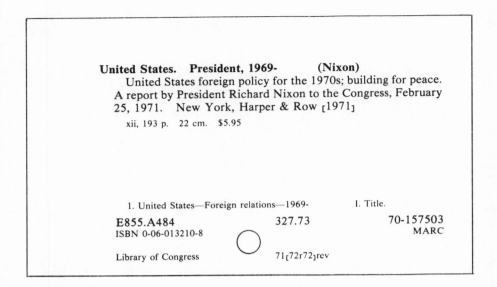

United States.   President, 1969-   (Nixon)
 United States foreign policy for the 1970s; building for peace.
A report by President Richard Nixon to the Congress, February
25, 1971.   New York, Harper & Row ₍1971₎

xii, 193 p.   22 cm. $5.95

1. United States—Foreign relations—1969-   I. Title.

E855.A484   327.73   70-157503
ISBN 0-06-013210-8   MARC

Library of Congress   71₍72r72₎rev

Example 6.20 *(continued)*.

Local Alternatives to LC Classification

In addition to the choices that are offered by LC on copy, there may be other situations where a local library may choose to assign classifications different from those given by LC. Local classification schemes may have been developed for use with certain kinds of materials — e.g., juvenile materials or local theses. These schemes may or may not be compatible with LC classification. There may also be local variations to the LC classification on an individual number basis. Certain LC classification numbers may be rejected in favor of a different number or a locally expanded run of numbers for that topic. For example, an expansion of the schedule for the local history of a state or community may have been devised. Also, there may be local approval for choice of a different number when the local cataloger disagrees with the number assigned by LC or other outside source. There may be series for which each title has been classified separately by LC but which the local library wishes to classify together as a group, or there may be series that LC has classed together, and that the library wishes to classify separately, but the copy predates the time when LC began supplying alternate numbers for series.

In any of these cases, the copy cataloger must be able to recognize situations where the LC classification will not be used locally or where a given alternative will be used instead. This may be done by annotating the classification schedules, if all classification numbers are checked before use. The decision on whether to use analytic or separate call numbers cannot be recorded in the schedule, however, because this decision can be called for with virtually any possible number. If all classification numbers are not checked before use, the library should limit the exceptions as much as possible and should then teach the copy catalogers to recognize those exceptions.

Type of Cuttering to Be Used

The Library of Congress number appearing on LC copy is, in the majority of cases, a complete *call number*. This differs from the suggested Dewey number, which is a classification number only. The LC call number consists of a classification number (which may, itself, contain a cutter number for an aspect of the subject), a cutter number that distinguishes the work in question from other works that have been assigned that classification number, often a date, and sometimes a part (i.e., volume, section, etc.) number. The LC call number represents the actual call number that the Library of Congress has assigned to its copy of the item. It is unique to that item because the cutter number and following parts of the call number were assigned at the official shelflist of LC and were constructed so as to fit it among other items in that classification without duplicating any call number already assigned.

One of the decisions that a library must make with LC call numbers on copy is whether LC's cuttering will be used or whether the local library will assign its own cutter numbers. Some libraries, in order to avoid duplication between LC call numbers and locally assigned call numbers, have made it a practice to assign their own cutter numbers, often according to the Cutter-Sanborn tables. If this is done, it is necessary to check the shelflist whenever a call number is assigned and leave some kind of notification there to hold the number until cataloging is finished and entered into the catalog. It is also necessary that the people who work with LC copy know the difference between a subject cutter and a cutter representing the main entry. They must know that only the main entry cutter of the LC call number should be dropped and replaced with the library's own cutter. They also need to know that if the classification calls for two cutters as part of the classification (*double cuttering*), LC does not add a third cutter for the main entry. Instead, the second subject cutter is adjusted to allow for alphabetizing the main entries (see Example 6.21, page 200). A library that does its own cuttering, and chooses to use more than two cutters, needs a procedure for readjusting the second cutter before adding a third one.

Many libraries use LC cuttering as is and then devise some means of marking the locally assigned call numbers so that if LC assigns the same cutter to another work later, it will not conflict. A common device is to affix an "x" to any LC-type cutter assigned locally, as shown:

TK6565
.L6
C6x
1987

Although there are a few instances in which there is no cutter to which an "x" can be suffixed, the system can be used anyway. For example, if the call number has no cutter, but ends with a date, the "x" must be added to the date; for example,

JX2373
1892x

```
OCLC: 1197847        Rec stat: n Entrd: 750128        Used: 870506
Type: a Bib lvl: m Govt pub:    Lang:  eng Source:    Illus: a
Repr:    Enc lvl:   Conf pub: 0 Ctry:  ke  Dat tp: s M/F/B: 10
Indx: 0 Mod rec:    Festschr: 0 Cont: b
Desc:    Int lvl:   Dates: 1973,
   1 010        73-980184
   2 040        DLC $c DLC $d m.c.
   3 043        fe-----
   4 050 0      HD3561.A6 $b E227
   5 082        334/.0967
   6 090        $b
   7 049        YCLM
   8 100 10     Hyd'en, Goran, $d 1938- $w cn
   9 245 10     Efficiency versus distribution in East African
cooperatives; $b a study in organizational conflicts $c [by] Goran
Hyden.
  10 260 0      Nairobi, $b East African Literature Bureau $c [1973]
  11 300        xix, 254 p. $b illus. $c 23 cm.
  12 504        Bibliography: p. 250-254.
  13 650 0      Cooperative societies $z Africa, East.
```

Example 6.21. The classification HD3561, in the run of numbers assigned to industrial cooperation by country, calls for double cuttering: first, ".A6" for general cooperative societies, which are then subdivided "by state, province, etc." The cutter "E227", therefore, stands both for East Africa and for the alphabetical arrangement of Hydén among other works on the subject, since LC does not assign more than two cutters to a call number. It will be noted that in a MARC record, the second cutter is placed in the "b" subfield of the 050 field, even though it partially represents the subject.

If a literary author is assigned an author cutter in the classification scheme and further subdivision is by date only, the "x" again should be added to the date; for example,

PQ6503
.B3
1947x

Also, where there are standard cutters to denote literary forms (e.g., A6 — Selections), the date following should be suffixed by the "x"; for example,

PS2587
.P5
A6
1899x

Otherwise, filing of such call numbers would throw the locally assigned ones out of natural sequence (see Example 6.34 on page 221). If such exceptions are successfully worked out, the complete call numbers assigned by LC can be used as they appear. It is not necessary to check the shelflist first, unless other procedures require it. LC occasionally duplicates its own numbers, but in one library employing this method, during a three-year period when 25,000 titles were cataloged each year, there were fewer than 12 duplicate call number problems a year. The time saved by not checking the shelflist was tremendous. Some libraries that began using Cutter-Sanborn numbers with LC classification have since switched to accepting LC's cutter numbers in order to make more efficient use of LC copy. These libraries have found that the two systems can be intershelved, but they have to be willing to accept the fact that items within a classification number will not fall in absolute alphabetical order.

Decisions Necessary When Using
LC Cuttering

If a library does accept complete LC call numbers, it must be willing to accept certain idiosyncracies of the system or work out procedures for changing certain of the call numbers.

Editions

There are a number of instances in which different editions of a work are not given successive call numbers by LC. The problem of editions being classified in different class numbers has already been discussed. There are also cases in which the main entry changes from one edition to the next. This can happen when a new author has done the revision or when the order of names has changed, signifying a change in principal author. The cutter of the later edition then may differ from that of the earlier (see Example 6.22, page 202). Main entry changes between editions have also happened quite often because of rule changes, first with the rule change in AACR 1 that no longer allowed an editor to be main entry, and then with the adoption of AACR 2 — particularly the drastic reduction in situations where a corporate body can be main entry. LC's policy prior to adoption of AACR 2 was to try to assign the same class number, cutter number, and subject headings to editions as long as the subject content of the editions did not vary significantly.[7] However, when the main entry changed, the cutter sometimes was different (as already seen in Example 6.22). With the adoption of AACR 2, LC announced that new editions of works cataloged according to AACR 2 would be assigned appropriate call numbers regardless of numbers assigned to editions cataloged before AACR 2 (see Example 6.23, page 203).[8] Editions were only given the same class and cutter numbers if subject content were the same and the main entry had not changed. However, for new editions of works whose earlier editions originally had been cataloged according to AACR 2, LC's policy returned to that prior to AACR 2 adoption. That is, when two editions of a work have both been cataloged according to AACR 2, an effort is made to use the same class number and cutter number, even if the choice of main entry changes.

It is possible for the cuttering to be so different when the main entry has changed that the editions are widely separated on the shelf, even though the classification number may be the same. If the library has decided that editions must stand together (see earlier discussion of this question), one possible compromise is to recutter the new to place it with the old when only the cutter differs, and to reclassify the old only when the classification number used for it is clearly inferior to the classification number that LC has assigned to the new edition. However, consideration should also be given to the fact that if LC's new call number is not used, these same decisions will have to be dealt with whenever future editions are acquired by the library.

A further instance in which editions are separated by LC's cuttering is much more difficult to circumvent than other situations mentioned. This problem

Record (a)

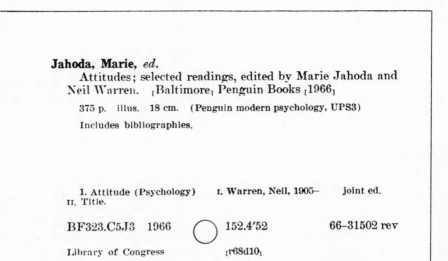

Jahoda, Marie, *ed.*
  Attitudes; selected readings, edited by Marie Jahoda and
Neil Warren. ₁Baltimore₁ Penguin Books ₁1966₁

  375 p.   illus.   18 cm.   (Penguin modern psychology, UPS3)

  Includes bibliographies.

  1. Attitude (Psychology)   ɪ. Warren, Neil, 1905–   joint ed.
ɪɪ. Title.

  BF323.C5.J3   1966   152.4′52   66–31502 rev

  Library of Congress   ₁r68d10₁

Record (b)

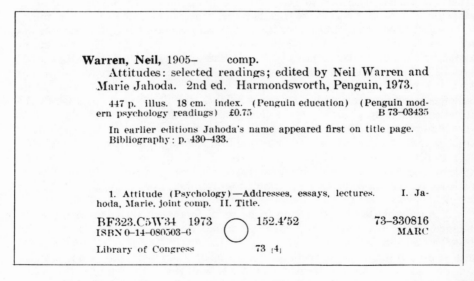

Warren, Neil, 1905–   comp.
  Attitudes: selected readings; edited by Neil Warren and
Marie Jahoda. 2nd ed. Harmondsworth, Penguin, 1973.

  447 p.   illus.   18 cm.   index.   (Penguin education)   (Penguin modern psychology readings)   £0.75   B 73–03435

  In earlier editions Jahoda's name appeared first on title page.
  Bibliography: p. 430–433.

  1. Attitude (Psychology)—Addresses, essays, lectures.   I. Jahoda, Marie, joint comp.   II. Title.

  BF323.C5W34   1973   152.4′52   73–330816
  ISBN 0–14–080503–6   MARC

  Library of Congress   73 ₁4₁

Example 6.22. Record (a) represents the first edition of the work and Record (b) represents
the second edition. The main entry has changed because the order of the editors' names on
the title pages changed. The first LC call number is cuttered with a "J" cutter and the
second has a "W" cutter. (It will be noted that if there were to be a third edition now, the
main entry would be title and would require yet a third cutter.)

Record (a)

```
OCLC: 6603069        Rec stat: c Entrd: 800723        Used: 870825
Type: a Bib lvl: m Govt pub:     Lang:  eng Source:     Illus:
Repr:       Enc lvl:     Conf pub: 0 Ctry:  pau Dat tp: s M/F/B: 10
Indx: 0 Mod rec:        Festschr: 0 Cont:
Desc: i Int lvl:       Dates: 1980,
  1 010          80-19484//r872
  2 040          DLC $c DLC $d m.c.
  3 020          0812107691 (pbk.)
  4 050 1        RC684.E9 $b A45 1980
  5 060          WE103 A514g
  6 082 0        615/.824 $2 19
  7 090              $b
  8 049          YCLM
  9 110 20       American College of Sports Medicine. $w cn
 10 245 10       Guidelines for graded exercise testing and exercise
prescription / $c American College of Sports Medicine.
 11 250          2d ed.
 12 260 0        Philadelphia : $b Lea & Febiger, $c 1980.
 13 300          xiii, 151 p. ; $c 20 cm.
 14 650  0       Exercise therapy.
 15 650  0       Heart $x Diseases $x Patients $x Rehabilitation.
 16 650  0       Exercise tests.
 17 650  2       Exercise test.
 18 650  2       Exercise therapy.
 19 650  2       Exertion.
```

Record (b)

```
OCLC: 12751162       Rec stat: c Entrd: 851009        Used: 870901
Type: a Bib lvl: m Govt pub:     Lang:  eng Source:     Illus:
Repr:       Enc lvl:     Conf pub: 0 Ctry:  pau Dat tp: s M/F/B: 00
Indx: 1 Mod rec:        Festschr: 0 Cont: b
Desc: a Int lvl:       Dates: 1986,
  1 010          85-24030//r87
  2 040          DLC $c DLC $d VET $d CUX $d m/c
  3 020          0812110226 (pbk.)
  4 050 0        RC684.E9 $b G85 1986
  5 082 0        615.8/24 $2 19
  6 096          WB 541 G946
  7 090              $b
  8 049          YCLM
  9 245 00       Guidelines for exercise testing and prescription / $c
American College of Sports Medicine.
 10 250          3rd ed.
 11 260 0        Philadelphia : $b Lea & Febiger, $c 1986.
 12 300          xii, 179 p. ; $c 22 cm.
 13 500          Rev. ed. of: Guidelines for graded exercise testing and
exercise prescription / American College of Sports Medicine. 1975.
 14 504          Includes bibliographical references and index.
 15 650  0       Exercise therapy.
 16 650  0       Heart $x Diseases $x Patients $x Rehabilitation.
 17 650  0       Exercise tests.
 18 650  2       Exercise Therapy
 19 650  2       Exercise Test
 20 650  2       Exertion
 21 710 20       American College of Sports Medicine. $w cn
 22 710 21       American College of Sports Medicine. $t Guidelines for
graded exercise testing and exercise prescription. $w cn
```

Example 6.23. Record (a), created prior to AACR 2, has a corporate body as main entry and is cuttered accordingly. Record (b) represents a later edition cataloged under AACR 2 with title main entry. The cutter is for title. The subject headings, however, have been revised on both records to match the latest form.

concerns the policy, begun in 1973, of assigning one cutter to be used for all publications entered under a particular corporate heading that have been assigned the same classification number.[9] The cutter is assigned disregarding all subheadings. The only distinction between call numbers for monographs on a particular subject entered under one corporate name is the addition of a date, and if dates are the same, addition of work letters to the date (see Examples 6.24 and 6.25, page 206). This part of the call number has traditionally served as the distinction between call numbers for *editions* of a work; but with this practice, it distinguishes between works of a parent corporate body. No attempt is made to draw together editions of a work. The only distinction between call numbers for serials in this situation is the addition of a work letter to the cutter (see Example 6.26, pages 207-8). If a library wishes to keep editions together, it is forced to abandon LC's call number for items with corporate main entries and assign its own cutter numbers. Let us say, for example, that a work first appears in 1973 and is assigned the call number

> H9000.4
> .O73
> 1973a

When the second edition appears in 1987, it may be assigned the call number

> H9000.4
> .O73
> 1987b

In the intervening years between editions, works entirely unrelated to the first one may have been assigned:

H9000.4	H9000.4	H9000.4	H9000.4	H9000.4	
.O73	.O73	.O73	.O73	.O73	etc.
1973b	1974	1974a	1974b	1975	

Even if a library decides to accept LC's system, it can be difficult to do so, because local original catalogers who are cuttering for a corporate heading have no way of guessing what cutter will be assigned by LC to that heading in that specific classification. Probably the best solution to the original cataloging dilemma is to use the practice followed before 1973 in which each work of a corporate heading was given a distinctive cutter. The one being assigned by the local cataloger is just one more of those distinctive cutters.

Record (a)

```
OCLC: 12612045      Rec stat: c Entrd: 850904       Used: 871009
Type: a Bib lvl: m Govt pub: f Lang:  eng Source:   Illus:
Repr:     Enc lvl:     Conf pub: 0 Ctry:  dcu Dat tp: m M/F/B: 10
Indx: 1 Mod rec:     Festschr: 0 Cont:
Desc: a Int lvl:     Dates: 1985,9999
  1 010        85-19854//r87
  2 040        DLC $c DLC $d GPO $d m/c
  3 043        n-us---
  4 050  0     Z695 $b .L695 1985
  5 051        Z663.78 $b .S65 1985 $c Copy 3.
  6 082  0     025.4/7 $2 19
  7 074        820-A
  8 086  0     LC 26.8/4:985 $z LC 30.25:Su 1/985
  9 090           $b
 10 049        YCLM
 11 110 20     Library of Congress. $b Subject Cataloging Division. $w cn
 12 245 10     Subject cataloging manual : $b subject headings / $c
Subject Cataloging Division, Processing Services.
 13 250        Rev. ed.
 14 260  0     Washington : $b Library of Congress, $c 1985-
 15 300        1 v. (loose-leaf) ; $c 28 cm.
 16 500        Includes index.
 17 610 20     Library of Congress. $b Subject Cataloging Division. $x
Handbooks, manuals, etc. $w cn
 18 650  0     Subject cataloging $x Handbooks, manuals, etc.
 19 650  0     Subject headings, Library of Congress $x Handbooks,
manuals, etc.
```

Record (b)

```
OCLC: 6719034       Rec stat: c Entrd: 850906       Used: 871006
Type: a Bib lvl: m Govt pub: f Lang:  eng Source:   Illus:
Repr:     Enc lvl:     Conf pub: 0 Ctry:  dcu Dat tp: s M/F/B: 10
Indx: 0 Mod rec:     Festschr: 0 Cont:
Desc: a Int lvl:     Dates: 1986,
  1 010        85-600211//r87
  2 040        DLC $c DLC $d MBU $d m/c
  3 019        12586525
  4 020        0844405108
  5 050  0     Z695 $b .L695 1986
  6 051        Z663.78 $b .S8 1986 $c Copy 3.
  7 082  0     025.4/9 $2 19
  8 086  0     LC 26:7:10/v.1-2
  9 096        Z 695 L697L 1986
 10 090           $b
 11 049        YCLM
 12 110 20     Library of Congress. $b Subject Cataloging Division. $w cn
 13 245 10     Library of Congress subject headings / $c Subject
Cataloging Division, Processing Services.
 14 250        10th ed.
 15 260  0     Washington : $b Library of Congress, $c 1986.
 16 300        2 v. (xxxi, 3543) ; $c 31 cm.
 17 500        Incorporates material through December 1984.
 18 650  0     Subject headings, Library of Congress.
 19 650  2     Subject headings
```

Example 6.24. The LC call numbers for these two works have identical classification and cutter numbers because they are works on the same subject that are the responsibility of the same corporate body. The result is that the *Subject Cataloging Manual* is shelved between editions of *LCSH*, to the confusion of librarians and library science students, alike! (It will be noted that LC remedied the problem for their own shelves when they assigned call numbers to their "Copy 3" of each title, as given in the 051 field.)

Record (a)

```
OCLC: 803321        Rec stat: c Entrd: 740114        Used: 870917
Type: a Bib lvl: m Govt pub:      Lang:  eng Source:    Illus:
Repr:     Enc lvl:   Conf pub: 0 Ctry:  fr  Dat tp: s M/F/B: 00
Indx: 0 Mod rec: m Festschr: 0 Cont: bs
Desc:     Int lvl:   Dates: 1973,
   1 010        73-180578//r85
   2 040        DLC $c DLC $d m.c.
   3 015        F***
   4 020        9264111050
   5 050 0      HD9000.4 $b .073 1973
   6 082        338.1/3
   7 090        $b
   8 049        YCLM
   9 110 20     Organisation for Economic Co-operation and Development. $w
cn
  10 245 14     The formation of food prices and their behaviour in times
of inflation.
  11 260 0      [Paris] $b Organisation for Economic Co-operation and
Development, $c 1973.
  12 300        123 p. $c 24 cm.
  13 350        $2.50 (U.S.)
  14 440 0      Agricultural products and markets
  15 504        Includes bibliographical references.
  16 650 0      Food industry and trade.
  17 650 0      Agricultural prices.
  18 650 0      Food prices.
```

Record (b)

```
OCLC: 760008        Rec stat: c Entrd: 740910        Used: 870720
Type: a Bib lvl: m Govt pub:      Lang:  fre Source:    Illus:
Repr:     Enc lvl: J Conf pub: 0 Ctry:  fr  Dat tp: s M/F/B: 00
Indx: 0 Mod rec: m Festschr: 0 Cont: s
Desc:     Int lvl:   Dates: 1973,
   1 010        74-172241
   2 040        DLC $c DLC $d OCL
   3 015        F***
   4 019        789267
   5 020        9264010920
   6 041 0      engfre
   7 050 0      HD9000.4 $b .073 1973a
   8 082        338.1
   9 090        $b
  10 049        YCLM
  11 110 20     Organisation for Economic Co-operation and Development. $w
ln
  12 245 10     Food consumption statistics, 1955-1971. $b Statistiques de
la comsommation des denr'ees alimentaires.
  13 260 1      Paris, $c 1973.
  14 300        xx, 290 p. $c 32 cm.
  15 350        $7.50 (U.S.)
  16 500        English and French.
  17 650 0      Food $x Statistics.
  18 740 1      Statistiques de la consommation des denr'ees alimentaires.
```

Example 6.25. The LC call numbers for these two works are identical, with the exception of the work letter "a" attached to the date of the call number in Record (b).

Record (a)

Canada. Parliament. Special Joint Committee on Canada's International Relations.
Minutes of proceedings and evidence of the Special Joint Committee of the Senate and of the House of Commons on Canada's International Relations = Procès-verbaux et témoignages du Comité mixte spécial du Sénat et de la Chambre des communes sur les relations extérieures du Canada. —
— Ottawa : Queen's Printer for Canada : Available from the Canadian Govt. Pub. Centre,

v. ; 27 cm.

Description based on: 33rd Parliament, 1st session, issue no. 11 (July 26,

(Continued on next card)

86-648056
AACR 2   MARC-S

[8610]

Canada. Parliament. Special Joint Committee on Canada's International Relations. — Minutes of proceedings and evidence of the Special Joint Committee of the Senate and of the House of Commons on ...   (Card 2)

1985); title from cover.
English and French.
Running title: Canada's international relations   —Relations extérieures du Canada

1. Canada—Foreign relations—1945-   —Periodicals.   I. Title.   II. Title: Procès-verbaux et témoignages du Comité mixte spécial du Sénat et de la Chambre des communes sur les relations extérieures du Canada.   III. Title: Canada's international relations.   IV. Title: Relations extérieures du Canada.

F1034.2.C273a   327.71'005—dc19   86-648056
                                                    AACR 2   MARC-S

Library of Congress   [8610]

Example 6.26. These records represent two different serial works coming out of different committees of Canada's Parliament. The only difference in LC call numbers between the two is the addition of work letters "a" and "b" to the cutter number. Record (b) is shown on page 208.

Record (b)

Canada. Parliament. House of Commons. Standing Committee on External Affairs and International Trade.
    Minutes of proceedings and evidence of the Standing Committee on External Affairs and International Trade = Procèsverbaux et témoignages du Comité permanent des affaires étrangères et du commerce extérieur. — 33rd Parliament, 1st session, issue no. 1 (April 14, 1986)- — Ottawa : Queen's Printer : Available from the Canadian Govt. Pub. Centre, 1986-

    v. ; 27 cm.

    Title from cover.
    English and French.
    Continues in part the Minutes of proceedings and evidence of the Standing

(Continued on next card)

86-645565
AACR 2   MARC-S

[8707]

Canada. Parliament. House of Commons. Standing Committee on External Affairs and International Trade. — Minutes of proceedings and evidence of the Standing Committee on External Affairs and International Trade ...   1986-
(Card 2)

Committee on External Affairs and National Defence and the Minutes of proceedings and evidence of the Standing Committee on Finance, Trade and Economic Affairs.

    1. Canada—Foreign economic relations—Periodicals.   2. Canada—Foreign relations—1945-   —Periodicals.   I. Title.   II. Title: Procès-verbaux et témoignages du Comité permanent des affaires étrangères et du commerce extérieur.

F1034.2.C273b   327.71'005—dc19   86-645565
AACR 2   MARC-S

Library of Congress   [8707]

Example 6.26 *(continued)*.

Translations

Cuttering of translations by LC presents some problems for the library using retrospective copy. Current practice seems relatively stable. Some parts of the classification schedules, especially in literature, dictate the treatment of translations. Other classifications, however, do not, so they are handled through the cutter number. With the exception of corporate body publications, which are treated in the same way as editions with corporate body authors discussed above, translations are given the cutter of the original edition with numbers added according to the following scheme:[10]

.x	Original work (x represents cutter assigned to the original)
.x12	Polyglot
.x13	English translation
.x14	French translation
.x15	German translation
.x16	Italian translation
.x17	Russian translation
.x18	Spanish translation

Only some of the main languages are listed. Other languages are fitted in alphabetically. For example, Danish could be given .x12; Japanese could be .x16 if .x17 were already used for Russian, or .x17 if .x16 were already used for Italian or some other language; Swedish could be .x18 or .x19, depending upon what was already used; and Ukrainian could be .x19. It would depend upon what languages were represented already. If LC does not own the original when they are classifying a translation, they determine what the number for the original would be and then add to it from the above scheme.

The scheme is only a guide, but it has been fairly closely followed since 1970. It has not always been followed, however, when a work has been translated into many languages. Before the late 1950s when this scheme was conceived, and currently for any work translated into many languages, a system of successive cutter numbering has been used. For example, the original could be assigned the cutter .C68 and translations could be assigned .C69, .C7, .C72, .C73, etc. Also, before 1970, the "1" was sometimes omitted when using the table; so that the original work could be assigned .C53, while its German translation might have been given .C535 instead of .C5315, and the Spanish translation might have been assigned .C538 rather than .C5318.

Another problem in using retrospective translation copy is that LC did not, in the past, assign a number for the original if they did not own it. They simply cuttered the translation like any other work. If a library that owns such a translation and uses LC's number then receives the original, the cutter for the original will have to be an adjusted form of that for the translation (e.g., translation .C3; original .C29) or the translation must be reclassified.

All these variations mean that if a library considers consistency important in the treatment of translations, it must cutter older titles locally rather than relying on LC's number. Use of LC's cutters, however, usually results in translations and originals being shelved together, if one can accept the inconsistencies. One constant problem, of course, is the local assignment of cutters to items that LC has not yet cataloged. It is sometimes difficult to adjust the cutter and at the same time second-guess what LC will do. The current method is easier to work with because if one knows, for example, that LC has assigned .C815 to a Greek translation, .C8 can then be given locally to the original, or .C813 can be given to the English translation.

Cuttering of Successive Entry Serials

If a library catalogs serials according to the practice of making a new catalog record when a title changes rather than keeping the catalog record for the entire serial under latest entry, LC's method of cuttering successive entries may cause some problems. If the serial does not change in subject content at the time of the entry change, and if it continues numbering as if there had been no change, the call number remains exactly the same (see Example 6.27). Continuous numbering in such a case could mean consecutive years (as in an annual) as well as consecutive numbers, letters, etc.[11] Some libraries cannot accept this because their shelflists or their online catalogs require that every catalog record bear a unique call number. In such a situation it may be necessary to add a digit to the cutter for each entry change that occurs. For example, the second title in Example 6.27 could be assigned the call number UF533.D461. It is possible to avoid having to alter the cutter by providing a message such as "For later volumes see next record" in the shelflist for each entry that has a successive entry following it in the shelflist. The successive entries may in turn be identified as such, so that it is clear why there are two or more entries in the shelflist with identical call numbers. If a serial begins new numbering with a changed title, LC assigns a new call number. If the subject content has remained the same, the new call number will not differ in classification, but will have a different cutter (see Example 6.28, page 213).

Record (a)

Defense systems management review. v. 1-3, no. 3; winter 1976-summer 1980.

ₜFort Belvoir, Va., Defense Systems Management College; for sale by the National Technical Information Service, Springfield, Va.ₜ

3 v. ill. 27 cm.

Quarterly.

"Distribution of this publication is controlled. Inquiries concerning distribution, or proposed articles, should be addressed to the Editor."

Disseminates information concerning new developments and effective actions taken relative to the management of defense systems programs and defense systems acquisition.

(Continued on next card)

77-648728
MARC-S

77ₜ8607ₜ

Defense systems management review ... (Card 2)

Continued by: Concepts (Fort Belvoir, Va.) ISSN 0279-6759, autumn 1980.
Supt. of Docs. no.: D 1.53:
GPO: Item 310-H
ISSN 0363-7727 = Defense systems management review.

1. Munitions—United States—Management—Periodicals. 2. United States. Dept. of Defense—Management—Periodicals. 3. Weapons systems—Management—Periodicals. I. Defense Systems Management College. II. United States. Dept. of Defense.

UF533.D46   355.8'2'0973   77-648728
MARC-S

Library of Congress   77ₜ8607ₜ

Example 6.27. When a new catalog record is made for a changed serial title, LC determines whether the new serial has the same subject content as the old serial. If so, *and* if the serial continues the previous numbering, the same call number is assigned to the new title, shown in Record (b) (page 212), as was assigned to the previous title, shown in Record (a).

Record (b)

Concepts (Fort Belvoir, Va.)
Concepts : the journal of defense systems acquisition management. — Vol. 3, no. 4 (autumn 1980)-v. 5, no. 4 (autumn 1982) — Fort Belvoir, Va. : Defense Systems Management College, ₍1980₎-1982.

v. : ill. ; 25 cm.

Quarterly.
Disseminates information concerning new developments and effective actions taken relative to the management of defense systems programs and defense systems acquisition.
Continues: Defense systems management review.
Supt. of Docs. no.: D 1.53:

(Continued on next card)

81-645840
AACR 2   MARC-S

₍8410₎

Concepts (Fort Belvoir, Va.) — Concepts ...   ₍1980₎-1982. (Card 2)

GPO: Item 310-H
ISSN 0279-6759 = Concepts (Fort Belvoir, Va.)

1. United States—Armed Forces—Procurement—Periodicals.   2. United States—Armed Forces—Management—Periodicals.   3. United States—Armed Forces—Weapons systems—Periodicals.   I. Defense Systems Management College.

UF533.D46   355.8'2'0973   81-645840
AACR 2   MARC-S

Library of Congress   ₍8410₎

Example 6.27 *(continued)*.

Record (a)

Journal of library automation. v. 1-14; Mar. 1968-Dec. 1981.
ₜChicagoₙ American Library Association.

14 v. ill. 26 cm.

Quarterly.
Official publication of the Information Science and Automation Division of the American Library Association, 1968-77; of the Library and Information Technology Association of the ALA, 1978-81.
Absorbed: JOLA technical communications, Mar. 1973 ISSN 0021-3748.
Continued by: Information technology and libraries, ISSN 0730-9295.
ISSN 0022-2240 = Journal of library automation

1. Libraries—Automation—Periodicals.   I. American Library Association. Information Science and Automation Division.   II. Library and Information Technology Association (U.S.)
ₜDNLM: 1. Automatic Data Processing—periodicals.   2. Information Systems—periodicals.   3. Libraries—periodicals.   Z 699.A1 J86ₙ

Z678.9.A1J68   025'.001'8   68-6437
                                                         MARC-S

Library of Congress   ₜ8801r82ₙrev

Record (b)

Information technology and libraries. — Vol. 1, no. 1 (Mar. 1982)-
— ₜChicago, IL : Library and Information Technology Association, c1982-

v. : ill. ; 24 cm.

Quarterly.
Title from cover.
Official publication of the Library and Information Technology Association.
Continues: Journal of library automation.
ISSN 0730-9295 = Information technology and libraries.

1. Information science—Periodicals.   2. Libraries—Automation—Periodicals.   I. Library and Information Technology Association (U.S.)
ₜDNLM: Z 699.A1 J86ₙ

Z678.9.A1I53   82-645170

                          025.3'028'54—dc19
                                              AACR 2   MARC-S
Library of Congress   ₜ8706ₙ

Example 6.28. This example shows a title change in which the numbering began anew with the new title. The LC call numbers have different cutters.

Addition of Dates and/or Volume Numbers
to Call Numbers

The last part of an LC call number may be the cutter, or a date or volume number (or both) may be added. When using LC's call numbers in a local library, there are cases where it may be desirable to delete or change what LC has used, or where it is necessary to add one of these notations when LC has not.

Dates

Beginning in April 1982, LC began adding the date of imprint to the call numbers for all monographs, with only a few rare exceptions.[12] Prior to that time dates were added or not added for a variety of reasons. For example, dates have traditionally been used to distinguish between editions. Before dates were added to call numbers for all monographs, the call number for a first edition often did not have a date, but that for a subsequent edition did (see Example 6.29). Records for many monographs cataloged before 1982 do not have dates appended to call numbers. Most libraries continue to use those older call numbers even though they are not consistent with current practice because using them will not result in shelflist conflicts, there will be more consistency between libraries in a network, and it is then not necessary to teach copy catalogers how to choose which date should be added.

The dates added to call numbers are sometimes modified with letters. When two or more editions are published in the same year, a letter is added to the date as can be seen in Example 6.29. When the only imprint date available is one in which only the decade or century has been surmised, the beginning year of the decade or century in question is used, and a "z" is appended to it (see Example 6.30, page 216). For a photocopy or facsimile, the date of the original followed by the letter "a" is used. As mentioned earlier, subsequent works of the same corporate body falling in the same classification use the date followed by letters starting with "a". Finally, there are cases where classification schedules call only for subarrangement by date. In these cases, also, work letters are added to the date (see Example 6.31, page 216).

Record (a)

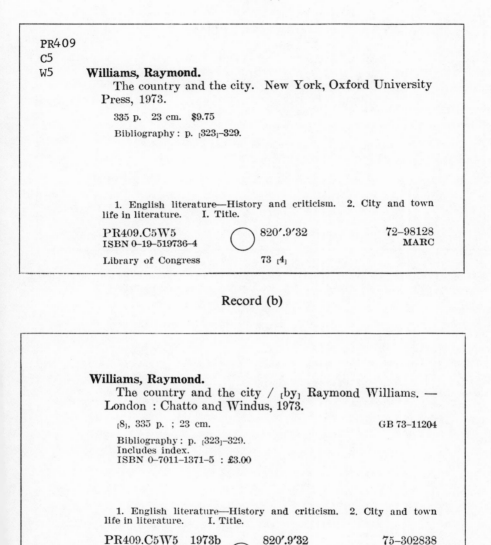

PR409
C5
W5 **Williams, Raymond.**
The country and the city. New York, Oxford University
Press, 1973.

335 p. 23 cm. $9.75

Bibliography : p. ₁323₁–329.

1. English literature—History and criticism. 2. City and town
life in literature. I. Title.

PR409.C5W5   820'.9'32   72–98128
ISBN 0–19–519736–4   MARC

Library of Congress   73 ₁4₁

Record (b)

Williams, Raymond.
The country and the city / ₁by₁ Raymond Williams. —
London : Chatto and Windus, 1973.

₁8₁, 335 p. ; 23 cm.   GB 73–11204

Bibliography : p. ₁323₁–329.
Includes index.
ISBN 0–7011–1371–5 : £3.00

1. English literature—History and criticism. 2. City and town
life in literature. I. Title.

PR409.C5W5 1973b   820'.9'32   75–302838
                                           MARC

Library of Congress   75

Example 6.29. Prior to 1982 LC monograph call numbers often did not have a date appended, as shown in Record (a). However, then, as now, if two or more editions were published the same year, as were the two editions represented in this example, the call numbers for the second and following editions were appended with the publication date plus a letter beginning with "b", as shown in Record (b).

Rittner, Gerhard, comp.
   Fröhlicher Kreis : Tanzrädlein, Volks- und Gemeinschaft-
stänze / hrsg. von Gerhard Rittner ; [musikalisch durch-
gesehen und gesetzt von Konrad Scheierling ; graphische
Gestaltung von Hildegard Hoefer]. — 1. bis 3. Aufl. —
München : V. Höfling Verlag, [195–?]

   55 p. : ill. ; 24 cm.

   Melodies with chord symbols ; in part with words.
   Includes directions for the dances.

   1. Folk dancing.   2. Dance music.   I. Title.

   GV1743.R57   1950z   75–572550

   Library of Congress   75

Example 6.30. When only the decade or century is known or guessed, the LC call number is appended with the first year of the decade or century followed by "z".

Record (a)

```
OCLC: 1218835        Rec stat: n Entrd: 750213        Used: 870521
Type: a Bib lvl: m Govt pub:     Lang:  eng Source:    Illus:
Repr:    Enc lvl:    Conf pub: 0 Ctry:  txu Dat tp: s M/F/B: 10
Indx: 1 Mod rec:     Festschr: 0 Cont: b
Desc: i Int lvl:     Dates: 1974,
 1 010       75-303128
 2 040       DLC $c DLC $d m.c.
 3 043       n-us---
 4 050 0     CS71.T827 $b  1974b
 5 082       929/.2/0973
 6 090       $b
 7 049       YCLM
 8 100 10    Trimble, David B., $d 1922- $w cn
 9 245 10    Hiestand family of Page County, Virginia / $c David B.
Trimble.
10 260 0     [San Antonio? Tex. : $b s.n., $c 1974]
11 300       314 p. ; $c 23 cm.
12 504       Includes bibliographical references and index.
13 600 30    Trimble family.
14 600 30    Hiestand family.
15 600 30    Boehm family.
```

Example 6.31. There are cases where the LC classification schedules themselves call for distinguishing between works only by adding a date to the call number. Records (a) and (b) in this example represent not editions of a work, but entirely different works that are on the same subject.

Record (b)

```
OCLC: 1218829        Rec stat: n Entrd: 750212        Used: 860516
Type: a Bib lvl: m Govt pub:      Lang:  eng Source:    Illus:
Repr:     Enc lvl:    Conf pub: 0 Ctry:  txu Dat tp: s M/F/B: 10
Indx: 1 Mod rec:      Festschr: 0 Cont: b
Desc: i Int lvl:    Dates: 1974,
   1 010        75-303120
   2 040        DLC $c DLC $d m.c.
   3 043        n-us---
   4 050 0      CS71.T827 $b   1974c
   5 082        929/.2/0973
   6 090         $b
   7 049        YCLM
   8 100 10     Trimble, David B., $d 1922- $w cn
   9 245 10     Southwest Virginia families / $c David B. Trimble.
  10 260 0      [San Antonio? Tex. : $b s.n., $c 1974]
  11 300        364 p. ; $c 23 cm.
  12 504        Includes bibliographical references and index.
  13 600 30     Trimble family.
  14 600 30     Buchanan family.
  15 600 30     Crockett family.
```

Example 6.31 *(continued)*.

There were cases in the past where editions were distinguished other than by the addition of dates. For example, when the edition was a multivolume work with an imprint date covering more than one year, LC assigned successive cutter numbers instead of adding the earliest volume's date as is done now (see Example 6.32, below and page 218). A copy cataloger who is expected to notice situations

Record (a)

```
OCLC: 939041         Rec stat: n Entrd: 731001        Used: 870922
Type: a Bib lvl: m Govt pub:      Lang:  eng Source:    Illus: cfh
Repr:     Enc lvl:    Conf pub: 0 Ctry:  enk Dat tp: m M/F/B: 10a
Indx: 0 Mod rec: m Festschr: 0 Cont:
Desc:   Int lvl:    Dates: 1967,1969
   1 010        67-83396//r852
   2 040        DLC $c DLC $d m.c.
   3 015        B67-6659 (v. 1)
   4 020        0049210106 (v. 1) varies
   5 050 0      B1649.R94 $b A32
   6 082        192 $a B
   7 090         $b
   8 049        YCLM
   9 100 10     Russell, Bertrand, $d 1872-1970. $w cn
  10 245 04     The autobiography of Bertrand Russell.
  11 260 0      London, $b Allen & Unwin, $c 1967-69.
  12 300        3 v. $b front., 8 plates (incl. ports.), facsim. $c 24 1/2
cm.
  13 505 0      [1] 1872-1914.--v. 2. 1914-1944.--v. 3. 1944-1967.
```

Example 6.32. In the past, LC used successive cutter numbers to distinguish between editions that consisted of multivolume sets published in more than one year, as shown in Records (a), (b) and (c) (page 218), rather than using dates.

Record (b)

```
OCLC: 228124        Rec stat: c Entrd: 720125        Used: 871009
Type: a Bib lvl: m Govt pub:       Lang:  eng Source:    Illus: ach
Repr:       Enc lvl: I Conf pub: 0 Ctry:  mau Dat tp: r M/F/B: 10a
Indx: 0 Mod rec: m Festschr: 0 Cont:
Desc:       Int lvl:      Dates: 1967,9999
   1 010          67-14453//r
   2 040          DLC $c URB $d SER $d OCL
   3 050 0        B1649.R94 $b A33
   4 082          828/.9/1203
   5 090           $b
   6 049          YCLM
   7 100 10       Russell, Bertrand, $d 1872-1970. $w 1n
   8 245 14       The autobiography of Bertrand Russell.
   9 250          [1st American ed.]
  10 260 0        Boston, $b Little, Brown $c [1967-
  11 300              v. $b illus., facsim., ports. $c 24 cm.
  12 500          "An Atlantic Monthly Press book."
  13 505 0        [1] 1872-1914.--[2] 1914-1944.
  14 870 19        $j 100/1 $a Russell, Bertrand Russell, $c 3d earl, $d
1872-1970.
```

Record (c)

```
OCLC: 2616382       Rec stat: c Entrd: 710623        Used: 870108
Type: a Bib lvl: m Govt pub:       Lang:  eng Source:    Illus: ac
Repr:       Enc lvl: 1 Conf pub: 0 Ctry:  onc Dat tp: m M/F/B: 10a
Indx: 0 Mod rec: m Festschr: 0 Cont:
Desc:       Int lvl:      Dates: 1968,9999
   1 010          68-141055//r85
   2 040          DLC $c DLC $d m.c.
   3 015          C***
   4 050 0        B1649.R94 $b A34
   5 082          192 $a B
   6 090           $b
   7 049          YCLM
   8 100 11       Russell, Bertrand, $d 1872-1970. $w cn
   9 245 04       The autobiography of Bertrand Russell.
  10 260 0        Toronto, $a Montreal, $b McClelland and Stewart, $c [1968-
  11 300          v.     $b illus., ports. $c 24 cm.
  12 350          $8.95 Can. (v. 2)
  13 505 1            --v. 2. 1914-1944.
```

Example 6.32 *(continued)*.

where the local library cannot follow LC's policies in assignment of call numbers, must know, in this case, that the omission of dates was not an error. If a local library decides not to accept such call numbers, a decision should be made about whether to add a date to the call number that LC has already adjusted for the new edition, or to find the first edition call number and add the date to it.

One problem with the addition of dates arises for local libraries because until April 1988 LC assigned the printing date rather than the date of first appearance of the edition of the work (see Example 6.33; see also the discussion of LC's use of printing dates in description in Chapter 2). This means that for books cataloged by LC before April 1988, if the book acquired in the local library is printed in a different year or shows no printing date at all, the call number date on the LC copy matches nothing in the local book being cataloged. One solution is to change the date in such call numbers to the date of first publication of that edition (LC's current practice) and add a letter to the date if necessary to distinguish it from another edition of the work published the same year.

Young, Louise B
    Power over people / Louise B. Young. — London ; New
York : Oxford University Press, 1973, 1974 printing.

    xi, 234 p. : ill. ; 21 cm. — (A Galaxy book ; 413)   GB***

    Bibliography: p. 225–234.
    ISBN 0–19–501830–3 : $2.95 (U.S.)

    1. Electric power-plants—Environmental aspects.   I. Title.

    TD195.E4Y68   1974   363.3   72–91020
                                                       MARC

    Library of Congress   ◯ 74 [4]

Example 6.33. The printing date was used in the call number of this work. If the local
library acquires a copy of the book that shows no printing date or else is printed in a
different year, the call number date then matches neither the copyright date nor the local
copy's printing date. (Under current practice LC would use "1973" as the date in this call
number.)

Libraries may also find that reprint and facsimile call numbers require
decisions. For a work judged to be a facsimile, it has already been pointed out
that the imprint date of the original plus the letter "a" is added. If, however, it is
judged to be a reprint, the date of reprinting is added. One problem with this is
that the criteria for determining facsimiles versus reprints at LC have changed
over the years. Until the adoption of ISBD at LC, an item was treated as a
facsimile if it called itself a facsimile or, occasionally, if the cataloger added a
note calling it a facsimile. This policy meant that many items that were really
reprints were given the date of the original with an "a" added. Following adoption
of ISBD, facsimile editions were redefined to include only those that have as their
"chief purpose to simulate the physical appearance of the original work."[13]
AACR 2 adds to that definition, "as well as to provide an exact replica of the
text."[14] The descriptive cataloger thus may identify as reprints those that describe
themselves as facsimiles but that by the current definition really are not. As a
result, the number of original dates followed by "a" has diminished greatly.
However, there has been increased use of dates followed by "a" for other
purposes. One example is LC's policy for cuttering works entered under
corporate headings, discussed above in the section on LC cuttering. Another is
the cuttering of conferences, symposia, etc., discussed below. If a copy cataloger
is expected to make any change in the date added to a call number by LC, or is
expected to add dates as well as cutters to incomplete bracketed classification
numbers, LC's use of dates and letters following dates must be fully understood.

Call numbers assigned to monographic publications of conferences,
symposia, etc., also have dates added. If the main entry is the name of the
conference, the date given is the date the conference was held instead of the
imprint date. If the main entry is the title, the imprint date is used, and the

following discussion of date letters does not apply. No date is added to the call number for serials. Serials are cuttered to precede individual monographic publications of a conference. Current practice, which began in 1970, is to distinguish between individual monographic publications by adding consecutive letters to the date in the call number. Publications of the conference are given letters "a" through "y", while "z" is reserved for books about the conference, individual books being given za, zb, etc.[15] (This "z" has no relationship to the earlier-mentioned appending of "z" to dates for decades or centuries when date is uncertain.)

Prior to 1970, practice for conference call numbers was to assign letters, each of which meant a certain kind of material. For example, the date alone signified proceedings, "a" meant papers read, "d" meant committee discussions, and so on. Call numbers assigned under these two systems do not conflict with each other and may be used side by side, although some libraries may be bothered by the inconsistency. The main problem is that if libraries try to follow LC's current practice when assigning local numbers, there is no way to guess which letter LC will use, since it is determined by accident of the sequence in which the items are shelflisted at LC. Even if the local library knows the classification, cutter, and date that will be assigned, it cannot know the letter; therefore, a system must be devised to avoid conflicts. For example, one could add "x" following the letter: 1975dx. Adding "x" to the cutter, however, could separate it from other publications of the conference, unless "x" is ignored in filing and shelving except where necessary to distinguish between duplicate numbers (see Example 6.34).

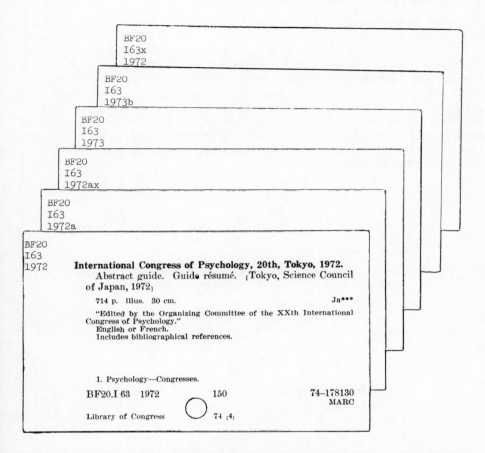

Example 6.34. In order to avoid conflict in assigning work letters to dates on call numbers of conferences, it is necessary to devise some method of assigning local letters. If it is deemed important to keep publications of the same conference together, then the adjustment must be made to the date, not to the cutter. In this example, the item with "x" affixed to the date files with other 1972 publications, but the item with "x" affixed to the cutter files after the 1973 publications and would file farther and farther away as more dates were added.

Volume Numbering

Numbering at the end of a call number usually signifies analytic cataloging. There are exceptions, however. For example, music call numbers often end with a number (see Example 6.35). Copy catalogers must be able to recognize the difference. In the case of analytics, a call number ending with numbering can be used only if the decision has been made to classify that series or set together. If the decision has been made to classify the parts of the series separately, a different call number must be assigned. On the other hand, the music call number that ends in a number but which is not an analytic can be used without change as the call number for that work.

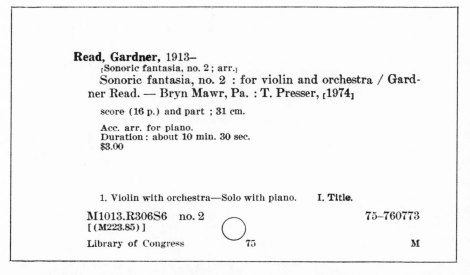

Read, Gardner, 1913–
 ₁Sonoric fantasia, no. 2 ; arr.₁
 Sonoric fantasia, no. 2 : for violin and orchestra / Gardner Read. — Bryn Mawr, Pa. : T. Presser, ₁1974₁

 score (16 p.) and part ; 31 cm.

 Acc. arr. for piano.
 Duration : about 10 min. 30 sec.
 $3.00

 1. Violin with orchestra—Solo with piano.   I. Title.

 M1013.R306S6   no. 2   75-760773
 [(M223.85)]
 Library of Congress   75   M

Example 6.35. Numbering at the end of some call numbers is called for by the classification scheme and does not signify analytic cataloging.

An analytic LC call number often can be recognized by the fact that the last cutter is for the series of which it is a part, not for the main entry of the individual work being cataloged. This cutter is followed by some device showing that the piece is only one part of a larger entity, usually numbering given in the language of the piece (see Example 6.36). Despite the fact that many people will not comprehend the meaning of some of the terms used, many libraries will want to go along with LC's policy. Others prefer to try to translate these terms into equivalent English terms. When the pieces use a numeral only, LC precedes the numeral in the call number with "no." or "vol." (see Example 6.17 on page 193). The device also can be a year, which is then often accompanied by a number (see Example 6.37, pages 224-25).

Record (a)

Chalard, Jacques.
Contribution à l'étude du Namurien du bassin houiller du Nord de la France / par Jacques Chalard. — ₍Douai₎ : Houillères du bassin du Nord et du Pas-de-Calais, 1960.

299 p., ₍12₎ leaves of plates : ill. ; 32 cm. & atlas (13 p., 66 fold. leaves of plates : ill.). — (Études géologiques pour l'Atlas de topographie souterraine : III, Stratigraphie ; fasc. 1)

Bibliography : p. ₍287₎-291.

1. Geology, Stratigraphic—Carboniferous. 2. Geology—France.
I. Title. II. Series.

QE640.E87 fasc. 1   551.7′00944 s   75-500660
[QE671]   [551.7′5′0944]   MARC
Library of Congress   75 ₍2₎

Record (b)

Van De Laar, Aart J   **M**
Report of an evaluation survey of university level manpower supply and demand in selected African countries, by Aart, J. M. van de Laar. ₍Addis Ababa?₎, United Nations₎ 1970.
1 v. (various pagings) 29 cm. (₍United Nations. Document₎ E/CN.14/WP.6/32)
At head of title : United Nations, Economic and Social Council, Economic Commission for Africa.
Includes bibliographical references.
1. Education—Economic aspects—Africa. 2. Manpower policy—Africa. 3. College graduates—Employment—Africa. I. United Nations. Economic Commission for Africa. II. Title. III. Series.

JX1977.A2   E/CN.14/WP.6/32   73-158491
[LC67.A33]   300′.8 s   [331.1′26]   MARC

Library of Congress   73 ₍4₎

Example 6.36. The language used in the work cataloged is used for the numbering in analytic call numbers. The work in Record (a) is called *fascicule*. "E/CN.14/WP.6/32" indicates the numbering on Record (b). The call number for Record (c) (page 224) uses "jild-i 1," although few library shelvers or filers in the United States would comprehend its meaning in a call number; on the other hand, users searching for volumes of this specific series would understand, since that is the terminology a citation would probably have.

Record (c)

Malbūbī, Muḥammad Bāqir.
(Māh-i mubārak-i Ramaẓān)

ماه مبارك رمضـان ، بقلم محمد باقر ملبوبى . قم ، كتابفروشى

خرد ‏[1962] 1341.

336 p. 25 cm. (**His** 1 جلد ، الوقايع و الحوادث)

1. Islamic Empire — Anecdotes, facetiae, satire, etc. 2. Months.
I. Title. II. Series: Malbūbī, Muḥammad Bāqir. al-Vaqāyi' va al
-ḥavādis, jild-i 1.

DS36.855.M35 jild-i 1   74–200006

Library of Congress   74 ‏[2]   N E

Example 6.36 *(continued)*.

Record (a)

```
OCLC: 678270        Rec stat: n Entrd: 730717      Used: 861029
Type: a Bib lvl: m Govt pub:   Lang:  eng Source:   Illus: f
Repr:   Enc lvl:   Conf pub: 1 Ctry:  wb  Dat tp: s M/F/B: 00
Indx: 0 Mod rec: m Festschr: 0 Cont: b
Desc:   Int lvl:   Dates: 1967,
   1 010      73-164479
   2 040      DLC $c DLC $d m.c.
   3 041 0    engfregerita
   4 050 0    N21 $b .I585 1964
   5 082      709/.4
   6 090      $b
   7 049      YCLM
   8 111 20   International Congress of the History of Art $n (21st : $d
1964 : $c Bonn) $w mn
   9 245 10   Stil und Uberlieferung in der Kunst des Abendlandes.
  10 260 0    Berlin, $b Gebr. Mann, $c 1967.
  11 300      3 v. $b plates. $c 24 cm.
  12 490 1    Akten des 21. Internationalen Kongresses fur
Kunstgeschichte in Bonn 1964
  13 500      English, French, German, or Italian.
  14 504      Includes bibliographical references.
  15 505 0    Bd. 1. Epochen europaischer Kunst.--Bd. 2. Michelangelo.--
Bd. 3. Theorien und Probleme.
  16 650 0    Art $x Congresses.
  17 830 0    International Congress of the History of Art. Acts, $v
1964.
  18 872 29   $j 111/1 $a International Congress of the History of Art,
$n 21st, $c Bonn, $d 1964.
```

Example 6.37. Occasionally the device that shows that a work is cataloged as part of a larger entity is simply the year. Record (a) shows such a case. "N21.I585" is the LC classification and cutter number assigned to the serial whose title is "Acts." A date used in this way to distinguish among volumes of a series may be accompanied by numbering, as shown on Record (b).

Record (b)

```
OCLC: 6761697          Rec stat: c  Entrd: 790925        Used: 850930
Type: a  Bib lvl: m  Govt pub:     Lang:  swe Source:     Illus:
Repr:      Enc lvl:    Conf pub: 0 Ctry:  sw  Dat tp: s M/F/B: 10
Indx: 0  Mod rec: m  Festschr: 0 Cont:
Desc: i  Int lvl:    Dates: 1974,
   1 010          75-570529//r852
   2 040          DLC $c DLC $d m.c.
   3 020          9138021986 : $c kr24.00
   4 043          e-sw---
   5 050 0        J406 $b .R15 1974:103
   6 090          $b
   7 049          YCLM
   8 110 10       Sweden. $b 1972 ars skatteutredning. $w cn
   9 245 10       Skatteomlaggning, 1976 : $b delbetankande / $c av 1972
ars skatteutredning.
  10 260 0        Stockholm : $b LiberForlag/Allmanna forlaget, $c 1974.
  11 300          163 p. ; $c 25 cm.
  12 490 1        Statens offentliga utredningar ; 1974 : 103
  13 650  0       Income tax $z Sweden $x Law.
  14 650  0       Pensions $x Law and legislation $z Sweden.
  15 830  0       Statens offentliga utredningar ; $v 1974:103.
```

Example 6.37 *(continued)*.

The device used for indicating that an item is part of a larger entity, which causes perhaps the most difficulty, is the abbreviation "subser.", used when the title being cataloged is a series within a serial (see Example 6.38, page 226). The result is identical call numbers for all subseries that occur in a given serial. "Subser." has been used only since the early 1970s. Formerly, subseries were given the call number of the serial of which they were part, with no further designation. This, of course, resulted not only in identical call numbers for all subseries, but also in numbers that were identical to the main series as well (see Example 6.39, pages 227-28). A multivolume monographic set that is part of a serial, however, is given the number of the first volume of the title followed by "etc." (see Example 6.40, page 229). The problem with all of these identification devices for subseries is that the only way a patron can locate these volumes is through the volume numbers at the end of the series statement in the description. Yet, for the items identified "subser.", LC does not even print the *first* volume number as part of the series statement. Any library that wants to help patrons find these items must add volume numbers to the series statement every time another volume of that subseries or set arrives in the library.

Record (a)

Australia. Dept. of Science. Antarctic Division.
Report—Department of Science, Antarctic Division.

Canberra, Govt. Printer.

    v. illus. 25 cm. annual. (Parliamentary paper)

1. Research — Antarctic regions — Periodicals. 2. Research — Australia—Periodicals.   I. Series: Australia. Parliament. The records of the proceedings and the printed papers.

J905.L3 subser.	328.94'01 s	74–646984
[Q180.A6]	[507'.2'0989]	MARC-S
Library of Congress	74 [2]	

Record (b)

Australia. Dept. of Supply.
Annual report.
Canberra, Commonwealth Govt. Print. Off.

    v. illus. 25 cm. (Parliamentary papers)

Report year ends June 30.

1. Australia—Armed Forces—Supplies and stores—Periodicals. 2. Australia. Dept. of Supply.   I. Series: Australia. Parliament. The records of the proceedings and the printed papers.

J905.L3 subser.	328.94'01 s	73–644600
[U265]	[355.6'21'0994]	MARC-S
Library of Congress	74 [2]	

Example 6.38. The current practice of identifying call numbers for series within a serial is to use "subser." following the call number. This results in identical call numbers for different works as is illustrated by the two cards in this example. Since the volume numbers are not included either in the series statement or in the call number, it would be extremely difficult for anyone to find these reports among all the other papers of this serial.

Record (a)

U. S. *National Bureau of Standards.*
Special publication. no. 1–
Washington, For sale by the Supt. of Docs., U. S. Govt.
Print. Off., 1918–

no. in   v. illus., maps. 16–72 x 112 cm.

No. 54 not published .
Title varies: No. 1–294, Miscellaneous publication (varies slightly).
Some numbers issued under a variant form of name: Bureau of Standards.
Some numbers issued in revised editions; some accompanied by supplements.
Some numbers are charts.

Record (a) *[continued]*

U. S. *National Bureau of Standards.*   **Special publication.**
1918–   (Card 2)

"About Dec. 1918 the Standards Bureau began this series entitled Miscellaneous publications, of which no. 21 was the first actually issued bearing series title and number. Number 21 was followed by nos. 1 and 19. Beginning with 39 the series title and numbers appear regularly on the publications ... Other numbers preceding 39 were arbitrarily assigned ... to publications issued before Dec. 1918 and which therefore do not bear series titles nor numbers."—Catalogue of the public documents of the Sixty-fourth Congress ... 1915/17, p. 2006–2097.

1. Weights and measures—U. S.—Collected works.   I. U. S. National Bureau of Standards. Miscellaneous publication.

QC100.U57   51–39294

Library of Congress   (r70b2) rev

Example 6.39. Before the early 1970s, call numbers for series within a serial bore no special designation. As a result, there were call numbers identical not only to those of other series—Records (b) and (c) (page 228)—but also to that of the main serial—Record (a) above.

Record (b)

U. S. National Bureau of Standards.
NBS frequency and time broadcast services. 1960–

Washington, For sale by the Supt. of Docs., U. S. Govt.
Print. Off.
  v. illus. 26 cm. (**Its Special publication, 236**)
  Title varies: 1960–   Standard frequency and time services of
the National Bureau of Standards (varies slightly).—
NBS standard frequency and time services.
  1. Time signals. 2. Frequency standards.   I. U. S. National
Bureau of Standards. Standard frequency and time services of the
National Bureau of Standards. II. U. S. National Bureau of Standards. NBS standard frequency and time services. III. Title.   (Series: U. S. National Bureau of Standards. Special publication, 236)

QC100.U57   384.54′4   61–60260

Record (c)

U. S. *National Bureau of Standards. Office of Standard
Reference Materials.*
  Standard reference materials. 1–
Washington, For sale by the Superintendent of Documents,
U. S. Govt. Print. Off., 1964–

  no. illus. 26 cm. ([U. S.] National Bureau of Standards.
Miscellaneous publication 260)

  Includes an unnumbered publication issued Oct. 1965 but intended
as the beginning of the series.

  1. Materials—Standards—Collected works.   I. Title.   (Series:
U. S. National Bureau of Standards. Special publication 260)

QC100.U57   64–62975

Library of Congress   [r70c2]   rev

Example 6.39 *(continued)*.

```
OCLC: 1258107      Rec stat: c Entrd: 750224        Used: 870825
Type: a Bib lvl: m Govt pub:     Lang:  fre Source:  Illus:
Repr:     Enc lvl:  Conf pub: 0 Ctry:  gw  Dat tp: m M/F/B: 10
Indx: 0 Mod rec:    Festschr: 0 Cont: b
Desc: i Int lvl:    Dates: 1974,1980
   1 010        75-501075//r82
   2 040        DLC $c DLC
   3 015        GFR***
   4 020        3770519167 (v. 2)
   5 050 0      P25 $b .I53 Bd. 21, etc. $a P121
   6 082        410
   7 090          $b
   8 049        YCLM
   9 100 10     Larochette, J.
  10 245 13     Le langage et la r'ealit'e / $c Joe Larochette.
  11 260 0      Munchen : $b W. Fink, $c 1974-1980.
  12 300        2 v. ; $c 21 cm.
  13 440   0    Internationale Bibliothek fur Allgemeine Linguistik ; $v
Bd. 21, 43
  14 504        Includes bibliographical references.
  15 505 0      1. Probltemes de linguistique g'en'erale et de linguistique
romane.--2. L'emploi des formes de l'indicatif en francais.
  16 650  0     Linguistics.
  17 650  0     Romance languages.
```

Example 6.40. This example shows cataloging for a multivolume monographic set that is part of an analyzed serial. The fact that there is more than one volume for this title is shown in the LC call number by "etc."

Completion of Partial LC Call Numbers and Related Problems

Established procedures must exist to handle the following situations: the assignment of call numbers locally, the lack of a call number on copy, presence of a bracketed classification number only, the decision to use an LC suggested alternative, or use of a local alternative.

When there is no call number at all, someone must assign one locally, if the item is to be retrievable by call number.

When there is *only* a bracketed number, the copy cataloger must first determine whether it is a complete call number or a classification number only. As can be seen in Example 6.41 (pages 230-31), an LC classification number can look like a complete call number. The classification number "E269.N3" has been assigned to many items about Blacks in the American Revolution. In order to make it into a complete call number, a cutter for Brannon should be added, and under current practice, the date "1974" should be added as well. The fact that the cutter does not match the main entry is a clue that the call number is not complete, but as has been seen from earlier examples, the last cutter does not always match the main entry in *complete* call numbers. Copy catalogers should probably be taught to refer such cases to someone with classification and call number experience.

When LC-suggested alternatives are given *in addition* to LC's complete call number, the bracketed alternatives are classification numbers only and must be completed locally, if chosen for local use. Occasionally LC acquires a "Copy 2" or later copy to which it assigns a different call number that is a complete call number and that may be used as is by the local library. It does not appear in brackets, but is identified as "— —— Copy 2" on cards, and is in field 051 of a MARC record (see Example 6.42, page 231, and Example 6.24 on page 205).

Record (a)

Learning Technology Incorporated.
How to talk with children about sex, by Learning Technology Incorporated, in consultation with Ronald K. Filippi. New York, Wiley ₁1973₁

vi, 122 p. illus. 28 cm.

1. Sex instruction.   I. Title.

[HQ57.L35]   612.6′007   72–8334
ISBN 0–471–52025–X   MARC

Library of Congress   73 ₁4₁

Record (b)

Brannon, Jean Marilyn.
Blacks in the American Revolutionary War. ₁Phonodisc₁ Conceived, narrated & recorded by Jean Brannon. Folkways FD 5576. ₁1974₁
2 s. 12 in. 33⅓ rpm.

Descriptive notes and text of the recording (₁6₁ p., ₁12₁ columns) inserted in slipcase.
CONTENTS: Introduction, Phillis Wheatley.—Crispus Attucks.—Black soldiers.—Black valor.—Black sailors.—Black achievers.

1. United States — History — Revolution, 1775–1783 — Negroes.
2. United States—History—Revolution, 1775–1783—Negro troops.

[E269.N3]   74–750612

Library of Congress   75   MN

Example 6.41. LC decided not to keep the edition represented by Record (a). It was cataloged, however, as a service to LC copy users, and was given in brackets the complete call number it would have been assigned if retained by LC. The bracketed number on Record (b), however, is not a complete call number. "N3" is a subject notation and an author cutter still needs to be added in order to make it a complete call number. Record (c) shows that when Record (b) was input into OCLC, the incomplete call number was not recognized as such. "E269.N3" should all be in subfield "a" of the 050 field, as subfield "b" is meant to contain the specific item cutter.

Record (c)

```
OCLC: 2878783        Rec stat: c Entrd: 770411        Used: 870923
Type: i Bib lvl: m Lang:  eng Source:    Accomp mat: bj
Repr:      Enc lvl: K Ctry:  nyu Dat tp: s MEBE: 1
           Mod rec: m Comp:  zz Format: n Prts: n
Desc:      Int lvl:   LTxt:  h Dates: 1974,
  1 010        74-750612
  2 040        DLC $c IEP
  3 007        s $b d $d b $e m $f m $g e $h n $i n
  4 043        n-us---
  5 045        v7v8
  6 050 1      E269 $b .N3
  7 092        973.34 $b B
  8 090        $b
  9 049        YCLM
 10 100 10     Brannon, Jean Marilyn.
 11 245 10     Blacks in the American Revolutionary War. $h [Sound
recording] $b  / $c Conceived, narrated & recorded by Jean Brannon.
 12 262        $b Folkways $c FD 5576. $d [1974]
 13 305        1 disc. $c 33 1/3 rpm. $e mono. $b 12 in.
 14 500        Descriptive notes and text of the recording ([6] p., [12]
columns) inserted in container.
 15 504        Includes bibliography.
 16 505 0      Introduction, Phillis Wheatley.--Chrispus Attucks.--Black
soldiers.--Black valor.--Black sailors.--Black achievers.
 17 651 0      United States $x History $y Revolution, 1775-1783 $x
Negroes.
 18 651 0      United States $x History $y Revolution, 1775-1783 $x Negro
troops.
```

Example 6.41 *(continued)*. (It will be noted that under current practice the subject subdivision "Negroes" should be changed to "Afro-Americans" in Records (b) and (c); however, LC decided not to make this change on pre-MARC records because of the large numbers of cards involved. Local libraries using such records must make the change themselves.)

United Nations. Dept. of Economic and Social Affairs.
   Implementation of the international development strategy.
New York, United Nations, 1973.

   2 v. illus. 29 cm. (United Nations. ₁Document₁ E/5267-E/5267/add.
1) (United Nations. ₁Document₁ ST/ECA/178-ST/ECA/178/add. 1) $6.50

   United Nations publication. Sales no: E.73.II.A.2.₁-3₁
   Includes bibliographical references.
—— ——Copy 2.   HD82.U482 1973

   1. Economic policy. 2. Developing countries—Economic policy. I. Title.
II. Series. III. Series: United Nations. Document ST/ECA/178-ST/E-
CA/178/add.1.

JX1977.A2ST/ECA/178   300'.8 s   74-185110
₁HD82₁   ◯   ₁338.91₁   MARC

   Library of Congress   76₁r85₁rev

Example 6.42. If a library chooses not to use the analytic call number for this item, it may use the number that LC assigned its Copy 2: "HD82.U482 1973." It is a complete call number.

Use of local alternatives to LC call numbers requires that copy catalogers be able to recognize all LC numbers that cannot be used as they appear. Then there should be written instructions recording local decisions made and explaining in what way the numbers will be changed. If such policies and instructions are not written and accessible (i.e., indexed in some fashion), there can be no hope for consistency in handling such call numbers.

If a library does not assign its LC numbers locally but purchases card sets with numbers already assigned, it should have made known its requirements to the commercial firm that supplies the cards. If the firm cannot supply cards with numbers desired locally, then the local library must either accept what can be supplied or arrange to receive certain types of cards with no call number supplied. In the latter case the library must be equipped with sufficient staff to supply its own call numbers. There is also the option of changing call numbers supplied by the outside source, but this is costly since supplied numbers would have to be erased on every card of the set before the locally assigned number could be typed.

DEWEY DECIMAL CLASSIFICATION

Some of the decisions that confront the library that uses Dewey classification differ from those faced by LC classification users. The source of the Dewey number has a definite impact on the decisions to be made. If a library has contracted with an outside source to provide precataloged books with preprinted cards and spine labels, undoubtedly it has decided to accept the numbers assigned. If a library purchases preprinted cards from a company that offers choices on such things as classification of fiction or biography, or length of numbers, this library, too, probably has decided to accept the numbers with only a minimum amount of change. Libraries that choose to purchase card sets without classification numbers in the margin and libraries that use Library of Congress cataloging (either card format or MARC format) as the basis for their catalog records must decide whether to accept or reject Dewey classification numbers suggested on that copy.

Accepting the Dewey Number
Given on Outside Copy

For most libraries using Dewey when LC copy is used, the only decision is whether to accept or reject suggested numbers. There are no decisions involving acceptance of suggested cutter numbers because none are given. Some commercial firms do offer to print one or more letters of the author's (or biographee's) name below the call number in the margin (see Example 6.43, pages 233-34). A library may choose to have this done, if it has decided to accept that form as a complete call number or to use the letter as the basis for adding a cutter to complete the call number. When member input copy is used from a network, there may be no Dewey number at all, or there may be a complete Dewey call number. In the latter case, there must be a policy about acceptance of cutter numbers, as well as classification numbers.

Record (a)

```
309.23
B          Berger, Peter L
               Pyramids of sacrifice: political
           ethics and social change [by] Peter L.
           Berger. New York, Basic Books [1975,
           c1974]
               xiv, 242 p. 25 cm.

               Includes bibliographical references.


               1.Underdeveloped areas--Economic
           policy. 2.Underdeveloped areas--Social
           conditions. 3.Political ethics. 4.
           Right and left (Political science) I.
           Title.
       HC59.7.B38804                     309.2'3'091724
       ISBN 0-465-06778-6                        74-78304
                                    014 114        LC-MARC
```

Record (b)

```
629.44   Billings, Charlene W
Bi            Space station; bold new step beyond
         earth.  Dodd 1986
            64p   illus

            Describes the design, functions, and
         possible methods of construction of the
         permanently manned space station pro-
         posed by NASA.

         1.Space stations I.Title
```

Example 6.43. Some commercial producers of card sets offer call numbers with one or more letters of the name of the author—Records (a), (b), and (c) (page 234)—or biographee—Record (d) (page 234)—under the Dewey number.

Record (c)

```
637
GIB        Gibbons, Gail.
                The milk makers / by Gail Gibbons.
             - New York : Macmillan ; London :
             Collier Macmillan, c1985.
                [32] p. : col. ill. ; 21 x 26 cm.

                SUMMARY: Explains now cows produce
             milk and how it is processed before
             being delivered to stores.




                1. Dairying.  2. Dairy cattle.
             3. Milk.  4. Cows.  I. Title.

637                                    84-20081 /AC MARCIVE®
ISBN 0-02736640-5
```

Record (d)

```
355.331 Mellor, William Bancroft.
  0924      General Patton: the last cavalier.
Pat       Putnam [1971]
             191 p. illus., port.
          (Lives to remember)

          A biography of the controversial com-
          mander of the Third Army in World War
          II.




             1.Patton, George Smith, 1885-1945—Juv.
          lit.  2.Patton, George Smith, 1885-1945.
          3.Military bio      graphy. I.Title
          355.3:31.0924        E745.P3M39 1971
          CARD CORPORATION OF AMERICA ©        75-108745
```

Example 6.43 *(continued)*.

The classification numbers supplied by commercial firms may be assigned wholly by the firms or may be based on the number suggested by LC, or a combination thereof. In all cases, however, the numbers are devised from the edition of Dewey or Abridged Dewey in effect at the time of cataloging and they are not reclassed to reflect changes in a later edition. Whether or not the numbers can be used just as they appear depends on the library's philosophy regarding whether call numbers should serve a location or collocation function. For example, a copy cataloger may have two books in the area of mathematics, one on trigonometry and one on topology. The number 514 could be suggested as a classification number for both of these, the former according to the 17th edition of Dewey and the latter according to the 18th edition of Dewey. In a library with open stacks, a mathematician might be disturbed, to say the least, to find books on topology and trigonometry together in 514 while also finding some books on trigonometry in 516.24 (18th edition) and some books on topology in 513.83 (17th edition).

Many libraries, of course, already have on their shelves numbers representing many more than two editions of Dewey. Through the 14th edition new numbers were almost always expansions or reductions of numbers with the same meaning as before, but later editions have contained many relocations. Even a relatively new library with numbers on the shelf from only one or two editions must cope with suggested Dewey numbers from several editions on retrospective copy if it intends to use outside copy for any older material it acquires.

Besides the changes that occur when a new edition appears, there may be changes between editions; these are first instituted by the Library of Congress and are usually followed in time by other commercial producers of cards. An example of this is the change made in January 1975, when LC began use of area notation −41 instead of −42 for British Isles, United Kingdom, Great Britain, while area notation for Scotland was changed to −411. Notation −42 is now assigned only to England and Wales. This was a logical and long overdue change, since the former arrangement implied that Great Britain was part of Scotland. It affects libraries of all sizes, however, because in the 900s, the basic three-digit history number for Great Britain appears on new cataloging as 941 and on old copy as 942. Scotland's history number is 941.1 instead of 941; so a library that uses the new numbers without reclassifying the old has quite a mixture in the 941 area. For larger libraries, which subdivide many subject areas by country, the area notation change can affect virtually every classification number in Dewey. However, with fewer materials at each spot, it is hoped that in most cases items stand so close together that the change is hardly noticed.

These changes were incorporated along with others into the 19th edition of Dewey, which was not implemented until 1980. More recent changes between editions have been the implementation of the expanded revision of "301-307 Sociology" in January 1982 and of the "004-006" schedule for computer science in May 1985. Such implementations are to be the norm from now on, with new editions of Dewey being issued farther apart.

Accepting Dewey Numbers
Assigned by LC

Because LC copy from MARC tapes, CDS Alert Service, cards, or *NUC* is the basis for cataloging by many commercial sources and by individual libraries, the idiosyncracies of Dewey numbers suggested by LC are discussed in this section.

As with LC class numbers, Dewey numbers assigned by LC are occasionally in error. In the study of LC cataloging mentioned earlier, Dewey numbers were checked against the third summary in the Dewey schedules that gives the meanings of numbers up to the decimal point. Again, the purpose was to find numbers that were completely out of place. It was found that 98 percent were fine at this level.[16] Examples 6.44 and 6.45 illustrate the kinds of errors found. But when one considers that 1,808 records were examined and 37 errors were found, one has to consider the relative value to the patron of holding up 1,771 items with good numbers in order to find 37 bad ones.

An understanding of how the Decimal Classification Division at LC operates is a useful asset for anyone who uses LC's suggested numbers. One of the pertinent points is that Dewey numbers are currently being assigned to only about 40 percent of all titles cataloged, the same percentage of titles that were assigned Dewey numbers in the mid-1970s. There was a concerted effort in the late 1970s and early 1980s to increase the proportion of titles being assigned Dewey numbers, and the percentage gradually increased to 70 percent by 1985, but budget cuts and procedure changes have caused it to decrease again. Another useful piece of information is that Dewey numbers on CIP entries, as well as on the finished cataloging available on cards, MARC, or in *NUC*, are those assigned from proofs, galleys, or front matter. The finished book is not checked by the Dewey Classification Division upon arrival of the book at LC, unless it was especially requested. It is also useful to know that there is little attempt to assign the same classification number to editions of a work (see Examples 6.4, 6.5, 6.32, and 7.7).

```
OCLC: 8239179      Rec stat: c Entrd: 820706        Used: 820917
Type: a Bib lvl: m Govt pub:     Lang:  eng Source:    Illus:
Repr:     Enc lvl:    Conf pub: 0 Ctry:  enk Dat tp: s M/F/B: 10
Indx: 1 Mod rec:     Festschr: 0 Cont:
Desc: a Int lvl:     Dates: 1981,
   1 010       81-193154
   2 040       DLC $c DLC
   3 015       GB***
   4 020       0631129332 : $c L6.50
   5 039 0     2 $b 3 $c 3 $d 3 $e 3
   6 043       ew------ $a e-uk---
   7 050 0     HC241.25.G7 $b R87
   8 082 0     331.24/22 $2 19
   9 090          $b
  10 049       IVEA
  11 100 10    Rutherford, Malcolm.
  12 245 10    Can we save the Common Market? / $c Malcolm Rutherford.
  13 260 0     Oxford : $b Blackwell, $c 1981.
  14 300       115 p. ; $c 23 cm.
  15 440  0    Mainstream series
  16 500       Includes index.
  17 610 20    European Economic Community $z Great Britain.
```

Example 6.44. This example shows a typographical error in the Dewey number. There is no "331.2422" in the 19th edition of Dewey. The correct number is "341.2422."

```
OCLC: 8081355        Rec stat: c Entrd: 820517        Used: 870903
Type: a Bib lvl: m Govt pub:      Lang:  eng Source:     Illus: a
Repr:      Enc lvl:      Conf pub: 0 Ctry:  enk Dat tp: s M/F/B: 10
Indx: 1 Mod rec:      Festschr: 0 Cont: b
Desc: a Int lvl:      Dates: 1981,
   1 010        82-107536//r842
   2 040        DLC $c DLC $d m/c
   3 015        GB***
   4 019        9038894
   5 020        0198545150
   6 039 0      2 $b 3 $c 3 $d 3 $e 3
   7 050 0      S593.2 $b .S6 1982 Suppl.
   8 082 0      552/.5 $2 19
   9 090        $b
  10 049        IVEA
  11 100 10     Smart, Peter. $w cn
  12 245 10     Electron microscopy of soils and sediments : $b examples /
$c Peter Smart and N. Keith Tovey.
  13 260 0      Oxford : $b Clarendon Press ; $a New York : $b Oxford
University Press, $c 1981.
  14 300        viii, 177 p. : $b ill. ; $c 25 cm.
  15 504        Bibliography: p. [170]-171.
  16 500        Includes indexes.
  17 650 0      Soil micromorphology.
  18 650 0      Sediments (Geology)
  19 650 0      Electron microscopy $x Technique.
  20 650 0      Soil micromorphology $x Atlases.
  21 650 0      Sediments (Geology) $x Atlases.
  22 700 10     Tovey, N. Keith. $w cn
```

Example 6.45. This example shows an error in content analysis. The Dewey number given, "552.5," stands for sedimentary rocks. The number would more properly be "631.43," which stands for soil physics and includes the topic "soil micromorphology."

The fact that not all LC cataloging receives Dewey numbers affects libraries more or less according to their size. LC assigns Dewey numbers to all CIP items, all English language items, and many items in the other major languages. Others are worked in as time permits. For many medium-sized and small libraries, the CIP and English items represent a high percentage of their acquisitions. Larger libraries and special libraries acquire and catalog foreign language materials, technical reports, retrospective materials, and nonprint items, for which a substantial percentage of the LC copy does not include a suggested Dewey number. Since most of this copy does have an LC call number or suggested LC class number, libraries may derive some benefit from locating that number in the LC classification schedules and then attempting to locate the comparable classification in Dewey. This at least saves "starting from scratch" in supplying Dewey numbers.

When the Dewey number is present, the length of the suggested number presents a situation that requires a policy decision in each library. If allowances for number-building provided by Dewey are followed, the length of the number can render it practically unusable (see Example 6.46, page 238). Since 1967, LC has provided guides to meaningful shortening of such numbers in the form of *prime marks*.[17] These appear as accent marks (') on cards and as slashes (/) in MARC records. With the adoption of the 11th abridged edition, the practices of segmentation were changed so that most of the time the first segment is the same as the number provided in the abridged edition. Most of the commercial firms that provide card sets based on LC copy allow libraries the option of cutting

```
OCLC: 1255586          Rec stat: c Entrd: 750226        Used: 820820
Type: a Bib lvl: m Govt pub:      Lang: eng Source:     Illus:
Repr:     Enc lvl:     Conf pub: 0 Ctry: enk Dat tp: s M/F/B: 10
Indx: 0 Mod rec:       Festschr: 0 Cont: s
Desc: i Int lvl:       Dates: 1974,
  1 010      75-304866//r82
  2 040      DLC $c DLC $d m.c.
  3 015      GB***
  4 041 0    eng $b fregerita
  5 043      e-------
  6 050 0    HD9696.C63 $b E75 1974c
  7 082      380.1/45/62138195094
  8 090      $b
  9 049      YCLM
 10 110 20   Frost & Sullivan. $w cn
 11 245 14   The European market for small business systems, 1974 to
1983.
 12 260 0    London : $b Frost & Sullivan, $c 1974.
 13 300      2 v. ; $c 29 cm.
 14 500      Added t.p. in French, German, and Italian.
 15 500      On spine: Small business computers in Europe.
 16 500      Summaries in French, German, and Italian; text in English.
 17 650 0    Computer industry $z Europe.
 18 650 0    Small business $x Data processing.
 19 740 1    Small business computers in Europe.
```

Example 6.46. Dewey numbers can be incredibly long. This one has 14 digits past the decimal point. However, *prime marks* show where the number can be meaningfully shortened for use in small libraries (first prime) or medium-sized libraries (second prime). Prime marks can also be used to shorten numbers in large libraries that have small or medium-sized collections in a particular subject area.

numbers at one of the primes. There is usually a limit, however, on the length of number they will print (e.g., one company cuts back to the closest prime if the number goes more than nine digits past the decimal point). Some libraries themselves set a limit on the number of digits that a cataloger may assign, or choose one of the primes at which they will usually cut a number. There may also be variation within a library on use of standard subdivisions to lengthen a number. In subject areas where the collection is very small, for example, material may not have further breakdown by form or place. In other areas, however, size of the collection may demand as much subdivision as possible.

There are fewer suggested alternatives to Dewey numbers on LC copy than there are for the LC classification numbers, but several past policies and practices necessitate decisions before older numbers are used. Between 1952 and 1958 numbers were given for both the 14th and 15th editions when they differed other than in length. The 15th edition number was starred.[18] This is the only time numbers from more than one edition have been given. Between 1961 and 1969 the *only* number given on many of the nonfiction materials for young people was assigned from the Abridged Dewey and designated "j". Now numbers are assigned from the latest full edition (see Example 6.47). During the time that the Abridged Edition was not a literal abridgement (editions 9 and 10), if the Abridged Dewey number was not the same as the digits to the left of the first prime, the abridged one was given in brackets following the regular one.[19] In 1968 LC began providing Dewey numbers for adult fiction for the benefit of those libraries that do not place all fiction in one section. At about the same time, they began to identify fiction for children with "[Fic]" and books for very young children with "[E]" (meaning Easy) (see Example 6.48, page 240).

Record (a)

The **Ants;** adapted from text by Edward S. Ross. Photos. by Edward S. Ross. Illus. by Robert Borja. ₁New ed.₁ Chicago, Childrens Press ₁1967, ᶜ1961₁

63 p. col. illus. 29 cm. (Adventures in nature and science)

Original issued under the same title by Colorslide nature and science program, Columbia Record Club, New York, 1961.
Bibliography : p. 60.

1. Ants—Juvenile literature. ɪ. Ross, Edward Shearman, 1915–

QL565.A65 1967   j 595.79   67–20109

Library of Congress   ₁12₁

Record (b)

Wheelus, Doris.
Baton twirling : a complete illustrated guide / Doris Wheelus. — New York : Lion Books, ₁1974, c1975₁

viii, 124 p. : ill. : 26 cm.

SUMMARY : Diagrams and text instruct the beginning, intermediate, and advanced twirler in the various techniques of baton twirling.
ISBN 0–87460–310–2. ISBN 0–87460–311–0 pbk.

1. Baton twirling—Juvenile literature. ₁1. Baton twirling₁
I. Title.

MT733.6.W5   785'.06'7108   74–22050
                                              MARC
                                               A C
Library of Congress   75   MN

Example 6.47. Between 1961 and 1969 Dewey numbers for nonfiction materials for children and young people through age 16 were assigned from the Abridged Dewey and designated "j", Record (a). They are now assigned from the latest full edition of Dewey, Record (b). Libraries wishing to classify them as a separate group must identify them and assign whatever classification or special designation is used locally.

Record (a)

```
OCLC: 1031213        Rec stat: p Entrd: 740808        Used: 870919
Type: a Bib lvl: m Govt pub:    Lang:  eng Source:    Illus: a
Repr:     Enc lvl:    Conf pub: 0 Ctry:  nyu Dat tp: c M/F/B: 00
Indx: 0 Mod rec:     Festschr: 0 Cont:
Desc:     Int lvl: j Dates: 1975,1973
   1 010        74-16386/AC
   2 040        DLC $c DLC $d m.c.
   3 020        0525610081
   4 050  0     PZ7.B75164 $b 014
   5 082        [E]
   6 090         $b
   7 049        YCLM
   8 100 10     Brennan, Nicholas. $w cn
   9 245 10     Olaf's incredible machine.
  10 260 0      [New York] $b Windmill Books $c [1975, c1973]
  11 300        [25] p. $b col. illus. $c 28 cm.
  12 520        When the machine he invents grows so large that it
threatens to take over the world, Olaf decides to get away from it all
in his balloon.
  13 650  1     Pollution $x Fiction.
```

Record (b)

```
OCLC: 1085907        Rec stat: p Entrd: 741005        Used: 870826
Type: a Bib lvl: m Govt pub:    Lang:  eng Source:    Illus:
Repr:     Enc lvl:    Conf pub: 0 Ctry:  pau Dat tp: s M/F/B: 11
Indx: 0 Mod rec:     Festschr: 0 Cont:
Desc: i Int lvl: j Dates: 1975,
   1 010        74-23568/AC
   2 040        DLC $c DLC $d m.c.
   3 020        0664325602
   4 050  0     PZ7.W137 $b Es
   5 082        [Fic]
   6 090         $b
   7 049        YCLM
   8 100 10     Walden, Amelia Elizabeth. $w dn
   9 245 10     Escape on skis / $c Amelia Walden.
  10 260 0      Philadelphia : $b Westminster Press, $c [1975]
  11 300        173 p. ; $c 22 cm.
  12 520        While training for the skiing olympics in Switzerland, Kim
Merrill is caught up in the intrigue surrounding the mysterious
disappearance of her fianc'e.
  13 650  1     Mystery and detective stories.
```

Example 6.48. Catalog records of items for very young children are assigned "[E]" in the Dewey classification field, as shown in Record (a), and fiction records for juveniles are assigned "[Fic]", as shown in Record (b).

As with LC classification, there are some cases where alternative classifications are provided. Since 1965 LC has supplied "[B]" following a subject classification number for biographical material. This was begun because the 17th edition began recommending that biographies be classified with the subject area associated with the biographee, rather than all together in the 920s. Biographies cataloged before 1965 bear 920 numbers[20] (see Example 6.49). Another application of alternative designations is with monographic series, which LC classifies as a set. At the time they started supplying alternative individual title numbers for LC classification (1972), they also began supplying the equivalent Dewey numbers in addition to the number for the series as a whole, which is identified

Record (a)

Eccles, Mark.
  Shakespeare in Warwickshire. Madison, University of Wisconsin Press, 1961.

  vi, 182 p. illus., maps. 23 cm.

  Bibliographical references included in "Notes" (p. ₁145₁–165)

  1. Shakespeare, William—Homes and haunts—Stratford-upon-Avon.
2. Shakespeare, William—Biog.   ɪ. Title.

                                      Full name: Mark Williams Eccles.

  PR2916.E25   928.2   61–5900
  Library of Congress   ₍5₎

Record (b)

Rowse, Alfred Leslie, 1903–
  Shakespeare the man ₁by₁ A. L. Rowse ₁London₁ Macmillan ₁1973₁

  xi, 284 p.   illus.   23 cm.   £4.95   GB***

  Includes bibliographical references.

  1. Shakespeare, William, 1564–1616—Biography.   I. Title.

  PR2894.R67   1973   822.3′3 [B]   73–173726
  ISBN 0–333–14494–5   MARC
  Library of Congress   73 ₍4₎

Example 6.49. Prior to the 17th edition of Dewey in 1965, biographies were given Dewey numbers in the 920s, Record (a). Since 1965 they have been classified in the subject area associated with the biographee and have been accompanied by the alternative designation B], Record (b).

by the letter "s" following it (see Record (a) in Example 6.17 on page 193). The alternative number appears in brackets below the series number on cards and in a second subfield "a" on MARC records. The "s" has been added to the whole series number only since 1969. Before 1959 such numbers were enclosed in parentheses, and between 1959 and 1969 they were not identified. This alternative number may also be followed by "[B]", thus providing two alternative designations to the series number. As with LC classification, most commercial sources of preprinted cards supply the number for the individual title, rather than the number for the series.

In December 1980 LC's Decimal Classification Division began assigning two numbers to works classed in "340, Law."[21] The first number is built by first indicating the branch of law, then the area notation for the jurisdiction, and last the notation for a subdivision of the branch of law. The second number is built according to Option B in Dewey and indicates first the jurisdiction, followed by the branch of law and the subdivision of the branch. If the library believes its users are best served by having works about a branch of law together, the first number should be chosen. If it would be more useful to have works about a particular country or other jurisdiction together, the second number should be chosen. When LC classes a legal series together, there are four Dewey numbers given: the collected set number and the specific analytic number for the first option, and the collected set number and the specific analytic number for Option B.

Because of the nature of LC copy available to Dewey libraries—specifically, the lack of any number at all on much of the copy, the lack of a means of drawing together materials on the same subject, and use of long numbers divided by prime marks—the use of Dewey classification can be quite expensive in terms of time and personnel required to maintain it. Even in a library that sees the call number strictly as a location device, the suggested number often is too long and must be cut, and a number must be supplied when the copy provides no suggested number. As a result, Dewey copy catalogers must be more sophisticated in classification than LC copy catalogers. A Dewey library may need to have a person or group of people responsible for classification of materials with copy; this group of people might be separate from the people who handle the description and entry (and possibly subject headings, although subject headings and classification often go together). Since this separate group of people is often professionally trained, and therefore more highly paid, large libraries that believe themselves to be committed to Dewey and commercial firms that supply Dewey numbers benefitted greatly from the Library of Congress' increase in the percentage of copy being assigned Dewey numbers from the mid-1970s to the mid-1980s, and it is unfortunate that budget cuts have again reduced the percentage.

Local Alternatives to Dewey Numbers

Most of the situations in which local libraries deviate from use of Dewey classification have been mentioned already. The more common ones include placing fiction together in a section given a label "F" or other such designation, and keeping biographies together either in the 920s or labeled "B". Juvenile materials may be marked in a special way above the classification or may not be classified at all.

Some libraries may wish to classify bibliographies with their subject areas instead of all in 016. This is quite easy to do with the suggested bibliography number, since one can simply move the decimal point three places to the right, remove 016 from the front of the number and put it on the end. Also, some libraries may wish to classify all literature of an author together instead of having it separated by form. Such a case requires massive local rewriting of the 800s, but it can be done. Most of the possibilities already mentioned earlier in the section on "Local Alternatives to LC Classification" can also apply in a Dewey library — local history may need expanding, certain numbers may be preferred locally to the one usually used for a subject by the outside cataloging source, and certain series may be locally classified together instead of as separate titles. These types of local differences should be written as policy if the library expects consistency in its cataloging practice.

Completing Dewey Call Numbers

Because all Dewey numbers on LC copy are classification numbers only, and because commercial firms do not offer cutter numbers as part of the call number on preprinted card sets, it is necessary to decide whether a unique call number is required for each item. If it is, procedures must be established for assigning cutters. It must be decided what level of personnel will do it, and any local variations from the standard way of assigning cutter numbers must be identified. In this situation, as well as when Dewey numbers are lacking, the LC call number may be used as a guide. Clues may be derived from LC's cuttering, addition of dates, and part numbers as to the work's relationship to other works or other editions. These then may be incorporated into the complete Dewey call number.

If a unique call number is not required, it must be decided whether a second line is needed to make a call number for each item. If so, then it must be decided whether this will consist of letters of the author's name (or biographee's name, when applicable), and how many letters will be used; or perhaps there is some other device to be used. In general, these decisions must be made before an outside source of copy is chosen, and definitely before preprinted cards are ordered.

SUMMARY

In the area of classification/call numbers, not only is it sometimes undesirable to use copy exactly as it appears, it also is sometimes impossible since no classification may be given. The LC call number sometimes is not complete, and the Dewey number is a complete call number only on commercial preprinted card sets (and then only if unique call numbers for each item are not necessary), or on member copy in a network (and then only if input or updated by a Dewey library). Therefore, many decisions must be made in this area when outside copy is used. The following questions should be considered:

1. Which classification scheme will be used?

2. Is the call number strictly a location device, or does it contribute to collocation by keeping related subject materials together?

   a. If the call number serves as more than a location device, will the classification number be double-checked in the classification schedules or local shelflist, or both?

   b. If call numbers are accepted without any checking, what percentage of duplicate numbers will be acceptable, and will procedures be needed to deal with such duplicates?

3. Is it necessary for each item to have a unique call number?

4. When new sections and/or revisions of the classification scheme appear, will materials already in the library be reclassified?

5. Is it necessary for editions to stand together on the shelf, or for translations to stand next to the original work?

6. Do all items require classification?

7. Do some items require a kind of classification different from the scheme chosen for the majority of the materials?

8. Where alternative classifications are suggested, which classification will be used?

9. Are there situations where local alternatives to the suggested classification are desirable?

10. What type of cuttering, if any, will be used to make a complete call number?

11. Are there situations where classification numbers on copy may be considered unacceptable? If so, what level of personnel will make this judgement?

12. Who may assign classification numbers and/or cutters when they are missing or unacceptable?

13. If the library uses LC classification, have the following questions been considered:

    a. If LC's complete call number is accepted, are there certain situations where the cutter assigned by LC will not be used?

    b. Are there times when a date on an LC call number should be changed locally or when a date should be added to the call number?

    c. Is LC's method of designating analyzed parts of a work in the call number acceptable?

14. If the library uses Dewey classification, have the following questions been considered:

   a. Which edition(s) of Dewey will be accepted locally?

   b. Are there certain revisions of Dewey, such as Phoenix schedules, which will not be accepted?

   c. Will Dewey numbers suggested by LC automatically be cut at one of the prime marks?

NOTES

[1]For example, Paul S. Dunkin, *Cataloging U.S.A.* (Chicago: American Library Association, 1969), 107-12.

[2]Arlene G. Taylor and Charles W. Simpson, "Accuracy of LC Copy: A Comparison between Copy That Began as CIP and Other LC Cataloging," *Library Resources & Technical Services* 30 (October/December 1986): 386.

[3]*Cataloging Service*, bulletin 90 (September 1970): 1.

[4]*Music Cataloging Bulletin* 12 (March 1981): 1.

[5]*Cataloging Service*, bulletin 104 (May 1972): 6.

[6]Ibid., bulletin 113 (Spring 1975): 5-6.

[7]Ibid., bulletin 112 (Winter 1975): 14-15.

[8]*Cataloging Service Bulletin*, no. 12 (Spring 1981): 62.

[9]*Cataloging Service*, bulletin 110 (Summer 1974): 6-8.

[10]Library of Congress, Subject Cataloging Division, *Subject Cataloging Manual: Shelflisting* (Washington, D.C.: Library of Congress, 1987?), G 150: 1-2.

[11]Ibid., G 1000: 1.

[12]*Cataloging Service Bulletin*, no. 19 (Winter 1982): 25-26.

[13]*Anglo-American Cataloging Rules. Chapter 6, Separately Published Monographs* (Chicago: American Library Association, 1974), 114.

[14]*AACR 2*, 566.

[15]*Subject Cataloging Manual: Shelflisting*, G 230: 2, 5.

[16]Taylor and Simpson, "Accuracy of LC Copy," 386.

[17]*Cataloging Service*, bulletin 78 (December 1966): 1-2.

[18]Ibid., bulletin 25 (December 1951): 1.

[19]Ibid., bulletin 86 (January 1969): 2.

[20]Ibid., bulletin 70 (June 1965): 1.

[21]*Cataloging Service Bulletin*, no. 11 (Winter 1981): 104.

NEAR AND CO-OP COPY

INTRODUCTION

In this book, *near copy* has been defined as the copy available from the usual outside cataloging source for some edition of the work other than that owned by the local library. *Co-op copy* has been defined as copy from other than the usual source. As explained earlier, this definition is broader than the traditional one because similar processing decisions are faced whenever outside copy from other than the usual source is integrated into a local catalog.

The preceding chapters have discussed description, choice and form of name and title access points, subject headings, and classification based on the assumption that the copy being used is *exact copy* for the edition of the work in hand and that it came from the usual source. All of the decisions required by use of exact copy are also required when using near and co-op copy, and there are additional questions as well. These fall into broad categories of deciding whether or not near and/or co-op copy will be used and, if so, to what extent. When the copy is obtained through an online cooperative cataloging source, further considerations also come into play. Because there can be a number of differences in use of near and co-op copy, they are discussed separately.

NEAR COPY

There are basically five situations when near copy, but not exact copy, may be available from the usual source of outside copy. All fall under the broad characterization of *differing editions*.

Revised Editions

This category applies to cases where information in a work has been revised, rewritten, updated, or changed from the information that appeared earlier. Such instances often are characterized by an edition statement (e.g., "Second edition," "Completely revised"), but not always. In some cases there is a new copyright date, although this in itself does not necessarily indicate a revised edition. In the case of many government publications that do not have copyright, there is simply another printing date to indicate a revision, although a new printing date in such publications does not always indicate revised material. The cataloging rules in effect when processing later editions often must be consulted in these cases. Other possible characterizations are differences in the physical description (e.g., number of pages in a book, frames in a filmstrip, etc.); new prefatory material; changes of author or editor, or in the order of author's names, etc.; and changes in title.

There are various reasons for the unavailability of exact copy. It may be that the outside source has not acquired and/or cataloged the revised material or the original. This can happen when changes made in the edition seem too slight to warrant new purchase or new cataloging. In the case of suppliers other than LC, the earlier edition may be the one for which copy is not available. If the later edition were cataloged, there would not be enough orders for the cataloging of the earlier edition to justify keeping it in stock. More often, though, the exact copy is not available because the outside source has not *yet* cataloged the item, and the local library may not wish to wait. In such cases, near copy can be used as a basis for local cataloging.

Although the bibliographic utilities have made both co-op and near copy from non-LC libraries more available, there are still types of materials for which even near copy is difficult to find. These include audiovisual materials, computer files, and some music items. The cataloging of special types of materials can be complicated and/or time consuming so that some libraries would rather wait for another library to be the first to catalog the item. Also, given the backlogs in most libraries, and the differences in priorities vis-à-vis processing, there will be times when copy just is not available and must be created by the local library in order to get some items processed.

As the participation of publishers in the CIP program has increased, the percentage of near copy being used for revised editions has decreased, at least for most printed materials. Other materials, such as computer files and audiovisuals, are still not receiving as much attention. For those who order cards, or obtain copy from a source other than online, CIP is of most benefit to those who acquire mainly current materials because much retrospective material does not contain CIP data. In some libraries, regardless of the technical source of copy, items with CIP are processed immediately without waiting for exact copy. This is easiest in libraries where MARC CIP can be found online. In such libraries, MARC CIP is routinely used to process materials because little information is missing from that copy and most utilities require its use rather than creation of a separate record. However, in libraries that reproduce card sets from LC card copy, use of CIP requires typing an entire card set or at least a master; thus, these libraries may use CIP only as a last resort.

When near copy is used for revised editions, many descriptive changes may be required. Usually an edition statement must be added or changed; publication date will differ; and paging usually changes. In addition to these three changes, which almost always occur, there may be changes in title or subtitle. The original author(s) may have been joined or superseded by another. Editors may change. Place and name of publisher might be changed. There may be new illustrations or a change in size. The new edition may be incorporated into or withdrawn from a series. If the title has changed, a note giving the original title would be in order. A multitude of other notes, applicable to the edition in hand but not to the one represented by the near copy, might have to be added (see Example 7.1). If one is physically altering a printed card, as shown in the example, it is necessary to be concerned about space available on the card. For example, when

Record (a)

National Information Center for Educational Media.
    Index to producers & distributors.   2d ed.   Los Angeles,
1973.
    vi, 134 p.   28 cm.

    1. Audio-visual materials—Catalogs.   I. Title.
    LB1043.Z9N3   1973   011   72-190636
                                                              MARC

    Library of Congress   (   ) 74

Record (b)

LB1043
Z9
N3   **National Information Center for Educational Media.**
1975   Index to producers & distributors. 3 d ed.   Los Angeles,
              1975.
              vi, 198 p.   28 cm.

              Cover title: Producers & distributors (non
              -book media).

        1. Audio-visual materials—Catalogs.   I. Title.   II. Title: Pro-
    ducers & distributors (non-book media).
                                                              MARC
        Library of Congress   ( ) 74

Example 7.1. Record (a) shows copy available for the second edition of the *Index*, which
was the nearest copy available at the time the local library wished to catalog the third
edition. Record (b) shows the adaptations necessary to use the near copy. Changes were
required in edition statement, publication date, paging, notes, added entries, and call
number.

copy for the first edition is the near copy being used to catalog a later edition, there may be no room on the copy for an edition area in the correct spot before the publication information, unless the first edition bore an edition statement. To avoid retyping copy that needs only a date and paging change in addition to the edition statement, the library could consider adding the edition statement as a note (see Example 7.2). In an online environment, a new record would be created with little editing involved.

The main entry for a revised edition also may change. When authors' names change order, or when a new author or editor takes over revision of a work, the main entry, as well as the description previously mentioned, may change according to appropriate rules in AACR 2. This often means added entry changes as well. Added entry changes or additions can also occur when there is no main entry change, and such changes must be identified by the person using near copy.

Subjects sometimes change enough between revised editions that the heading assigned to the edition represented by near copy may not be the best available to describe the contents of the edition in hand. This is usually determined by scanning prefatory matter to see whether the current edition's coverage is the same as in other editions. All of the subject heading problems mentioned in Chapter 5 can occur, but the two most apt to apply are out-of-date headings and lack of new headings which did not exist when the near copy was cataloged. The older the near copy, the greater the likelihood of finding outdated, inadequate headings.

Classification numbers may be affected in the same way as subject headings. In addition, libraries that use LC call numbers or Dewey call numbers from a source that cutters for them, will need to adjust the call numbers given on near copy if it is necessary that call numbers be unique. When the call number on the near copy is used as the call number for the revised edition, it will conflict if that number is now or later used for the edition represented by the near copy. The usual change consists of adding or substituting the date of the edition being cataloged (as in Examples 7.1 and 7.2). There may also be a cutter change if the main entry differs and if editions are not to be kept together in the local library. Also, if LC practice is followed, the cutter should be altered for an abridged edition. If the dates of the editions are the same, a letter should be added to the date in the call number.

Record (a)

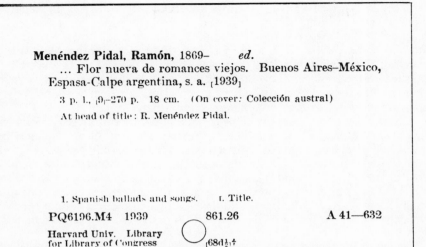

Menéndez Pidal, Ramón, 1869–   *ed.*
   ... Flor nueva de romances viejos. Buenos Aires–México,
Espasa-Calpe argentina, s. a. ₁1939₁

   3 p. l., ₁9₁–270 p. 18 cm. (On cover: Colección austral)

   At head of title : R. Menéndez Pidal.

   1. Spanish ballads and songs.   ɪ. Title.

   PQ6196.M4   1939   861.26   A 41—632

   Harvard Univ.   Library
   for Library of Congress   ₁68d½₁†

Record (b)

PQ6196
M4
1952

Menéndez Pidal, Ramón, 1869–   *ed.*
   ... Flor nueva de romances viejos. Buenos Aires–México,
Espasa-Calpe argentina, s. a., **c1952.**

   250 p.   18 cm. (On cover: Colección austral)

   At head of title : R. Menéndez Pidal.
   9. ed.

   1. Spanish ballads and songs.   ɪ. Title.

   PQ6196.M4   1939   861.26   A 41—632

   Harvard Univ.   Library
   for Library of Congress   ₁68d½₁†

Example 7.2. The nearest official source copy available when cataloging the ninth edition
of this work was copy with no edition statement, Record (a). In order to avoid having to
retype the copy to insert the edition area, the edition statement was added as a note,
Record (b).

Editions Published by Different Publishers

This category covers works whose informational content is unchanged, but which have been published by different publishers. Included are the following cases: a) the same work is published simultaneously in different countries; b) a work has been published in a hard cover edition and another publisher or a branch of the original publisher brings it out in paperback; c) a work has gone into the public domain and several publishers have published editions of it; and d) the government or perhaps a university publishes an item without copyright, which is later published by a commercial publisher.

Exact copy often is not available for one or another of these editions for the same reasons it may not be available for revised editions. Near copy may be the best source of cataloging data; although due to the availability of MARC records from those countries where simultaneous publishing occurs quite frequently, copy for the edition in hand is becoming more readily accessible. Such copy must be treated like co-op copy, however, because its source probably is not the one usually used by the local library, and the cataloging practices can, at times, vary considerably. CIP is not as likely to appear in books from foreign countries, but when it does, it, too, must be treated like co-op copy.

When using near copy for an edition published by a different publisher, the only change needed in description is often in the publication area. This is usually true when two editions of a work are published simultaneously in different countries (see Example 7.3). However, it may also be necessary to make other changes. For example, an edition statement (e.g., "1st American ed.") may be called for. In such a case, the library that reproduces card sets from LC card copy may wish to consider adding it as a note rather than in the edition area, as suggested in the preceding section, in order to avoid retyping most of the description. Conversely, it may be necessary to remove an edition statement (see Example 7.4, page 254). In all these situations it may also be necessary, depending upon the policies of the library, to make changes because of the passage of time and the resultant changes in heading forms, rules, and policies. In Example 7.3, for example, it might be necessary to add Picasso's death date, 1973, to the two headings for his name in the tracing. A uniform title consisting of the original title followed by "English" would also be desired in some libraries. However, adding a uniform title to card copy requires either moving the main entry up a line or typing the uniform title in the upper right corner or elsewhere on the card.

Record (a)

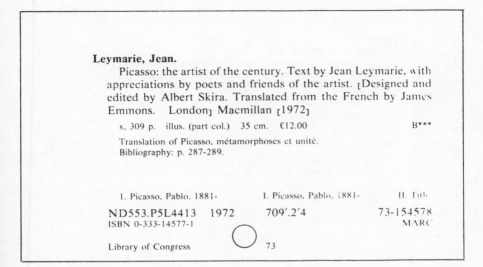

Leymarie, Jean.
　　Picasso: the artist of the century. Text by Jean Leymarie, with appreciations by poets and friends of the artist. [Designed and edited by Albert Skira. Translated from the French by James Emmons.　London] Macmillan [1972]
　　　　x, 309 p.　illus. (part col.)　35 cm.　£12.00　　　　　　B***
　　　　Translation of Picasso, métamorphoses et unité.
　　　　Bibliography: p. 287-289.

　　　1. Picasso, Pablo, 1881-　　　1. Picasso, Pablo, 1881-　　II. Title

　　　ND553.P5L4413　1972　　　709'.2'4　　　　　73-154578
　　　ISBN 0-333-14577-1　　　　　　　　　　　　　　　　MARC

　　　Library of Congress　　　　　　73

Record (b)

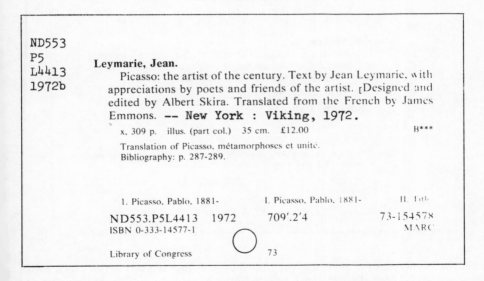

ND553
P5
L4413
1972b

Leymarie, Jean.
　　Picasso: the artist of the century. Text by Jean Leymarie, with appreciations by poets and friends of the artist. [Designed and edited by Albert Skira. Translated from the French by James Emmons. -- New York : Viking, 1972.
　　　　x, 309 p.　illus. (part col.)　35 cm.　£12.00　　　　　　B***
　　　　Translation of Picasso, métamorphoses et unité.
　　　　Bibliography: p. 287-289.

　　　1. Picasso, Pablo, 1881-　　　1. Picasso, Pablo, 1881-　　II. Title

　　　ND553.P5L4413　1972　　　709'.2'4　　　　　73-154578
　　　ISBN 0-333-14577-1　　　　　　　　　　　　　　　　MARC

　　　Library of Congress　　　　　　73

Example 7.3. Editions of this work were published in both London and New York the same year. When the local library acquired the New York edition, the nearest copy available was for the London edition, Record (a). Record (b) shows the required changes in imprint and call number necessary to adapt the near copy to the edition in hand. Other changes might also be required in some libraries. (In the card examples in this chapter, ISBD-style punctuation is used whenever a change being made necessitates using punctuation. Otherwise, punctuation is left as it appears. This is a matter of policy for each library to decide.)

Record (a)

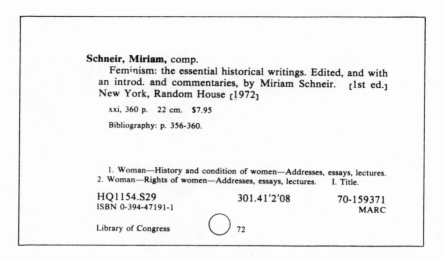

Schneir, Miriam, comp.
  Feminism: the essential historical writings. Edited, and with
an introd. and commentaries, by Miriam Schneir. [1st ed.]
New York, Random House [1972]

  xxi, 360 p.   22 cm. $7.95

  Bibliography: p. 356-360.

  1. Woman—History and condition of women—Addresses, essays, lectures.
2. Woman—Rights of women—Addresses, essays, lectures.   I. Title.

HQ1154.S29   301.41'2'08   70-159371
ISBN 0-394-47191-1   MARC

Library of Congress   72

Record (b)

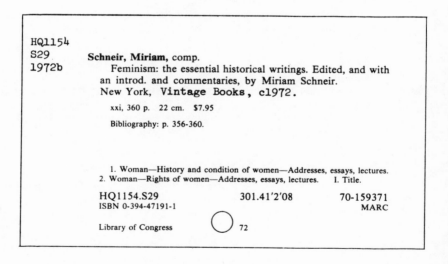

HQ1154
S29   Schneir, Miriam, comp.
1972b   Feminism: the essential historical writings. Edited, and with
             an introd. and commentaries, by Miriam Schneir.
             New York, Vintage Books, c1972.

  xxi, 360 p.   22 cm. $7.95

  Bibliography: p. 356-360.

  1. Woman—History and condition of women—Addresses, essays, lectures.
2. Woman—Rights of women—Addresses, essays, lectures.   I. Title.

HQ1154.S29   301.41'2'08   70-159371
ISBN 0-394-47191-1   MARC

Library of Congress   72

Example 7.4. Record (a) shows LC copy for the hard cover edition, which called itself
"First edition." When the paperback edition appeared, it bore a different publisher (a
division of the hard bound publisher) and did not have the edition statement. Record (b)
shows adjustments necessary in edition area, publication area, and call number when using
the near copy for cataloging the paperback. It will be noted, also, that under AACR 2 the
main entry would be the title with an added entry for Schneir. Few libraries, however,
would find it necessary to make this change, especially if card copy is being used. In
addition, the terminology in the subject headings is out-of-date, and many libraries would
change these in the tracing as well as on the subject heading cards. The current LC headings
are: "Feminism—History" and "Women's rights—History."

Most bibliographic utilities require separate records for editions of a work. Separate records are called for by both AACR 2 and inputting standards. Therefore, the kinds of alterations possible when manipulating card sets as exemplified by Examples 7.1-7.4, would result in the need for separate records online. A paperback issued at the same time as the hardcover edition, or later in the same year, however, could easily appear on the same record (see Example 7.5).

```
OCLC: 12371478      Rec stat: p Entrd: 850724          Used: 871020
Type: a Bib lvl: m Govt pub:     Lang:  eng Source:    Illus:
Repr: d Enc lvl:    Conf pub: 0 Ctry:    mau Dat tp: s M/F/B: 11
Indx: 0 Mod rec:    Festschr: 0 Cont:
Desc: a Int lvl:    Dates: 1985,
  1 010        85-17669
  2 040        DLC $c DLC $d m/c
  3 020        0816139407 (lg. print)
  4 020        0816139415 (pbk. : lg. print)
  5 050 1      PS3557.R358 $b V5 1985b
  6 082 0      813/.54 $2 19
  7 090           $b
  8 049        YCLM
  9 100 10     Greeley, Andrew M., $d 1928- $w cn
 10 245 10     Virgin and martyr / $c Andrew M. Greeley.
 11 250        [Large print]
 12 260 0      Boston, Mass. : $b G.K. Hall, $c 1985.
 13 300        653 p. ; $c 25 cm.
 14 440  0     G.K. Hall large print book series
 15 650  0     Large type books.
```

Example 7.5. In this example, both the hardcover and paperback for the same title were published in the same year by the same publisher. According to the LC rule interpretation on what governs a new edition, this situation only requires one record.

When different publishers have published editions of a work other than simultaneous publication in different countries, there are likely to be more extensive changes on near copy. Physical description and series differences may occur. There may be cover title changes, or other differences that require notes (see Example 7.6, pages 256-57).

Record (a)

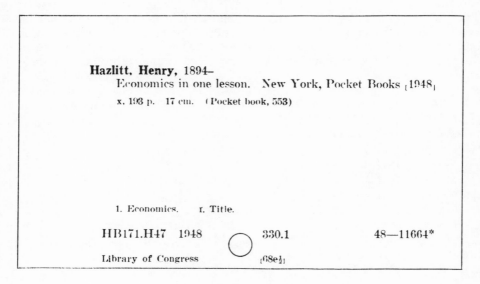

Hazlitt, Henry, 1894–
Economics in one lesson. New York, Pocket Books ₁1948₁

x, 193 p. 17 cm. (Pocket book, 553)

1. Economics. ɪ. Title.

HB171.H47 1948   330.1   48—11664*

Library of Congress   ₁68e½₁

Record (b)

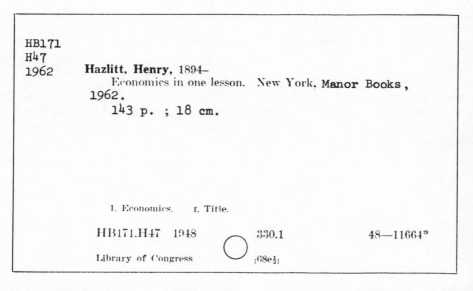

HB171
H47
1962

Hazlitt, Henry, 1894–
Economics in one lesson. New York, Manor Books,
1962.
143 p. ; 18 cm.

1. Economics. ɪ. Title.

HB171.H47 1948   330.1   48—11664*

Library of Congress   ₁68e½₁

Example 7.6. Records (a) and (c) show the nearest cataloging that was available for two works at the time they were received by the local library. In order to adapt the copy for the edition acquired locally, Record (a) required changes in publication area, physical description, series, and call number, as shown on Record (b). Record (c) required change of one word in the statement of responsibility in addition to the publication area, series, and call number changes, shown on Record (d). If this adaptation were being done now, it would also be necessary on Record (d) to consider whether the subject heading requires change to AACR 2 form or whether "Paris" and "Paris (France)" can be interfiled.

Record (c)

Rougerie, Jacques.
    1871 ₁i. e. Dix-huit cent soixante et onze₁ : jalons pour une histoire de la Commune de Paris. Préparé sous la direction de Jacques Rougerie avec la collaboration de Tristan Haan, Georges Haupt, et Miklos Molnar. Assen, Van Gorcum, 1973.
    x, 621 p. illus. 24 cm. (Publications on social history issued by the International Instituut voor Sociale Geschiedenis, 7)   Ne***
    Erratum slip inserted.
    English, French, or German.
    Includes bibliographical references.
    1. Paris—History—Commune, 1871—Addresses, essays, lectures. I. Title. II. Series: International Institute for Social History. Publications on social history, 7.

DC316.R7 1973   944'.36'081   73–163739
ISBN 90–232–1046–8   MARC
Library of Congress   ( ) 73 ₁4₁

Record (d)

DC316
R7
1973b
    Rougerie, Jacques.
    1871 ₁i. e. Dix-huit cent soixante et onze₁ : jalons pour une histoire de la Commune de Paris. Publié sous la direction de Jacques Rougerie avec la collaboration de Tristan Haan, Georges Haupt, et Miklos Molnar. -- Paris : Presses Universitaires de France, 1973, c1972.
    x, 621 p. illus. 24 cm.
    Erratum slip inserted.
    English, French, or German.
    Includes bibliographical references.
    1. Paris—History—Commune, 1871—Addresses, essays, lectures. I. Title.

DC316.R7 1973   944'.36'081   73–163739
ISBN 90–232–1046–8   MARC
Library of Congress   ( ) 73 ₁4₁

Example 7.6 *(continued)*.

Sometimes the title itself differs because different publishers may believe that a certain title will sell better than another in a particular locale. Thus, the card version near copy is usable only for some notes, added entries, subject headings, and classification unless the titles in question are very nearly the same length and other parts of the description differ so slightly that corrections can be typed to fit on the copy. This type of copy is very useful as online copy because much can be retained when creating a new record.

Occasionally, the information may be set up on the title page in such a way that the main entry should be different if the AACR 2 entry rules are followed. For example, a collected edition of two or more works by different authors may be given a collective title by one publisher, but not by another publisher. In the first case entry would be under title, and in the second it would be under the author of the first work (see Example 7.7). It is also possible that information given in prefatory matter can lead to different main entries (see Example 7.8, page 260). Finding the near copy in these cases might perhaps occur only by accident unless the titles are identical and search is by title. If found, only notes, added entries, subject headings, and classification will be usable.

Access points can vary when different publishers produce the same work. One may indicate an editor while the other does not. Added title and/or series entries may apply to one but not the other. However, there should be few occasions when subject headings on near copy of this type would not be the proper ones for the work in hand. One such rare occasion might be a book to which one publisher added a bibliography that covers a special topic and is large enough to warrant not only a note, but an additional subject heading. However, the same intellectual contents should call for the same subject analysis, no matter what the physical appearance, although one may find a number of *outdated* headings.

Classification numbers, too, should remain the same. Libraries using LC call numbers may need to adjust the call numbers in the same way as for revised editions. Application of the same date to the call numbers for simultaneous publication of the same work in different countries occurs frequently. If the near copy has "1976b" at the end of the call number, the library must decide whether to drop the letter, add "c", or resort to some other measure.

Record (a)

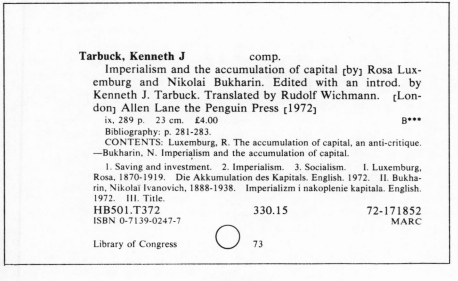

Tarbuck, Kenneth J   comp.
    Imperialism and the accumulation of capital ₍by₎ Rosa Luxemburg and Nikolai Bukharin. Edited with an introd. by Kenneth J. Tarbuck. Translated by Rudolf Wichmann. ₍London₎ Allen Lane the Penguin Press ₍1972₎
    ix, 289 p.   23 cm.   £4.00   B***
    Bibliography: p. 281-283.
    CONTENTS: Luxemburg, R. The accumulation of capital, an anti-critique. —Bukharin, N. Imperialism and the accumulation of capital.

    1. Saving and investment.   2. Imperialism.   3. Socialism.   I. Luxemburg, Rosa, 1870-1919.   Die Akkumulation des Kapitals. English. 1972.   II. Bukharin, Nikolaï Ivanovich, 1888-1938.   Imperializm i nakoplenie kapitala. English. 1972.   III. Title.

HB501.T372   330.15   72-171852
ISBN 0-7139-0247-7   MARC

Library of Congress   73

Record (b)

Luxemburg, Rosa, 1870-1919.
    The accumulation of capital—an anti-critique, by Rosa Luxemburg. Imperialism and the accumulation of capital, by Nikolai I. Bukharin. Edited with an introd. by Kenneth J. Tarbuck. Translated by Rudolf Wichmann.   New York, Monthly Review Press ₍1973, c1972₎
    ix, 289 p.   22 cm. $9.50
    Translation of Die Akkumulation des Kapitals ... Eine Antikritik, and Imperializm i nakoplenie kapitala, respectively.
    Bibliography: p. 281-283.
    1. Capitalism.   2. Imperialism.   I. Tarbuck, Kenneth J., comp.   II. Bukharin, Nikolaï Ivanovich, 1888-1938.   Imperializm i nakoplenie kapitala. English. 1973.   III. Title.

HB501.L9813   332'.01   72-81768
ISBN 0-85345-265-2   MARC

Library of Congress   73

Example 7.7. These records represent cataloging for two books with identical contents. The British and American publishers, however, constructed the titles and title pages so differently that different main entries were required. At the time of cataloging of Record (a), items with collective titles required entry under a compiler named on the title page. Now, entry would be under title. In either case, Record (a)'s entry would differ from the main entry required for Record (b) where there is no collective title. In this case, main entry under the entry required for the first-named work is still proper. [Note: The current LCAF record for Rosa Luxemburg gives her birth year as 1871. It is interesting to note that subject headings and Dewey classification numbers vary between Records (a) and (b).]

Record (a)

The **Study** of total societies.   Edited, with an introd., by
Samuel Z. Klausner.   New York, F. A. Praeger ₁1967₁

xx, 220 p.   illus.   22 cm.

Papers originally presented at a conference held in Washington,
July 28 and 29, 1965, under the auspices of the Bureau of Social Sci-
ence Research, and sponsored by the Army Research Office of the
Dept. of the Army through the Special Operations Research Office of
American University.
Includes bibliographical references.

1. Social sciences—Addresses, essays, lectures.   2. National state—
Addresses, essays, lectures.   I. Klausner, Samuel Z., ed.   II. Bureau
of Social Science Research, Washington, D. C.   III. American University, Washington, D. C.   Special Operations Research Office.

H35.S844   1967   67–66367

Library of Congress   ₁5₁

Record (b)

Klausner, Samuel Z.
       The study of total societies.   Edited, with an introd., by
Samuel Z. Klausner.   ₁1st ed.₁   Garden City, N. Y., Anchor
Books, 1967.
       xix. 220 p   18 cm.
       1. Social sciences—Addresses, essays, lectures.   2. National state—
Addresses, essays, lectures.   I. Title.
H35.K57   300′.8   67–12852

Example 7.8. It is possible for items published by two different publishers to be cataloged
with different main entries. Praeger identified the papers as coming from a conference,
while Anchor Books did not. Under the most current rules, Record (b) would now also be
entered under title, not editor, but the added entries relating to the conference would still
be lacking, and a library that uses LC copy to catalog the Anchor Books edition will find
that Klausner is still given as main entry. LC records are not reissued to change choice of
main entry after rules have changed. It will be noted that the corporate bodies given as
added entries II and III on Record (a) are not in AACR 2 form. In both cases
"Washington, D.C." should be in parentheses.

Reprint and Facsimile Editions

Included in this category are works for which the original publication has gone out of print but which have been copied and published by a reprint publisher for the purpose of making the information again available to the public. Early serial issues sometimes are republished in this manner, and a library that did not subscribe to a serial from the first may occasionally acquire back issues from a reprint publisher. Also in this category are those newly published items that seek to reproduce as closely as possible in binding, paper, and print, the original editions that they copy (i.e., facsimiles). Reprint editions are distinguished here from later printings. The publisher of a *reprint* edition is different from the publisher of the original edition. If the original publisher prints another issue after an edition has been out of print, it is treated as a *later printing*, not a reprint, when using outside copy. A third item in this category is the single or *on-demand* photoreproduction of an item that is not mass-produced as an edition of the work. These may be acquired from a commercial firm, such as University Microfilms International, or from some other library known to own a copy of the original.

Near copy is often used for cataloging reprints, facsimiles, or photocopies when copy is available only for the original edition. This happens fairly often if the library uses LC copy and if there is much retrospective buying. LC copy for many reprints published from about 1968 to 1971 is not available. LC copy is usually not available at all for photocopies because these types of materials are usually not added to LC's collection. Photocopies usually must be cataloged from near copy because they often are produced only as a result of a local request. This is one instance in the online environment where near copy can be found for a reproduction in the same format (e.g., paper photocopy if what one is cataloging is a paper photocopy, or microfiche if what one is cataloging is microfiche, etc.) and need only be slightly altered in order to reflect the publication data of the item held by the local library rather than creating a new record online. According to AACR 2, these are considered printings, not true editions or reprints.

The use of near copy in card format for a reprint or facsimile edition calls for changing the publication area and adding a note, unless the local policy is different (see Example 7.9, page 262). There may also be other differences from the original that must be changed or noted. The new title page, for example, is sometimes simpler than the original. Near copy found online would also require very little editing in order to create copy for the reprint edition.

Record (a)

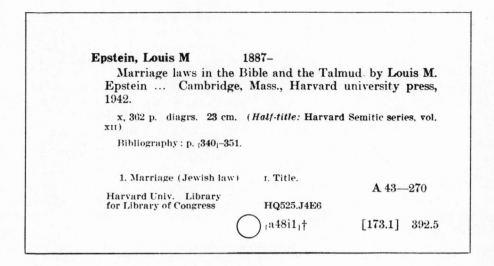

Epstein, Louis M   1887–
    Marriage laws in the Bible and the Talmud. by Louis M.
Epstein ...   Cambridge, Mass., Harvard university press,
1942.

    x, 362 p. diagrs. 23 cm. (*Half-title:* Harvard Semitic series, vol.
XII)

    Bibliography : p. ₍340₎–351.

    1. Marriage (Jewish law)   I. Title.
                                                          A 43—270
    Harvard Univ. Library
    for Library of Congress   HQ525.J4E6
                          ◯ ₍a48i1₎†   [173.1]   392.5

Record (b)

HQ525
J4
E6   Epstein, Louis M   1887– 1949.
1968   Marriage laws in the Bible and the Talmud. by Louis M.
        Epstein. — New York : Johnson Reprint, 1968,
        c1942.

            x, 362 p. diagrs. 23 cm. (*Half-title:* Harvard Semitic series, vol.
        XII)

            Bibliography : p. ₍340₎–351.
            Reprint of the ed. published by Harvard
        University Press, Cambridge, Mass.
            Includes index.
            1. Marriage (Jewish law)   I. Title.
                                                              A 43—270
        Harvard Univ. Library
        for Library of Congress   HQ525.J4E6
                              ◯ ₍a48i1₎†   [173.1]   392.5

Example 7.9. In this example, copy for the original edition, Record (a), is used as the basis
for cataloging a reprint of that edition, Record (b). Changes were required in publication
and notes areas and in call number. The author's death date was also added.

For libraries cataloging according to current LC policy, use of copy for an original work to catalog the photoreproduced edition usually requires only addition of a note describing the reproduction, since the original is described in the body of the entry[1] (see Example 7.10, page 264). Items from the National Technical Information Service (NTIS) present particular problems because they are obviously photocopies, yet they are mass-produced in the same way as reprint editions. They also are assigned "PB" numbers, which are used in some libraries as retrieval devices. They have seldom been cataloged by LC or other outside sources in the past, although LC has done more recently. When cataloged for OCLC, NTIS publications are considered to be reprints, not photocopies, and therefore the reprint publication data must be placed in the publication area rather than in a note (see Example 7.11, page 265).

If the near copy used in this category is that for the original edition, while the piece in hand has been photocopied or reprinted, the access points should all remain the same, except that a change in rules may dictate that the choice of main entry should be different, and, of course, forms of names and terminology for subjects may be different. If the near copy used is for an edition other than the original one that has been reprinted, the potential changes in entry and tracings mentioned in the two preceding sections may apply.

Classification should remain the same if copy for the exact original is used. Here, too, possible exceptions arise with outdated copy. If LC's call numbers are used, the local library will probably wish to adjust the call number on the near copy to fit the reprint, facsimile, or photoreproduction being cataloged. This will mean adding a date or a letter to a date, or altering the cutter, depending upon the situation and on local practice. Examples 7.9, 7.10, and 7.11 demonstrate some possible adjustments for LC call numbers.

Record (a)

Parker, Franklin, 1921–
    George Peabody, founder of modern philanthropy.
[Nashville? 1956]

    3 v. (xlv, 1219 l.)   29 cm.

    Thesis—George Peabody College for Teachers.
    "Errata sheet" : 4 leaves inserted.
    Bibliography : leaves 1092–1219.

    1. Peabody, George, 1795–1869.

    HV28.P4P29   923.673   56—40830

    Library of Congress   ◯   [a74b2]

Record (b)

HV28
P4
P29
1956a
    Parker, Franklin, 1921–
        George Peabody, founder of modern philanthropy.
    [Nashville? 1956]

        3 v. (xlv, 1219 l.)   29 cm.

        Thesis—George Peabody College for Teachers.
        "Errata sheet" : 4 leaves inserted.
        Bibliography : leaves 1092–1219.

    Photocopy of typescript. Ann Arbor, Mich. :
Xerox University Microfilms, 1974. -- 21 cm.

        1. Peabody, George, 1795–1869.

    HV28.P4P29   923.673   56—40830

    Library of Congress   ◯   [a74b2]

Example 7.10. In order to adapt the copy for the original thesis, Record (a), to show that the local library owned a photocopy of it, it was necessary only to add a note and to add the date to the call number, Record (b). It will be noted that according to current LC subject heading practice another subject heading should be added for this work: "Philanthropists — Biography."

Record (a)

National Conference on State and Local Manpower Planning, Salt Lake City, 1971.
    Proceedings. Conference leaders and editors: R. Thayne Robson ₍and₎ Garth L. Mangum. ₍Salt Lake City₎ University of Utah ₍1971₎

    vii, 280 p. 27 cm.

    "Sponsored by Manpower Administration, U. S. Department of Labor ₍and₎ Human Resources Institute, Center for Economic and Community Development, University of Utah."

    Includes bibliographical references.

    1. Manpower policy—United States—Congresses.   I. Robson, R. Thayne, ed. II. Mangum, Garth L., ed. III. United States. Dept. of Labor. Manpower Administration. IV. Utah. University. Human Resources Institute.

HD5724.N235 1971   331.1'1'0973   73–623388
                                          MARC

Library of Congress   ◯ 74 ₍4₎

Record (b)

HD5724
N235 **National Conference on State and Local Manpower Planning, Salt Lake City, 1971.**
1971x

    Proceedings. Conference leaders and editors: R. Thayne Robson ₍and₎ Garth L. Mangum. -- Springfield, Va. : National Technical Information Service, [1971?].

    vii, 277 p. ; 27 cm.

    "Sponsored by Manpower Administration, U. S. Department of Labor ₍and₎ Human Resources Institute, Center for Economic and Community Development, University of Utah."

    Includes bibliographical references.

    "PB 212 199."

    Reprint of the document published by University of Utah.

HD5724.N235 1971   331.1'1'0973   73–623388
                                          MARC

Library of Congress   ◯ 74 ₍4₎

Example 7.11. One possible way of cataloging NTIS publications using near copy is to treat them as reprints. Record (b) shows the changes and additions necessary to do this. The tracings were transferred to the back of the main entry card in order to leave room for the notes. Depending upon how a library is handling conference qualifiers under AACR 2, the main entry heading may need to be changed to "National Conference on State and Local Manpower Planning (1971 : Salt Lake City, Utah)." In addition, the AACR 2 form for added entry IV is "University of Utah. Human Resources Institute."

Original and Translated Editions

There are times when a local library acquires a translation for which only the original and/or another translation has been cataloged by the outside source. It may likewise acquire an original edition for which only a translation has been cataloged. Exact copy is often unavailable for all translations when a popular work has been translated into many languages, and there may not be exact copy for a translation of an English work into a lesser-known language or for an original in a lesser-known language when an English translation is available. It is highly unlikely, in such cases, that the near copy itself will be used for card reproduction. It can be used as the basis for new copy in either manual or online systems, however, since main and some added entries, subjects, and classification should remain the same even though the language has changed.

Description of original and translated editions usually must be completely redone when near copy is used. Only if the titles are cognates can the copy be used as demonstrated in the examples already shown. However, much of the information can be used in the new cataloging. For example, if only original language copy is available when cataloging a translation, the title on the copy can be used for the uniform title and, if the information is not available anywhere in the translation itself, for the "Translation of ..." note. Subject headings, added entries, and classification can be used; and the LC call number can be adjusted to fit the translation by adding digits to represent the language.

When using translation copy for cataloging the original work, all access points except translator and/or series can be used, classification should remain the same, and the LC call number often can be adjusted by dropping the translation digits. When using translation copy to catalog another translation, in addition to the usable items just mentioned, the "Translation of ..." note can be retained for the new cataloging.

Editions Produced in Different Physical Forms

A local library may acquire a work in a physical form different from the one cataloged by the outside source. One of the most common of such cases is the acquisition of microform versions of material for which the only available cataloging copy represents the hard copy edition. Serials, including newspapers, are often acquired by local libraries in microform.

Other types of format differences occur when a recording appears as an LP-disc, tape, or compact disc; when videorecordings (in color or in black and white) appear on film, videotape (in Beta or VHS), or videodisc; and when computer data files can be acquired on tape, disk, or CD-ROM. From 1971 through early 1978, LC provided cataloging for sound recordings with several lines of physical description, each representing a different format in which the recording was known to exist[2] (see Example 7.12). These were called multicarrier entries, and they required that a local library draw a line through the physical description for the formats not owned, mark the format owned, or indicate in some other fashion which format the local patron could expect to find. As was done prior to 1971, cataloging is now prepared by the Library of Congress for every format they add to their collections. "Formats not owned by LC will be indicated in notes if the information is readily available."[3]

Record (a)

Rimskiĭ-Korsakov, Nikolaĭ Andreevich, 1844–1908.
₍Scheherazade₎ Phonorecord.
Scheherazade; symphonic suite, op. 35.   RCA ₍Red Seal.
1973₎
   disc ARD1–0028.   2 s.   12 in.   33⅓ rpm.   quadraphonic.
   cartridge ARS1–0028.   3¾ ips.   stereophonic.
   cartridge ART1–0028.   3¾ ips.   quadraphonic.
   cassette ARK1–0028.   2½ x 4 in.   stereophonic.

   Norman Carol, violin; Philadelphia Orchestra; Eugene Ormandy,
   conductor.
   Duration: 47 min., 46 sec.
   Program notes by R. D. Darrell on slipcase.

   1. Suites (Orchestra)   I. Ormandy, Eugene, 1899–   II. Philadelphia Orchestra.   III. Title.

   [M1003]   72–750879

   Library of Congress   73 ₍2₎   R

Record (b)

Future of wildlife ₍videorecording₎ / West Wind Productions, Inc.
— Boulder, CO : West Wind Productions, 1980.

   1 videocassette (15 min.) : sd., col. + 1 fact sheet.

   Title from data sheet.
   Credits: Bert Kempers.
   Issued as 1/2 in. or U-matic 3/4 in.
   Issued also as motion picture.
   Summary: Focuses on what can be done to ensure a safe future for America's
   wildlife.
   For sale ($245.00)

   1. Wildlife conservation—United States.   ₍1. Wildlife conservation₎   I.
   West Wind Productions.

   ₍QL84.2₎   333.95—dc11a   81-707147
                                                   AACR 2   MARC
   West Wind Productions
   for Library of Congress   ₍8204₎   F

Example 7.12. From 1971 to early 1978, LC provided multicarrier entries for recordings
when they had all formats in hand or knew about their existence at the time of cataloging,
as shown in Record (a). A local library that acquires only one of these formats, and can
find only multicarrier copy, will probably wish to indicate in some way which physical
description applies to the format owned. Record (b) illustrates LC's current practice of
making separate records for each format added to their collections, referring to other
formats in a note.

With physical form differences, as with reprint and photocopy editions, the entries, subjects, and classification should not differ. Unless the near copy is old, it should therefore be useful for these elements and may sometimes require relatively few changes in description outside the physical description and "notes" areas. If the LC call number is used, the library may wish to adjust it with date, date letter, or cutter change in the same manner as other editions; or it may be desirable instead to add a form designation to distinguish it from the original form and to identify its location if such media are housed separately (see Example 7.13).

Record (a)

Reptiles and amphibians (*Motion picture*)   National Geographic Society.   Released by McGraw-Hill Book Co., 1969.

54 min.   sd.   color.   16 mm.

With teacher's guide.
Summary: Explores the world of reptiles and amphibians, and compares their prehistoric existence with their existence today as lower life forms.

1. Reptiles.   2. Amphibians.   r. National Geographic Society, Washington, D. C.   ii. McGraw-Hill Book Company.

919.4   73–701850

McGraw-Hill Book Co.
for Library of Congress   69 [2]   F

Example 7.13. When the videocassette of the above title was received, the only cataloging copy available was copy for the motion picture, Record (a). Record (b) shows possible adjustments in order to use the card copy for cataloging the videocassette. It should be noted that these adaptations were made according to revised Chapter 12 of AACR 1, and would look somewhat different using AACR 2. In addition, the AACR 2 form for added entry I is "National Geographic Society (U.S.)". In an online environment a new record would have to be created for this videorecording, rather than adapting the near copy.

Record (b)

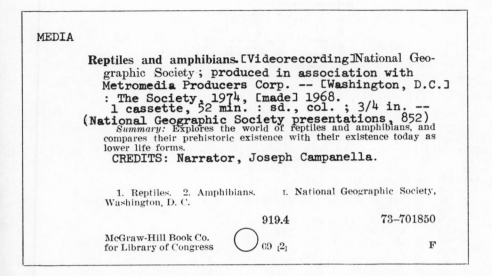

MEDIA

Reptiles and amphibians. [Videorecording]National Geographic Society ; **produced in association with Metromedia Producers Corp. -- [Washington, D.C.] : The Society, 1974, [made] 1968.
1 cassette, 52 min. : sd., col. ; 3/4 in. --
(National Geographic Society presentations,** 852)
Summary: Explores the world of reptiles and amphibians, and compares their prehistoric existence with their existence today as lower life forms.
CREDITS: Narrator, Joseph Campanella.

1. Reptiles. 2. Amphibians.   ɪ. National Geographic Society, Washington, D. C.

919.4   73–701850

McGraw-Hill Book Co.
for Library of Congress   69 [2]   F

Example 7.13 *(continued)*.

Local Use of Near Copy

Use of near copy depends to some extent on the kind of catalog and, if it is a card catalog, on the means of acquiring and/or reproducing copy for card sets. If cataloging is meant for a book, microform, or online catalog, the near copy can be used as a reference point. Parts that do not match can be dropped and replaced when cataloging is prepared, using basically the same methods as those for exact copy. The same is true when cataloging is going into a card catalog, and the card preparation method is reproduction from a master record prepared in-house. Unusable parts of the near copy are simply eradicated, and changes and/or additions of any length are inserted.

The advent of computer-based cataloging systems has greatly enhanced the ability of libraries to make use of near copy. Card sets do not have to be manually altered to adjust the bibliographic information in order to match the edition or rendition in hand; thus, much time is saved in the creation of a record from near copy. Erasing and typing in data as in Example 7.13 is more easily achieved online. Near copy from *NUC*, such as an LC non-MARC record or an LC cooperative record, can be used as a reference when creating a new record, or can be converted to MARC format based on the standards of a particular utility (see Example 7.14, page 270). The record can then be used as the basis for creating a new record for the edition in hand, as explained in Chapter 8.

Record (a)

Minkowski, Hermann, 1864–1909.
  Briefe an David Hilbert/ Hermann Minkowski. Mit
Beitr. u. hrsg. von L. Rüdenberg u. H. Zassenhaus. —
Berlin, Heidelberg, New York: Springer, 1973.
    165 p.: ill.: 24 cm.   DM32.00   GFR 73–A
  1. Minkowski, Hermann, 1864–1909. 2. Hilbert, David, 1862–1943.
  3. Mathematicians—Correspondence, reminiscences, etc.   I. Hil-
  bert, David, 1862–1943. II. Rüdenberg, Lily, ed. III. Zassenhaus,
  Hans, ed.
  QA29.M523A33 1973   510'.92 [B]   73–75263
  ISBN 3–540–06121–5

Record (b)

```
OCLC: 1025933        Rec stat: c Entrd: 741001        Used: 871008
  Type: a Bib lvl: m Govt pub:    Lang:  ger Source:    Illus: a
  Repr:     Enc lvl: I Conf pub: O Ctry:  wb  Dat tp: s M/F/B: 10b
  Indx: 0 Mod rec: m Festschr: 0 Cont:
  Desc: i Int lvl:    Dates: 1973,
    1 010        73-75263
    2 040        DLC $c OSU $d OCL $d SER $d m/c
    3 015        GFR73-A
    4 020        3540061215 : $c DM32.00
    5 050 0      QA29.M523 $b A33 1973
    6 082        510/.92 $a B
    7 090         $b
    8 049        YCLM
    9 100 11     Minkowski, H. $q (Hermann), $d 1864-1909. $w cn
   10 245 10     Briefe an David Hilbert / $c Hermann Minkowski. Mit Beitr.
u. hrsg. von L. Rudenberg u. H. Zassenhaus.
   11 260 0      Berlin, $a Heidelberg, $a New York : $b Springer, $c 1973.
   12 300        165 p. : $b ill. ; $c 24 cm.
   13 600 10     Hilbert, David, $d 1862-1943. $w cn
   14 650 0      Mathematicians $x Correspondence, reminiscences, etc.
   15 700 10     Hilbert, David, $d 1862-1943. $w cn
   16 700 11     Rudenberg, Lily, $e ed.
   17 700 11     Zassenhaus, Hans. $e ed. $w cn
   18 870 19      $j 100/1 $a Minkowski, Hermann, $d 1864-1909.
```

Example 7.14. The *NUC* copy shown in Record (a) was converted to MARC format and input into OCLC in 1974, shown in Record (b). At the time of input no changes to the record content or access points were necessary because the cataloging rules in effect were the same as the ones LC used to create the record. Later, AACR 2 conversion brought the 100 field up-to-date.

When the library reproduces its own cards from LC copy or orders complete card sets, however, more thought must be given to the usability of near copy for these purposes. When complete card sets are ordered, any changes in main entry and description must be made on every card of the set. In some cases this can be more time consuming than typing a complete new set of cards. Libraries in this situation should consider carefully whether they wish to receive card sets when only near copy is available. It may depend on the kind of changes that will be required. If the only change is addition of a "Photocopy" note, for example, then the near copy is probably desirable.

The library that reproduces its cards from paper copy will find that some changes can be made directly on the copy, and then a card set can be reproduced from that master. In many cases, however, the changes will not fit. These must be treated essentially as original cataloging. Therefore, a decision should be made as to whether *all* near copy will be photocopied from *NUC*, ordered from LC, or acquired by other means for use by the copy cataloger. It may be that only certain kinds of near copy will be used in this way; if this is so, the instances of its use should be clearly defined.

A decision also should be made about which personnel will handle items for which only near copy is available. In some libraries original catalogers handle all near copy; in other libraries copy catalogers handle both exact and near copy. If the latter route is chosen, it must be remembered that the copy catalogers will require much more training and skill than they need for work with exact copy only. This is so because more knowledge of rules for description and access points is required, along with greater expertise in the areas of subject headings and classification.

When a library participates in a cooperative cataloging system, such as a bibliographic utility or a regional database, the use of near copy is also affected by responsibilities to others in the cooperative. The responsibilities are twofold: the holdings information must be accurate for resource sharing purposes, and a certain standard of quality required by that utility or network must be met when creating/not creating new records from near copy. In some instances, the level of expertise of the individual using the near copy may be dictated by the agreement among members of that cooperative group.

A note of caution concerning near copy for certain kinds of material: successive symposiums, for example, may seem to be good candidates for use of near copy; but even when they have the same title, there can be numerous other differences. In Example 7.15 (pages 272-75), the first symposium had been cataloged by LC under the name of the editor and was so entered in the local catalog. It was later revised by LC to be entered under the name of the symposium, but the local library was not aware of this. When the second symposium arrived, the local library located the revised copy for the first symposium and attempted to use it as near copy. In addition to the changes in number, symposium date, imprint date, and paging, there should have been the following changes: change of third editor and tracing III; addition of "2" following title in the body of entry and in the first note; change of date and grant number in second note, along with deletion of one of the corporate bodies mentioned. Instead of adding the last note, the first symposium should probably have been recataloged and both should have been cuttered with S9 instead of B7. When so many differences are involved, the near copy can really be used only as a reference point. Even in an online cataloging environment, deriving a new record from an existing record, as explained in Chapter 8, needs to be done selectively; and successive symposia involve some of the more complicated cataloging decisions.

A final note of caution should be given to libraries that have used near copy in card format in the manner shown in Examples 7.1 through 7.13. In most of these examples the LC Card Number (LCCN) was not changed and thus still represents the edition for which the cataloging was originally done. Retrospective conversion projects, in which manual records are converted to MARC records, have often been carried out by matching LCCNs from card shelflists against the LC MARC database and downloading all records for which a match is found. It can be seen that if this procedure is carried out unquestioningly, records will be downloaded that do not match the items they are supposed to represent.

Record (a)

TX556
M4
B7

Briskey, Ernest Joseph, 1931–   *ed.*
 The physiology and biochemistry of muscle as a food.
Edited by E. J. Briskey, R. G. Cassens ₍and₎ J. C. Trautman. Madison, University of Wisconsin Press, 1966.
  xii, 437 p. illus. 25 cm.
  "Proceedings of an international symposium, sponsored by the
University of Wisconsin, July, 1965, with the support of United States
Public Health Service research grant EF–00727–01, from the Division
of Environmental Engineering and Food Protection, and a special
grant from the American Meat Institute Foundation."
  Includes bibliographies.
  1. Muscle—Congresses. 2. Meat—Congresses.   i. Cassens, R. G.,
joint ed. ii. Trautman, Jack Carl, 1929–   joint ed. iii. Wisconsin.
University. iv. Title.
  TX556.M4B7   641.306   66–22849

○

Record (b)

**Symposium on the Physiology and Biochemistry of Muscle
as a Food, 1st, University of Wisconsin, 1965.**
 The physiology and biochemistry of muscle as a food,
edited by E. J. Briskey, R. G. Cassens ₍and₎ J. C. Trautman. Madison, University of Wisconsin Press, 1966.

  xii, 437 p. illus. 25 cm.

  Half title: Muscle as a food.
  "Proceedings of an international symposium sponsored by the University of Wisconsin, July, 1965, with the support of United States
Public Health Service research grant EF–00727–01, from the Division of Environmental Engineering and Food Protection, and a
special grant from the American Meat Institute Foundation."

        (Continued on next card)

○   66–22849
 rev
 ₍r71b2₎

Example 7.15. One must be careful about what is used as near copy. This example shows
misuse. Record (a) represents the first LC copy for the 1965 symposium. It was used by the
local library just as it appeared. This copy was then revised by LC, Record (b). The revised
copy for the 1st symposium was then used by the local library as near copy for cataloging
the 2nd symposium, Record (c) (page 274). The LC cataloging for the 2nd symposium,
which came later, Record (d) (page 275), is shown in order to show what else ought to have
been changed on Record (c).

Record (b) *[continued]*

Symposium on the Physiology and Biochemistry of Muscle as a Food, 1st, University of Wisconsin, 1965. The physiology and biochemistry of muscle as a food ... 1966. (Card 2)

    Includes bibliographies.

    1. Muscle—Congresses. 2. Meat—Congresses.   I. Briskey, Ernest Joseph, 1931–   ed. II. Cassens, R. G., ed. III. Trautman, Jack Carl, 1929–   ed. IV. Wisconsin. University. V. Title. VI. Title: Muscle as a food.

TX556.M4S9   1965   66–22849

Library of Congress   rev
                          ₍r71b2₎

Example 7.15 *(continued)*. It will be noted that the AACR 2 form for both symposia would have changes in the qualifier. In addition the AACR 2 form for added entry IV is "University of Wisconsin," and the current form for subject 1 has been changed to the plural: "Muscles."

Record (c)

TX556
M4
B7
1969

Symposium on the Physiology and Biochemistry of Muscle as a Food, 2d, University of Wisconsin, 1969.
The physiology and biochemistry of muscle as a food, edited by E. J. Briskey, R. G. Casséns ₍and₎ J. C. Trautman. Madison, University of Wisconsin Press, 1970.

843 p. illus. 25 cm.

Half title: Muscle as a food.
"Proceedings of an international symposium sponsored by the University of Wisconsin, July, 1965, with the support of United States Public Health Service research grant EF–00727–01, from the Division of Environmental Engineering and Food Protection, and a special grant from the American Meat Institute Foundation."

Record (c) *[continued]*

Symposium on the Physiology and Biochemistry of Muscle as a Food, 2d, University of Wisconsin, 1969. The physiology and biochemistry of muscle as a food ... 1970. (Card 2)

Includes bibliographies.
First symposium entered under Briskey, Ernest Joseph, 1931– ed.

1. Muscle—Congresses. 2. Meat—Congresses. I. Briskey, Ernest Joseph, 1931– ed. II. Cassens, R. G., ed. III. Trautman, Jack Carl, 1929– ed. IV. Wisconsin. University. V. Title. VI. Title: Muscle as a food.

TX556.M4S9 1965 66–22849

Library of Congress rev ₍r71b2₎

Example 7.15 *(continued)*.

Record (d)

Symposium on the Physiology and Biochemistry of Muscle as a Food, 2d, University of Wisconsin, 1969.
The physiology and biochemistry of muscle as a food, 2, edited by E. J. Briskey, R. G. Cassens ₍and₎ B. B. Marsh.   Madison, University of Wisconsin Press, 1970.

xvi, 843 p.   illus.   25 cm.

Half title: Muscle as a food, 2.
"Proceedings of an international symposium sponsored by the University of Wisconsin, 1969, with the support of United States Public Health Service research grant 7D-00158 and a special grant from the American Meat Institute Foundation."

◯

Record (d) *[continued]*

Symposium on the Physiology and Biochemistry of Muscle as a Food, 2d, University of Wisconsin, 1969.   The physiology and biochemistry of muscle as a food, 2 ... 1970.   (Card 2)

Includes bibliographies.

1. Muscle—Congresses.   2. Meat—Congresses.   I. Briskey, Ernest Joseph, 1931-   ed.   II. Cassens, R. G., ed.   III. Marsh, Benjamin B., 1926-   ed.   IV. Wisconsin.   University.   V. Title.   VI. Title: Muscle as a food, 2.

TX556.M4S9   1969   641.3'06   76-25241
                                                                    MARC

Library of Congress   ◯ 71

Example 7.15 *(continued)*.

CO-OP COPY

Co-op copy may be available from a number of sources. For example, any commercial cataloging other than that usually used could be a source of copy for items not available from the usual source. One source of co-op copy is the *National Union Catalog*. Copy printed there from any library other than LC is co-op. Co-op copy also becomes available to any library participating in a computerized cataloging system. Any original cataloging input into the system by any of the local libraries can be used as co-op copy by the other libraries.

The major decisions most libraries face concerning co-op copy are whether or not they will use it and, if so, how it will be used. A number of important factors must be considered when these decisions are made.

Standards for Description and Access on Co-op Copy

If a library has decided on certain standards for description and access points and has chosen an outside cataloging source accordingly, copy from any other source may vary. If a library normally uses simplified cataloging from companies such as Baker & Taylor, for example, copy from LC has unnecessary detail in description and form of entry. LC's added entries for corporate bodies or series may be unnecessary, and subject headings might be too specialized. On the other hand, a library that follows AACR 2 more closely would find that simplified cataloging from another source requires much expansion.

The quality of co-op copy can also vary—especially that available from networks and *NUC*. Because each library tends to have its own local standards for original cataloging, the copy sent in to *NUC* or keyed into a master file from an individual library reflects that library's practice. Forms of access points may vary; there may or may not be a uniform title; certain areas of description may be truncated or given in great detail; a series may be traced by one library but not by another, etc. On some *NUC* co-op entries, tracings do not appear at all, so there are no added entries with which to agree *or* disagree. Libraries in networks learn which cooperating libraries have local policies similar to theirs, and they find that copy from those libraries can be used most efficiently. Also, as the networks have developed, they have attempted to standardize the contributed cataloging so that the variations above do not occur as often. The adoption of AACR 2 has greatly contributed to higher standards and uniformity in cataloging practices in co-op copy.

Subjects on Co-op Copy

Subjects on co-op copy from a commercial source may not be usable if the subject authority is not the one used locally. However, the local library that knows what authority the outside source uses can adjust accordingly. The problem with co-op copy from networks is that subject analysis practices differ and may not exactly coincide with that of the local library. Also, since libraries have different cut-off points for subdividing main headings, the subdivision of headings on co-op copy varies—some are divided as much as possible, and others have no subdivision at all. Because of such differences, it may be decided that close scrutiny will be the norm. This can be done as long as the copy cataloging staff has the appropriate training, or the original catalogers have the time. However, the greatest benefits from co-op copy can be realized when, as often as possible, the local library trusts the cataloging of other libraries in order to save time and resources locally. Given current standards in most utilities, extensive changes to network co-op copy can be kept to a minimum as discussed further in Chapter 8.

With *NUC* copy, in addition to the above problems, the lack of any subject headings at all on some copy can cause problems for libraries. Also, when subject headings *are* used in *NUC* copy, one may not know whether the headings are from *Sears*, LC, or some other subject authority, or whether they simply reflect that library's local practices. The copy found in *NUC* that resulted from cooperative projects with LC or LC non-MARC records, however, will be more useful.

Call Numbers on Co-op Copy

As with subjects, the call numbers on commercial co-op copy are based on an announced classification scheme. Co-op copy available through networks often provides a call number based only on the classification scheme used by the library from which the copy originated. If the library wishing to use the copy follows a different scheme, there may not be a call number in the record that the library can use. Even if the classification scheme is the same, the local library may employ a different method of cuttering.

Most co-op copy available from *NUC* has no call number or classification number at all. Some of the co-op copy in the *Pre-1956 Imprints* bears call numbers and, when it does, it presents the same problems as network co-op copy.

Local Use of Co-op Copy

On the positive side of the picture, it can be said that using co-op copy is generally better than having no copy at all. It at least gives the local cataloger an idea of what one other library thought the cataloging ought to be. This gives something to react to, which is easier than beginning in a vacuum. If tracings and/or call numbers are given, the same principle holds true.

If co-op copy is used, a library must decide which level of personnel will handle it. When much of it requires addition of tracings and/or call numbers, it is usually given to people trained for original cataloging.

Co-op copy overlaps with near copy in a way that may be used to advantage in some libraries; in some cases co-op copy is available for the exact edition being cataloged when only near copy is available from the usual outside source. If these are used together, they can be handled by the same staff members who process near copy. The co-op copy can be used for the description, and the tracings and classification from the near copy can be added to it in the same way as when near copy alone is used (see Example 7.16, pages 278-79). This is feasible only in libraries that prepare their own masters for card set reproduction or use online copy. It would not be economical for a library to order a printed card set of the near copy to be used in this fashion.

Record (a)

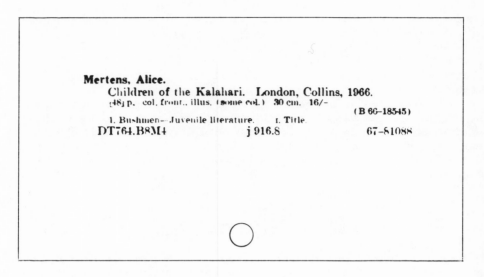

Mertens, Alice.
    Children of the Kalahari. London, Collins, 1966.
    [48] p. col. front., illus. (some col.) 30 cm. 16/-
                                                  (B 66-18545)

    1. Bushmen—Juvenile literature.   I. Title.
    DT764.B8M4   j 916.8   67-61088

Record (b)

Mertens, Alice.
    Children of the Kalahari.   Indianapolis,
Bobbs-Merrill, 1966.
    [48] p. col. front., illus. (some col.) 30 cm.
    1. Bushmen.   I. Title.
                                       NUC69-103985

Example 7.16. Only co-op copy is available for the American edition of this work, shown as Record (b). There is LC copy for the British edition, Record (a). If Record (a) is used as near copy when making a local card set for the American edition, the physical description, as well as the publication area, will have to be retyped, even though the physical description correctly describes the book, as shown in Record (c). This is true because the publication area for the British edition does not have room for the longer American imprint. However, if the co-op copy is used in conjunction with the near copy, no descriptive changes are

Record (c)

```
DT764
B8
M4
1966b     Mertens. Alice.
               Children of the Kalahari. -- Indianapolis, Bobbs
           -Merrill, 1966.
               [48] p. : ill. ; 30 cm.




               1. San (African people)--Juvenile literature.
           I. Title.
```

Record (d)

```
DT764
B8
M4         Mertens, Alice.
1966b          Children of the Kalahari.   Indianapolis,
           Bobbs-Merrill, 1966.
               [48] p.  col. front., illus. (some col.)  30 cm.

                                          NUC69-103985



               1. San (African people)--Juvenile literature.
           I. Title.
```

required. Ordinarily the subject headings from the near copy could be used as found, except that when an enlarged photocopy from *NUC* is used, as in Record (a), tracings often have to be moved to allow space for descriptive changes. In addition to this being a problem in the example shown here, the subject heading on the near copy reflects out-of-date (and prejudicial) terminology. Thus, it would have needed to be changed in any case. On both Records (c) and (d) the near copy LC call number has been used with date and date letter added.

Example 7.16 *(continued)*.

National Library Copy

The situation shown in Example 7.16 becomes more prevalent with the increased availability of records of other national libraries, such as the British Library (UKM), the National Library of Canada (NLC), and the National Library of Medicine (NLM). In the OCLC database, where records for the same titles cataloged by the national libraries can coexist, the local library is faced with deciding to which record their symbol should be added. Records may differ in details of description. Forms of name and title access points can differ markedly. Choice of subject analysis may also affect one's decision. UKM records supply LC classification and Dewey classification numbers only—not complete call numbers. LC subject headings are given but are often different from those assigned by LC. PRECIS (Preserved Context Indexing System) subject strings are provided in 69x fields (which display in 886 fields in OCLC). NLC records provide LC call numbers (in 055 fields) and LC subject headings, but, in addition, they assign subject headings in French (second indicator 6 in the 6xx fields) and NLC headings in English (second indicator 5 in the 6xx fields). NLM records assign NLM call numbers (in 060 fields) and NLM subject headings (second indicator 2 in 6xx fields). In Example 7.17, three different records for the same title have been input by LC, NLM, and UKM. It will be noted that the form of name of the main entry is different on each record and that the LC class numbers differ between LC and UKM. NLM subjects and classification, of course, differ from the other two. Nonmedical libraries in the United States tend to add their symbols to the LC record. Medical libraries select either the NLM record or the LC record, although the NLM record is often more current in NLM call number and subject headings than the LC record. British libraries lean toward the UKM record. How a copy cataloger is to deal with this situation should be clearly outlined so as to avoid confusion and delays in processing.

Record (a)

```
OCLC: 6760973       Rec stat: n Entrd: 800911       Used: 860621
 Type: a Bib lvl: m Govt pub:      Lang:   eng Source: d Illus: a
 Repr:       Enc lvl:      Conf pub: 0 Ctry:   enk Dat tp: s M/F/B: 10
 Indx: 1 Mod rec:      Festschr: 0 Cont:
 Desc: i Int lvl:      Dates: 1980,
  1 010       79-41324
  2 040       NLM $c NLM
  3 020       0192611534
  4 060       WG 100 W488c 1980
  5 069 0     8008544
  6 090       $b
  7 049       YCLM
  8 100 10    Werf, Tjeerd van der.
  9 245 10    Cardiovascular pathophysiology / $c  Tjeerd van der Werf.
 10 260 0     Oxford ; New York : $b Oxford Univ. Press, $c 1980.
 11 300       xiv, 296 p. : $b ill.
 12 650  2    Cardiovascular Diseases $x physiopathology
```

Example 7.17. Records (a), (b), and (c) illustrate the coexistence of national library records for the same title. The local library needs to prepare the copy cataloger to take the appropriate course of action. As in Example 7.16, the information from records not used can be borrowed so as to make these records as useful as possible, and so as not to narrow the responsibilities of the copy cataloger needlessly. (The 653 field in Record (c) includes the terms used in the PRECIS subject string but does not include the codes that explain the relationships among terms. The latter are included in line 19.)

Record (b)

```
OCLC: 6278342        Rec stat: c Entrd: 800211        Used: 870821
Type: a Bib lvl: m Govt pub:    Lang:  eng Source:    Illus: a
Repr:      Enc lvl:    Conf pub: 0 Ctry:  enk Dat tp: s M/F/B: 10
Indx: 1 Mod rec:      Festschr: 0 Cont: b
Desc: i Int lvl:     Dates: 1980,
  1 010       79-41324
  2 040       DLC $c DLC $d CHS $d CUX
  3 015       GB80
  4 020       0192611534 : $c L10.00
  5 020       0192612298 (pbk.) : $c L5.00
  6 050 0     RC667 $b .W43
  7 060       WG 100 W488c 1980
  8 082       616.1/07
  9 090         $b
 10 049       YCLM
 11 100 10    Werf, T. van der.
 12 245 10    Cardiovascular pathophysiology / $c Tjeerd van der Werf.
 13 260 0     Oxford ; $a New York : $b Oxford University Press, $c 1980.
 14 300       xiv, 296 p. : $b ill. ; $c 23 cm.
 15 504       Includes bibliographies and index.
 16 650 0     Cardiovascular system $x Diseases.
 17 650 0     Physiology, Pathological.
 18 650 2     Cardiovascular System $x physiopathology
 19 650 2     Cardiovascular Diseases
 20 650 2     Cardiovascular Diseases $x physiopathology
```

Record (c)

```
OCLC: 16493619       Rec stat: n Entrd: 801117        Used: 870815
Type: a Bib lvl: m Govt pub:    Lang:  eng Source: d Illus: a
Repr:      Enc lvl:    Conf pub: 0 Ctry:  enk Dat tp: s M/F/B: 10
Indx: 1 Mod rec:      Festschr: 0 Cont:
Desc:      Int lvl:     Dates: 1980,
  1 010       gb80-12374 $z 79-41324
  2 040       UKM $c UKM
  3 015       GB80-12374
  4 020       0192611534 : $c L15.00:
  5 020       0192612298
  6 050 1     RC669
  7 082 0     616.1/07 $2 19
  8 090         $b
  9 049       YCLM
 10 100 20    Van Der Werf, Tjeerd.
 11 245 10    Cardiovascular pathophysiology / $c Tjeerd Van Der Werf.
 12 260 0     Oxford : $b Oxford University Press, $c 1980.
 13 300       xiv, 296 p. : $b ill. ; $c 24 cm.
 14 504       Includes bibliographies and index.
 15 500       ISBN 0-19-261229-8 Pbk: L6.95.
 16 650 0     Cardiovascular system $x Diseases.
 17 650 0     Physiology, Pathological.
 18 653       Man $a Cardiovascular system $a Diseases $a Physiological
aspects
 19 886 2       $2 UK MARC $a 690 $b 00 $z 10030 $a man $z p1030 $a
cardiovascular system $z 20030 $a diseases $z 20020 $a  $z 31030 $a
physiological aspects
 20 886 2       $2 UK MARC $a 691 $b 00 $a 0655392
 21 886 2       $2 UK MARC $a 692 $b 00 $a 0000906
 22 886 2       $2 UK MARC $a 692 $b 00 $a 0000930
 23 886 2       $2 UK MARC $a 900 $b 10 $a Werf $h Tjeerd van der $x See
$a Van Der Werf, Tjeerd $z 100
 24 886 2       $2 UK MARC $a 900 $b 20 $a Der Werf $h Tjeerd van $x See
$a Van Der Werf, Tjeerd $z 100
```

Example 7.17 *(continued)*.

Example 7.18 illustrates the simultaneous publishing of the same title by different publishers. There is only one record for each edition: one LC and one UKM. It will be noted that the call numbers and subject headings are not in agreement in these two records. When using the UKM record, a cataloger might evaluate the call number and subject heading to determine acceptability. Alternatively, the call number and subject headings could be borrowed from the LC record. If this is done it would be advisable to add a work letter to the date in the call number in case the U.S. imprint is actually acquired later.

Record (a)

```
OCLC: 12949921      Rec stat: p Entrd: 851120        Used: 871029
Type: a Bib lvl: m Govt pub:     Lang:  eng Source:    Illus:
Repr:     Enc lvl:    Conf pub: 0 Ctry:  nyu Dat tp: s M/F/B: 10
Indx: 1 Mod rec:     Festschr: 0 Cont:
Desc: a Int lvl:     Dates: 1986,
  1 010        85-29705/MN
  2 040        DLC $c DLC $d m/c
  3 020        019520509X (set) : $c $95.00
  4 043        e-uk-en
  5 050 0      ML1731.8.L7 $b G36 1986
  6 082 0      782.81/0941 $2 19
  7 090        $b
  8 049        YCLM
  9 100 10     Ganzl, Kurt. $w cn
 10 245 10     British musical theatre / $c Kurt Ganzl.
 11 260 0      New York : $b Oxford University Press, $c 1986.
 12 300        2 v. ; $c 24 cm.
 13 500        Includes indexes.
 14 650  0     Musical revue, comedy, etc. $z England $z London.
```

Record (b)

```
OCLC: 16083489      Rec stat: c Entrd: 870506        Used: 870924
Type: a Bib lvl: m Govt pub:     Lang:  eng Source: d Illus:
Repr:     Enc lvl:    Conf pub: 1 Ctry:  enk Dat tp: s M/F/B: 10
Indx: 1 Mod rec:     Festschr: 1 Cont:
Desc: a Int lvl:     Dates: 1986,
  1 010        gb86-7592
  2 040        UKM $c UKM $d OCL
  3 015        GB86-7592
  4 020        0333398394 (v.1) : $c L60.00
  5 020        0333397444 (v.2) : $c L60.00
  6 050 1      ML1950
  7 082 0      782.81 $2 19
  8 090        $b
  9 049        YCLM
 10 100 10     Ganzl, Kurt. $w 1n
 11 245 14     The British musical theatre / $c Kurt Ganzl.
 12 260 0      Basingstoke : $b Macmillan, $c 1986.
 13 300        2 v. (various pagings) ; $c 24 cm.
 14 500        Includes index.
 15 650  0     Musical revue, comedy, etc. $x History and criticism.
 16 653        Musical shows in English, 1866-1979
 17 886 2       $2 UK MARC $a 690 $b 00 $z 11030 $a musical shows in
English $d 1866-1979
 18 886 2       $2 UK MARC $a 691 $b 00 $a 2578212
 19 886 2       $2 UK MARC $a 692 $b 00 $a 0026778
```

Example 7.18. These records show cataloging for the same title published in the United States and Great Britain by two different publishers. LC has cataloged the U.S. edition, Record (a), and the British Library the U.K. edition, Record (b). As in Example 7.16, the call number and subject heading can be used from the LC copy if needed.

NLC records do not as often duplicate records from other national libraries in cataloging for the same title. This is true because of an agreement between LC and NLC that all Canadian publications and publications about Canada will be cataloged by NLC, and NLC's cataloging will then be accepted by LC. However, another library may catalog the same title, as shown in Example 7.19 (pages 284-85). In this case the copy cataloger must choose between two versions of co-op copy.

SUMMARY

Near and co-op copy can be used as an aid in the cataloging process when exact copy is not available. When and how such copy is used depends on each local library's answers to the following questions:

1. How economical is it to search and acquire near or co-op copy, balanced against its ultimate usefulness in terms of cataloging time saved?

2. Are there situations in which near or co-op copy will be used only as a guide for aid in original cataloging?

3. Are there situations in which near or co-op copy will be used as a substitute for exact copy when the latter is not available?

4. Will co-op cataloging from certain identified libraries be used as if it were exact copy?

5. If near copy is used for revised editions, will entries, subjects, and classification, as well as description, be examined for needed changes?

6. How does the format of the catalog or the method of acquiring copy affect usability of near or co-op copy?

7. If near and/or co-op copy is used in the same way as exact copy, which staff members will handle it?

8. Are there situations where co-op and near copy can be used together for cataloging the same title?

Record (a)

```
OCLC: 16048353        Rec stat: p Entrd: 861028          Used: 871019
Type: a Bib lvl: m Govt pub:        Lang:  fre Source: d Illus:
Repr:     Enc lvl:    Conf pub: 1 Ctry:  onc Dat tp: s M/F/B: 00
Indx: 0 Mod rec:      Festschr: 0 Cont: b
Desc: a Int lvl:      Dates: 1987,
   1 010        cn86-90337
   2 040        NLC $b fre $c NLC
   3 015        C86-90337-0
   4 020        2760301516 : $c 15,95 $
   5 043        n-cn--- $a n-us---
   6 055 00     PQ3897 $b A98 1987
   7 055 01     PQ3897
   8 082 0      840.9/97 $2 19
   9 090         $b
  10 049        YCLM
  11 245 04     Les Autres litt'eratures d'expression francaise en
Am'erique du Nord / $c sous la direction de Jules Tessier, Pierre-Louis
Vaillancourt.
  12 260 0      [Ottawa] : $b 'Editions de l'Universit'e d'Ottawa, $c 1987.
  13 263        8701
  14 300        164 p. ; $c 23 cm.
  15 490 1      Cahiers du CRCCF ; $v 24
  16 500        R'eunit les textes pr'esent'es †a un colloque tenu †a
Cornwall, Ont. en mars 1984. Cf. p. [5]
  17 504        Comprend des bibliogr.
  18 650 6      Litt'erature canadienne-francaise $y 20e si†ecle $x
Histoire et critique.
  19 650 6      Litt'erature  am'ericaine (francaise) $x Histoire et
critique.
  20 650 5      Canadian literature (French) $y 20th century $x History and
criticism.
  21 650 0      French-American literature $x History and criticism.
  22 700 10     Tessier, Jules, $d 1941-
  23 700 10     Vaillancourt, Pierre-Louis.
  24 830 0      Cahiers du Centre de recherche en civilisation canadienne-
francaise ; $v 24
```

Example 7.19. These records show cataloging for the same title completed by the National Library of Canada, Record (a), and by a member of OCLC, Record (b) A copy cataloger in a library that uses LC copy as its usual source must choose here between two versions of co-op copy.

Record (b)

```
OCLC: 16874067      Rec stat: n Entrd: 871019         Used: 871021
Type: a Bib lvl: m Govt pub:    Lang:  fre Source: d Illus:
Repr:    Enc lvl: I Conf pub: 1 Ctry:   onc Dat tp: s M/F/B: 00
Indx: 0 Mod rec:    Festschr: 0 Cont: b
Desc: a Int lvl:    Dates: 1987,
   1 010
   2 040       ORU $c ORU
   3 020       2760301516
   4 090       PQ3897 $b .A97 1987
   5 090          $b
   6 049       YCLM
   7 245 04    Les Autres litt'eratures d'expression francaise en
Am'erique du Nord / $c sous la direction de Jules Tessier, Pierre-Louis
Vaillancourt.
   8 260 0     [Ottawa] : $b 'Editions de l'Universit'e d'Ottawa, $c 1987.
   9 300       164 p. ; $c 23 cm.
  10 490 1     Cahiers du CRCCF ; $v 24
  11 500       Contains the papers presented at a conference held in
Cornwall, Ontario in March 1984.
  12 504       Includes bibliographical references.
  13 650  0    French-American literature $x History and criticism.
  14 700 10    Tessier, Jules, $d 1941-
  15 700 10    Vaillancourt, Pierre-Louis.
  16 710 20    University of Ottawa. $b Centre de recherche en
civilisation canadienne-francaise.
  17 830  0    Cahiers du Centre de recherche en civilisation canadienne-
francaise ; $v 24.
```

Example 7.19 *(continued)*.

NOTES

[1]*Cataloging Service Bulletin*, no. 14 (Fall 1981): 56-58.

[2]Music Library Association, *Music Cataloging Bulletin* 2, no. 11 (November 1971): 3; vol. 3, no. 11 (November 1972): 3.

[3]Music Library Association, *Music Cataloging Bulletin* 9, no. 4 (April 1978): 2.

COMPUTER-BASED
COPY CATALOGING

INTRODUCTION

When libraries decide to move from traditional means of catalog copy to a computer-based source, they must decide what system(s) will offer the services and products they have in mind, provide the best response rate for their type of library, and be at a price they can afford. Some will find this combination of ideal qualities in any number of the systems available on the market today, while others will find that they must compromise in order to process materials through a computer-based system.

Another decision concerns how much of the work currently done offline will be transferred to an online process. Some institutions spend only a few hours per day on the terminal, doing much of the time-consuming, labor-intensive work offline, leaving the terminal time for production. Others process a title from beginning to end, including marking the pieces, temporary shelflists, and/or worksheets as they catalog the item online. If the local catalog is also online, even shelflisting can be performed without ever leaving the workstation, if the online shelflist is set up adjacent to the terminal or is actually part of the cataloging system used. The division between online and offline activity might also be based on the number of workstations available, the hours of operation of the library, and the number of staff members requiring online access. To make the best use of terminal time when online time is at a premium, specific hours can be scheduled for working online, and the online activities can be divided by this measure as well. In other words, as many noncomputer-based processing opportunities as necessary should be provided not only to keep employees busy when the system is unavailable but also to allow for variation in day-to-day procedures. One institution actually keeps a few book trucks around with Library of Congress printouts in each book (because much of the work can be done offline) which provides offline cataloging activities when needed.

The intent of the automated, cooperative, cataloging process as stated by Frederick Kilgour in 1976 was to make it "possible for libraries to set an objective for reducing the rate of per-unit cost in descriptive cataloging.... [O]nly one library participating in the network does first-time descriptive cataloging of an item; others subsequently cataloging the item employ the cataloging information already in the system."[1] The main objective still holds true today. When using records for cataloging, whether in a network/utility, a micro-based stand-alone system, or a turnkey system, the idea is to process an item with that record in a timely, efficient, and cost-effective manner. Based on this premise, this chapter offers suggestions and recommendations toward achieving that goal by addressing the following areas:

1. Training the staff

2. Searching for the appropriate record

3. Using the bibliographic record

4. Exact copy not found and the use of near copy

5. Entering a new record online

6. Authority control and Library of Congress authority records

TRAINING THE STAFF

There are so many variables involved in the training of staff (e.g., education and responsibilities of an individual), as well as so many different systems to choose from for cataloging copy that to attempt to give step-by-step training instructions would likely prove more confusing than helpful. This section, therefore, is not a detailed outline on how to train someone to use a specific system in a specific manner, but rather it provides ideas and considerations to apply when designing training sessions, exercises, and/or manuals.

Training Materials

Before spending time creating training materials for the system being used (e.g., tagging, basic use of the system), the trainer should first look to the utility, the literature, and other users of the same system for guidance. Computer-based training (CBT) packages, online tutorials, predesigned exercises, or manuals that can aid in the structure and design of training sessions and materials may already exist. There are also user groups from whose meetings one can gather suggestions and thus benefit from the experiences of others. There may be periodic workshops on various aspects of the system offered by the database provider or other organizations, free of charge or for a small fee, which employees may attend. This would be particularly helpful when all staff members are new to the system, or the system itself is a newcomer to the field. The library staff may then use the workshop information as a basis for the design of its own sessions and materials. Most often the one-time fee pays for itself manifold. Another option would be to hire another user of that system on a consulting basis to do the training.

Whether one is training a large or small group of staff members, a workshop atmosphere can be very effective. Overhead transparencies, videotapes (perhaps available through interlibrary loan or from the utility), and other types of media work well in this setting. There is also much that employees can do in preparation for the workshop, such as assigned reading, and exercises performed both at the terminal and at their desks.

System Documentation

Staff should be acquainted with all relevant documents available from the utility even if they are not all covered in-depth in the training sessions. It is very difficult to teach staff all there is to know about a system — this is a monumental task, for which the utility designs documentation. It is useful for staff members at least to know that documentation exists that can aid them in their day-to-day operations. This knowledge will provide the means for them to learn more about the system on their own after having been trained in the basics of searching, editing, and/or ordering offline products, etc. This knowledge can also reduce the number of queries the supervisor will have to answer. Providing staff members with significant preliminary readings, giving them special guidance in the usage of the documents relevant to their positions, and alerting them to the existence of additional documentation will benefit all involved.

The Machine-Readable Cataloging
(MARC) Record

Much has been written over the years about MARC and its origins, uses, system-specific versions, and how it has changed the way libraries order, process, and provide services to their patrons. A good understanding of the world of MARC, as well as a good basis for a lecture on the MARC format, is Walt Crawford's *MARC for Library Use: Understanding the USMARC Formats* (White Plains, N.Y.: Knowledge Industries, 1984). Although this edition is somewhat out of date due to changes to the MARC format, it still provides correct, basic, and detailed information for use as an introduction to MARC for staff training or for suggested reading. Some systems provide a mnemonic display of a MARC record, but facility in the use of the system can be greatly enhanced if staff members have at least a basic understanding of the MARC record.

When preparing training materials, the ideal place to start is with the format for book records. It contains all of the basic elements of the MARC format and forms a solid foundation for all other types of materials that are cataloged online. This may seem a waste of time if some of the people being trained are, for example, only maps catalogers. However, if all attend a basic books session, they will learn the fundamentals of the MARC format (i.e., tags, indicators, etc.) because it is the same for many areas of the bibliographic record (e.g., author fields, subject headings fields). Then specific instruction for the nonbook materials and the fields that are specific to those materials can be provided.

As part of this training, the vocabulary associated with the MARC format can be emphasized. One should include such terms as tag, field, indicator, subfield, fixed field, variable field, etc. There is also system-specific vocabulary to note, such as *derived copy, workform*, etc.

For those already familiar with the catalog card, showing the relationship between the catalog card and the MARC fields from which catalog card data is created can make the transition to use of an online bibliographic system a little smoother. For those who are not familiar with the catalog card but work in an environment where the public card catalog and/or shelflist are still in use, a preliminary reading assignment and/or a basic explanation of the catalog card could also be helpful in their achieving an understanding of how the data fields work.

SEARCHING FOR THE APPROPRIATE RECORD

The means of accessing bibliographic records online varies from system to system. Whatever the form of the search query, staff should be trained to search independently, thoroughly, and with good judgement. Therefore, the more they know about searching for records in a database (the straightforward as well as the idiosyncratic), the more accurate the search results can be. For example, in the OCLC system it is not enough to show the staff member the author search key and how to construct it. How the system indexes authors with a surname of MacDonald or Macdonald, for example, is vital information for accurate record retrieval. Familiarity with the file structures in RLIN is essential to avoid searching for materials in inappropriate files.

Exhaustive searching for records needed for processing can help to avoid duplication of effort. Because searching varies from system to system, it is difficult to recommend specific search patterns. One commonality among all online or MARC based systems, however, is the existence of numeric fields in the record. Numbers like the LCCN, ISBN, and ISSN, are one source of more or less unique access to bibliographic records. Although such numbers may retrieve more than one record, the list is brief enough that the appropriate record is easily discerned. Therefore, if a title bears a number that is indexed by the system in use, this is always the best place to start. The best approach to take if a numeric search query is fruitless varies from system to system, based on the capabilities of that system.

If the person searching for bibliographic records has not been given enough training to be able to determine the most logical search key appropriate to the material, a list of search keys or queries, in a recommended order, will save the searcher much time in deciding how to proceed. Such a list is also helpful when using systems that charge per search or when accessing the system through dial access, since fewer searching attempts will be necessary and connect-time charges can be kept to a minimum. Valuable perspectives on preferred and tested searching logic and techniques can be found in the literature and by user groups and other contacts within the library community who use the system.

Recognizing the Correct Record

An individual given the task of searching for appropriate copy does not necessarily have to know how to catalog in order to make certain fundamental decisions. Good instruction on the comparison of item and record is enough for searching the system for the correct record. However, this is an area where an understanding of the basic elements of the MARC record is recommended.

The fields discussed below can be taken into account when choosing the correct record for an item in hand. It is not necessarily an exhaustive list, nor is the order appropriate to all works—this varies by material type. Also, it should be kept in mind that each field suggested below should not be used alone as criteria for matching but should instead be used in combination with the other suggested fields as appropriate. For example, simply finding matching ISBNs does not preclude the need to check the 245 and 260 fields.

The level of staff member who initiates the search for the appropriate record online varies from library to library and ranges from student or volunteer to catalog librarian. The description in this section is most appropriate to those who receive basic instruction in reading the MARC record and are trained to make one-to-one comparisons. For trained copy catalogers or librarians, there are, of course, short-cuts.

Type and Bibliographic Level

These fields are the positions 6 and 7 in the Leader in MARC, the "Type:" and "Bib lvl:" elements in the OCLC fixed field, and "BLT:" in RLIN.

The first thing to check is the Type code in conjunction with the Bibliographic Level. This indicates if the record is for a book, serial, map, etc. The format for audiovisual materials may also require the noting of field 008, position 33, "Type of material," when evaluating the record for its appropriateness to the piece in hand. After awhile, the type of record will become recognizable to the searcher by other elements of the record (e.g., the general material designation in the 245 field), precluding the need to check these two positions.

Form of Reproduction

This code appears in position 23 of MARC field 008, as the "Repr:" code in the OCLC fixed field, and as "REP:" in RLIN.

In some formats it is necessary to check this code to be certain that it is an exact match according to form of material. For example, if one has the paper copy of a title (coded as a blank in the "Reproduction" fixed field), and the record being evaluated is for a microfiche edition (coded "b"), this would not be an exact match. If no other copy is available, this record could be used as near copy for creating an original record (see "Exact Copy Not Found and the Use of Near Copy" later in this chapter).

010 Field
Library of Congress Control Number (LCCN)

If the item contains an LCCN, in particular as part of Library of Congress Cataloging-in-Publication (CIP) data, this would not only be a good field to compare with the piece in hand, but also it could have been the search key used. If this search key was used, however, one would still want to glance at a few other fields in the record to be sure this is truly the same title since these numbers are at times printed incorrectly or have typographical errors. The former occurs from time to time, for example, when a new edition of a work is published and the publisher continues to use the previous edition's LCCN and/or CIP.

020, etc. Fields
International Standard Book Number (ISBN),
or Other Standard or Publisher Numbers

If the item bears a number, in particular a type that is of standard usage by the publishers of that type of material, it is most often a unique identifier, and therefore one of the key elements to compare (and search by).

There are many reasons why the number on the piece may not match the number in the record, not all necessarily meaning that the record is inappropriate. For example, some publishers may print incorrect numbers, numbers with more digits than the standard calls for, or the search key may have been entered incorrectly. The latter could be checked and reentered, although the others may require using a different search key instead. Whatever the reason for the discrepancy, when the numbers do not match, one should check some of the other recommended fields as well before deciding that more searching is necessary or deciding that the record is, or is not the appropriate one.

245 Field
Title Statement

After comparing the above fields, the next step would be to compare the title field with the chief source of information of the item in hand. Comparison of this field would include the title, the other title information, and the statement of responsibility, as well as any other subfields present. Variations between text and record should be closely evaluated since this is one of the primary areas that could result in the need for a new record. Searchers should be instructed not to be concerned with most punctuation and subfield codes at this point, but they should know that order of information is important. A thorough comparison of this field precludes the need for checking the 1XX fields since the data in the latter fields are established by the cataloger.

250 Field
Edition Statement

The edition statement is a particularly troublesome area. When comparing most English language publications, this area should be the same as what appears on the item in order to consider the record an exact match. An exception arises in older copy where, due to the difference in cataloging rules over the years, this statement may not have been transcribed, in which event, the publication date becomes very important. Foreign language publications are not as consistent in their usage of the term *edition*, causing the retrieved record to look like near copy. Treatment of records for such publications is a local decision. Some institutions create new records, while others use these records and change the edition statement if they feel that the publisher's statement of edition was really a printing statement. Use of these records depends upon the country of publication and one's knowledge of the practices of publishers there, together with the input standards of the online system. If edition statements disagree, or one or the other is actually lacking a statement, the searcher should question whether the record and piece actually match, because even though the transcription of an edition statement is required by AACR 2 and the utilities, it is sometimes inadvertently missed by the cataloger. When there is unresolved doubt, the searcher should seek guidance from the utility or its documentation.

260 Field
Publisher, Distribution, etc.

If all of the above fields match, the next area to compare is the publication information field. Unfortunately, it may not always match exactly, even when the correct record has been retrieved. Due to changes in cataloging rules over the years, varying interpretations of older and current rules, as well as improper interpretations, the 260 field can prove to be one of the more confusing areas. If the differences consist of more than punctuation or orthographics, the following recommendations may help in evaluating this field:

1. If the publication information on the piece appears in the 260 field, but the order or selection of publisher and place varies slightly, the titles and standard numbers match, and this is the only record available, continue comparing other fields with the piece in hand. If order is the only discrepancy, the item can then be passed on to a higher level staff member for evaluation. For example, based on typography, one library may consider the first place of publication to be different from what another library has recorded, resulting in a variation of transcription of the 260 field. After more detailed evaluation a cataloger may discover that the only difference in the record is the interpretation of AACR 2.

2. If the publication information does not match but nearly everything else does (in particular the 245 field), and this is the only record found, this record will probably still be useful for creating a new record. Whether it can be used as it is depends on many factors, such as the current cataloging rules and the standards for creating a new record in a particular system. This, too, can be passed on for further evaluation.

300 Field
Physical Description

Subfields $a, $c, and $e are the most important to check in the physical description. The form in which this publication is issued, both in pagination and format, should match. If, for example, the only record available is for a particular title issued in a single volume, but the item in hand consists of a two-volume set, that record is not describing the same item. Bibliographically, the item in hand and the title described would be considered two different entities and a unique record would be required. As another example, some items are published with or without plates inserted. If, for example, the piece in hand lacks plates, but the only record found includes reference to plates, one would need to make sure that the copy was explicitly published this way (i.e., not just missing the plates) before creating the new record that such a difference would require.

In the area of accompanying material, there are rare instances where one format or another may be equally appropriate. For example, a book with slides could be cataloged on a books workform, identifying the slides in the 300 field as accompanying material. The other option would be to catalog the slides on an audiovisual media workform, noting the book as the accompanying material. The treatment of such items must be based on local and national practices as well as the standards established by the utility a library may be using.

4XX (Series) and 5XX (Note) Fields

There are two other groups of fields that should be looked at when deciding if a record is appropriate. The first group covers the series fields 400, 410, 411, 440, and 490. If these fields match, both in name and numbering of the item, and everything else matches including the next group of fields, the record is probably the right one. However, if a series appears on the piece but not in the record, or vice versa, this discrepancy should be questioned.

The notes area (5XX) is the other group of fields of which to be aware. This is particularly true for materials that can be reproduced in other formats. Library of Congress rule interpretation prescribes nonadherence to Chapter 11 in AACR 2 for microform reproductions and for on-demand reprints (i.e., following AACR 1 by cataloging the original and then describing the reproduction in a note), if the fixed field is not coded properly for the reproduction, and if there is no General Material Designation (GMD), the record could actually match the piece in hand exactly until a 533 or other note is found. Although not specifically listed here as an area to check, the "Dates" element in the 008 field can also be glanced at when evaluating the record, especially in this case because it can also be a clue to the format of the item being described (i.e., the reproduction date is always first). When a microform reproduction is involved, assuming that the "Form of reproduction" code is correct, checking this code first can be a time saver and will be a clue to the searcher to look for a note of some kind.

There are other situations where only a note may identify another edition. Example 8.1 (page 294-95) illustrates a case where the only real difference between two works exists at the head of the title. The difference in the catalog records for those titles is only really evident in one of the 500 notes, reflecting in each case the corporate body that housed the exhibition. The other differences in description merely reflect subjective decisions as to whether the note on the title page should be transcribed in the statement of responsibility or in a quoted note, and whether or not a list of other exhibition catalogues published by Olivetti belongs in the bibliography note.

Record (a)

```
OCLC: 12678992      Rec stat: c Entrd: 851016         Used: 871022
Type: a Bib lvl: m Govt pub:      Lang:  eng Source: d Illus: ao
Repr:    Enc lvl: I Conf pub: 0 Ctry:  it  Dat tp: s M/F/B: 10
Indx: 1 Mod rec:     Festschr: 0 Cont:  c
Desc: a Int lvl:     Dates: 1984,
   1 010
   2 040      ZPM $c ZPM $d OCL $d m/c $d OCL
   3 090      N7952 $b .T7 1985
   4 090        $b
   5 049      YCLM
   6 245 04   The Treasury of San Marco, Venice / $c photography: Mario
Carrieri; catalogue design: Egidio Bonfante; catalogue translation: Jane
Clarey [et al.]; edited by David Buckton with the help of Christopher
Entwistle and Rowena Prior.
   7 260 0    Milan : $b Olivetti, $c c1984 $g (1985 printing)
   8 300      337 p. : $b ill. (some col.) ; $c 26 cm.
   9 500      "The exhibition has been organized by Olivetti's Cultural
Relations Department, the Procuratoria of San Marco, the R'eunion des
mus'ees nationaux in Paris, and the Metropolitan Museum of Art in New
York."
  10 500      At head of title page: The Metropolitan Museum of Art.
  11 504      Bibliography: p. 315-327.
  12 500      Includes index.
  13 610 20   Basilica di San Marco (Venice, Italy) $x Exhibitions. $w cn
  14 650  0   Christian art and symbolism $z Italy $z Venice $x
Exhibitions.
  15 700 10   Buckton, David. $w cn
  16 710 20   Metropolitan Museum of Art (New York, N.Y.) $w cn
```

Example 8.1. Record (a) represents an exhibition catalog for the Metropolitan Museum of Art in New York. This same exhibit travelled to Los Angeles, and an exhibition catalog, Record (b), was also published for that exhibit. These two records are describing the exact same text. However, for each separate museum the appropriate heading appeared at the top of the title page. There are differences in description that resulted from different interpretations by two catalogers on transcription of the title page and on pages to be included in the bibliography, but these do not distinguish between the two editions. The distinction is made only by the "At head of title" note (and, of course, the subsequent added entries).

Record (b)

```
OCLC: 13216648      Rec stat: c Entrd: 851104         Used: 871031
Type: a Bib lvl: m Govt pub:     Lang: eng Source:    Illus: a
Repr:    Enc lvl:    Conf pub: 0 Ctry:  it Dat tp: s M/F/B: 00
Indx: 1 Mod rec:     Festschr: 0 Cont: cb
Desc: a Int lvl:    Dates: 1984,
   1 010       85-670244
   2 040       DLC $c DLC
   3 019       12007443 $a 12595257 $a 13870019 $a 13885359
   4 041 1     engita
   5 043       e-it---
   6 050 0     NK520.I8 $b V467 1985
   7 082 0     730/.094/074 $2 19
   8 090        $b
   9 049       YCLM
  10 245 04    The Treasury of San Marco, Venice / $c [the exhibition has
been organized by Olivetti's Cultural Relations Department .... et al. ;
photography, Mario Carrieri ; catalogue design, Egidio Bonfante ; catalogue
translation, Jane Clarey ... et al. ; edited by David Buckton with the help
of Christopher Entwistle and Rowena Prior].
  11 260 0     Milan : $b Olivetti, $c c1984 $g (1985 printing)
  12 300       337 p. : $b ill. (some col.) ; $c 26 cm.
  13 500       At head of title: Los Angeles County Museum of Art.
  14 504       Bibliography: p. 315-325.
  15 500       Includes index.
  16 650  0    Decorative arts $x Exhibitions.
  17 610 20    Basilica di San Marco (Venice, Italy) $x Exhibitions.
  18 700 10    Carrieri, Mario, $d 1932-
  19 700 10    Buckton, David.
  20 700 10    Entwistle, Christopher.
  21 700 10    Prior, Rowena.
  22 710 20    Ing. C. Olivetti & c. $b Cultural Relations Dept.
  23 710 20    Los Angeles County Museum of Art.
```

Example 8.1 *(continued)*.

Choosing the Most Appropriate Record

Regardless of the cooperative cataloging system being used (unless records are being created in a local database with standards for unique records), the searcher will from time to time have to choose from more than one acceptable record. In systems that provide access to multiple versions of the same record as a matter of course, this becomes a routine part of the searching process. Procedures for selecting the preferred record can be established in advance for all levels of users to apply, and will most often be based on the following:

1. Originator of the cataloging record

2. The encoding level (completeness) of that record

3. Appropriateness of call number and/or subject headings to the local library

Originator of the Cataloging Record (040 Field)

Listed in the 040 field, in subfield $a, is the library that created the cataloging data. In systems where libraries also appear in the subfield $d for various reasons, this subfield needs to be taken into consideration as well. Additionally, in serial records, the 042 field provides the authentication characteristics of the record and can be consulted for level of authoritativeness of the record. The local library may create a list, in priority order, of libraries whose cataloging is acceptable in order to make this selection easier for the searcher. Most often, Library of Congress cataloging is always accepted and is considered the preferred copy when deciding between two or more cataloging records for the same item. Given the number of records produced by LC and the high response rate experienced by those who search for this copy, this criterion alone can make selection of the record a simpler task. To make the task even easier, a library may add other libraries to the list (e.g., some of the libraries who participate in cooperative cataloging projects with LC and who, by essence of their size and reputation, input or catalog a relatively large number of titles with high quality). A library may choose also to include libraries with whom they process materials cooperatively or whose cataloging practices tend to be similar to their own. This policy may require study of the records of these libraries, as some libraries have done, as well as periodic reevaluation because of staff turnover and possible changes in practices. Another way to establish such a list of acceptable libraries would be that of expressly forming a cooperative cataloging and/or acquisitions group where libraries in a geographic or topical area agree to acquire and/or catalog materials based on agreed-upon standards and guidelines and could thus explicitly accept the cataloging of other members in the group. A list of acceptable or preferred libraries works especially well for those who are members of utilities such as RLIN and Utlas where the cataloging of other member libraries is accessible. In this case, a list in priority order would be the most useful, although in Utlas a user's display can actually be profiled to appear in such an order.

Encoding Level of the Record

The encoding level of the record appears in position 17 of the Leader in MARC, in OCLC's fixed field element "Enc lvl:", and in RLIN's "EL:".

Most libraries select the record that has the highest encoding level. This information is coded in some systems in a non-MARC field (e.g., RLIN's Cataloging Category Code), which may preclude the need to check this code in the fixed field. Lower level cataloging can still be a good basis for cataloging, although it may require higher level staff to deal with it.

Call Number and Subject Headings

Ideally, the record should have both call number and subject headings appropriate to the local library. If none of the records include both, the following priority of selection might be applied:

1. Select the record with the subject headings
2. Select the record with the call number

The reverse order may be more appropriate to some libraries, based on the level of training of the copy cataloger, although this order will work well for those who feel that the selection of a call number by using the subject headings on a record can be easier (and quicker) than assigning subject headings.

It may be worthwhile also to list all of the records that exactly match the item in hand (but each of which only has one of the above) to give the copy cataloger more to work with. In those utilities where there are as many versions available as there are holdings symbols attached, listing those records could be too time consuming. However, listing a few combinations of records with each needed element could significantly help the staff member using the copy.

USING THE BIBLIOGRAPHIC RECORD

This section addresses the editing of exact copy. Following this section are sections that address creating records from near copy and entering new records online.

Establishing Procedures

The procedures established for staff when using a bibliographic or authority record—i.e., what to ignore, what to evaluate, what to look for, what to add, etc.—should be documented in some fashion. A library can create, for instance, an in-house manual with specific instructions provided for each MARC field the copy cataloger will encounter on the screen. With this type of manual there could be little question as to how to deal with any field within a record. The manual could be arranged either numerically according to tag number (based on some of the system manuals, with each field being given separate treatment), or the fields could be grouped into like areas, such as all of the personal name fields (i.e., 100, 400, 600, 700, 800). The latter approach would require provision of a brief index to the appropriate areas of the manual. The former type of manual may be more easily accessed, although the latter type of manual may be easier to construct. Also to be taken into account are the separate formats being cataloged and the division of tasks within the department.

Because some of the MARC fields are specific to certain materials, a general, overall editing manual could be designed with supplementary manuals covering specific types of material. Already existing manuals, such as the *CONSER Editing Guide* could serve as a basis for the internal manual.[2] However, before embarking on such a project, one should be aware of how much information is already provided in the utilities' documentation and attempt to restrict the manual to local practices rather than merely repeat the system's guidelines.

Because separation of tag and bibliographic areas can be difficult, given their intricate relationships in the automated cataloging process, another option is to write an in-house cataloging manual, rather than a tagging or editing manual, and intersperse the tags, etc., where appropriate. In the latter choice, an index, including the fields as access points, is a necessity. Of course, any manual benefits from an index and/or a table of contents.

Checking Fields in Bibliographic Records

Due to the preponderance of rules, rule revisions, bibliographic standards, and local and national interpretations over the years, copy catalogers encounter catalog records reflecting these varying cataloging practices. Decisions necessary for dealing with the cataloging practices reflected in the copy in hand are addressed in Chapter 2. Decisions that must be made because the copy is found online in MARC format are discussed below.

Decisions to be made when checking MARC fields fall into several categories and these will be addressed individually. There is one step, however, that should be taken regardless of the decision premise the local library choses to follow. This step is very straightforward: Read the record carefully enough to detect typographical errors. This probably seems very simple, and very basic, and it is. Those who enter records into a database can, and will, make typographical errors that can go undetected. Even the Library of Congress records, the primary source of MARC records today, need to be read, for their records, too, include inputting errors. Of course, those fields that are read routinely in order to check the elements of the record against the piece in hand will be looked at. Yet even here errors can go undetected if not enough care is taken when reading these fields.

The fields that the copy cataloger is not responsible for authoritatively should also be read. For example, when using Library of Congress records, the subject headings may be given only a cursory glance (if they are being accepted without question), or not even read at all. However, this is one area where errors can occur and much work would have to be done to correct them later. Therefore, it is recommended that the copy cataloger be instructed to read even those areas they are not required to verify.

Usefulness of Fields for
Present and Future Catalogs

If the catalog is a card catalog and no online or microform catalog exists at this time, the primary, current concern is correct card production. The fields that are important in this area are covered later. However, as cards are being produced electronically, local libraries are preparing themselves for online, microfiche, or microfilm catalogs. In many systems the image of the record is being saved on an archival tape which the local library can procure periodically or at a later date when they are ready to create a catalog in a form other than on cards. If the library ever intends to make use of that MARC record, it is never too soon to begin to prepare for that day. It is recommended that:

1. Libraries become familiar with some of the possibilities available in an online environment and proceed accordingly;

2. Libraries document as much as possible. For example, libraries should keep track of methods for indicating holdings, means for knowing which version of the record should be the online catalog version as more copies are added to the collection and the record is used again, or any other local idiosyncracies that will make processing archival tapes easier.

Those libraries that are not yet online should consult with other libraries that are and learn from their experiences. By following the above recommendations, the local library can begin to predetermine what fields or fixed field elements will be important to the online catalog design and displays, and instruct the copy catalogers accordingly.

Local libraries should take into account that there are some fields in the record that, unless they are currently used for processing (i.e., card production, microfiche, etc.), cause absolutely no harm if they remain in the record, even if they are incorrectly coded. Example 8.2 illustrates an LC record where the fixed field code in position 32 of the MARC field 008 ("M" of OCLC element "M/F/B:" and RLIN-"MEI:") should really be coded "1", indicating that the main entry is in the body of the entry (i.e., the 245 field). If a library does not make use of this in an online environment (and it is doubtful that it will), it is unnecessary even to look at this code, let alone to verify it. Another example is provided by the fields in the record that contain other classification numbers from schemes that the local library does not use. When tapes are processed for creation of a catalog, the vendor is instructed to use the call number field(s) used by that library. It will ignore all of the other extraneous fields. Deleting all of the other classification fields can be time consuming (especially in LC records), truly unnecessary, and even undesirable, if, as in some libraries, these fields may be considered for alternative indexing of the records.

```
OCLC: 7841390      Rec stat: c Entrd: 820412        Used: 870630
Type: a Bib lvl: m Govt pub:      Lang:  eng Source:    Illus:
Repr:    Enc lvl:  Conf pub: O Ctry:  cau Dat tp: s M/F/B: 00
Indx: 1 Mod rec:   Festschr: O Cont: b
Desc: a Int lvl:   Dates: 1981,
   1 010        81-50790//r863
   2 040        DLC $c DLC $d m/c
   3 019        7848709
   4 020        0804711070
   5 050  0     K230.H3652 $b M3
   6 082  0     340/.109 $2 19
   7 090        $b
   8 049        YCLM
   9 100 10     MacCormick, Neil. $w cn
  10 245 10     H.L.A. Hart / $c Neil MacCormick.
  11 260  0     Stanford, Calif. : $b Stanford University Press, $c 1981.
  12 300        184 p. ; $c 23 cm.
  13 490  1     Jurists--profiles in legal theory
  14 504        "List of works by H.L.A. Hart": 8th prelim. page.
  15 504        Includes bibliographical references and index.
  16 650  0     Jurisprudence.
  17 600 10     Hart, H. L. A. $q (Herbert Lionel Adolphus), $d 1907- $w cn
  18 600 10     Hart, H. L. A. $q (Herbert Lionel Adolphus), $d 1907- $x
Bibliography. $w cn
  19 830  0     Jurists--profiles in legal theory (Stanford, Calif.)
```

Example 8.2. As can be seen in the 245 field, the main entry is indeed in the body of the entry, although the fixed field element (M/F/B:) has a zero in the first position. This fixed field element currently is not used for any automatic displays, printing, etc., and tends to be one of the least used elements of the fixed field. There are also two class numbers in this record. One of the two will probably be selected, but the other can still remain in the record since a local system vendor can merely ignore extraneous fields when processing the local library's tapes.

There are some fields, however, that can be used at a later date. For example, the index code (MARC field - 008/31; OCLC - "Indx:"; RLIN - "II:") is coded according to whether an index is available for the item. Example 8.3 illustrates a record that obviously has an index, according to the note on line 13, but whose fixed field code is "0", indicating no index. Therefore, even when an inputting library provides the correct notes, the fixed field can be incorrect. The local library needs to decide if this is a code that has to be correct or not. Although this author knows of no library that currently employs this code for any online display, it could conceivably be used in a short record display (translated mnemonically, of course) to indicate that the item has an index.

```
OCLC: 6132903        Rec stat: n  Entrd: 800423         Used: 871013
Type: a  Bib lvl: m  Govt pub:    Lang:  eng Source:    Illus: b
Repr:    Enc lvl:    Conf pub: 0  Ctry:  vau Dat tp: s  M/F/B: 10
Indx: 0  Mod rec:    Festschr: 0  Cont: b
Desc: i  Int lvl:    Dates: 1980,
    1 010        80-65162
    2 040        DLC $c DLC $d m.c.
    3 020        0913312215
    4 043        e-ur---
    5 050  0     Z6739.R9 $b A44 $a HD9506.R85
    6 082        016.3337/0947
    7 090         $b
    8 049        YCLM
    9 100 10     Alexandrov, Eugene A. $w cn
   10 245 10     Mineral & energy resources of the USSR : $b a selected
bibliography of sources in English / $c compiled by Eugene A.
Alexandrov.
   11 260  0     Falls Church, Va. : $b American Geological Institute, $c
1980.
   12 300        xv, 91 p. : $b map ; $c 25 cm.
   13 500        Includes indexes.
   14 650  0     Mines and mineral resources $z Russia $x Bibliography.
   15 650  0     Mineral industries $z Russia $x Bibliography.
   16 650  0     Power resources $z Russia $x Bibliography.
   17 710 20     American Geological Institute. $w cn
```

Example 8.3. The 500 field indicates that there are indexes included in this item, but the fixed field element "Indx:" indicates otherwise. This is an element of the fixed field in the MARC format that tends to be left at the system default, since it is an optional field in the standards of most utilities.

Another example of MARC data that can be important to online retrieval of a MARC record is the filing indicator position in title fields. Example 8.4 illustrates a 245 field where the filing indicator position has not been coded. This is common in older MARC records since it was not always required to code this indicator position. Some online catalogs make use of this code for indexing within their own systems, although for card production this code is not used. This again becomes a local decision, although this is one area that would not take much editing time or extensive knowledge of the MARC format.

```
OCLC: 71592          Rec stat: n Entrd: 700508      Used: 871114
Type: a Bib lvl: m Govt pub: _ Lang:  eng Source:    Illus: ac
Repr:     Enc lvl:   Conf pub: 1 Ctry:  ctu Dat tp: s M/F/B: 00
Indx: 0 Mod rec:   Festschr: 0 Cont: b
Desc:    Int lvl:   Dates: 1969,
    1 010       76-12028
    2 040       DLC $c DLC
    3 050  0    PS169.T7 $b M5
    4 082       191
    5 090        $b
    6 049       YCLM
    7 245  0    The Minor and later transcendentalists; $b a symposium. $c
Edited by Edwin Gittleman.
    8 260  0    Hartford, $b Transcendental Books $c [1969]
    9 300       72 1. $b illus., port. $c 29 cm.
   10 504       Includes bibliographies.
   11 650  0    Transcendentalism (New England)
   12 700 10    Gittleman, Edwin, $e ed.
```

Example 8.4. In the early days of MARC it was not required to code the filing indicator (i.e., second indicator position) in the 245 field. For those local libraries that intend to use these filing indicators in their local online systems, coding this correctly is important. In this example the indicators "04" should follow "245."

The above examples illustrate how very local the decisions are when instructing copy catalogers as to what to check, correct, or ignore when using a MARC record. In summary, the following basic options are available to the local library when making MARC record decisions for the non-card catalog environment:

Option 1: The copy cataloger edits only those fields appropriate to the currently used offline products, such as cards or online catalog archival tapes. Going in this direction will still provide many fine features of the MARC record, but inconsistencies will exist in fields that are not checked now but that the library may decide to use at a later date.

Option 2: The copy cataloger edits records both for the current catalog and in anticipation of specific fields being of use at a later date either when the institution goes online or when a current online catalog develops new features. This option is recommended only if extensive work is done in discerning what the possibilities are and if the time involved in making the appropriate changes is truly justifiable.

Option 3: The copy cataloger evaluates the entire record, making sure even the optional fields are accurate so that the MARC records will contain the entire realm of possibilities. This last option is the most time consuming and may be possible only with appropriate staffing levels. Also, because this option requires a much greater knowledge of the MARC formats, copy catalogers would have to be more highly trained.

Usefulness of Fields for the
Card Catalog and/or Shelflist

The production of catalog cards dictates a certain part of the evaluation and manipulation of the bibliographic record. In this area, the following should be given particular attention:

1. Call number fields

2. Fields that print as notes, in particular those with print constants

3. Fields providing or not providing access points (i.e., used to generate added entries) — this includes all subject, author, and title added entries

4. Missing necessary fields — some levels of records provide less information than others

5. Extraneous fields

Call Number Fields

To ensure the proper production of card sets, most utilities require the call number to be one from a classification scheme for which a library has been profiled. It is also required that it be entered correctly. For example, if a library has been profiled as a Dewey library on OCLC, only the 099, 098, or 092 call number fields (in that order of priority) will print when catalog cards and/or shelflist cards are produced. Instructing copy catalogers to look for and use only certain call number fields will ensure proper card production.

The call number fields that are not used for card production can be ignored and left in the record, for they will in no way affect card production, although they can appear on archival tapes. Some institutions are actually intentionally retaining all call number fields in anticipation of using more than one classification scheme as an indexing tool for their online public access catalogs.

Also, the cataloger should be aware of the possibility of the call number being input incorrectly. For example, in the Library of Congress call number fields (050 and 090 fields) in OCLC the decimal and the cutter numbers must be in the appropriate places in order for call numbers on catalog cards to print properly. Even in an online public catalog this could prove important when programming is done to process bibliographic records. Inaccuracies can cause misplaced call numbers and/or added staff time to reconcile problems noted by the vendor when processing the local library's tapes. Very few libraries have known the luxury of going online without a transition from the catalog card, so ensuring proper card production will continue to be important even as a library begins to go online.

Fields That Print as Notes

Fields that print as notes, in particular those having *print constants*, should be evaluated for their validity as well as the accuracy of the print constant being generated. However, just as differences between cataloging rules for punctuation and other minor descriptive issues should not take up valuable cataloging time, the structure of a note should not be the burden of the copy cataloger. As long as the note is conveying accurate information regarding the item, editing it either to switch the order of certain elements or to add a word or two when the meaning of the note remains the same is unnecessary and could require a higher level of copy cataloger. For example, there is little difference between "In Catalan, French, and Spanish," and "Catalan, French, and Spanish."

In serials, where the positions of dates in notes has changed slightly according to AACR 2, a library needs to decide whether or not changing the note to bring it to AACR 2 standards is worthwhile. This should only be done if the rest of the record is entered according to AACR 2 as well.

Another decision needed here involves whether the copy cataloger should be concerned with the order of the note fields. (This is not a problem for serials because the notes appear in MARC tag order.) According to AACR 2, notes should appear in a certain order. Given the differences between local library practices, some records will not be in accordance with this strict order. A library needs to decide if this order is important enough to take time to evaluate and adjust. Because it is so easy to move fields around online, this could be a great temptation, but may result in needless editing.

Perhaps the most important concern here is about print constants. Print constants are words such as "Summary" or "Indexed by" that introduce certain kinds of notes. As noted above, some fields provide print constants at the time the notes are printed on catalog cards (the print constants usually do not appear on the archival tape). The printing of some of the fields themselves can be controlled through the library's profile. However, control of the printing of print constants for those fields cannot be profiled. This must be done by properly coding the indicators for those fields. If the print constant indicator is coded to print, and the word itself is also typed into the text of the field before the cards are produced, two introductory words result (see Example 8.5, page 304). Another example can be found in serials format notes in the card production processes of some utilities. A note can be created automatically by the merging of two linking entry fields through the appropriate setting of the indicators. Improperly coded indicators can cause duplicate information in the catalog record (see Example 8.6, page 305). These kinds of errors may appear in records and can go undetected; therefore, copy catalogers should be advised to check these indicators for their accuracy.

Record (a)

```
OCLC: 9017458        Rec stat: n Entrd: 811020        Used: 850711
Type: g Bib lvl: m Govt pub:     Lang:  eng Source: c Leng: 027
        Enc lvl: 1 Type mat: m Ctry:  nyu Dat tp: s MEBE: 0
Tech: 1 Mod rec:          Accomp mat:
Desc: a Int lvl: g Dates: 1980,
    1 010        80-700973/F
    2 040        Time-Life Video $c DLC $d m/c
    3 007        m $b r $c u $d b $e a $f a $g a $h d
    4 020         $c For sale ($400.00)
    5 050        PN1995.9.C55 $b H57 1980
    6 082 1      791.43 $2 11
    7 090         $b
    8 049        YCLM
    9 245 00     Harold Lloyd's world of comedy $h [motion picture] / $c
produced by Harold Lloyd.
   10 260        New York : $b Time-Life Video, $c 1980.
   11 300        1 film reel (27 min.) : $b sd., b&w ; $c 16 mm.
   12 500        Title from data sheet.
   13 500        Intended audience: General.
   14 500        Issued also as videorecording.
   15 520        Summary:  Presents excerpts from numerous shorts and
feature-length films starring Harold Lloyd.
   16 650  0     Comedy films.
   17 650  1     Comedy films.
   18 700 11     Lloyd, Harold, $d 1894-1971. $w cn
   19 710 21     Time-Life Video. $w cn
   20 740 01     World of comedy.
```

Record (b)

```
PN1995.9
.C55 H57   Harold Lloyd's world of comedy [motion
1980           picture] / produced by Harold Lloyd.
           -- New York : Time-Life Video, 1980.
           1 film reel (27 min.) :  sd., b&w ; 16
       mm.
           Title from data sheet.
           Intended audience: General.
           Issued also as videorecording.
           Summary: Summary: Presents excerpts
       from numerous shorts and feature-length
       films starring Harold Lloyd.


           1. Comedy films.  2. [Comedy films.]
       I. Lloyd, Harold, 1894-1971.  II. Time-
       Life Video.  III. Title: World of
       comedy.

                            O

                                      80-700973
```

Example 8.5. The last note on Record (b) occurred because the first indicator, which controls the print constant for the 520 field, in line 15 of Record (a) was blank, meaning that it was set to print. In addition the cataloger had inserted the word "Summary:" in the note itself. (This record was edited to include this word; it is correct in the OCLC online file.) Some local online systems do not translate these indicator positions to provide print constants, so that some institutions input the print constants and leave them in the record. The first indicator in the 520 field should be "8" if the print constant should not be printed.

Record (a)

```
OCLC: 7536275      Rec stat: c Entrd: 810627        Used: 871030
Type: a Bib lvl: s Govt pub:    Lang:  eng Source: d S/L ent: 0
Repr:   Enc lvl: I Conf pub: 0 Ctry:  nyu Ser tp: p Alphabt: a
Indx: u Mod rec:   Phys med:    Cont: $   Frequn: m Pub st:  d
Desc: a Cum ind: u Titl pag: u ISDS:      Regulr: n Dates: 1914-1931
  1 010
  2 040       AZS $c AZS $d IUL $d DLC $d OCL
  3 019       8182023
  4 090       L11 $b .N74
  5 090         $b
  6 049       YCLM
  7 245 00    Normal instructor and primary plans.
  8 260 00    Dansville, N.Y. : $b F.A. Owen, $c 1914-1931.
  9 300       18 v. : $b ill. ; $c 36 cm.
 10 310       Monthly (except July and Aug.)
 11 362 0     Vol. 23, no. 7 (May 1914)-v. 40, no. 7 (May 1931)
 12 580       Merger of: Normal instructor (Dansville, N.Y. : 1906); and,
Primary plans.
 13 650  0    Education $x Periodicals.
 14 780 04    $t Normal instructor (Dansville, N.Y. : 1906) $w (DLC)sf
82005036 $w (OCoLC)8690878
 15 780 04    $t Primary plans $w (DLC)   06016936 $w (OCoLC)3417580
 16 785 00    $t Instructor (Dansville, N.Y.) $w (DLC)a   40002787 $w
(OCoLC)1753307
 17 936       May 1931
```

Record (b)

```
fL
11
N74          Normal instructor and primary plans. --
                Vol. 23, no. 7 (May 1914)-v. 40, no.
                7 (May 1931). -- Dansville, N.Y. :
             F.A. Owen, 1914-1931.
             18 v. : ill. ; 36 cm.
             Monthly (except July and Aug.)
             Merger of: Normal instructor
             (Dansville, N.Y. : 1906); and, Primary
             plans.
                Formed by the union of, Normal
             instructor (Dansville, N.Y. : 1906)
              and: Primary plans.
                Continued by: Instructor (Dansville,
             N.Y.).

             EDUCATION--PERIODICALS.
```

Example 8.6. The two notes beginning "Merger of" and "Formed by" in Record (b) are actually saying the same thing: One is from the 580 field and the other was generated by the print program settings in the two 780 fields in Record (a). A first indicator "0" in these fields generates the note beginning with "Formed by." A first indicator "1" turns off this feature. Record (a) is actually correct in the OCLC online file. It was edited here for the purpose of this example.

Fields Providing Access Points

For access points there are two major areas of concern: proper use of the indicators to generate added entries and correct usage of subfields.

Title fields—and most author fields—create added entries through the coding of the indicators. Example 8.7 shows a 100 field with a second indicator of "1". This indicator will generate a subject added entry card for that heading. In a dictionary card catalog, both headings would file in the same place. If the local subject cataloging policy prohibits this, copy catalogers should check this indicator every time to be sure it is set in accordance with local policy. The 245 field in this example shows a first indicator of "1". This generates the necessary title added entry. However, there may be titles for which it is not desired that an added entry be generated from this field (e.g., the generic title "Bulletin") so that the indicator in this position also should always be checked for its accuracy. It should especially be checked in cases of title main entries, for at times, the indicator may be inadvertently coded as a "1", which results in a title added entry card in addition to the title main entry card. This can occur when someone is creating a new record from an existing record and the main entry has changed to a title main entry (see "Exact Copy Not Found and the Use of Near Copy" later in this chapter). It is very easy to forget to set this indicator to zero when using existing copy and the main entry changes from author to title.

```
OCLC: 292490      Rec stat: c Entrd: 720410      Used: 871106
Type: a Bib lvl: m Govt pub:      Lang: eng Source:    Illus:
Repr:      Enc lvl:  Conf pub: 0 Ctry: nyu Dat tp: r M/F/B: 00a
Indx: 0 Mod rec:    Festschr: 0 Cont:
Desc:     Int lvl:  Dates: 1973,1912
 1 010        72-2120//r83
 2 040        DLC $c DLC $d m.c.
 3 020        0838314791
 4 041 1      engswe
 5 050 0      PT9814 $b .L3813 1973
 6 082        839.7/2/6 $a B
 7 090         $b
 8 049        YCLM
 9 100 11     Strindberg, August, $d 1849-1912. $w cn
10 240 10     Legender. $l English
11 245 10     Legends; autobiographical sketches.
12 260 0      New York, $b Haskell House Publishers $c 1973.
13 300        245 p. $c 23 cm.
14 500        Reprint of the 1912 ed.
15 500        Translation of Legender.
```

Example 8.7. The above example, with "1" in the second indicator position of the 100 field, would result in a subject added entry for Strindberg. Including a 600 entry for Strindberg would result in two identical subject added entries. LC does not follow the above practice in current cataloging, but instead provides the exact subject added entry. The use of the above method of adding a tracing is only appropriate when no subdivisions are required.

Subfield codes are of particular importance in subject heading (6XX) fields. Subfield codes $x, $y, and $z in these fields must appear in the field in order for the appropriate intervening punctuation (i.e., --) between headings and their subdivisions to print correctly on cards. None of the other subfields valid in these fields, such as subfields $n and $p, will generate this punctuation. On printed cards, the lack of the appropriate subfield-generated punctuation may not be catastrophic. However, the appropriate subfields may become more important when using the MARC record in a local online system, for it will be necessary to be able to tell the system vendor where to insert the punctuation (i.e., preceding or following which subfields), and such errors would be more apparent in the local system display.

Missing/Incorrect Data

From time to time, even though it has been determined that the record in fact describes the title in hand, the record may be found to be accurate but bibliographically incomplete or incorrect according to either cataloging rules, local policy, or both. Some of the most common missing or incorrect elements found in bibliographic records are as follows:

1. No 300 field (or missing elements in this field)

2. No 020 or 022 field

3. Incomplete contents notes for multivolume sets with distinct titles that an institution includes routinely

4. Miscoded reproduction code in the 008 (or fixed) field

5. Missing or inaccurate edition statements

6. Dates in the 260 field and the fixed field not in agreement in the nonserial formats

7. Various added entries, including subjects and series, missing or inaccurate

8. Mistagged fields and incorrect subfield codes

Copy catalogers should be instructed about how to handle these and other such variances when they arise.

Extraneous Fields

Extraneous fields (i.e., those that have no effect on card production and are not deemed necessary for present or future online catalog displays or access, particularly those input for local use by national libraries only) require some instruction to copy catalogers, though little or no manipulation or decision-making on their part regarding the content of these fields need occur. A general checklist for those not worth noting could help copy catalogers and speed up automated processing. However, this list should be given special consideration and should be created only after a thorough evaluation of the printing/non-printing fields in the system being used, coupled with some understanding of online catalogs.

EXACT COPY NOT FOUND
AND THE USE OF NEAR COPY

When a record does not exist for the title and format in hand, the next step is to search for near copy (including near co-op copy) online. The instances where near copy can be used to create new records by altering cards or card sets is covered in detail in Chapter 7. In the online, cooperative environment, where the unique description of a title is important, in many cases a completely new MARC record would be created for the new title. One must become familiar with the guidelines for creating new records in the utility being used, and also with current cataloging rules, in order to avoid duplication of effort and to avoid adding the library's holding symbol to inappropriate records.

The creation of a new record online can be much easier than altering catalog cards by hand. In the OCLC database, for example, a special online command prepares a record to be added to the database, retaining much of the MARC record that made it near copy to begin with. Example 8.8 (pages 309-10) illustrates how this works. In this use of near copy, there was little difference between the cataloging records for the first and second editions. Other than bringing the description up to AACR 2 standards, little editing was necessary. The LC-established Dewey call number could be used as the basis for the 092 field, and the subject heading was retained. The imprint statement, with minor alterations, was acceptable, as was the note field and the main entry. The fixed field was also very similar and merely needed to be recoded to reflect the new publication date, local cataloging codes, and a new level and type of description. Unfortunately, creating a new record from near copy is not always this simple and there are times when starting from scratch may seem easier than altering near copy.

If a new record is created for a cooperative cataloging system such as OCLC or RLIN, the level of expertise of copy catalogers should include categories 4-18 from Table 1 in Chapter 1, because original cataloging is being prepared. Some institutions do not give this type of work to copy catalogers, although others do. This is a local decision based on how well, and in what areas, copy catalogers are trained. If a copy cataloger holds this responsibility, it is a good idea to have an original cataloger or other staff member of high expertise look over the new record being added to the database. This can be a usual procedure or one to follow until the copy cataloger has become proficient in the use of near copy.

Record (a)

```
OCLC: 134702        Rec stat: c Entrd:  710419         Used: 851011
Type: a Bib lvl: m Govt pub:     Lang:  eng Source:     Illus: b
Repr:    Enc lvl:    Conf pub: 0 Ctry:  gw  Dat tp: s M/F/B: 10
Indx: 0 Mod rec: m Festschr: 0 Cont:
Desc:    Int lvl:    Dates: 1969,
   1 010       77-550069
   2 040       DLC $c DLC $d m.c.
   3 015       GDB***
   4 043       e-gx---
   5 050 0     CS614 $b .F7
   6 082       929.1/0943
   7 092       $b
   8 049       TRNN
   9 100 10    Friederichs, Heinz F. $q (Heinz Friedrich) $w cn
  10 245 10    How to find my German ancestors and relatives, $c by Heinz
F. Friederichs.
  11 260 0     Neustadt [West Germany] $b Degener, $c 1969.
  12 300       16 p. $b map. $c 21 cm.
  13 500       Cover title.
  14 651  0    Germany $x Genealogy.
```

Record (b)

```
OCLC: NEW          Rec stat: n Entrd:  851011         Used: 851011
Type: a Bib lvl: m Govt pub:     Lang:  ___ Source: _  Illus:
Repr:    Enc lvl: _  Conf pub: 0 Ctry:  xx  Dat tp: _ M/F/B: 10
Indx: 0 Mod rec:   Festschr: 0 Cont:
Desc: _ Int lvl:    Dates: ____,
   1 010
   2 040        $c TRN
   3 092        $b
   4 049        TRNN
   5 100 10     Friederichs, Heinz F. $q (Heinz Friedrich) $w cn
   6 245 10     How to find my German ancestors and relatives, $c by Heinz
F. Friederichs.
   7 260 0      Neustadt [West Germany] $b Degener, $c 1969.
   8 300        16 p. $b map. $c 21 cm.
   9 500        Cover title.
  10 651  0     Germany $x Genealogy.
```

Example 8.8. These three records illustrate how to create a new record from existing copy on OCLC. This capability is available in all of the major networks, and many of the smaller systems. Record (a) for the original edition is called up and a specific command is used, resulting in Record (b), which retains much of what appeared in the original record. In order to create Record (c) (page 310), the only fields that had to be added were the call number and the edition statement. Also, the date had to be adjusted appropriately, ISBD punctuation was added, and AACR 2 rules were followed. In addition fixed field information was filled in.

Record (c)

```
OCLC: 12662287     Rec stat: n Entrd: 851011        Used: 851011
Type: a Bib lvl: m Govt pub:    Lang:  eng Source: d Illus: b
Repr:    Enc lvl: I Conf pub: 0 Ctry:  gw  Dat tp: s M/F/B: 10
Indx: 0 Mod rec:    Festschr: 0 Cont:
Desc: a Int lvl:    Dates: 1985,
   1 010
   2 040      TRN $c TRN
   3 092      929.10943 $b F912h, 1985
   4 092      $b
   5 049      TRNN
   6 100 10   Friederichs, Heinz F. $q (Heinz Friedrich) $w cn
   7 245 10   How to find my German ancestors and relatives / $c by Heinz
F. Friederichs.
   8 250      2nd ed.
   9 260  0   Neustadt [West Germany] : $b Degener & Co., $c 1985.
  10 300      16 p. : $b map ; $c 21 cm.
  11 500      Cover title.
  12 651   0  Germany $x Genealogy.
```

Example 8.8 *(continued)*.

It is also necessary to search one more time immediately preceding the adding of a new record to any database when creating that record from a near copy workform. One last search should be performed to ensure nonduplicated records and, thus, fewer multiple responses to the searching done by other users of the system.

ENTERING A NEW RECORD ONLINE

Depending on the type of library and the source of cataloging being used, most libraries will have a relatively good hit-rate (i.e., percentage of records found online) and will not be creating many original records. In cases where a title will most likely be cataloged by the Library of Congress within a short or acceptable period of time, and if there is no particular urgency for processing the title, the item may be set aside to wait for the record to be created by LC or other library. Some institutions wait a designated period of time (e.g., 10 weeks) and then automatically search again for a record. If a record is not found after the second search, the item may be sent to the original cataloging department or put into the backlog for searching at a later designated time. For some local materials, such as theses and in-house publications, no matter how long one waits for copy the appropriate record may never appear online and original cataloging ultimately will be needed to process the title.

For titles whose publication dates precede the issuing of MARC records by the Library of Congress (i.e., 1968 for English language monographs; later dates for various other languages), the *National Union Catalog (NUC)* can be a viable source for paper copy. Copy found there can be used as a basis for MARC copy, either transcribed exactly or altered, and input into the online system for record production (see Example 7.14 on page 270). Users of online systems, however, have found so many titles online that although *NUC* can still be helpful for some foreign language titles, particularly those in non-Roman scripts, *NUC* is not often being searched as an alternative source of copy for current Roman script items unless there is good reason to believe that copy can be found.

AUTHORITY CONTROL AND
LIBRARY OF CONGRESS AUTHORITY RECORDS

For all name and subject headings, the preceding individual chapters dealing with each of these areas of the bibliographic record can be applied to machine-readable copy as well. Fortunately, in most systems, authority files for name headings and series titles are usually made available online. Subject authority records are currently available on OCLC and Utlas. Authority records are also available as CD-ROM products or on microfiche.

If authority work is performed in the local library, it must be decided how much authority work is to be done at the terminal. Some institutions check all headings online as they catalog. Others who, for example, have online catalogs, might accept all headings as they find them online and then correct any outdated headings in the local online system through postcataloging operations. In the latter instance, the verification of all headings could be done at the same time instead of individually as the records are produced. Institutions that order card sets from a master unit record often prefer to check the headings before producing cards in order not to have to correct them manually later on. When establishing procedures, the following should be taken into account:

1. The processing environment (for example, terminal time may be at a premium and therefore used most efficiently when authority work is not part of processing)

2. The expertise of the copy cataloger

3. The format (e.g., paper versus online) and location of the local authority file

4. The expected use of the authority file to update older headings, etc.

5. The location and format of the Library of Congress authority files (e.g., online versus microfiche)

If maintaining authoritative headings on MARC records is an objective of the local library, vendors who provide authorities services may be considered for the process of cleaning up local archival tapes. Some actually perform authorities conversions of archival tapes and provide a subscription for this service. Another maintains the bibliographic records online and, for a fee, updates the headings on the bibliographic records themselves as changes occur in the authority record. The only problem with the latter service is the inability to create local headings that appear as references in LC authority records (i.e., a local library may wish deliberately to use a form that LC has chosen as a reference rather than the form LC has chosen as the heading). This cannot be done when using a vendor for authorities because every time a global replace takes place, the locally assigned headings will be replaced by another heading. Maintaining consistency and documenting all procedures used in producing local catalog records will help to assure a cleaner local online authority file when that day comes.

When using an LC authority record to verify a heading, there are a few basic fixed field elements and/or headings that are important to note. These are addressed below. If headings are not found in the file, they can be created based on AACR 2 rules and the evaluation of the records for other similar headings.

The use of LC authority records can be a complicated matter. Provided here are some pointers on evaluating the records and instructing copy catalogers in using them. Depending on which type of authority record is being used (i.e., name, uniform title, subject, or series), the fields that a copy cataloger needs to address vary, although not greatly. Many of the fields to look at are the same, with only some slight variations. In the interest of clarity, name headings are discussed separately from uniform title headings, series, and subjects below.

Name Authority Records

The following specific fields need to be addressed when verifying a heading in a bibliographic record with an LC authority record.

Rules

The code for the cataloging rules followed can be found in MARC field 008/07, in the OCLC fixed field as "Rules:", and in RLIN as "CRC:".

The copy cataloger should look first for code "c" or "d" in this fixed field element. If the code is "c" or "d", it indicates that the main heading in the record has been established in accordance with AACR 2 practice. Other codes, such as "a" or "b", indicating headings based on older rules, must be dealt with as well. If the heading is not AACR 2, a more complex type of evaluation may be necessary. The rules by which the heading in the bibliographic record was established must first be considered. If that heading is already in AACR 2 form, and it conflicts with the authority record that is not coded AACR 2, a local method for dealing with this situation must be established. Some possible choices (not an exhaustive list, however) are as follows:

1. The bibliographic heading, if in AACR 2 form, could override the non-AACR 2 heading in the authority file

2. The heading, by essence of being in the authority file, could be considered authoritative

3. In all such discrepancies, the title could be handed over to an original cataloger for evaluation

There is, unfortunately, a small problem with each of the above choices, which should be pointed out. If choice number 1 is used, one must assume that the heading in the bibliographic record is, in fact, in AACR 2 form when the description is coded as such. In other words, the description level can be coded as AACR 2, but the heading may not be correctly established or may not conform with local practices. There may be some telltale signs of an AACR 2 heading (e.g., the use of forenames in parentheses in personal name headings), but it may otherwise take some high level evaluation to confirm that a heading is, indeed, AACR 2. Whether copy catalogers can perform this task depends upon the extent of their training. Choice number 2 means taking a heading that is actually stated as being pre-AACR 2 and adding it to the local catalog, although the pre-AACR 2 form in the authority record may or may not eventually be established as the AACR 2 heading. Studies show that only 15 to 18 percent of pre-AACR 2 headings are established differently under AACR 2, so this may not be a bad choice.[3] The copy cataloger would have to know how to establish AACR 2 headings in order to make this evaluation. If choice number 3 is selected, it would require staff time that might not be available. However, the counterbalance to this is the extra work that may be required later by other staff due to the possible addition of incorrect headings to the local catalogs because of choice 1 or 2.

1XX, 4XX, 5XX Fields

The 1XX fields (here being 100, 110, 111) are the fields in which the established heading is found. The 4XX fields (400, 410, 411) contain "see from" references that are either pre-AACR 2 form of names or variant forms. The 5XX fields contain "see also from" references for earlier, later, or otherwise related names. Sometimes, of course, the heading in the work might appear in either the 4XX or 5XX fields, and the copy cataloger needs to be instructed on some of the idiosyncracies of headings in order to know what direction to take. For example, line 11 in Example 8.9 (page 314) gives an earlier form of name for this institution for which an authority record may or may not have been made. If this is the form on the piece, the copy cataloger would need to look at that record instead. In this example, there actually is not a separate record for the name in this 510 field. It is a related society for which LC has not yet created an authority record. It is worth noting the use of the subfield $w in 5XX fields to indicate whether the heading is an earlier or later one (see Records (b), (c), and (d) in Example 4.10 on pages 115-16). The letter "a" in such a subfield $w indicates an earlier name, while the letter "b" indicates a later name. When establishing headings for serials, which sometimes cover long periods during which the corporate body has changed names once or twice, these indications can become very useful.

667 and 670 Fields

The 667 and 670 fields are two notes fields in authority records. The copy cataloger looking for a heading and only finding one record for a corporate body, for example, that has obviously changed names over the years, should be instructed to look for information in these fields. In Example 8.9, earlier headings not established in authority records of their own are found in the

667 field. This field can be used as verification of the AACR 2 heading. In some cases, the 670 field can also contain very valuable information (see discussion of this field for series authority records below).

```
ARN: 296843      Rec stat: n      Entrd: 840819       Used: 840819
Type: z          Geo subd: n      Govt agn: _ Lang:   Source:
Roman: _         Subj: a          Series: n ‾ Ser num: n Head: aab
Ref status: a    Upd status: a    Auth status: a      Name: n
Enc lvl: n       Auth/Ref: a      Mod rec:            Rules: c

   1 010      n  79063901
   2 040         DLC $c DLC
   3 110 20      Institution of Electrical Engineers.
   4 110 20      Institution of Electrical Engineers, London $w nnaa
   5 410 20      Society of Telegraph Engineers (London, England)
   6 410 20      Society of Telegraph Engineers and Electricians (London,
England)
   7 410 20      Institute of Electrical Engineers (London, England)
   8 410 20      Angliiskii institut inzhenerov-elektrikov (London,
England)
   9 410 20      IEE
  10 410 20      I.E.E.
  11 510 20      Northern Society of Electrical Engineers
  12 667         The following headings for earlier names are also valid
AACR 2 headings: Society of Telegraph Engineers; Society of Telegraph
Engineers and Electricians.
  13 670         Angliiskii ...
  14 670         LC data base 10/18/83 $b (hdg.: Institution of Electrical
Engineers, London)
```

Example 8.9. This corporate name authority record shows a related name that does not have a record of its own and also two earlier names that LC has not established separately.

Authority Records for Uniform Title Headings

1XX Field

Uniform title headings can appear in 100, 110, 111, or 130 fields of authority records. When the heading consists of a name and a title, it is coded 100, 110, or 111, depending upon the type of name. The title then appears in the subfield "$t" of that same field (see Record (a) in Example 8.10, pages 315-16). These headings can be confusing for the novice because when they are used as main entries, they are not transcribed into a bibliographic record in the same way they appear in the authority record. Instead, the title part of the uniform title heading from subfield "$t" (and any subsequent subfields) of the authority record is transcribed into field 240 of the bibliographic record, as shown in Record (b) of Example 8.10. When used as added entries or subject entries, however, they are transcribed into single 6XX or 7XX fields, as shown in Record (c) of Example 8.10, line 24 (page 316).

Record (a)

```
ARN: 1084760      Rec stat: n      Entrd: 840830           Used: 840830
Type: z           Geo subd: n      Govt agn: _ Lang:       Source:
Roman: _          Subj: a          Series: n  Ser num: n   Head: aab
Ref status: a     Upd status: a    Auth status: a          Name: a
Enc lvl: n        Auth/Ref: a      Mod rec:                Rules: c

  1 010       n  82257958
  2 040       DLC $c DLC
  3 100 10    Capote, Truman, $d 1924- $t Breakfast at Tiffany's
  4 400 10    Capote, Truman, $d 1924- $t Breakfast at Tiffany's and
three stories
  5 670       His Breakfast at Tiffany's and three stories, 1983, c1958.
```

Record (b)

```
OCLC: 10825536      Rec stat: n Entrd: 840516         Used: 870123
Type: a Bib lvl: m Govt pub:       Lang: eng Source:   Illus: fa
Repr:     Enc lvl:    Conf pub: 0 Ctry:  pau Dat tp: c M/F/B: 11
Indx: 0 Mod rec:     Festschr: 0 Cont:
Desc: a Int lvl:     Dates: 1983,1958
  1 010       83-113742
  2 040       DLC $c DLC $d m/c
  3 050 0     PS3505.A59 $b B7 1983
  4 082 0     813/.54 $2 19
  5 090       $b
  6 049       YCLM
  7 100 10    Capote, Truman, $d 1924- $w cn
  8 240 10    Breakfast at Tiffany's
  9 245 10    Breakfast at Tiffany's and three stories / $c Truman Capote
; illustrated by Kenneth Francis Dewey.
 10 250       A Limited ed.
 11 260 0     Franklin Center, Pa. : $b Franklin Library, $c 1983, c1958.
 12 300       174 p., [6] leaves of plates : $b ill. ; $c 20 cm.
 13 440  4    The Collected stories of the world's greatest writers
 14 500       "Notes from the editors" (22 p.) laid in.
 15 505 0     Breakfast at Tiffany's -- House of flowers -- A diamond
guitar -- A Christmas memory.
```

Example 8.10. Record (a) is for a uniform title heading. The name of the author is required for a complete heading. When used as a main entry, the heading appears in two fields (100 and 240) of the bibliographic record, Record (b). When used as an added entry, it is transcribed into one field, shown in line 24 of Record (c) (page 316).

Record (c)

```
OCLC: 12913526      Rec stat: c Entrd: 840420      Used: 870815
Type: i Bib lvl: m Lang:  eng Source:   Accomp mat:
Repr:      Enc lvl:    Ctry:  nyu Dat tp: s MEBE: 0
           Mod rec:    Comp:   nn Format: n Prts: n
Desc: a Int lvl:       LTxt:    f  Dates: 1983,
  1 010       83-740016/R
  2 040       DLC $c DLC $d OCL $d m/c
  3 007       s $b d $c u $d b $e s $f m $g e $h n $i n $j m $k p $l l $m u
  4 019       10106738
  5 020       0898451469
  6 028 02    SBR-502 $b Caedmon
  7 050 1     PS3505.A59
  8 050 0     Caedmon SBR-502
  9 090       $b
 10 049       YCLM
 11 245 00    Breakfast at Tiffany's $h [sound recording].
 12 260 0     New York, N.Y. : $b Caedmon, $c p1983.
 13 300       3 sound discs (146 min.) : $b 33 1/3 rpm, stereo. ; $c 12 in.
 14 306       022600
 15 500       "A Novel Approach recording"--Container.
 16 500       Dramatized with music and sound effects.
 17 500       Adapted by Jane Tannehill from Truman Capote's novel of the
same title.
 18 511 1     Elizabeth Ashley (Holly Golightly), David Dukes (narrator),
Caedmon Players with Larry Robinson, Jerry Terheyden, Maggie Albright.
 19 500       Automatic sequence.
 20 520       Tells the story of a bright and brittle Manhattan playgirl,
the men who love her, and her dreams of a romantic, sophisticated life
in Brazil.
 21 700 10    Tannehill, Jane. $w cn
 22 700 10    Ashley, Elizabeth, $d 1939- $w cn
 23 700 10    Dukes, David. $w cn
 24 700 11    Capote, Truman, $d 1924- $t Breakfast at Tiffany's. $w cn
 25 710 20    Caedmon Players. $w cn
```

Example 8.10 *(continued)*.

When a uniform title heading consists of a title only, it is recorded in field 130 of the authority record (see Example 8.11). In this case it is transcribed into a single 130, 630, or 730 field of a bibliographic record as it appears in the authority record. The first indicator position (filing indicator) is blank because LC does not code this position due to system restrictions in their inhouse systems. As a result they must establish uniform title headings in the 130 field without initial articles.

Other Fields

All other fields of uniform title records (e.g., fixed field for rules used, 4XX, 5XX, 667, and 670) serve the same functions as described under name authority records.

Record (a)

```
ARN: 1082805      Rec stat: n      Entrd: 840830          Used: 840830
Type: z           Geo subd: n      Govt agn: _ Lang:      Source:
Roman: _          Subj: a          Series: n  Ser num: n  Head: aab
Ref status: a     Upd status: a    Auth status: a         Name: n
Enc lvl: n        Auth/Ref: a      Mod rec:               Rules: c

  1 010       n  82255602
  2 040       DLC $c DLC
  3 130  0    Bible. $p N.T. $p Mark. $l French.
  4 430  0    Bible. $p Evangile selon Marc
  5 430  0    Bible. $p N.T. $p Marc
  6 430  0    Evangile selon Marc
  7 670       Standaert, B. L'Evangile selon Marc, 1983.
```

Record (b)

```
OCLC: 11235338       Rec stat: n Entrd: 830912        Used: 861107
Type: a  Bib lvl: m  Govt pub:    Lang:  fre Source:    Illus:
Repr:    Enc lvl:    Conf pub: 0  Ctry:  fr  Dat tp: s  M/F/B: 10
Indx: 0  Mod rec:    Festschr: 0  Cont: b
Desc: a  Int lvl:    Dates: 1983,
  1 010       83-199202
  2 040       DLC $c DLC $d m/c
  3 020       2204019623 : $c 45.00F
  4 050  0    BS2585.3 $b .S69 1983
  5 082  0    226/.307 $2 19
  6 090        $b
  7 049       YCLM
  8 100 10    Standaert, Beno^it. $w cn
  9 245 12    L'Evangile selon Marc : $b commentaire / $c Beno^it
Standaert.
 10 260  0    Paris : $b Editions du Cerf, $c 1983.
 11 300       141 p. ; $c 18 cm.
 12 490  0    Lire la Bible, $x 0588-2257 ; $v 61
 13 504       Bibliography: p. [137]-138.
 14 630 00    Bible. $p N.T. $p Mark $x Commentaries.
```

Example 8.11. Record (a) is for a uniform title heading that does not have a name as its main entry. The heading has been used as the basis for the subject heading in Record (b). As is the practice for subject headings, the language designation has been omitted.

Series Authority Records

Series headings are also established as uniform title headings, but they can be transcribed into additional fields of bibliographic records. They are treated separately here because series authority records contain additional fields that provide important data.

130 Field

Most series appear in 130 fields of authority records (see Example 8.12). However, in bibliographic records, they can be transcribed into 440 or 830 fields in addition to any uniform title fields. Just as for uniform titles, series titles are established by LC without initial articles. However, the copy cataloger needs to be aware that if an initial article appears in the series area of the bibliographic record as the established heading, it is not necessarily incorrect. It probably reflects the AACR 2 description of the item in hand. LC has recently begun using the article in the bibliographic record, even if the heading is being, or has been, established in the authority record without it. It is up to the local library to decide if the copy cataloger should add the articles back into earlier LC copy or leave the copy as is.

```
ARN: 1795592      Rec stat: c      Entrd: 870311           Used: 870325
Type: z           Geo subd: n      Govt agn: _ Lang:       Source:
Roman: _          Subj: a          Series: a  Ser num: a Head: aaa
Ref status: a     Upd status: a    Auth status: a          Name: n
Enc lvl: n        Auth/Ref: a      Mod rec:                Rules: c

 1 010        n  86701074
 2 040        DLC $c DLC $d DLC
 3 130   0    IEE energy series.
 4 410  20    Institution of Electrical Engineers. $t IEE energy series
$w nna
 5 642        2 $5 DLC
 6 643        London, U.K. $b Peter Peregrinus
 7 644        f $5 DLC
 8 645        t $5 DLC
 9 646        s $5 DLC
10 670        Dunn, P.D. Renewable energies, c1986: $b ser. t.p.
```

Example 8.12. This is an example of a series authority record. Some fields are similar to those found in name and uniform title authority records, but it also has a few unique fields or messages that need to be dealt with separately when instructing copy catalogers.

Rules

This code is found in MARC field 008/07, in OCLC's fixed field element "Rules:", and in RLIN as "CRC:". The same guidelines as for name authority records can be applied here.

643 Field

This field indicates the place of publication of the series as it appears on the item from which it was established. There will be more than one of these fields if the publication information changes during the life of the series.

644, 645, and 646 Fields

These fields are specific to series records. The 644 field indicates whether the individual volumes of the series are analyzed (i.e., given bibliographic records of their own). The letter "f" means the volumes are to be analyzed in *full*.

Other options in this field are "p" for analyzed in *part*, and "n" for *not analyzed*. The 645 field indicates whether a series is traced ("t") or not traced ("n"). There are occasionally two 645 fields indicating LC's tracing decision before and after the adoption of AACR 2. The 646 field indicates whether the individual volumes of the series are classified separately ("s"), as a collected set ("c"), or with the main series ("m").

670 Field

The 670 field provides the source of the heading, or other notes, as in other authority records. However, this information can be especially helpful in deciding if this is truly the series in which the work has been published. For example, if the place of publication of the series has changed since the establishment of the heading (and LC has not yet updated the record to reflect this), the publisher in the work being cataloged may differ from that in the 643 field. In this case it is appropriate to question whether the series is the same one. One way of solving the mystery is to check a list of the titles in that series (often that can be found right on the item) to determine whether the title listed in the 670 field also appears on that list. The ISSN is sometimes also listed as well (see Example 8.13), which can also serve as a checkpoint.

```
ARN: 1557202      Rec stat: n      Entrd: 860430        Used: 860430
Type: z           Geo subd: n      Govt agn: _ Lang:    Source:
Roman: _          Subj: a          Series: a _ Ser num: b Head: aaa
Ref status: n     Upd status: a    Auth status: a       Name: n
Enc lvl: n        Auth/Ref: a      Mod rec:             Rules: c

  1 010       n  86733782
  2 022       0275-875X
  3 040       DLC $c DLC $d DLC
  4 130    0  Wiley series on marketing management.
  5 643       New York $b Wiley
  6 644       f $5 DLC
  7 645       t $5 DLC
  8 646       s $5 DLC
  9 670       Crompton, J. L. Marketing government and social service,
c1986: $b ser. t.p.
```

Example 8.13. This record includes the ISSN of the series (field 022), a practice by LC since 1986. Therefore, only records created since that time will have this field present.

Subject Authority Records

In order to make efficient use of the LC subject authority records, it is important to understand what can and cannot be found there. OCLC *Technical Bulletin* no. 180 (November 1987), page 2, which preceded OCLC's loading of these records in December 1987, provides a good synopsis of what the user of these records needs to know:

SCOPE OF THE LC SUBJECT AUTHORITY FILE*

The MARC Distribution Service described the scope of the LC Subject Authorities File in a 1986 MARCH memorandum that announced the availability of the file:

"Under current [LC] policy, authority records are created only for those heading and heading-subdivision combinations which are to be printed in *Library of Congress Subject Headings* [LCSH]. Records are not created for every unique heading-subdivision combination assigned to a bibliographic record.

"Categories which currently are not printed and for which no MARC subject authority records are created are:

(1) names of persons, unless used as a pattern or example, or unless a subdivision must be printed;
(2) names of corporate bodies and jurisdictions, unless used as a pattern or example, or unless a subdivision must be printed;
(3) headings incorporating free-floating subdivisions, unless needed for use as a reference to another heading, or followed by a nonfree-floating subdivision;
(4) phrase headings created by incorporating free-floating terms (e.g., ... Region, ... Valley, ... in art, ... in literature).

[NOTE: Name authority records are created and distributed for categories 1 and 2 above].

"The file does **not** contain:

(1) records for subdivisions.... No LC policy has been developed for any possible future implementation of subdivision records.
(2) records for non-LC authority systems (e.g., MESH, NAL, NLC);
(3) records for LC juvenile headings. The Library of Congress will not maintain authority records for these headings as part of its internal automated authority system. Printed lists of these headings will be available [from LC]. The headings will continue to be used in bibliographic records in the Annotated Card program." ...

Additionally, you should note the following about LC subject authority records:

...

(2) Dewey Decimal Classification numbers are not yet included in the records.
(3) Source data information (e.g., 670 fields) may not be present in all existing authority records. However, newly created records will carry source data.
(4) ... "Narrower" term references are not being carried in LC subject authority records....

This file does not replace or duplicate LCSH. Cross-references needed to link subject headings formerly used (and still found in older OCLC records) to the form now used may or may not be present.

---

*Excerpted with permission from OCLC.

What this statement points out is that having access to the LC subject authority records does not eliminate the need for *LCSH*, nor does it make subject analysis and the assigning of subject headings any easier. The authors believe that given the complications of interpretation of these records, and given that they must be used in combination with the fiche or paper copy of *LCSH*, a copy cataloger would have to be highly trained in order to use these records accurately. Even the checking of old records to determine whether subject headings are still valid, or what their new forms would be, cannot be done easily because, as stated in the last paragraph of the above OCLC excerpt, the references necessary to make the connection may or may not be there.

The data covered in the following sections include those fields necessary for understanding the information provided by these records. There are other elements of these records that address the use of headings as subjects, but because those elements are not really necessary when deciphering an authority record, they are not noted here.

Direct/Indirect Geographic Subdivision Code

These codes appear in MARC field 008/06, "Geo subd:" in OCLC, and "DID:" in RLIN.

In name, series, and uniform title records this area is coded as "n", meaning "not applicable." In subject records, however, two different values predominate. For those headings that can be subdivided geographically, code "i" is assigned. The code applies to the heading, or to the heading and established subdivision combination, as shown in Example 8.14, Records (a) and (b) (page 322). The code for headings and heading/subdivision combinations that cannot be subdivided geographically is a "blank." At the time of this writing, "Geo subd:" in OCLC is followed by a *fill* character when geographic subdivision is not authorized (see Example 8.15, page 322). "Reference records," discussed below, also contain a fill character in the "Geo subd:" of the fixed field in OCLC.

Record (a)

```
ARN: 2033242    Rec stat: c      Entrd: 871218           Used: 871218
Type: z         Geo subd: i      Govt agn: _ Lang:       Source:
Roman: _        Subj: a          Series: n ¯ Ser num: n  Head: bab
Ref status: a   Upd status: a    Auth status: a          Name: n
Enc lvl: n      Auth/Ref: a      Mod rec:                Rules: n

 1 010       sh 85086804
 2 040       DLC $c DLC $d DLC
 3 150     0 Money market funds
 4 450     0 Funds, Money market
 5 550     0 Mutual funds $w g
```

Record (b)

```
ARN: 2033259    Rec stat: n      Entrd: 871218           Used: 871218
Type: z         Geo subd: i      Govt agn: _ Lang:       Source:
Roman: _        Subj: a          Series: n ¯ Ser num: n  Head: bab
Ref status: n   Upd status: a    Auth status: a          Name: n
Enc lvl: n      Auth/Ref: a      Mod rec:                Rules: n

 1 010       sh 85086807
 2 040       DLC $c DLC
 3 150     0 Money market funds $x Reserves $x Law and legislation
```

Example 8.14. The code "i" is assigned in the "Geo subd:" fixed field of both of these records. Thus, geographic subdivision is authorized at the end of each string. For example, the heading in Record (a) could be subdivided "Money market funds – New York," and the heading in Record (b) could be subdivided "Money market funds – Reserves – Law and legislation – New York."

```
ARN: 2137108    Rec stat: n      Entrd: 871219           Used: 871219
Type: z         Geo subd: _      Govt agn: _ Lang:       Source:
Roman: _        Subj: a          Series: n ¯ Ser num: n  Head: bab
Ref status: b   Upd status: a    Auth status: a          Name: n
Enc lvl: n      Auth/Ref: a      Mod rec:                Rules: n

 1 010       sh 85126519
 2 040       DLC $c DLC $d DLC
 3 053       PE1147 $b PE1153 $c English
 4 150     0 Spelling reform
 5 450     0 English language $x Spelling reform
 6 450     0 Orthography
 7 450     0 Simplified spelling
 8 550     0 English language $x Orthography and spelling $w g
 9 680       $i Here are entered works dealing with the effort to
reform English orthography. Works on orthography, spelling, and spelling
reform in languages in general are entered under $a Language and
Languages--Orthography and spelling. $i Works dealing with orthography,
spelling, and spelling reform in specific languages or groups of
languages are entered under the name of the language with subdivision $a
Orthography and spelling, $i e.g. $a French language--Orthography and
spelling.
10 681       $i Notes under $a Language and languages--Orthography and
spelling; Phonetic spelling
```

Example 8.15. This record has a fill character in the "Geo subd:" fixed field. The heading in this record, "Spelling reform," may not be subdivided geographically.

It should be noted that even though a heading and subdivision combination may not be authorized for geographic subdivision after the subdivision, the heading itself may be authorized for geographic subdivision, in which case a geographic subdivision could be inserted between the heading and the topical subdivision (see Example 8.16). It should also be noted that even when a heading is coded "i", and therefore may be subdivided geographically, there may be restrictions on use or meaning that are apparent only if one reads the notes in the 680 fields, which are discussed further below (see Example 8.17, page 324).

Record (a)

```
ARN: 2094669    Rec stat: n     Entrd: 871218        Used: 871218
Type: z         Geo subd: i     Govt agn: _ Lang:    Source:
Roman: _        Subj: a         Series: n _ Ser num: n Head: bab
Ref status: b   Upd status: a   Auth status: a       Name: n
Enc lvl: n      Auth/Ref: a     Mod rec:             Rules: n

 1 010          sh 85119438
 2 040          DLC $c DLC $d DLC
 3 053          GN495.2 $c Primitive
 4 053          HS
 5 150   0      Secret societies
 6 360            $i names of individual secret societies
 7 450   0      Fraternities
 8 550   0      Hazing $w g
 9 550   0      Rites and ceremonies $w g
10 550   0      Ritual $w g
11 550   0      Societies $w g
12 550   0      Sociology $w g
13 550   0      Initiations (into trades, societies, etc.)
```

Record (b)

```
ARN: 2094682    Rec stat: n     Entrd: 871218        Used: 871218
Type: z         Geo subd: _     Govt agn: _ Lang:    Source:
Roman: _        Subj: a         Series: n _ Ser num: n Head: bab
Ref status: b   Upd status: a   Auth status: a       Name: n
Enc lvl: n      Auth/Ref: a     Mod rec:             Rules: n

 1 010          sh 85119439
 2 040          DLC $c DLC
 3 053          HS155 $b 8
 4 150   0      Secret societies $x Rituals
 5 360            $i subdivision $a Rituals $i under names of individual
secret societies
 6 550   0      Ritual $w g
```

Example 8.16. The code "i" is assigned in the "Geo subd:" fixed field of Record (a), meaning that it is permissible to subdivide this heading geographically (e.g., "Secret societies – New York"). In Record (b) the code is represented by a fill character. Thus, a geographic subdivision may not be placed at the end of the string. However, because it is permissible to geographically subdivide the main part of the heading, a geographic subdivision may be placed between the main heading and the subdivision (e.g., "Secret societies – New York – Rituals").

```
ARN: 2082400      Rec stat: n      Entrd: 871218          Used: 871218
Type: z           Geo subd: i      Govt agn: _ Lang:      Source:
Roman: _          Subj: a          Series: n ¯ Ser num: n Head: bab
Ref status: b     Upd status: a    Auth status: a         Name: n
Enc lvl: n        Auth/Ref: a      Mod rec:               Rules: n
```

```
 1 010       sh 85013838
 2 040       DLC $c DLC $d DLC
 3 053       Z1001 $b Z9000
 4 150   0   Bibliography
 5 360           $i names of literatures, e.g. $a American literature; $i
and subdivision $a Bibliography $i under names of persons, places and
subjects; also subdivision $a Bibliography--Methodology $i under
specific subjects, e.g. $a Medicine--Bibliography--Methodology; $i and
subdivision $a Imprints $i under names of countries, states, cities,
etc.
 6 450   0   Book lists
 7 450   0   Lists of publications
 8 450   0   Publication lists
 9 450   0   Publications
10 550   0   Documentation $w g
11 550   0   Abstracts
12 550   0   Books
13 550   0   Cataloging
14 550   0   Library science
15 550   0   Printing
16 550   0   Publishers and publishing
17 680           $i Under this heading, when subdivided by place and
appropriate topical subdivision, are entered works which discuss the
theories, methods, history, etc. of the discipline of bibliography
practiced within a particular region or country, e.g. $a Bibliography--
United States--History; Bibliography--United States--Methodology.
18 680           $i Works on the technique of compiling national
bibliographies, i.e. lists of titles produced in one country, lists of
titles produced in the language of one country without regard to place
of publication, lists of titles produced by citizens of one country
whether residing in that country or elsewhere, or lists of titles about
one country, are entered under $a Bibliography, National $i with country
subdivision, e.g. $a Bibliography, National--United States.
19 680           $i Actual lists of titles published in a particular
country are entered under the name of the country with subdivision $a
Imprints, $i e.g. $a United States--Imprints.
20 680           $i Actual lists of titles published in the language of one
country without regard to place of publication are entered under phrase
headings of the type $a English imprints.
21 680           $i Actual lists of titles about a particular country are
entered under the name of the country with subdivision $a Bibliography,
$i e.g. $a United States--Bibliography.
```

Example 8.17. The code "i" is assigned to this record in "Geo subd:", meaning that the heading can be subdivided geographically. However, the notes in lines 17 through 21 restrict the meaning of such subdivision and give alternate heading forms to use when other meanings are desired.

150, 151 Fields
Authority/Reference Record Code

The authority/reference record code data are found in MARC authorities as 008/09, in OCLC as "Auth/Ref:", and in RLIN as "ARR:".

The 150 field contains a topical subject heading, and the 151 field contains a geographic name that is used as a subject. However, a heading found in a 150 field is not always an established heading. This field must always be looked at in combination with the Authority/Reference record code and the 260 field. The code assigned here indicates, as does its name, whether the record is an authority record (code "a") or just a reference record (code "b" or "c"). Example 8.18 shows the reference record for the invalid heading, "Orthography." Also included in all reference records is a 260 field, which is the *see* reference for the invalid heading. When LC prints the fiche and the book-form *LCSH*, the information in the 260 field is preceded by the word "use." Not all references have a reference record, however, but only those that do not have one-to-one correspondences with specific headings. When there is one-to-one correspondence with one or more established headings, the nonauthorized form is listed in a 4XX field on the record(s) for the authorized heading(s).

Record (a)

```
ARN: 2101633    Rec stat: n    Entrd: 871218        Used: 871218
Type: z         Geo subd: _    Govt agn: _ Lang:    Source:
Roman: _        Subj: n        Series: n  Ser num: n Head: bbb
Ref status: n   Upd status: a  Auth status: n       Name: n
Enc lvl: n      Auth/Ref: b    Mod rec:             Rules: n

 1 010          sh 85095796
 2 040          DLC $c DLC
 3 150    0     Orthography
 4 260          $i subdivision $a Orthography and spelling $i under names
of languages, e.g. $a English language--Orthography and spelling
```

Example 8.18. The record in this example is a reference record rather than an authority record. The term "Orthography" is not to be used as a heading on bibliographic records. This is indicated by the code "b" in the "Auth/Ref:" fixed field, and by the presence of a 260 field.

360 Field (General Explanatory See Also Reference)

The 360 field, also unique to subjects, is present in records of valid authority headings (appearing in the 1XX fields) when a longer explanation is needed than can be generated by a 550 reference field. It actually serves the same purpose in a subject authority record (Auth/Ref: a) as the 260 field in a reference record. When LC prints the fiche and book-form *LCSH*, the information in the 360 field is preceded by "SA", meaning "see also." For an example of this field, see Example 8.19, page 326).

450, 451, 550, and 551 Fields

These fields (see Example 8.19) provide "see from" (4XX) and "see also from" (5XX) references in the same manner as do the 4XX and 5XX fields in other authority records. A code used in the 550 field (i.e., "g" meaning "broader term") will be seen in a subfield "$w" when the heading is hierarchically broader than the heading in the 1XX field. In the paper and fiche versions of LCSH, the tag for this reference is "BT", for "broader term," and the tag for the 550 references that do not contain "g" in subfield "$w" is "RT", meaning "related term."

```
ARN: 2156809      Rec stat: n       Entrd: 871219         Used: 871219
Type: z           Geo subd: _       Govt agn: _ Lang:     Source:
Roman: _          Subj: a           Series: n   Ser num: n Head: bab
Ref status: b     Upd status: a     Auth status: a        Name: n
Enc lvl: n        Auth/Ref: a       Mod rec:              Rules: n
```

```
 1 010        sh 85074530
 2 040        DLC $c DLC
 3 150   0    Language and languages $x Orthography and spelling
 4 360           $i subdivision $a Orthography and spelling $i under names
of languages or groups of languages, e.g., $a English language--
Orthography and spelling
 5 450   0    Language and languages $x Spelling reform
 6 450   0    Orthography
 7 450   0    Spelling
 8 550   0    Writing $w g
 9 680        Here are entered works on orthography, spelling, and spelling
reform in languages in general. Works dealing with the effort to reform
English orthography are entered under Spelling reform. Works dealing with
orthography, spelling, and spelling reform in specific languages or groups
of languages are entered under the name of the language with subdivision
Orthography and spelling, $i e.g. $a French language--Orthography and
spelling.
10 681        $i Note under $a Spelling reform
```

Example 8.19. This record provides an example of a 360 explanatory reference field, 450 and 550 reference fields, as well as a 680 scope note field, and a 681 tracing field. A reciprocal tracing field appears in the record for "Spelling reform," shown in Example 8.15 on page 322.

680, 681 Fields

The 680 (Scope note) field describes the usage of a subject heading and may also indicate overlapping headings (see Example 8.19). The 681 field refers the cataloger to a note or examples under other valid headings. A reciprocal 681 field appears in the record for the heading(s) being referred to (see Example 8.15 on page 322).

SUMMARY

When a library processes its materials online, particularly in a cooperative environment, many factors need to be taken into consideration and decided upon both in advance and as the future dictates. Some of these factors can be addressed by answering the following questions:

1. Which database will best suit the library's needs bibliographically, economically, and for products and services?

2. What effect does the form of the present public catalog have on online copy cataloging procedures?

3. What effect do future automation plans for the library have on processing records that are being captured on tape?

4. What effect does participation in a cooperative network of libraries — either statewide, nationally, or internationally — have on copy cataloging?

5. How will local copy cataloging policy decisions be documented?

6. Of what will training consist? How will computer considerations affect the length of the training period before copy catalogers are released to work on their own without review?

7. How much of the cataloging process will take place online? offline? Will editing be done directly online or from printouts?

8. Which tags, indicators, subfield codes, and fixed fields must be checked? Which must be retained in the record for current/later use?

9. Who will be responsible for near copy cataloging when a new record is required? If copy catalogers prepare new records from copy, will these records be reviewed by an original cataloger? If so, for how long?

10. What kind of online authority work will be expected of copy catalogers?

NOTES

[1]Patricia A. Becker and Ann T. Dodson, comps., and Lois L. Yoakam, ed., *Collected Papers of Frederick G. Kilgour: OCLC Years* (Dublin, Ohio: OCLC Online Computer Library Center, Inc., 1984), 362.

[2]Library of Congress, Serial Record Division, *CONSER Editing Guide* (Washington, D.C.: Library of Congress, 1986).

[3]Arlene Taylor Dowell, *AACR 2 Headings: A Five-Year Projection of Their Impact on Catalogs* (Littleton, Colo.: Libraries Unlimited, 1982), 28-31, 50.

MERITS AND PROBLEMS OF
COPY CATALOGING
A Summary

INTRODUCTION

Efficient use of outside cataloging becomes increasingly important as libraries grow and as it becomes more difficult to obtain money for increasing staff size. At the same time, it is the author's belief that outside cataloging must be integrated into existing local systems. It has been shown throughout this book that it is possible to use outside copy exactly as it appears *only* if the library and its users are willing to accept the potential consequences. There are occasionally appearances on copy of the following kinds of discrepancies: varying forms of entry; lack of some locally needed access points; subject separation of editions and other related materials; errors or discrepancies that cause misfiling or that convey misinformation; widely variant classification for the same subject, editions, or translations; insufficiently complete call numbers; and incorrect coding and/or tagging of MARC records. If these consequences are considered unacceptable, local catalogers must be provided the opportunity to compensate for them.

POTENTIAL CONSEQUENCES OF A
NONINTEGRATED CATALOG

Because so many other decisions hinge on this one, there must be an early decision about whether the potential consequences of using unchanged outside copy can be tolerated. Considering the difficulties involved in changing new copy, changing previous cataloging, or connecting entries with references, one is tempted to wonder whether the patron really cares. If, for example, a woman has written some books under her birth name and others under her married name, do patrons really expect to find them all listed together; or are they annoyed at being referred to the married name for a book that has the birth name on the title page? There are claims for both views, and this theoretical point will be contested for years. Recent online catalog use studies have indicated that patrons would like better and more consistent subject access,[1] and we have learned that users are sometimes frustrated by the lack of collocation of names in various databases.[2] However, we do not really know what patrons expect from the catalogs in various kinds of libraries.

A tempting solution is simply to use whatever appears in the piece being cataloged, or on the outside copy, without attempting to reference the other forms. One can justifiably argue that it is not possible to refer from every variation a patron may think of. For example, the user searching for an author believed to be named Wilson will go away unsatisfied if the author's name is actually spelled Willson, because a reference would not normally be made in such a case. (Interestingly, many libraries with printed catalogs file McDonald and MacDonald together, but not Wilson and Willson or any other such spelling variations, a practice that is confusing and misleading.)

On the other side, it can be asked why a patron does not deserve to be told that a corporate body, for example, has changed its name and that more recent materials therefore are found under the newer name. Is it the patron's responsibility to keep up with such things? Can a patron, or even the library's reference staff, really be expected to find, without aid of a reference, a vernacular entry such as Nihon Keizai Kenkyū Sentā when there are also entries in the catalog under its English equivalent, Japan Economic Research Center? Can it be assumed that library users are sophisticated enough to locate early materials on a subject under an antiquated term when materials are also listed under a more current term? These questions are all part of a larger one: What responsibility does the library, particularly the cataloger, have in making materials accessible, beyond placing them where they can be seen, taken from shelves by interested persons, and circulated? Is the primary purpose to "get the books out" in *any* fashion that avoids bogging them down behind the scenes where they cannot be circulated; then to point proudly to statistical figures representing the number of items "added to the collection"? If so, it can be accomplished by circulating the materials uncataloged, or by taking the outside copy exactly as it appears, asking no questions, and making no changes. Or is the primary purpose to provide adequate means of retrieving the item intershelved somewhere on one of the shelves in one of the ranges on one of the floors of the stacks in the library—or perhaps one of its branches?

The dilemma outlined here is not a new one. It was first posed by Charles Hastings soon after the advent of printed cards from LC:

> They seem to have thought that when they began to order printed cards their troubles in the cataloging line were practically over.... Nothing has been more plainly manifested during the past year than the fact that if a librarian doesn't know how to catalog without printed cards, she won't know how to catalog with them. She can make up a rough author list with them at a famous rate but to make a respectable dictionary or subject catalog is a vastly different matter.[3]

However, later in the same report Hastings made the following observation:

> There has been much progress also I think in the method of using the cards.... Libraries which were at first inclined to work over the L.C. cards and make them conform as much as possible to their style of cataloging are coming to see their mistake.... [The] objection to the use of the cards as they are printed, like the objections to the use of them in general, comes largely from the *a priori* bias of the cataloger and not from the users of the catalog.[4]

Thus, Hastings, in 1903, identified the twin considerations of the need to use LC cards as printed if they were to be economically feasible, and at the same time, integrating them into a unified whole if they were to be usable. There is a middle ground between the opposing extremes at which both administrators and catalogers often find themselves on this question. Compromise is possible if people are willing to talk with each other about the issues.

A basic question in copy cataloging, then, is, Should access points in the catalog and shelflist match, be referenced, or neither? In choosing among these options, the library must weigh projected staff time and costs required to implement each method as well as the philosophical considerations just discussed.

METHODS OF ACHIEVING AN INTEGRATED CATALOG

If an integrated catalog is desired in a library, there are three basic ways of handling integration when variations occur between new copy and the catalog: by changing the new copy; by changing the previously completed cataloging; or by making *see also* references. All of these have certain drawbacks as well as advantages.

Changing New Copy

Two of the potential problems of using outside cataloging can be corrected only by adjusting the new copy: lack of needed access points, and errors or discrepancies on copy. Changing new copy is one of the options available to cope with other problems as well. As discussed in earlier chapters, it is possible to change access points and classification/call numbers on new copy when these do not agree with what has already been used in the past. This approach generally means continuing to change that entry or classification for each new item using it.

The physical change for each item cataloged may involve corrections on a master or at a terminal, or it may mean making the change on every card of a set. Such changes are easily made when the cataloging system is online. In other systems, however, changes are made with more difficulty, in varying degrees. When an access point is changed on new copy, the procedure is repeated each time the access point appears on new copy, because the outside source rarely returns to the form used originally or locally. If a call number is changed on new cataloging, there is no physical difference from methods used when there is no change, unless items are purchased preprocessed and/or cards are purchased with preprinted call numbers. When new materials come already processed, *any* change will require remarking either the new acquisition or existing holdings. This negates somewhat the advantage of altering the new item.

Although the physical process is relatively simple, changing new copy is quite time consuming. It involves checking access points and the shelflist before cataloging, and repeatedly verifying that the new form applies to the same name, subject, etc., already in the catalog.

Changing Previously Completed Cataloging

The second method of integrating the catalog is to change previous cataloging to agree with the new form. Each time such a change is necessary, the cataloger and/or the typist may suspect that it might be easier to change the new copy to agree with entries already in the catalog rather than to change the latter to agree with the copy. But is it really easier? And, if so, does it better serve the library's purpose in the long run? This must be determined by evaluating the time required to change previous cataloging, so that subsequent new copy can be used unchanged, opposed to the time required to continue changing new copy in the future.

Physical change of previous cataloging varies in complexity with the type of catalog and with the part of the cataloging being changed. If the change involves a main entry, many libraries with printed catalogs deem it necessary to change that main entry at every secondary entry for the set. If the change affects an added or subject entry, the official tracing record is usually corrected in addition to the heading itself. If a classification/call number is involved, the change must be made on the physical item as well as at every catalog entry.

The format of the library's catalog must be considered because the ease of changing existing records varies with the type of catalog. In a card catalog, card sets must be located, pulled out, corrected, and refiled; or a new set of cards must be generated to replace the old cards. If there are several catalogs in branches as well as the main library, the complexity of the process is multiplied. A library with a book or microform catalog often has a master list in which all changes are recorded. All entries must be located in it and tagged for change, and a change notice or new entry must be generated so that the next supplement or new cumulation or edition of the catalog will incorporate the change. The public must wait for the new catalog or supplement, but in a large system this may take no longer than it would take for cards to be filed or refiled in a public card catalog following a similar change. Existing records in an online computer system are easiest to alter because the change can be made on the master record (i.e., main entry) at a terminal, all files are automatically updated, and the new information then may be instantly available to the public.

Making *See Also* References

The third method of integrating the local cataloging with new copy is to leave both the old and the new as they are and to connect them by means of *see also* references. This is a compromise between changing new copy or changing previous cataloging, but it is not without its own problems. A simple form-of-name change is easy enough to deal with this way, from a cataloging viewpoint. When there are multiple changes in the name, however, it becomes more complicated. For example, with two changes, three references must be made, each referring from one of the names to both of the others. With corporate names, which may have various cataloging name forms as well as actual name changes, mergers, and splits, the complications can be extensive. The relationships of actual name changes are difficult enough for a cataloger to explain on a reference without having also to explain variant cataloging forms. Also, the user experiences a certain frustration when directed to so many different places.

The usefulness of *see also* references may be affected to some extent by the type of catalog. They are less likely to be overlooked by the patron in a book or microform catalog than in a card catalog because it is easier to spot them while scanning a page than to find them while flipping cards. A reference card filed in front of an entry form may be overlooked if the patron assumes that once a card for the entry is found, all library holdings for that entry will be together under one form of name. This also causes problems when earlier/later name references and history cards are used. *See also* references for different cataloging forms are seldom used in online catalogs because changing unused forms is so easy. They are still necessary, however, for actual changes of corporate names and serial titles, for linking pseudonyms used by the same person, for connecting related subjects, and for other situations.

See also references can also be used in the shelflist and on blocks in the stacks as a compromise when classification schedules are revised. These, too, may be overlooked, and explanations can be complicated when multiple changes are involved.

Combining the Methods

In recent times libraries, particularly those with card catalogs, have combined the above methods of achieving an integrated catalog. Especially with the advent of AACR 2 heading changes, many libraries determined a specific number of entries for an access point below which all entries would be changed to the new form and above which *see also* references would be made to connect differing forms.

Whichever approach or compromise is selected, it is extremely important that *all* personnel involved in making changes understand why the changes are needed. Unnecessary resentment is often felt by staff, especially typing or keyboarding personnel, when they know that what they painstakingly do today may come back to them to be changed in a month, or a year. If the library's policy has been carefully thought through, there should be no reason to fear explaining it. An understanding of the reasoning behind policies can do wonders for staff morale.

OBSERVATIONS ON COPY CATALOGING

When a library has decided to use outside cataloging, the decision-making staff should be aware of a few general considerations.

Using the Newest Copy Available

One observation about copy cataloging, which is a problem only with LC copy, and then only if it is retrieved from the *NUC*, concerns revised copy. If a library's goal is to use copy with as little change as possible, whatever this may mean in each library, the library should take advantage of the changes, additions, and corrections already made by LC itself when copy is first located locally. This is usually no problem in a computer-based system because most are programmed so that revised copy supersedes the earlier version. However, if the copy one finds is pre-MARC LC copy input by a member library, it is possible that the latest version was not used. For example, the record in OCLC for the symposium shown in Example 7.15 (pages 272-75) is the original cataloging shown in Record (a) of that example, not the revised cataloging shown in Record (b).

In a manual file of records from the CDS Alert Service, too, revised copy should supersede earlier copy. When card sets are ordered, revised copy should be sent, although most catalogers can tell of instances where it was not. However, in the printed book catalog and in the more recent microform version of *NUC*, revised copy supersedes earlier copy only when the two happen to fall in the same period of cumulation. Copy originally done in 1975 and revised in 1976 appeared in both annual cumulations. When the quinquennial was cumulated for 1973-1977, the later copy alone was printed, but for several years the dual copy situation existed. There are also many cases of copy from one quinquennial appearing again in a revised form in a later quinquennial.

In order to be certain of finding the latest revision when searching LC's book and microform catalogs, every issue following the first one where copy is found must be searched. If all issues are being searched anyhow, a small saving can be made by searching latest first, but the problem here is that references in earlier cumulations may not be repeated in later ones. If search is from latest to earliest and a reference is found, the search may have to be repeated. The dilemma is in choosing between the time required to resolve conflicts arising from unrevised copy and then changing it locally, versus the time required to search subsequent issues of *NUC* even though most items will have no revised copy. There is no easy answer. Local priorities must be delineated.

Whether these systems are computer or manual, none of them flag and replace copy that has already been processed and entered into a local catalog. LC's revision must be noticed by a local cataloger who then decides whether or not the change should be made locally.

Changing from One Outside Source to Another

A potential problem for libraries that use a source other than LC for outside copy concerns the possible necessity of changing sources. A prime example of such a situation was the demise of H. W. Wilson cards, which served small libraries with simplified cataloging from 1935 to 1975. One of the reasons for its demise was that sales of cards had dropped precipitously—presumably a number of libraries had already switched sources voluntarily. But libraries still using Wilson cards at the beginning of 1975 faced the necessity of finding a new source of cards.

If required to change the official outside source of copy, a library should consider again its needs. Its requirements may have changed since the decision was last made. Such factors as growth rate and staff size may differ. Also to be considered is the ease with which copy from a new source may be integrated into the existing catalog containing copy from the previous source. If meshing entries is important, a source that provides similar depth of entry and description should be chosen. Equivalent classification also is usually a requirement.

Libraries should periodically reevaluate the copy source, even when such an appraisal is not forced, to ensure that the source being used is the best one for that library at that time. Commercial cataloging sources that seem to be thriving are those that send materials fully processed with cards ready to file. Some newer companies may not have been available when a library chose its source of outside copy; they should be considered not only when a forced change takes place, but also as procedures and/or financial situations are reassessed.

Copy Cataloging Units

When it is decided that processing should be local, it is possible to process materials with outside copy quickly and efficiently through a copy cataloging unit, while retaining ability to maintain an integrated catalog responsive to the needs of local users. Such a unit can function using card sets or master copy, either printed or appearing on a computer screen. A first step is to decide on copy cataloging policies. As a starting point, lists of questions are provided at the ends of chapters 1 through 8 of this book.

Even the library with well-established cataloging policies should reexamine them at the time it joins a cataloging network or undergoes any major change. This is especially important because a dedicated line to a network is cost effective only if it is used to near-maximum capacity. Time cannot be spent determining fine points of policy while copy waits on the screen for action. Another reason for establishing clear-cut cataloging policies before joining a network is that such policies are reflected in the cataloging that the library will contribute to the system. Policies, therefore, come under scrutiny of every other library in the network — right there for everyone to evaluate and to use as a basis for forming an opinion about the library! More important, however, is the need for cataloging contributed to a network to be usable as copy by other libraries, and a library's policies can affect the usability of the cataloging it contributes.

A second step is to document policy decisions, including the reasoning used, and to organize them in such a fashion that they can be retrieved easily for reference, especially by the copy cataloger. Procedures, too, should be written in step-by-step format, and specific points should be easily accessible. A training manual for new copy catalogers is essential so that there is consistent practice, especially if turnover is high in these positions, and so that the trainee is not expected to remember detailed verbal instructions given once or twice. Written instructions can be referred to as often as needed until the procedure has been learned, so that the trainee does not need to interrupt the supervisor constantly. The written manual also helps relieve the trainer of some of the awesome responsibility of remembering to explain to each new cataloger every step in a quite complicated process.

A final requirement for a successful copy cataloging unit is supervision by a person thoroughly familiar with cataloging, with the importance of creating an integrated local catalog, with local policies and procedures, and with the organization of the written manual. The supervisor must interpret cataloging rules, subject heading lists, classification schedules, local policies and procedures, and, often, MARC formats and network policies and procedures. This person also is called on to answer questions concerning past cataloging practices and priorities, both local ones and those of the outside source. Resolution of the more complicated conflicts falls here, and there are always instantaneous decisions to be made on topics that seem not to have been covered by any policy decision, and that must not conflict with any policy already in existence. In addition to all of the abilities mentioned, the supervisor should also have good management skills, but that is the subject of another book!

CONCLUSION

With careful planning, copy cataloging can be, for the local library, the best possible means of serving patrons. It can help speed the appearance of bibliographic data in the catalog. If certain kinds of decisions are made ahead of time, the processing of the majority of available outside copy can become semi-routine. This, in turn, frees the original cataloger to spend time on solving problems, resolving conflicts, and working out means of satisfying the special needs of local patrons. If the local user can have both earlier availability of materials and better access to them via the local catalog, the library has improved two of its basic functions.

NOTES

[1]See, for example, Karen Markey, *Subject Searching in Library Catalogs before and after the Introduction of Online Catalogs* (Dublin, Ohio: OCLC, 1984).

[2]See, for example, David M. Pilachowski and David Everett, "What's in a Name? Looking for People Online ...," *Database* 8 (August 1985): 47-65; 9 (April 1986): 43-50; and 9 (October 1986): 26-34.

[3]Charles M. Hastings, "Report on the Card Distribution Work of the Library of Congress," *Library Journal* 28 (October 1903): 708.

[4]Ibid., 709-710.

SELECT BIBLIOGRAPHY

Barnard, Henry. "Law Book Copy Cataloging on OCLC: Potholes and Pitfalls." *Cataloging & Classification Quarterly* 5 (Summer 1985): 79-84.

Bloomberg, Marty, and G. Edward Evans. *Introduction to Technical Services for Library Technicians.* 5th ed. Littleton, Colo.: Libraries Unlimited, 1985.

Charbonneau, Gary. "A Comparison of Rates of Patron Utilization of Library Materials Receiving Original Cataloging and Materials Receiving Copy Cataloging." *Collection Management* 8 (Spring 1986): 25-32.

Dowell, Arlene Taylor. "Discrepancies in CIP: How Serious Is the Problem?" *Library Journal* 104 (November 1, 1979): 2281-87.

Dowell, Arlene Taylor. "What You Buy and What You Have: Integrating Outside Cataloging Copy into an Existing System." *Catholic Library World* 48 (May/June 1977): 416-18.

Hickey, Doralyn J. "Search for Uniformity in Cataloging: Centralization and Standardization." *Library Trends* 25 (January 1977): 565-86.

Hogan, Allan D. "Acceptance of Cataloging Contributed by OCLC Members." In *OCLC: A National Library Network*, edited by Anne Marie Allison and Ann Allan. Short Hills, N.J.: Enslow Publishers, 1979, 121-38.

Hudson, Judith. "Copy Cataloging Activities: Report of a Survey." *Cataloging & Classification Quarterly* 7 (Fall 1986): 63-67.

Hudson, Judith. "On-the-Job Training for Cataloging and Classification." *Cataloging & Classification Quarterly* 7 (Summer 1987): 69-78.

Hudson, Judith. "Revisions to Contributed Cataloging in a Cooperative Cataloging Database." *Journal of Library Automation* 14 (June 1981): 116-20.

Leung, Shirley W. "MARC CIP Records and MARC LC Records: An Evaluative Study of Their Discrepancies." *Cataloging & Classification Quarterly* 4 (Winter 1983): 27-39.

McDonough, Joyce G., Carol Alf O'Connor, and Thomas A. O'Connor. "Moving the Backlog: An Optimum Cycle for Searching OCLC." In *Library Acquisitions: Practice and Theory* 6, no. 3 (1982): 265-70.

Metz, Paul, and John Espley. "The Availability of Cataloging Copy in the OCLC Data Base." *College & Research Libraries* 41 (September 1980): 430-36.

Ohmes, Frances, and J. F. Jones. "The Other Half of Cataloging." *Library Resources & Technical Services* 17 (Summer 1973): 320-29.

Ryans, Constance C. "A Study of Errors Found in Non-MARC Cataloging in a Machine-Assisted System." *Journal of Library Automation* 11 (June 1978): 125-32.

Salas-Tull, Laura, and Jacque Halverson. "Subject Heading Revision: A Comparative Study." *Cataloging & Classification Quarterly* 7 (Spring 1987): 13-22.

Struble, Carol A., and Paul B. Kohberger, Jr. "Statistical Survey to Determine Availability of Cataloging Copy on OCLC." *Cataloging & Classification Quarterly* 7 (Spring 1987): 13-22.

Taylor, Arlene G., and Charles W. Simpson. "Accuracy of LC Copy: A Comparison between Copy That Began as CIP and Other LC Cataloging." *Library Resources & Technical Services* 30 (October/December 1986): 375-87.

Valentine, Phyllis A. "Increasing Production in Cataloging While Decreasing Cost." *Technicalities* 4 (July 1984): 10-13.

INDEX

090 copy. *See* Co-op copy
AACR 2. *See Anglo-American*
Cataloguing Rules, 2nd ed.
Abbreviations, 35, 36, 44-45
Abridged Dewey Decimal Classification,
170, 235, 237, 238
Abridgement of title added entries, 88
Access points. *See also* Added entries
choice of, 66-92
in co-op copy, 276
definition, 66
form of entry, 93-134
MARC fields, 306-7
Accompanying material, 36, 293
Acquisition groups, cooperative, 296
Added copies
classification/call numbers, 182, 219,
229
printing differences, 48-49, 184
Added entries, 66-92
choice of, 69-92
on co-op copy, 276
definition, 69
deletion from copy, 69-71
filing, 71
Library of Congress procedures, 69,
71, 74, 78-79, 83, 84, 86-88, 306
in "limited cataloging," 41-43, 74, 89
local addition, 16-17, 68-69, 71-92
MARC fields, 71, 306-7
in minimal level cataloging, 43-44,
74-75, 78
name/title, 69, 74, 78-83
names, 67-77, 84, 93-127
on near copy, 249, 258, 266
series, 30, 42, 71, 89-91, 120,
130-31, 258, 276
subjects, 140-67, 306

titles, 23, 69, 84-88, 127-32, 250,
258, 306
translations, 32, 39, 78
uniform, 78-83
Alternative classification numbers
Dewey Decimal Classification, 238-42
Library of Congress Classification,
190-99, 229-32
local, 183-84, 191, 198-99, 229-32,
242-43
Alternative subject headings, 135-37
Analytical entries, 74
classification/call numbers, 194, 198,
222-29, 231, 242
series added entries, 71, 89
Anglo-American Cataloguing Rules, 2nd
ed., 14-15
on access points and notes, 42
on added entries, 69, 84, 88, 127, 268
changing data to, 308, 332
in co-op copy, 276
in near copy, 249, 258
on conferences, congresses, etc., 273
on edition statement, 36, 292
on editions, 201, 255
on holdings, 57, 60
on imprint, 48-49
interpretation of, 292
ISBD standards application, 34
and Library of Congress, 93, 105-8,
201, 293, 319
adopted by, 36
on main entry, 67-69, 127, 201, 258
on names, 8, 27, 94-95, 96, 312, 313,
314
corporate, 111, 113, 116, 121
personal, 100, 104, 105-8
on notes, 303